To Bill

Enjoy the Journey

Clint Frederick

WORLD WAR II:

A Legacy of Letters

ONE SOLDIER'S JOURNEY

CLINTON
FREDERICK

Zonicom Press LLC
% Clinton Frederick
7807 E Oberlin Way
Scottsdale, AZ 85262
zonicompress@msn.com

Library of Congress Cataloging-in-Publication Data

Frederick, Clinton.
 WWII, a legacy of letters : one soldier's journey / Clinton Frederick.--
1st ed.
    p. cm.
 Includes index.
 ISBN-13: 978-0-9778493-0-7
 ISBN-10: 0-9778493-0-7
 1. United States. Army. Cavalry Division, 1st. 2. World War,
1939-1945--Regimental histories--United States. 3. World War,
1939-1945--Campaigns--Oceania. 4. Frederick, George Frederick,
1914---Correspondence. 5. World War, 1939-1945--Personal narratives,
American. 6. Soldiers--United States--Correspondence. I. Title: World War
II, a legacy of letters. II. Title: World War 2, a legacy of letters. III.
Title: World War Two, a legacy of letters. IV. Frederick, George Frederick,
1914- V. Title.
 D769.308.F74 2006
 940.54'26581--dc22

                                   2006006871

Printed in Canada

——Produced by Five Star Publications, Inc.
—— Linda F. Radke, President
www.FiveStarPublications.com

—— Editor: Gary Anderson
 Project Manager: Sue DeFabis
 Cover design: Kris Taft Miller
 Interior design: Janet Bergin

CONTENTS

PREFACE

The events in this book happened. Names have not been changed. The people are real. Like Tom Brokaw's books, *The Greatest Generation Speaks,* and *An Album of Memories,* this book traces one soldier's life through World War II, his romance, his ethics, and his heroism.

I knew my father and grandfather had served in the South Pacific in World War II. My father is mentioned in two books: *The Army Air Forces in World War II, Vol. IV: The Pacific: Guadalcanal to Saipan August 1942 to July 1944,* by W. F. Craven and J. L. Cate and *CARTWHEEL: The Reduction of Rabaul,* by John Miller, Jr. Since I knew my father had seen action in the Admiralty Islands, I found another book, as well, titled *The Admiralties, Operations of the 1st Cavalry Division, 29 February–18 May 1944.*

Through the years, I've collected a number of books on WWII. I thought it might be interesting to trace the letters home with the events of the time. I started my research by searching web sites, collecting more books, and buying old issues of *Yank* magazine. I also used the Internet, searching for people who might have served with my father in World War II. Also, I wanted to type out the letters so they would be easier to read and give copies to our daughters and to my mother for Christmas. My mother is still living in Ft. Scott, Kansas.

The First Cavalry Division has a web site and was featured in a recent movie *We Were Soldiers,* starring Mel Gibson. I was able to become an associate member and attended their convention in Texas. There I was able to meet some of the men who served with my father in the Admiralty Islands.

Unfortunately, none of them could remember my father, although they were in the same battle as he was.

One of my high school classmates established a web site for our class. One classmate was George Lampe, who had retired as a General from the military. I contacted General George, as I call him, and asked if he could help me with some research on my father's military career, since all his records had been destroyed. He suggested I contact Maxwell Air Force Base.

"The records for the army air force are all stored there," he responded. "Those guys love to do research. Why don't you contact them and see what they find?"

General George was also helpful in answering some technical questions I had about the military.

Dr. Kitchens at Maxwell AFB answered my request. Amazingly, he found *Historical Study No. 86*, titled "Close Air Support in the War Against Japan," containing a chapter on the action in the Admiralty Islands that centered on my father and the 12th Air Liaison Party (ALP). The study had been written by the USAF Historical Division, Research Studies Institute, in 1955, and was stamped *Confidential*. On the web site for Maxwell AFB, the historical studies can now be downloaded. Searching other historical studies, I also found him in study number 43, and a few of the men I know my father served with were also mentioned. What a wealth of information. Dr. Kitchens also found morning reports concerning thirty-four days of action in the Admiralty Islands that had been retained in the files. Morning reports were like journals and were stamped *SECRET*, but have since been declassified. They had been written by my father.

I asked my cousin Bobby Frederick if his father ever mentioned the events of WWII, but the response was negative.

"My father never mentioned WWII. I don't even know where he served. I think he was in ordnance," Bobby told me.

My mother had told me a few stories about the WWII era. Over the Christmas holidays of 2004, I read the letters to my mother, asking her to tax her memory and tell me as much as she could remember. When she mentioned that Lt. Laird was best man at their wedding, I searched the Internet for a Lt. Laird and found him still living in Maryland. His daughters, Rose and Diane, and granddaughter, Renee Brown, were able to supply me with some of the pictures in this book.

From my conversations with Lt. Laird in the spring of 2005, I found him as feisty as he must have been in WWII, although his wife stated, "I clipped his wings!"

Acknowledgement should also be given to Ed Gammill and Ira Chaub, who served with the 5th Army Air Force, and Jack Sloan, who served on the *USS Swanson* during World War II. Another thank you to Quinn and Tony Fiske, whose father served with the 7th Cavalry during WWII and supplied information from the compilation of *The 1st Cavalry Division in WWII* by Major B. C. Wright, and to Russ Blaise whose father served with the Alamo Scouts during WWII and was able to clarify my research.

I also contacted the Military History Institute in Carlisle, Pennsylvania, requesting information. The request was too voluminous for them, so they suggested that I contact a local researcher. A special thank you goes to Carolyn Lacky of Carlisle, Pennsylvania, for her prompt response in finding *The Diary of the Admiralty Island Campaign*, written a month after the Admiralty Islands battle in 1944 by the 1st Cavalry headquarters staff, various newspaper clippings from that time, and the papers of Chaplain Charles Trent.

I know I'm forgetting some people who helped in my research and in the publication of this story.

I should thank Joanne Nelson, my sister-in-law, for an initial edit, but "I couldn't finish it because I started crying," she said. Kari Frederick, my daughter, performed another edit and had valuable suggestions. A special thank you to Fred Campbell, my mother's cousin in Ft. Scott, Kansas, for his encouragement and assistance to my mother in gathering information.

Linda Radke and her staff at Five Star Publications, Inc. also deserve my gratitude for their encouragement and diligent attention. Gary Anderson for editing, Kris Taft-Miller for her work on the cover, Janet Bergin for layout and design and Sue DeFabis who kept it all together.

My cousin, Mary Anne, provided initial cover design layout and worked with Five Star Publications, Inc. to create the cover. Mary Anne was an inspiration for this book. "The story needs to be told."

Finally, and most valuable, were the suggestions from my wife, Kathy. She read some of the initial drafts and, with an uncritical comment, suggested a different format, a different presentation, or a sentence restructuring. She has an unequaled gift of prose and expression. This story would never have been written without her encouragement.

For my Daughters:
Randi
Kim
Kari

October 2002—To New Jersey

I t was a balmy Wednesday afternoon in early October when I found myself sitting on a National Airlines flight from Las Vegas to Philadelphia. I had received an invitation to attend my cousin Bobby Frederick's wedding to Julia. The only one of my father's generation still living at the time was my father's younger sister, Eleanor, but she'd had a stroke and wasn't doing very well.

Mary Anne, my other cousin, was only two months older than I. As children, we'd been very close, since we were all about the same age, but we'd pursued our separate careers, and it had been many years since we'd all seen each other. I was in the west and my cousins in the east. I called Mary Anne and we hatched a scheme. I'd show up at the wedding and surprise Bobby, Julia, and the rest of the family. I wouldn't be expected, and it would be a big surprise. Mary Anne lived in our grandparents' house, where they had lived during WWII, in Laurel Springs, New Jersey.

"You need to see my mother," Mary Anne chided. "You know she's not doing very well. Besides, Clint, you need to come back here and go through all those trunks in the attic."

I had purchased a new digital camera just before the trip and figured I could keep busy on the three-hour trip learning how to operate it. I figured wrong. In thirty minutes, I'd learned all the functions of the camera I wanted to know. I leaned my seat back and reminisced about playing in the attic of my grandparents' house with Mary Anne and Bobby. I remembered trunks filled with treasures of knickknacks, papers, and memorabilia. There were rifles, swords, and all sorts of military items.

My grandfather, at the outbreak of WWII, had joined the military after his retirement from a railroad company and then traveled the world until his second retirement in the early 1950s. My grandmother had joined him after WWII in Japan. He was transferred to Germany, then to the Philippines and back to Japan before he retired from the Air Force as a colonel. He had bought a 1948 Buick between his stints in Japan and Germany. I remembered that Buick as having traveled around the world with him, from Philadelphia to Germany, the Philippines, Japan, and San Francisco before they drove it back to the East Coast. They had stopped to visit us in Kansas on their way to Philadelphia.

My father had served in WWII, but I didn't know much about it. I knew that he'd received several medals, had been in the 5th Army Air Force, and had seen action in the South Pacific. Our house had burned in December 1945, and any letters or souvenirs that my father had sent from his service in WWII had been destroyed. One time, when I was in St. Louis and had some time, I visited the National Archives, where military information about those who had served in WWII is kept. I learned that the archives had also caught fire, and any records of my father's service in WWII had been destroyed. What treasures of the past would the attic reveal?

While I was dreaming of treasures in the attic, the plane touched down in Philadelphia. After picking up my luggage and renting a car, I started toward Laurel Springs. Although it had been at least twenty years since I'd been there, I felt that once I got across the Delaware River, I could find the house at 535 Beech Avenue without getting lost. If it was still daylight, I was sure I could find it, but it was dark, which made it even more of a challenge.

Mary Anne still had the same telephone number my grandparents had used. I wondered if there was some kind of record for retaining the same telephone number. I knew it had been the same for at least sixty years, and probably another twenty-plus years before that. Entering Laurel Springs, I turned down a street that looked familiar. Another car turned on the same street and started following me. There the house was, on the corner. I pulled in next to the curb as the car following me pulled into the driveway. What timing! Mary Anne had been at a meeting and was just getting home.

Mary Anne gave me a tour of the house.

"Except for remodeling the basement and the attic, the house is the same," she said as we walked around the dining room where I remembered my grandmother serving spaghetti and eating the noodles rolled up on a spoon. I flashed back to the time I first had lobster. I didn't like it then, but I love it now. There's nothing like fresh Maine lobster.

Mary Anne hadn't changed a thing. It was like stepping back in time, to when my grandparents had occupied the house, more than fifty years earlier. The furniture, the pictures on the wall, and the knickknacks on the fireplace mantle were all as I remembered. Was it the same as when my father was a child, I wondered?

We adjourned to the bar in the basement to catch up on the last twenty years and to brag about how well our kids were doing. As teenagers, her Collingswood High School was bigger and better than my podunk school in Pittsburg, Kansas. I'm sure it was bigger, but not any better.

When she came to Kansas, just after I'd started driving at fourteen, we picked her and Bobby up at the Joplin, Missouri airport. Of course, I had to drive to show off for my eastern cousins, so on the way to the farm, we drove through Pittsburg. I pulled into Kansas State Teachers College and told Mary Anne it was my high school, explaining each of the buildings.

"That building houses the music department, the building next to it is the art department, and that's the stadium where we play our football games," I had bragged.

With our preliminary bragging over, I told Mary Anne the one thing I really wanted to do was dig into the old trunks in the attic.

"Remember when we used to play in the attic?" I asked.

"Yeah, we couldn't have been more than nine or ten years old," she responded.

"I remember some rifles and swords up there. Of course, that's what would interest me at that age. But I also remember there were a number of trunks. Some were locked and some were empty. Do you know what was in them?"

"Clinton, I have no idea what's in those old trunks. When we remodeled the attic, I told the workers just to shove everything under the beams in the crawl space. I've never looked up there or in the trunks. You can sleep in my son Jimmy's bedroom. There should be a panel you can remove to get into the crawl space. Beth Anne's bedroom is on the other side, and there should be a panel to access the other side of the attic there. Did I tell you that Jimmy and Beth Anne formed their own music company and write music for The History Channel?" she bragged for the tenth time.

It was past midnight eastern time before Mary Anne finally said that she needed to go to bed, since she had to work the next day.

"Don't wake me up," I said. "I'm on western time and three hours behind you."

I woke up just as Mary Anne and her roommate, Joyce, were leaving for work. May Anne was the head of the art department at a school and Joyce worked for a car agency. Both had been married, but their marriages had ended in divorce.

I stumbled downstairs and found a fresh pot of coffee waiting for me. I took the coffee to the screened-in front porch that wrapped around the southwest corner of the house. I chuckled at the memories of playing office on the porch. Of course, Mary Anne had to be president. Grandpa Frederick had rigged a speaker under the porch from the basement and had surprised us with his deep baritone voice as he started talking while we were playing. Today was going to be a beautiful fall day in Laurel Springs.

Back in the attic, I looked for the panel Mary Anne told me could be removed. It was behind the bed, so I rearranged the furniture and removed the panel. There, right in front of me, was a trunk. I put my head through the opening and could see the silhouettes of other trunks under the beams. I went back downstairs and looked for a flashlight, but couldn't find one, but I did find an extension cord.

Returning to the attic, I plugged a small lamp into the extension cord, removed the shade, and crawled through the opening, knocking down cobwebs and sneezing from the dust.

I opened the lid of the first trunk and peered in. A bedpan and a glass urinal - now that's a real find! What had possessed my grandmother to keep a bedpan and a glass urinal? I opened another trunk. Inside were boxes containing letters and pictures. I closed the trunk and went to an upright wardrobe trunk. I couldn't open it very far because of space, but it looked empty. Holding the lamp, I continued crawling around, looking inside trunks. Several were empty, and one was filled with parachutes. Lying on the floor were two rifles and a Samurai sword. There should be more than one sword, I thought. I remembered several from childhood, but maybe there weren't. That had been fifty years ago.

Returning to the trunk with boxes of letters and pictures, I opened one of the boxes. There in front of me were letters from my father. I pulled the box out and sat on the floor of the bedroom, reading them. It looked as if my grandmother had saved every letter my father had written to her during World War II. There was V-mail in small handwriting and judging from the postmark on the envelope or return addresses, letters written from different bases around the nation while he was in training. The letters usually identified his location as "Somewhere in the Woods" or "Somewhere in New Guinea." A letter postmarked March 30th caught my eye. It was typewritten, so I opened it and read it.

"I got two Japs the first hour we were on shore…and have souvenirs to remember the occasion by…"

I pulled the rifles and Samurai sword from the attic into the bedroom so I could look at them better. The rifles were Japanese.

"Were these the souvenirs my father alluded to in his letter?" I wondered.

One looked new, but the other one had fourteen notches carved in the stock. Visions of fourteen allied men meeting their death from the rifle hopped through my mind. I tried to pull the sword from the sheath, but I couldn't. Finally, I found a small button on the sheath. I pressed the button and it released a shiny razor-sharp sword.

I put the sword down and crawled back into the crawl space. With some difficulty, I finally managed to pull the trunk containing the letters and pictures into the bedroom. Sitting on the floor, I glanced through the letters.

Besides the letters, there were legal documents, newspaper articles that had been clipped, a diary that my grandmother had kept in several small little red books; a diary my grandfather had kept; letters from my grandfather, my father, Uncle Harry, Aunt Eleanor; and old pictures that must have been taken in the early 1900s. Maybe Mary Anne would know who some of these people were. I needed some air. Besides, it was now past noon and I was getting hungry.

If I remembered right, there was a little restaurant in Laurel Springs where I'd had my first poor boy sandwich. I wondered if that restaurant was still there. I drove downtown to see if I could find it. I found the old train station, where people commuted to Philadelphia, and across the street, on the corner, was the deli. I went in, got a poor boy, and drove back to the house.

Upstairs I grabbed some letters and took them downstairs to the porch, where I sat digesting the letters and documents while nibbling on the sandwich.

My father was born December 14, 1914, in Philadelphia to Harry (no middle name) Eisenstein and Mary Louisa Frederick. Eisenstein? Leaving the documents that I had carried to the porch, I ran back up the stairs and started fumbling through the trunk again. I found some baby pictures and looked on the back. George Frederick Eisenstein had been written on one of them. An attempt to scratch out Eisenstein had been made, but hadn't been successful. Frederick had been written below Eisenstein.

A legal document caught my eye. My grandfather had legally changed his name from Eisenstein to Frederick in 1925. That explains why my father's middle name was Frederick. He had originally been named George Frederick Eisenstein. I had always been told it was because a Frederick had married a Frederick, which explained why he was named George Frederick Frederick, but secrets hid in the attic revealed the true story.

I perused some other documents. My grandfather Harry was born on January 23, 1895, in Philadelphia, and my grandmother about a year earlier, in 1894. My grandfather graduated from Central High School in 1912 and attended Pierce Business College, pursuing a major in business administration. He became an assistant chief clerk for the Lehigh Valley Railroad of New York. Did he commute to New York, I wondered?

Picking up another document, I read that he'd been a stock transfer agent, had paid bond interest, and had prepared financial statements for the board of directors. I always thought he was a conductor, but he must have held a high level position, since he earned a salary of $3,600 a year. That was a lot of money in the 1930s. He apparently had retired from Lehigh Valley Railroad Company in 1941, after some twenty-three years.

Another document showed my grandfather had joined the 57th Infantry Brigade of the New Jersey National Guard on October 21, 1924. He was honorably discharged in October 1929. A month later, he reenlisted and became a first lieutenant on January 3, 1933 and a captain on December 5, 1939. He was ordered to active duty on September 16, 1940, along with his sons, Second Lt. George Frederick and Sgt. Harry Frederick. That explained why he had retired from the railroad company and started a second career in the military. The New Jersey National Guard was activated before Pearl Harbor. The Department of Defense must have been anticipating war with Japan and Germany.

My father joined the National Guard on February 17, 1933, after his graduation from Haddon Heights High School on June 16, 1932. He also attended Pierce Business College. He became a second lieutenant on November 28, 1938. What other jobs he held wasn't revealed in the documents. Apparently he did well, since he was able to buy a new 1941 Oldsmobile.

My grandmother, Mary Frederick, was born to William and Louisa Frederick. William lived at 1535 Palmer Street in Philadelphia and was a fisherman. He was always mortgaging the property and paying off loans, since there were several mortgage documents. His sisters, Annie and Carrie, lived in the house until the 1950s. They were simply referred to as the aunts in some of the letters I'd read that morning. I remembered Aunt Carrie as a robust woman with white hair, and Aunt Annie as frail with brown hair. Apparently they were schoolteachers and had never married. A memory of a black Buick, narrow streets, and stairs to a second floor flat flashed through my mind.

Before I knew it, Mary Anne and Joyce came home.

"We're going into Philadelphia to an art gallery," Mary Anne told me. "Some of my students are showing their art there and I need to make an appearance. We can find a place to eat there."

I told Mary Anne what I'd found and showed her the document concerning our grandfather's 1925 name change. I also told her about the house at 1535 Palmer and how our great-grandfather William was always mortgaging the property.

"That's right by where we are going tonight. Now it's a very historic and trendy area. It has art shops, restaurants, and bars. Some of the streets are still cobblestone," she said.

We found a restaurant within walking distance of the art studio where Mary Anne's students were showing their art. After dinner, we walked to the studio and were introduced to a few of her students. They started asking Mary Anne questions about some of the other art on display.

"Dr. Morgan," one girl asked, "what is the artist trying to depict in this painting?"

Mary Anne studied the painting for a moment.

"Well, I see—" she said as she started a dissertation about the painting.

Joyce and I slipped out to the street while Mary Anne stayed with her students, but it wasn't long until she came out.

"What a bunch of BS. They hung on every word I had to say. I had no idea what that artist was trying to convey," she exclaimed with a twinkle in her eye.

But I knew different. Mary Anne didn't have a doctorate in art for nothing, and I could always tell when she was joking.

The next day would be another day of work for Mary Anne and Joyce. Mary Anne told me to bring what I wanted to go through out of the attic and spread it out in the living room.

"Are you sure you don't mind?" I asked. "Some of it might be pretty dirty."

"It'll clean," Mary Anne said.

The next morning, I was up a little earlier.

"I must be getting used to the time difference," I thought.

I started taking items downstairs and sorting them into piles around the living room. Back in the attic, I explored more of the trunks. Another trunk apparently housed mementos of our grandparents' travels. I pulled the trunk out so I could open it better. There wasn't enough space to pull it out of the crawl space, so I just started taking the contents downstairs to the living room. On the other side of the attic, I found a loose panel where I could access the crawl space from Beth Anne's bedroom. I still hadn't located a flashlight, but was able to find a spear that was more than seven feet long and another shorter spear by feeling around on the floor.

"How did they ever ship this from the South Pacific?"' I wondered.

I stopped exploring the attic and continued carrying items that might be of interest down to the living room. I was anxious to thumb through the diaries and read the letters, but I was also getting hungry and needed a break.

I left the house and drove by 315 W. Atlantic Avenue, where Aunt Eleanor lived. Mary Anne had told me that her mother wasn't well and that they'd hired a full-time nurse. I didn't stop, since we'd see her the next day at the wedding. I drove down White Horse Pike and found a restaurant. It was amazing how some things don't change. The last time I'd driven around the area was 1961, in the '55 Buick my grandfather had bought after he retired from the military. He died of a heart attack a few years after he retired. That was more than 40 years ago.

Back at the house, I started scanning through the letters and diaries. My grandfather had started a diary in September 1944, when he boarded a ship in New York, bound for the South Pacific. After a brief stop in Florida, the ship had cruised through the Panama Canal and then zigzagged across the Pacific, stopping at various islands until they reached New Guinea. The trip had taken nearly six weeks. The entries in the diary stopped, so I picked up another diary and started reading. That one was from 1949, and told about flying from Florida to an air force base in Panama. From there, he had gone to Peru, Chile, and finally, to Buenos Aires. He mentioned that he was learning to speak some Spanish, since it would be required there. I stumbled onto one of his letters from about the same time, in which he said that he hoped Grandmother Frederick could join him there.

Apparently he wasn't in South America very long, since the next correspondence I read was from my grandmother to the aunts from Germany. She told of a dinner, sitting next to a German official. The fellow had apologized for his English not being very good. My grandmother told him that was OK, since she could speak German. Immersed in the letters, diaries, and documents, it seemed like only a few minutes until Mary Anne came home.

"Mary Anne, did you know our grandparents spoke German?" I asked.

"Yeah. When they argued, they spoke German so we wouldn't understand what they were saying," she replied. "And if they were really mad at each other, they spoke in Japanese. It was pretty funny."

"There are some letters to our grandmother from your parents while they were in the Philippine Islands that you might want to go through," I said, showing her a pile of documents. "It appears that either our grandmother used to draft out letters before she sent them, or she wrote letters that she didn't send."

For the next several hours, we both read letters and tried to trace events.

Saturday was Bobby and Julia's wedding. I had no idea where it would be, so I trusted Mary Anne and Joyce to get us there, but we got lost and didn't make it to the church until after the ceremony started. We were seated in the back of the church, where Bobby and Julia would turn right in front of us on the way out. As predicted, when they turned in front of us, Bob was shocked to see me there and stopped the wedding procession for a few minutes while we hugged each other. I couldn't have planned the reunion better.

Aunt Bonnie, Bobby's mother, rode with us to the reception. On the way over, Mary Anne asked her if she knew how our grandparents had met.

She said, "Well, your grandmother went to a carnival and saw a fortune-teller, and he told her that she was going to marry someone with the initials HE. She met your grandfather and they rode the ferris wheel. The rest is history." Aunt Bonnie then turned to me and said, "You know, your dad was always pulling stunts like the one you pulled today. He'd just show up unannounced. Eleanor was always talking about the time she thought he was off someplace and he just showed up and took her to lunch!"

I was overcome with emotion at the wedding reception, being it was my father's family, from whom I'd been separated for too many years and too many miles. I met Bobby's children from his previous marriage. I'd never met them, but here they were, grown up and with families of their own.

Bobby and Julia came by, and we were able to visit briefly between the dancing and cake cutting. They were scheduled to leave for their honeymoon in the Caribbean after the reception. The nurse had brought Aunt Eleanor to the reception, but not to the wedding. I sat with her at her table for a while and tried to visit with her, but she could hardly speak. I know she recognized me, since I was conscious of her sparkling eyes being glued to my every move.

Sunday we looked at all the pictures, in an attempt to identify who various relatives or friends might be. Mary Anne, being more familiar with the pictures, was able to identify several distant relatives. From the letters I had reviewed, it was obvious that my father had been married before. I remembered that my mother had mentioned it, but it was never discussed. According to Mary Anne, my father had apparently eloped with a girl named Ruth, who was a friend of her mother. It hadn't lasted very long.

I took Mary Anne to the attic and pointed out other trunks that were empty or had meaningless items in them. I showed her the trunk with the bedpan and the glass urinal.

"Oh, ick," she exclaimed. "This stuff should be thrown away." But as she picked up the glass urinal, her eyes suddenly sparkled. "No, the bar. I can fill it with wine!"

She jumped up with the urinal and ran downstairs to wash it.

Surrounded by letters and documents, Mary Anne and I sat in the living room, reading letters. Mary Anne read letters regarding her mother. I sorted the letters and memorabilia into chronological order, using the postmarks on the envelopes. I was able to trace his life, particularly from the time the New Jersey National Guard was activated, through his service in the South Pacific.

The first record of my father's life, besides his baby picture, was his certificate of credits from Haddon Heights High School.

Perusing the credits, I asked Mary Anne, "Didn't your folks also go to

Haddon Heights?"

"Yes," she replied. "That's where they met. They were childhood sweethearts. My mother was a cheerleader and my father was a jock. He lettered in baseball, diving, and football."

"I remember reading about a George Wells who graduated from Haddon Heights in 1937. I remember it because I knew my father attended the same school, but figured, because of his age, that he would have graduated before George Wells," I said.

"So what's the story with George Wells? My folks graduated in 1937, so they would have been in the same class," Mary Anne said as she looked for a yearbook.

"George Wells held the record for the most bombing missions during WWII. He was in the European theater, though. When he reached ninety-nine, his buddy Fred Dyer was also a pilot with ninety-nine, so they got permission to fly together for the record-breaking 100th mission. They flipped a coin to see who would fly as pilot, and George Wells won. They flew the mission in a plane that was also on its 100th mission. They returned to lots of media coverage. Someone said that another pilot had flown 101 missions, fifty in the Pacific, and fifty-one in Europe, so they got permission to fly two more missions together so they could set the record at 102."

Some records indicated that my father had attended Pierce Business College, but the date was unclear. Apparently he was looking for a job, since the following letter was found in the mass of documents.

Laurel Springs, N.J.
December 9, 1932

Employer'S Exchange
1328 Chestnut Street
Philadelphia, Pa.

Dear Sir:

I received your letter today stating that I owe you $6.10, for a position you secured for me. I do not think I should pay you this money because I did not receive that much myself. I was informed about the position on Nov. 28 and on Nov. 29 the office was closed until January. Therefore I worked only two days, and received only two dollars pay.

If you wish to verify this statement you may call Camden 2470. This is the office telephone number and altho no one is supposed to be there, it is possible that someone will be there, when you call.

However, if I am taken back when the office reopens, as I am supposed to be, you may trust me that I will send you the $ 6.00.

I enclose the ten cents for the telephone call you made and I thank you for securing the position for me, even though it lasted only two days.

Very truly yours,

George Frederick

Sitting back in a chair, I became immersed in the letters. With the aid of my knowledge of WWII in the South Pacific I could imagine the events. As I read the letters, I felt pride in the accomplishments of my father, suffered his disappointments and frustrations, and shared his love for travel. Although they had never been communicated to me, I could understand and sense his inner feelings.

"Was it heredity?" I wondered.

LETTERS HOME

From the time it was activated in September 1940 until October 1941, the New Jersey 57th Infantry Brigade was stationed at Ft. Dix. There are no letters home until October 1941, when the brigade was transferred to participate in war games southeast of Charlotte, North Carolina. Apparently the Frederick family had friends who lived in Charlotte. George had always gone to church and Sunday school. In New Jersey, he was active in the youth activities and was an officer of the church. When he wasn't home he attended churches of different denominations.

Oct 27, 1941

Dear Mom,

Received your letter yesterday after I returned from an enjoyable weekend in Charlotte. Mr. & Mrs. Helms and the family sure treated us swell. They were sorry they didn't ask us to bring Harry over but they didn't know he was down here, so next time we get a chance to go over we are to take Harry over with us.

That sure is surprising about Ed not wanting a Red-Blue party. If I'm not mistaken he was the one who suggested one in the first place and now that we have a nice basement why not use it? I'm glad to hear that church is coming along OK and only wish I could be there. Dad and I and Herb Suther (Mrs. Helms' son-in-law) attended the First Methodist Church in Charlotte yesterday. There were 150 in the Bible class in Sunday School and between 1500 and 2000 to church but the choir only had 14 in it so we don't do so bad at home.

Did Dad tell you the new set-up we have? He doesn't have to go out on the maneuvers and the rest of us work with the regiment as assistants to the corresponding officers on the regimental staff. I wouldn't be surprised if they broke the brigades up when we get back to Dix. All the new high-ranking officers coming in are Regular Army so it looks like we are on our way out.

Since I don't have time to do much writing, please tell Mr. & Mrs. Reiner that I am thinking of them.

Well, we haven't had any rain yet but today it really is blowing. The dirt is flying all over the place and we can't keep anything clean.

I guess there isn't any more news now so I'll close.

Loads of love and kisses,
George

2

"SOMEWHERE IN THE U.S.A."
In the woods,
Friday, Nov. 14, 1941

Dear Mother:

Received your letter last Monday and now have time to answer it. Yes, I was company commander for two weeks, but now I am not even with the 57th Brigade. I am acting as understudy to the Adjutant of Special Troops, 44th Division, as the adjutant there expects to get out in a few weeks. Major Ivins suggested my name to Colonel Schrodor and he asked me if I wanted to come over with him. I thought it over and decided I have a better chance for promotion with special troops than I had if I stayed with Brigade, so here I am. As adjutant, I have command of the headquarters detachment, which is only eight men, but a lot of property. When I mentioned it to the general, he said it was up to me. He said he wanted to keep me as company commander and S-2, but if I wanted to go over to Special Troops or if I thought I had a better chance there, he wouldn't stand in my way. Incidentally, where I was with Dad before, now I am in the same outfit as Harry. In fact, when we are in the field the truck he rides in, follows immediately in the rear of the one I ride in.

I know that if you have charge of the Ladies Aid this month, it will go all right. Mrs. Fellman and Mrs. Sanning are both very helpful and I know they will work together OK with you. I am a little concerned about the Ladies Aid if Mr. Bramhall keeps putting his foot down on them doing anything. I think what they ought to do is not to hold whatever they want to and ask the church trustees for permission, regardless of what Mr. Bramhall says or thinks.

On the piano situation, there was supposed to be one put down there. We got an extra piano from Mrs. Maision to be placed in the basement but I guess like everything else, you just can't get anyone together to do anything unless it's for their own benefit. That's a good idea on the curtain and I will write to Mr. Reiner and see if he can arrange something like it.

Just now we are out in the woods waiting for our last phase of the field maneuvers to start. This is the one that's supposed to be the all out maneuver. There is quite a force assembled against us but I guess we can beat them, at least we can try.

Well, there's no more news at present. I hope you are feeling fine and I expect to be home by this time next month.

Loads of love and kisses

George

3/4 mile SW Pageland, SC
November 28, 1941

3   *Dear Mother:*

Received your letter yesterday. Boy, it sure takes a long time to get mail from Jersey. Yours is postmarked the 23rd and I got it the 27th.

Dad gave me that insurance blank and I'll take care of it OK so you can forget it.

I'm glad the Ladies Aid is going to continue the luncheons. I think they are a fine thing and help to keep the Ladies active around church. Gee, what did we spend money on a nice basement for anyway, if we can't use it?

As to the Deason's not wanting suppers, it seems to me that Ralph Townsend never objected and neither did Dad, so that's two out of four, and two of the older members of the church besides.

If Mrs. Willis keeps up her arguing she will tear down everything we have built up. That Ladies class is constantly growing but if they're going to have arguments at their class meetings, I guess it will fall apart like everything else. If Mrs. Willis can't do any better than that she ought to stay home, in my opinion.

Ed Kalix sent me an airmail letter telling me all about the contest. They went over the 100-dollar mark in money and the Sunday school attendance has been over the 90 mark the last couple of Sundays so it was a very successful contest. I thought that was nice of him to let me know so promptly.

This war is nearly over. We have advanced 50 miles since Sunday night and if it keeps up, we'll be out of the maneuver area so we'll have to stop soon. I thought we would have a chance to go to Helm's in Charlotte this week-end but I guess not now, because we won't be back in camp until tomorrow night.

Our Thanksgiving dinner was good considering we were out in the woods, not even in base camp. It rained all day and our services were held in the rain, as well as our dinner so you can imagine what it was like. That was the first time I ever stood to eat my Thanksgiving dinner, but it was the only way we could eat it. The ground was too wet to sit on, so we stood at the crude tables we made out of logs. We had turkey, of course, but the rest was just plain food. The menu they had in the paper sounded good, but the only ones that had that were the ones in the permanent camps.

I had dinner with Harry but Dad was back in base camp. I imagine he faired better than we did, because he at least had a table to sit at. I saw Dad Saturday night at See's in Wadesboro. He had come in for a bath and since we were only ten miles away, I managed to get in also for the same purpose.

How has the weather been? It has been cold and warm here. During the day it gets up to about 60 and at night goes down to about 25. I sleep with my clothes on, as does everyone else, so we are not too cold.

Tell Eleanor I said to write. She owes me a letter but maybe I'll get a chance to write one to her anyway.

No word as to the close of the battle yet but it's eleven o'clock and everyone seems to think it's about over, so I'll close now.

Loads of love and kisses,

George

IN THE PRECEDING MONTHS, Japan had expanded its holdings into Indochina to obtain and secure supplies it felt were essential for its self-defense. Their move into Indochina was intended to accelerate the settlement of their war with China. Japan stated their motivating policy was for defensive purposes, since the means of its existence was being threatened. Japan viewed the actions and measures that had been taken by the United States as inimical to a peaceful settlement in the Pacific area. Japan and the

United States were attempting, through negotiations, to restore peace in the Pacific. Japan stated that "it is sometimes difficult to ascertain when an event is a cause and it is a consequence."[i] Of course, one of the items under discussion was the amount of oil the United States would ship to Japan.

Secretary of State Hull laid out to Ambassador Nomura what would restore peace in the Pacific. Among the provisions were: a mutual non-aggression treaty between Japan, United States, Russia, and other countries; equality of economic treatment and a reciprocal trade agreement between Japan and the United States; and an agreement by Japan to evacuate its forces from China and to recognize no support other than that of Chiang Kai-Shek. The United States and Japan would also unfreeze each other's assets in their respective countries. Japan viewed the terms as "humiliating."

Meanwhile, the United States was intercepting diplomatic messages to and from Japan. These messages gave every indication that war was imminent. For example, a record was being kept by Japan of all ships that traveled through the Panama Canal, as well as ships entering and leaving U.S. west coast ports, Manila, Pearl Harbor, Midway, and other ports in the Pacific. Messages were also intercepted from Japanese representatives who'd had meetings with Mussolini in Italy and with Hitler's foreign minister, Ribbentrop, in Berlin.

As early as October, a message from Japanese Ambassador Nomura stated, "U.S.–Japanese relations are now fast approaching a critical crossroad. The United States is gradually strengthening its wartime structure."

Nomura continued by stating it was doubtful that war would break out over the China problem alone, but that it would be impossible for the United States to impose terms on China that it would itself endure. The United States wanted agreements covering preservation of peace for the entire Pacific area, and not a patchwork of hit-or-miss local agreements.

Nomura completed his communiqué by stating, "If we depend on immediate settlement...by insisting upon our freedom of action, we must have our minds made up that not only will these negotiations be terminated, but that our national relations will be severed."

An intercepted message on November 25 to Tokyo from Hanoi stated that they'd been advised by the military to have a reply from the United States regarding the negotiations for peace and that the Japanese cabinet would make a decision between war and peace within the next day or two. It said that if the negotiations were successful, "various enterprises shall be launched in accordance with the plans which have been laid down in advance…and if not…all preparations for the campaign have been completed, our forces shall be able to move within the day."

A most glaring warning of Japan's impending actions was intercepted by the United States three days later, on November 28. The transmission from Tokyo to Washington complimented the ambassador's superhuman efforts, but that the negotiations were "de facto ruptured," and ordered, "Do not give the impression that negotiations are broken off."

Another message on December 2 revealed the intentions of Germany in a transcribed message relating a meeting between the Japanese ambassador to Germany and Germany's foreign minister Ribbentrop. Ribbentrop had just come from a meeting with Hitler, Goering, and other bigwigs, so the meeting didn't happen until late in the evening. In the meeting, Ribbentrop revealed their plans for the war in Russia and Europe. They wouldn't invade England, but would acquire their territories jointly with Japan and Italy. Germany would retain Europe and colonies in Africa, Italy would have the rest of Africa, and Japan would have the Pacific colonies. If war broke out between Japan and the United States, they would join with Japan against the United States.

Ribbentrop concluded the meeting by revealing that Hitler had stated, "If Japan reaches a decision to fight Britain and the United States, I am confident that that will not only be to the interest of Germany and Japan jointly, but would bring about favorable results for Japan herself."

A communiqué the next day from Tokyo instructed the Japanese ambassador to convey to Germany "very secretly that there is extreme danger that war may suddenly break out between the Anglo-Saxon nations and Japan through some clash of arms and that the time of the breaking out of this war may come quicker than anyone dreams."

Also on December 1, Tokyo sent instructions on how to destroy codes to Washington and other locations. It instructed its Hawaiian office observing Pearl Harbor to report the presence of ships in Pearl Harbor on a day-by-day basis, to let them know if there were observation balloons over the harbor and if the warships were provided with anti-mine nets.

On December 3, the Japanese ambassador to Italy met with Mussolini, saying, "If Japan declares war on the United States" that Italy would do so also and promised military aid. On December 5, Japan ordered their U.S. ambassadors to send certain individuals home by airplane in the next few days and the ambassadors told Tokyo that all but one of their code machines had been destroyed.

On December 6, the Washington office was advised by Tokyo that it would send a response to the United States concerning their proposal. They stated it was a very long message, in fourteen parts, and to "make every preparation to present it to the Americans just as soon as you receive instructions." They were also advised that absolute secrecy be maintained and not to use a "typist."

A message from Tokyo to Bangkok stated the notice would be given on the 7th, and from Tokyo to Honolulu, a note said, "Please wire immediately re: the latter part of my #123 [a] the movements of the fleet subsequent to the fourth."

Also on December 6, President Roosevelt sent a personal message to Emperor Hirohito, stating because of the "deep and far-reaching emergency which appears to be in formation," a situation that was freighted with "tragic possibilities," he hoped that the emperor would join him in an effort to restore the traditional amity that had existed between the United States and Japan. As the message was being delivered that evening, President Roosevelt received the first parts of the fourteen-part message. He read the message and then handed it to Harry Hopkins, who was with him and had been pacing slowly back and forth a few feet away from Roosevelt's desk.

"This means war," Roosevelt exclaimed.

Hopkins agreed and suggested that since war was inevitable at any moment, it was too bad the United States couldn't strike the first blow and prevent any sort of surprise.

Roosevelt replied, "No, we can't do that. We're a democracy and a peaceful people. But we have a good record."

Transmission of the fourteen-part memorandum reply concluded on December 7, with the final paragraph stating:

...the earnest hope of the Japanese Government to adjust Japanese-American relations and to preserve and promote the peace of the Pacific through cooperation with the American Government has finally been lost. The Japanese Government regrets to have to notify hereby the American Government that in view of the attitude of the American Government it cannot but consider that it is impossible to reach an agreement through further negotiations.

A separate Tokyo message to Washington instructed: "Will the Ambassador please submit to the United States Government (if possible to the Secretary of State) our reply to the United States at 1:00 p. m. on the 7th, your time."

Japan attacked Pearl Harbor, and even before Germany declared war, Hitler issued orders for his navy to destroy American ships wherever and whenever they were found. Germany and Italy declared war on the United States, and we were officially at war with Japan, Germany, and Italy.

In late 1941, the Japanese Army numbered approximately 1.7 million. They were determined to win their war with China and by driving west to eventually isolate China from the rest of the world. Although Russia was not viewed as an immediate threat it was not being ignored. They intended to capture or drive General MacArthur and the US forces out of the Philippines and also to destroy the US Pacific Fleet. By driving south the Japanese would obtain the valuable resources in the islands of Indonesia.

Japanese military might increased with the synergy of their expanding mineral rich conquests. Left for them was the establishment of an impenetrable defensive perimeter, holding the populace of their conquered territories in slavery, and a longer range objective of isolating Australia and forcing it to surrender.

The Japanese attack on Pearl Harbor very nearly accomplished the objective of destroying the US Pacific Fleet; however the aircraft carriers were saved as they were out to sea. The attack and invasion of the Philippine Islands to capture or drive General MacArthur and the US Forces out of the Philippines was launched on December 8th. The US forces are virtually defenseless from the Japanese air attacks and immediately lose over half of the 160 airplanes that are stationed on Luzon. Capture of the Philippines would also ensure Japans fuel flow of petrol from the East Indies.

The Japanese attack from both the north and south; virtually surrounding Luzon. With time running out MacArthur consolidates his forces on the Bataan Peninsula. Because of his familiarity with the terrain from having spent so much time in the Philippines he is able to establish a series of defensive perimeters that stall the Japanese attack. MacArthur's' plea for reinforcements or for a mass exodus from a southern location are ignored in Washington.

IN NEW JERSEY, the Frederick Family, my father, grandparents, Uncle Harry and his fiancée Bonny, and Aunt Eleanor and her beau, Warren, celebrated the holidays. With Warren joining the navy, war in both the Pacific and Europe, and all the men in the family in the military, there was an undercurrent of feelings, not said, but prevalent, wondering if it would be the last time the family would be together. My grandfather would be stationed in Philadelphia, putting in radar sites up and down the East Coast. George and Uncle Harry drove my father's new blue 1941 Oldsmobile two-door coupe to Camp Claiborne in central Louisiana in early January 1942.

War with Germany, Italy, and Japan had been declared but one month. The country was gripped with anxiety over the challenges ahead. The Pacific Fleet was severely crippled, saved only by the vulnerable aircraft carriers having been out to sea when Pearl Harbor was attacked. Only a few pessimists thought the war couldn't be won, but the news of German submarines (U-Boats) sinking supply ships to England faster then they could be built, General MacArthur's retreat from the Philippine Islands, and the enemy's control of more and more of the world's resources was depressing. The news only deepened the American resolve to pull together in the quest for ultimate victory. Prices rose on all goods, if you could get them. Gas, oil, nylon, and many other products were rationed. Rumors abounded—the Japanese were in submarines off the coast of California.

George and Harry drove to Camp Claiborne, filled with anticipation of what was ahead of them. Their dreams of a peaceful existence, surrounded by family and friends in the suburbs of Philadelphia, had been shattered and left behind. They were anxious to do their part and prove that they weren't afraid of battle.

LIFE MAGAZINE, in its October 6, 1941 issue, had run an article on Camp Claiborne with the headline, "Big Maneuvers Test U.S. Army; in Swamps and Forests of Louisiana, 350,000 Soldiers Stage Greatest Sham Battle in History." Army officials sought to make the maneuvers as close to real battlefield conditions as possible.

General George C. Marshall served as Chief of Staff of the Army. Marshall felt that the United States military lagged behind other countries in manpower, equipment, and field training. Marshall ordered the Louisiana maneuvers put into operation. Throughout World War II, Marshall chaired the JCS[ii] (Joint Chiefs of Staff) at the newly constructed Pentagon. Shortly after the war, Marshall retired from the Army and accepted the position of Secretary of State in the Truman Administration.

The Louisiana maneuvers in the fall of 1941 were a landmark in the development of the U.S. Army's strategy and planning for war, because they proved the usefulness of tanks in modern warfare. General Joseph Stilwell commanded a "blitzkrieg" invasion of Louisiana, just as Hitler's forces had used to slice through France. The 1941 maneuvers further revealed the weakness of conventional defenses against armored might when General George S. Patton proved that tanks could operate effectively even in the marshes of Louisiana. In addition, Army planners learned about reconnaissance and troop supply problems encountered in battlefield situations.

All branches of the Army had their leadership skills tested in the maneu-vers. Performance of officers from all branches of the Regular Army and the National Guard, from infantry to air corps, from general to corporal, were evaluated. Many of these officers would have distinguished military and civilian careers during and following the war. Some notable officers who par-ticipated in the 1941 maneuvers were General Eisenhower, Henry Kissinger, General Omar Bradley, General Walter Krueger, and General Innis P. Swift.

Lt. General Walter Krueger served as commander of the Blue Third Army during the Louisiana maneuvers. Krueger took command of this army in May 1941, and soundly defeated the opposing Red Army. Krueger was a professional soldier, beginning his military career as a private in 1898. Krueger was recognized as one of the U.S. Army's best educated and percep-tive officers, who kept pace with the changes of the art of war. In February 1943, Krueger was promoted to Commanding General of the Sixth Army in the Southwest Pacific Theater of Operations, including the Philippine Islands. Krueger was promoted to the rank of full general in March 1944, due to his outstanding leadership in the Pacific.

Major General Innis P. Swift served in the Louisiana maneuvers as the commanding general of the 1st Cavalry Division. The Louisiana maneuvers were the last campaign for the mounted cavalry units of the U.S. Army. Swift commanded his cavalry troopers through all the battles and skirmishes, including the crossing of the Sabine River as the 1st Cavalry attacked the Red Second Cavalry at Zwolle, Louisiana, and started turning the western flank for Krueger. After the maneuvers, Swift led the 1st Cavalry to the Southwest Pacific, where they engaged in the fighting for the Admiralty Islands in 1944. Later, the division entered the fighting in the Philippine Islands as General MacArthur fulfilled his promise to return and liberate the Philippine people.

AT CAMP CLAIBORNE, George signed up to become a pilot and Uncle Harry applied for Officers Candidate School.

Camp Claiborne, LA
January 23, 1942

4

Dear Mother:

This is the first opportunity I have had to write a letter, as my eyes have not been good the last couple of days.

We arrived here last Friday without any mishaps and immediately went to work cleaning out the area we moved into—the 34th Division that was here had to move out on 12 hours notice and they left quite a lot of rubbish around.

On Monday I had to take an additional physical examination for the air corps application. This time they gave me a complete flying examination and I passed OK in Class No. 1, which is required for pilot training. All I need now is approval of the Chief of the air corps, so I hope I get that and get in the air corps.

I had drops put in my eyes for the dilation test and therefore had to stay at Barksdale Field over Monday night. I got back here Tuesday night but it takes two or three days to get your eyes back to normal and that is why I haven't written a letter sooner.

I didn't ask Harry whether he wrote or not, but in case he didn't, he is fine and yesterday passed his physical examination for appointment to Officers Candidate School. He now has to go before a Board for his mental qualifications which he shouldn't have any trouble passing.

I sent Dad something for his birthday from Harry & I and forgot to put a card in it so I hope he gets it OK and tell him who it is from. Tell him several of the officers have asked me about him and are anxious to hear how he is making out.

Well, I guess that's all for the present.

Loads of love and kisses,

George

PS: My address:
Lt. George F. Frederick
Hq Special Troops
44th Division
APO 44
Camp Claiborne, LA

Camp Claiborne, LA
Feb. 1, 1942

Dear Mother:

Received your letter today and those others you sent me yesterday.

I haven't heard anything yet on my air corps application, even though there was a telegram sent by General Muir requesting the status of the application. He wanted to know because under the new set-up, I won't have any job, as Special Troops will be disbanded. There goes my one big chance for promotion too, because Col. Schroeder was going to recommend me for Captain today under the new method of promotion by selection because I'm doing a Captain's job, but since this job is to be abolished, he can't.

I suppose I'll be shifted over to a new job that won't rate Captain and then I'll be stuck as far as promotion goes. But you never can tell, maybe I'll get a better job. I asked to be assigned to a new outfit, the 44th Cav. Reconnaissance Troop, but I don't know how I'll make out on that. It's to be formed using the 57th Brigade Hq Co as a nucleus, so maybe I should have stayed with them.

You can see now why I'm anxious to get in the air corps, at least when you become a pilot you know what your job is and don't get shifted around from job to job.

Say is Eleanor sick? I haven't heard a word from her. Didn't she get my letter? Let me know.

I got a letter from Dad a couple of days ago and he says he is kept rather busy. I'm glad he's in Philadelphia, though, because at least he is close to you even if he can't actually get home all the time.

I received a letter from Freddie Hufner and he sails for somewhere next week but doesn't know where. I also got a letter from Marion Fried but none from Ruth Reiner. Well, if she doesn't want to write she doesn't have to but if she is sick or something let me know. Maybe Eleanor can find out for me and write.

Harry borrowed the car today to go into Alexandria to attend a wedding. His papers for Officers Candidate School are going thru here all right so I guess he'll be ordered to appear before the examining board soon. I hope he passes OK and I believe he will. Under this new set-up, if Col. Edmunds was fair, Harry should get a promotion, but he says the Colonel won't promote him as he wants to transfer a couple of men from the Ordnance Company. I put a word in for him anyway but don't know what good it will do.

Well, I guess that's all the news from here just now.

Lots of love & kisses,

George

44th Division Special Troops
Camp Claiborne, Louisiana
Feb. 11, 1942

Dear Mother:

I received your letter yesterday. I wish I knew when this free mail is going to start. I didn't know anything about it, as the papers down here *are only 10 pages and have very little news in them.*

On my air corps application, I'm not worrying because I've been praying every night that it will come thru and I know it will. I understand that a class for officers is supposed to start March 2nd so if I am chosen for that class I should hear something next week. The trouble seems to be that they have expanded so rapidly there is no room to put anyone until another class is graduated.

I'm glad that Dad has gotten something where he can be active because I know he hates to be inactive.

Did I tell you Mr. Reiner sent me a beautiful ring? It is made out of a solid bar of Morel metal and he did the work on it and then had it engraved with my initials. It really is swell and everyone here is admiring it.

By the way, how is the weather at home? It has been raining here the last couple of days and yesterday was cold but today it warmed up so that I didn't need to wear a jacket when I went to supper.

We move into the new area next week. It is worse than Fort Dix was in the tent area but we are used to that so I suppose we will build another camp like we did back at Dix.

Well, that's all the news. Harry has my car tonite. He went into Alexandria with some of the fellows.

Loads of love & kisses,

George

As predicted, George's application for flight training came through the next week. George took his Oldsmobile away from his brother and drove to San Antonio to start flight training at Kelly field while Harry stayed at Camp Claiborne.

IN DECEMBER, NEARLY SIMULTANEOUS with their attack on Pearl Harbor, the Japanese invaded the Philippine Islands in the northern regions of Luzon. The inexperienced and underequipped Filipino troops were no match for the 57,000 well-equipped veteran Japanese troops of the 14th Army, who immediately installed three air bases. In January, General MacArthur retreated to the Bataan Peninsula, which in the original battle plan was to "lay down a bunt" by stalling the Japanese advance as long as possible. It was designed to buy time in order to rebuild the American Pacific Fleet.

Despite a shortage of food, medicine, gasoline for the few trucks and tanks, and ammunition, the Filipino troops, most of whom had never fired a weapon, were thrown into frontline combat against the highly trained Japanese veterans. Americans from non-combatant outfits, such as air corpsmen and civilians, were formed into infantry units. Plagued by disease, malnutrition, and fatigue, the Bataan defenders continued to hold the Bataan peninsula during February. On February 22, General MacArthur was advised by General Marshall that President Roosevelt had personally directed him to leave Bataan and escape to Australia.

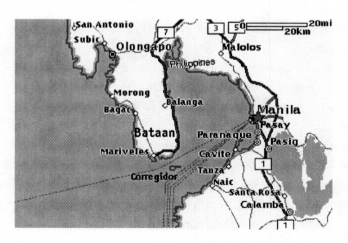

In February, the Far East Air Force was redesignated the 5th Army Air Force. They ceased operations in Brisbane, Australia, and moved to Java, an island east of Singapore, and south of Borneo and the Bataan peninsula.

31

A LEGACY OF LETTERS

Their ground echelon was entrenched with the troops on Bataan.

In San Antonio, George must have spent one night in the Plaza Hotel, since the next night he was in the bachelor quarters at Kelly Field. He was stationed at Kelly Field only one month. The telegrams that were sent weren't found in the trunk.

The Plaza Hotel
Tom L. Powell, Manager
San Antonio, Texas

Feb 25, 1942

Dear Mother:

Well, here I am. I arrived here last nite and came out to Kelly Field this morning.

All day we have been getting ourselves arranged and quartered. I have a room in the Bachelor Officers Quarters similar to the one I had at Fort Dix, except this is a nice bright corner room and is painted inside.

Our classes don't begin until Saturday. We are supposed to be here until April 1st and then we go to another field for our basic or primary training. It is supposed to be a 30-week course for us but they may shorten it. All we get here is classwork & athletics, so as to harden us up for the flying training, which is really tough.

In that telegram I sent you, I put the wrong address so I hope you didn't mail anything to it yet. The correct address is:
Lt. George F. Frederick
Squadron 10

Pilot Replacement Center
San Antonio, Texas

 This part of the field that we are on is much higher than the rest of the area and from our rear window of our quarters we can see San Antonio which is about 3 miles from here.
 I guess that's all I have to say now, except I hope you are well. I'll write Dad & Eleanor as soon as I can.

Love and kisses,

George

IN EARLY MARCH 1942, a lone Japanese airplane attempted to bomb Honolulu, but dropped its bombs short of the city. Pursuit planes of the 7th AAF lost the plane in the clouds. Japanese forces captured Rangoon, dealing China a blow by cutting off supplies from Burma along the Burma Road.

The *USS Canopus*, a destroyer tender, off the coast of Corregidor, was loaded with explosives and radio equipment. The radio equipment on Corregidor was from one of the secret locations where Japanese radio messages were intercepted, sent to Washington and decoded. Anthony Kruszyna, a cook on board the *Canopus*, was ordered off the boat, along with the rest of the crew, and joined the forces on Corregidor to defend the island. The *USS Canopus* was deliberately blown up and sunk, destroying all evidence of the ability to intercept and decode Japanese messages. Kruszyna, eventually became a prisoner of the Japanese, was transported to Japan on a "Hell Ship," and wasn't freed until Japan surrendered in 1945. He never recovered from the damage caused him physically or mentally, and died at an early age. Dan,[iii] his only child, became a very competent electrician in Phoenix, Arizona.

By March 11, General MacArthur had retreated to the island of Corregidor, which was surrounded by the Japanese navy. MacArthur, having ignored General Marshall, received a direct order from President Roosevelt to escape to Australia and leave General Wainwright behind with 11,000 troops. MacArthur wrote a letter of resignation, with the intent of becoming a civilian volunteer to the army on Bataan. His chief of staff, Major General Richard Sutherland, pointed out the closing lines of the president's cable, saying he was to assume command of all United States troops in the South Pacific.

"It's not a retreat, but the first step in defeating the Japanese," Sutherland pointed out. "You are needed to build and lead the army that will ultimately drive the enemy out of the Philippine Islands."

General King took Wainwright's place as Commander of the Filipino-American forces, and General Wainwright took MacArthur's position as Commanding General in the Philippines. MacArthur arranged for four decrepit PT boats to take himself , his family and fifteen officers to the Del Monte airfield on Mindanao, an island in the southern Philippines. The airfield was so-named because it belonged to the Del Monte Corporation.

Arriving at the muddy Del Monte airfield, they had to wait for their B-17s to take them to Batchelor airfield in the northern territory of Australia. Using spare parts three B-17's had been salvaged from the Philippines and flown to Australia for repair. These three B-17s took off to pick up MacArthur and his entourage. One had to turn back because of engine trouble. One, flown by Captain Goodman, was unable to complete the flight and crashed into the sea near Mindanao, with the loss of two of his crew. Only one was able to land on the dimly lit runway, and it had to be ground looped because it had lost its brakes. MacArthur was furious, and even more so when he saw Lt. Harl Pease[iv] jump from the plane.

"He's only a boy," MacArthur muttered.

He wouldn't allow anyone to board the decrepit planes and demanded experienced airmen.

MacArthur had to wait at Del Monte until General Brett was able to 'borrow' B-17s from the Navy in southern Australia. The B-17s were overloaded at Del Monte and MacArthur had to leave some of his luggage. Even so, four people managed to stow away on the plane for the flight to Australia.

After a harrowing five-hour flight within a few miles of Japanese airbases, the entourage arrived at Batchelor Field, forty-five miles south of Darwin, Australia, at nine a.m. on March 18th.

MacArthur remarked to his chief of staff, General Sutherland, "It was close, but that's the way it is in war. You win or lose, live or die—and the difference is just an eyelash."

MacArthur asked an American officer about the build-up of troops to retake the Philippines and was told there were but a few troops.

MacArthur was shocked and said to Sutherland, "Surely, he is wrong."

MacArthur and family left Batchelor on two Australian National Airways DC-3s in the midst of a Japanese air raid warning, which led to a bumpy departure. Arriving at Alice Springs, Australia, Mrs. MacArthur refused to fly any more. MacArthur sent his officers on south by plane while he boarded a special narrow-gauge train for the seventy-hour trip to the Terowie Railway, 220 kilometers north of Adelaide, arriving at 2 p.m. on March 20. His "secret trip" was met by a crowd of local people and the Australian press.

It was here that MacArthur stated, "I came out of Bataan and I shall return."

In early April, General King, commanding the Filipino-American forces holding Bataan, was forced to surrender to the Japanese, and early in May, Corregidor fell to the Japanese.

General Wainwright sent a cable to Washington D.C., stating: "There is a limit of human endurance and that limit has long since been passed. Without prospect of relief, I feel it is my duty to my country, and to my gallant troops, to end this useless effusion of blood and human sacrifice. With profound regret and continued pride in my gallant troops, I go to meet the Japanese commander. Goodbye, Mr. President."

Thus began the infamous Bataan Death March, where thousands of American prisoners lost their lives.

Meanwhile, General MacArthur found that he had only about 32,000 Allied troops at his disposal in Australia, though he thought he'd have a whole army. He had less than 100 airplanes, and many of those were clothbound and had to be started by handspinning the propellers. It was his greatest shock of the whole war.

"God have mercy on us!" he muttered.

MacArthur initially set up his headquarters in a hotel in Melbourne. One of his first acts was to fire Major General George H. Brett for the "miserable job" he'd done on MacArthur's rescue and for failing to reinforce Bataan. Unbeknownst to MacArthur, Brett had recommended him as Supreme Commander of the Southwest Pacific Area. MacArthur formally assumed command on April 18, 1942, and moved his headquarters to Brisbane.

ON MARCH 25, George left San Antonio and drove to Tulsa, Oklahoma, to take flight training at the Spartan School of Aviation. It didn't take him long to get settled into an apartment with two other officers. He wrote to his mother on March 25, and to his kid sister, Eleanor, on the 30th about her upcoming marriage.

March 25, 1942

Dear Mother:

Just have time to drop a line to see how you are and, as usual, ask you to do something for me.

Because we are moving around from place to place, it is rather inconvenient to keep shipping my steamer trunk so I decided to send it home. I can carry everything I have here in my car and therefore there isn't much use in paying every time I go somewhere.

I am enclosing the keys to it because I want you to open it when it comes. In the top drawer you will find a little something for your birthday and also a little knick-knack for Eleanor as a souvenir of San Antonio.

In the bottom drawer there is a box containing one service of a din-

ner set. Each officer was given one when the Special Troops broke up and I hope they carried OK. To get the bottom three drawers open it is necessary to pull the top drawer all the way out and then move the latch in the back to unlock the others.

It was shipped express collect, so let me know how much it will be and I'll send it to you.

We leave tomorrow morning for Dallas and then arrive at Tulsa, Okla. on Friday. We start training Monday so here's hoping I make out OK.

Oh, yes, the rest of the junk in the trunk can stay there as far as I am concerned.

Well, I guess I'll close now and I hope you are well.
Lots of love & kisses,

George

March 30, 1942

Dearest Eleanor:

Received the invitation to your wedding today. Golly it doesn't seem possible—my "kid" sister getting married.

I am sure I won't be able to make it because we are flying seven days a week. I go up for my first flight tomorrow at 8:00 a.m. so by the time you get this, I'll have been up for the first time in my life. We go up in open cockpit planes, so it is an additional thrill—also we hold the stick to get the feel of the controls.

We have 5 in our group. Two officers and three cadets. Each group of 5 has a separate instructor and he is with us throughout the entire course of our primary school. We get 60 hours of flying—about half of it solo. If we get thru this we have a good chance of going all the way thru to get our *wings. I'll let you know more about the course in my next letter.*

We drew our flying togs yesterday and they are the summer issue and golly, it is cold here. It was 32° this morning—quite a change from San Antonio. We live in Tulsa, as there are no accommodations at the airport—which incidentally is the Tulsa Municipal Airport, where all the liners come in.

Yesterday I spent touring Tulsa in the afternoon, as we had to report to the field in the morning. They have a swell park here and a zoo, so we went to the zoo.

I am living with two other officers in a three- room apartment plus bath and dinette. We pay $70 a month rent, which includes maid service, linen, and dishes. We are going to cook breakfast and supper and we have to eat lunch at the airport restaurant.

It is in a swell location and is called "Trenton Terrace." It reminds me a lot of my old Oaklyn apartment except it is bigger. There are three other officers living in other apartments in the same building. They are all married, so we have arranged to use our cars alternately, so as to save wear on the tires. Two of the fellows don't own cars so they are going to pay. It is only 7 1/2 miles to the field from here and since we have to be there at 7:45 a.m. we get up at 6:00 a.m. so as to cook and eat breakfast.

I guess it will work out OK but right now it is funny. We are trying to borrow money from the bank down here for 30 days so we can have enough money to eat. That sounds odd, but all of us are in the same boat. Since we changed stations at the end of the month, we won't get paid until the 20th of April and we had all the expense of coming up here to put out, besides laying in a food supply. You should see us. We all stay in at nite because we are all broke and can't go out. Everybody is trying to borrow from everyone else and we are all in the same fix. We aren't worried too much—yet.

Well, so much for me—now how about you? I guess you must be pretty well along the way with your plans by now, aren't you?

By the way, did you send an invitation to the McKeevers? Eleanor writes to me regularly and she has asked about you several times and I thought you may have forgotten her.

Gee, honey, I don't know what to write—for once. I mean about you and Warren. You know you have my sincerest and deepest prayers that your marriage will be a success—just the opposite of mine and I know with you two loving each other as you do—it is bound to be a success.

Eleanor, if you want to take a bit of advice from your older brother, and this is for Warren and you, and I speak from experience, I know, that I made plenty of mistakes when I was married, but I think the biggest mistake of all that I made, and one that many a couple make, and that is this:

Marriage is a give-and-take proposition. There will be times when you get discouraged, but don't let it get you down. Warren will share your worries and you'll share his. You know how it is to come home from work, tired and longing for the companionship of your home and wife or husband as the case may be. True, El, sometimes you may have had a tired, dull day, but always save a little bit of sunshine for Warren when he comes home from work, and he'll appreciate it and will show it in the way he treats you. That was the one thing that I missed—Ruth was for Ruth and no one else—you can't be like that, I know.

Another, and perhaps the biggest thing of all. Many a time you will be worried over something, and sometimes it will be money that you can't seem to get from anywhere. Don't worry. There is an answer to that problem and I know it will work because it worked for me and it will for you as long as you have faith in God. Eleanor, I probably don't have to tell you this, but I will and that is pray—and pray every night that the Lord will keep you and bless you and supply your every need—and believe me, Eleanor, He will.

I was hoping, as you know, to be able to get home so that I could say this to both of you—so you both could benefit from my mistakes, but maybe this letter will convey some of my feelings.

Remember, too, Eleanor, that anytime I can do anything—and I mean anything—even money, if I have it. You'll always be my "kid" sister and you and Warren will always be dear to me.

I don't know whether I'll have a chance to get you anything that I can send as a wedding present, so until I do, will you consider the furniture that I said is yours as a wedding present from me? It is all yours, any and all of it, if you want.

I guess that's all I have to say now. Write when you can, but I know you are real busy so I'll forgive you if you don't write for awhile.

Again, to you and Warren all my prayers and blessings for your happiness.

Loads of love & kisses,

George
PS
My new address:
ACTD
Spartan Aircraft Co.
Tulsa, Oklahoma

April 4, 1942

Dear Mother:

Well, if it isn't one thing it's another. My jaw and face are all healed, but I'm in the hospital again. Nothing to be alarmed about, however, as I am merely under observation. Every time I went up since Tuesday, I have been getting sick and had a peculiar feeling in the back of my head. I thought maybe I bumped it or something, so I went to the flight surgeon and asked to be examined. He told me he would keep me in the hospital for a week under observation and he is giving me some strong pills. I won't be able to fly for 21 days at least, until the effects of the pills wear off, so that means that I won't graduate with this class but will have to wait until the next class, which will be four weeks later.

I like flying so far, although I'll admit I get a little nervous up in a plane. That's why the doctor thinks I get sick and this treatment may cure me.

I've been up now a total of three hours and nine minutes and most of the time I've done the flying myself with the instructor telling me what to do. I've done straight & level flying, 90-degree turns, shallow & steep banks, stalls, and spins. These planes are very safe because if you leave the controls alone they will pull out of a spin themselves and they practically fly themselves. My instructor told me I was doing fine, so that made me feel good.

I am living at the Trenton Terrace Apts in Tulsa with two other fellows. It costs me $25 a month and this includes maid service, linens, and dinnerware. That's not bad for the three of us, each paying $25; we really get what amounts to hotel service. I've been doing the cooking in the morning and we have been eating the other two meals out, so it is not too expensive that way and we make sure of getting one good meal anyhow. We have a bedroom with double bed and a large living room with a Murphy bed and a dinette & kitchen. Then there is an extra large closet and a bathroom. It is in a beautiful neighborhood and it really is quiet, too, because it is near a large hospital. There are three other fellows living in the same building but they have separate apartments, as they are all married and have their wives along. We get paid our rental allowance because of having to live in town so it doesn't mean any more expense. The only thing was that we had to pay our rent in advance, however, so since we were all broke and haven't gotten paid yet, either our March pay or our travel pay, we got a joint loan from the bank for thirty days, or else I don't know what we would have done. We borrowed $125.00 altogether and the bank gave it to us without any security, since we were army officers. It cost $2.00 interest.

I hope the flowers you got from me were pretty and I sure wish I had been able to be home for Easter. I didn't even get to church, as I am in the hospital, so it didn't seem like Easter to me except for the cards I got. That was a pretty one you sent me.

I received a letter from Harry and I'm glad to see he got his promotion. That will mean a little increase in pay too. I sure hope he don't get gypped out of Officers Candidate School. He deserves it and I know he will make good, if they'll send him.

Well, I guess there isn't any other news now.

Loads of love & kisses,

George

New address:
ACTD
Spartan Aircraft Co.
Tulsa, Okla.

Spartan School of Aeronautics
Tulsa, Oklahoma

April 27, 1942

Dear Mother:

It was nice to hear your voice on the telephone the other night. I sure was surprised when the nurse told me I was wanted on the phone. I couldn't imagine who it could be as there is no one here that I know, but when the operator said "Laurel Springs calling," I knew who it was.

I wrote you a letter the same time I wrote Aunt Carrie, so I don't understand why you haven't received it. Maybe you have it by this time.

I was out again yesterday afternoon. One of the other officers here loaned me his car so I and another patient here went for a ride. There isn't anything particular to see as the country around here is very flat and there isn't any scenery to speak of. We did see some of the Indian schools that are here, but that is all.

I expect to get back to Tulsa and resume training on Wednesday. I'm beginning to get restless now, so I guess I am well.

I am enclosing the certificate which shows that I have a policy of $10,000 National Life Insurance, which is the Government Insurance, so put it with the rest of my papers. When I receive the policy, I will mail it to you, but in the meantime this is as good as a policy.

Well, there isn't any other news, so I'll close.

Lots of love,

George

George continued his flight training until June 17. Apparently he didn't finish flight training, since many pilots who didn't make it through the course became navigators or bombardiers. In June, he left Tulsa and went to bombardier school back at Kelly Field in San Antonio.

MEANWHILE, IN THE SOUTH PACIFIC, the Japanese extended their holdings. They landed at Rabaul in New Britain, south of the Bismarck Sea and east of New Guinea, and started construction of a major base of operations that would house more than 100,000 Japanese troops. To protect their eastern flank, they occupied Kavieng on New Ireland and extended south to Bougainville in the Solomon Islands.

On February 15, the British army suffered one of its worst defeats of WWII with the fall of Singapore, on the southern end of the Malay Peninsula. The British compound was considered an impregnable fortress, having been completed in 1938. It was a vital military base, protecting Britain's other possessions in the Far East. The defeat demonstrated that Japan would be a difficult force to overcome, since the British felt the power they could call upon would have fended off any possible attack by the Japanese.

On the same day that General MacArthur assumed command on the 133rd day of the outbreak of war with Japan, the citizens of Tokyo woke to a clear and quiet morning. An air raid drill was staged in the morning, but little attention was given to it. On April 18, 1942, the citizens went about their business, working, shopping, attending baseball games, or visiting parks. The people felt safe from enemy attack. After all, no enemy attacker had set foot on their sacred soil since Kublai Khan in1281, and his invading army had been driven back by a violent storm. The Japanese called it kamikaze, or "divine wind."

Japanese troops had smashed into Hong Kong, Malaya, and the Dutch East Indies. They had captured Wake and Guam. The fall of the Philippines was at hand. The Hawaiian Islands would soon stand as America's last Pacific outpost. U.S. authorities even feared that Japanese forces might strike the American mainland. Day after day, all of the news was bad. The Japanese felt invincible, but on that Sunday at noon, sixteen American B-25s dropped bombs on Tokyo. It was called the Doolittle Raid, after their leader, Lt. Col. Jimmy Doolittle. The raid restored American morale, destroyed the Japanese sense of ultimate victory, and signaled a new course for the war in the Pacific.

In May, the Japanese attempted to capture Port Morseby, on the southeastern coast of New Guinea. Establishment of a Japanese air base there would drive Australia out of the war and enhance the defense of Japan's enlarged Pacific empire. The U.S. Navy, aware of the impending invasion because of their superior intelligence, dispatched two aircraft carriers, the Lexington and the Yorktown, plus cruisers, destroyers, submarines, and land-based bombers. After two days of combat in early May, the United States had lost the Lexington and the Yorktown was severely damaged. A destroyer was also lost, along with several support vessels. The naval battle became the first sea battle in which the principle ships didn't exchange shots—it was all done by air.

Two large Japanese aircraft carriers, the Shokakua and the Zuikaku, both

29,800-ton carriers, were damaged. They also lost a light carrier, a destroyer, and several smaller ships. The Coral Sea battle stopped the Japanese from obtaining an airbase at Port Morseby. Although the Americans had broken the Japanese code, lack of communication between the Navy and the Army Air Force was evidenced by friendly bombing by the Air Force of their own ships. That led to improved communications in future battles.

In the spring of 1942, Japanese navy generals conceived "Operation FS." The plan called for the isolation of Australia, thereby denying United States access to a counter-offensive against Japan. The plan called for the occupation of Port Moresby on the southern coast of Papua New Guinea, capturing the island of Tulagi, an island north of Guadalcanal, and extending their holdings south to the Fiji Islands and Samoa. The Japanese intended to establish forward air and navy bases among the islands in the Solomon chain and heavily patrol the islands. A direct invasion of Australia had not been ruled out but the Japanese felt an invasion would over-extend their army. They had already called for Australia to surrender in early 1942. The blockade would enable Japan to "bully" Australia into submission by isolating it completely from the United States, or to invade at their convenience.

Admiral Yamamoto, who planned the invasion of Pearl Harbor, had studied at Harvard University, and served as the Japanese naval attaché to the United States in the 1920s, feared that American aircraft carriers would breach Japan's defensive perimeter in the Central Pacific and launch a retaliatory strike on Tokyo itself. His fear was justified as a result of the Doolittle Raid on April 18. American aircraft carriers also hindered their invading forces on the eastern coast of New Guinea and thwarted the invasion of Port Morsey in the battle of the Coral Sea. Rear Admiral Ugaki proposed an "Eastern Operation" that would destroy the American Pacific Fleet at Midway. Admiral Yamamoto endorsed the plan, as it would enable the Japanese to also invade Hawaii. Yamamoto knew that Japan had to try to end the Pacific War before the United States could gather its military strength. He believed that total annihilation of the Pacific Fleet at Midway would permit the fate of Hawaii to be used as a bargaining chip to draw the United States into peace talks that would recognize Japan's claim to domination of the western Pacific, including Australia.

Senior staff officers were reluctant to grant approval of Admiral Yamamoto's Midway invasion plan. They argued that a much better plan would be to confront the American Pacific Fleet in the South Pacific near Rabaul, where they could combine an attack with their land-based aircraft. They viewed Midway as a risky gamble because of its proximity to Pearl Harbor. Yamamoto was stubborn and obstinate and insisted on the approval of the venture, threatening to resign if the confrontation didn't take place at Midway. Reluctantly, but spurred on by the Doolittle Raid, the Japanese navy general staff gave Midway a high priority, but wouldn't agree to commit resources that had already been allocated to Operation FS.

Japan had been shaken by the Doolittle Raid, but remained euphoric over the initial easy victories from its surprise attacks on British and American outposts. The approval of Midway dispersed Japan's navy throughout the Pacific, from the Aleutian Islands to the southern Pacific, with Midway being a major campaign in the Central Pacific. Japan, in its arrogance, felt invincible, despite the Doolittle Raid.

In early June 1942, the Battle of Midway occurred and was considered the decisive battle of the war in the Pacific. The Japanese were on the offensive, capturing territory throughout Asia and the Pacific. They planned to capture Midway for use as an advance base and an impregnable eastern shield of defense in the Central Pacific. Rationale for capturing Midway rested with Japan's ability to pursue its Asian policies. The plan called for an attack on the Aleutian Islands by light carriers. With their large carriers and battleships waiting unseen west of Midway, they would ambush and wipe out the U.S. Pacific Fleet when they responded to the attack. Midway could then be maintained as a forward outpost, providing ample warning of any future American threat.

Thanks to code breaking efforts, the U.S. was fully aware of the Japanese plan. Monitoring of Japanese radio traffic had been set up in Australia, Hawaii, and on the island of Corregidor in the Philippines before it fell into Japanese control. The one missing element was exactly where the Japanese attack would occur. A fake message concerning water supply was sent that confirmed the code "AF" was Midway, and that the attack would be on June

4. Because of the communication intelligence, the U.S. Pacific Fleet was able to turn the tables on the Japanese with a surprise attack.

Due to American intelligence, judicious aircraft carrier tactics, and more than a little luck, the U.S. Navy inflicted a smashing defeat on the Japanese. The pilots and crew won the battle through courage and determination. The Japanese lost the four large carriers that had attacked Pearl Harbor, while the Americans only lost the Yorktown. The Japanese lost a high proportion of their experienced and trained carrier pilots, who couldn't be replaced.

Recognizing this defeat for what it was, Admiral Nagumo's chief of staff later wrote, "I felt bitter...I felt like swearing."

In a larger strategic sense, the Japanese offensive in the Pacific was derailed and their plans to advance on New Caledonia, Fiji, and Samoa were postponed. The balance of sea power in the Pacific shifted from Japan to an equitable balance between America and Japan. The battle enabled the U.S. to take the offensive in the Pacific.

In June, Prime Minister Winston Churchill met with President Roosevelt and made plans to conduct atomic research. A joint statement, issued simultaneously from London and Washington, gave an optimistic outlook for the war. The announcement concluded with the statement: "The Prime Minister and the President have met twice before, first in August 1941 and again in December 1941. There is no doubt in their minds that the overall picture is more favorable to victory than it was either in August or December of last year." On June 25, General Eisenhower was appointed to command the U.S. land forces in Europe.

Mayfair Hotel
Ross at St. Paul
Dallas

Wednesday June 17, 1942
Dear Mother:

Just a line to let you know I left Tulsa this morning. Received your letter OK and also when you talk to Aunt Carrie, tell her I received her letter and thank her for the gift she sent me. I'll write when I find out my new address.

I have to go back to Kelly Field to take tests to determine my qualifications for bombardier or navigator. I don't know how long I'll be there, but I hope it's not long as it is plenty hot there I guess. It is 92 here in Dallas this afternoon and tonite is nearly as warm.

I had a job getting a room as there is a JAYCEE convention here and all the big hotels are filled up. This one is nice enough but it is not air conditioned — only has a [letter torn] They [torn] rather large. Mr. [torn] office in it and it has a swell [torn] in porch on the side that is really cool. I was there to see them Monday evening and also to show them my films.

Well, it's too hot to write anymore. Hope Harry is getting thru OK. I haven't written him because I don't have his address so tell him in your next letter I am praying for him that he will succeed and I know he will. Lots of love & kisses,

George

Rice Hotel
Houston, Texas

June 24, 1942

Dear Mother:

Just a word to let you know I arrived safely in Houston. Will report out to field tomorrow to begin or at least find out when I begin to take bombardier training.

I passed my qualifying tests OK and am assigned to the Air Force Preflight School, Ellington Field, Texas.

As far as I know, my new address will be AAFPS (Bombardier) Ellington Field, Texas. If there is any change, I'll let you know.

I received your letter today before I left. That's two I haven't answered yet, so this will be an answer to both.

As far as that furniture goes, I told Ruth in the letter that it was up to Eleanor to decide. She didn't answer it so I wondered if she called Eleanor. I think as long as Eleanor is satisfied to have the desk and not the dinette set, then have her call Ruth up and tell her she will let her send after it provided she sends the desk over. Personally, I don't care what happens about the bedroom suite but it burns me up to think she is getting away with so much.

I did tell Mrs. Snuffin last year that she could have the refrigerator and I told Ruth that in the letter, so I can't very well ask for it back now unless she voluntarily gives it up—which I doubt she'll do because they are hard to get nowadays. Let me know if she tries to do anything about the furniture (Ruth I mean).

As for associating with people from the church, that is surprising unless it is with Thelma Whitaker—is that who? I can't give any other guess because she never acted friendly with anyone else—at least when I was with her.

Well, there's not much else. I guess you got my card from Mexico. That was some trip—hot & dusty, but it was worth it as I may not have the chance again. I took some pictures, but couldn't take any movies as I had to leave my camera on this side because it already had film in it and you can't take film over unless it is developed. My still camera was empty so that was OK.

Tell Aunts and Helen I am here and I will write when I get a chance.

Love & kisses,

George

Air Corps Advanced Flying School
Ellington Field, Texas

July 6, 1942

Dearest Mother:

14

Prepare for a shock! I am not going to take bombardier training after all! I haven't told you before because I didn't know whether I could qualify or not, but I received orders today to proceed to Randolph Field, Texas, to begin training or assignment to a training school. (I'm not sure which) for a course as glider pilot. It is a new field and there should be plenty of opportunity for advancement because they are practically crying for officers. I like it also because it is only a ten weeks course. We get 5 weeks on a "Cub" plane and then 5 weeks on a glider and then we get our wings as glider pilots.

I talked to several officers in post headquarters and they seemed to think it was a splendid opportunity, so since I had only just had 3 days on the bombardier business, I applied and was accepted. Another officer from here is going with me and several of the cadets. They have a waiting list of 100 so far, but they put us at the top because they need trained officers.

We will get wings when we finish, so maybe I'll get wings after all. I still like bombardier but I believe this offers a better opportunity for advancement, being a new organization.

I received your letter today and also the one with the money order from the club. I answered it to Mrs. Kitchen.

I know it was my fault on the furniture, so I told Eleanor in a letter that whatever she does is OK so long as it gets settled once and for all.

I got a letter from Dad yesterday but he didn't mention about any changes yet. I guess he will after they occur.

Also I nearly forgot, in my excitement of getting the order for Randolph Field, that I received the shirt & tie OK. They are swell, thanks a lot.

When you talk to Aunt Carrie, tell her that I received both her letters but haven't had a chance to answer yet. I will as soon as I get to Randolph Field.

I didn't go anywhere this weekend, even though we had nothing to do because it rained all day Saturday, Sunday & today. They call this place Ellington Lake now because actually according to the weather bureau 6 inches of rain fell in 48 hours.

There is water all over the place; it even stalled my car because I went through one puddle that came through the door.

Well, that's all the news now. Don't think I'm crazy for not taking bombardier training because I still like it and can still take it if I don't complete this course but I believe there is a good future in gliding and being a glider pilot.

Lots of love & kisses,

George

In July 1942, the Japanese beat the Allied plans to establish a base at Gona, located on the eastern shore of New Guinea. Port Morseby, the administrative center and the main port into New Guinea, is located on the western shore, across the Owen Stanley Mountain Range. The Japanese pushed west, taking an airfield near Kokoda at the foot of the mountain range. The loss was considered crucial by the Allies. The Kokoda Trail, over a treacherous mountain range and through a jungle, was between the 20,000 advancing Japanese troops and the retreating militia. The Australian 7th Infantry Division, trained for desert fighting, was dispatched to fend off the advancing Japanese army. The Aussies found the jungle as treacherous as the advancing Japanese did, and both sides suffered from disease. The Japanese continued to supply reinforcements as their forces dwindled because of fighting to the death.

On July 28, Lt. Gen. George C. Kenney was designated Commander of the Allied Air Forces and arrived in Australia. Kenney was born in Nova Scotia in 1889, but raised in Brookline, Massachusetts, where he attended school and spent three years at Massachusetts Institute of Technology. In World War I, he flew seventy-five missions, shot down two German planes, was shot down himself, and was awarded the Distinguished Service Cross and the Silver Star. In peacetime, he concentrated on aeronautical development and slowly advanced to Commanding Officer of the Fourth Army Air Force prior to being assigned to the Southwest Pacific under General MacArthur.

He took Brigadier Gen. Ennis C. Whitehead with him as his deputy commander. "Whitey," as he was called, joined the Army in 1917 and quickly joined the Air Service, where he earned his wings. He was sent to France, but since he was an excellent pilot, he was made a test pilot and saw no combat. In 1927, he was involved in a mid-air collision over Buenos Aires and in 1931, he set an air speed record from Miami to Panama.

With the crushing defeat of Japan at Midway, the Allies attacked Tulagi and Guadalcanal in early August. Except for MacArthur's retreat on the Bataan peninsula, it would be the first major land-based battle by the United States in World War II.

GEORGE MEETS CLEO

George arrived in Pittsburg, Kansas, in mid-July 1942 to start glider pilot training. He lived in a house close to the college campus on the southern part of town, but took his flight training at a small municipal airport on the northwest edge of town. He roomed in a private home with Lt. Wilbert G. Laird, whom he'd met in Tulsa during flight training. The house where George and Lt. Laird lived was two blocks south of where Cleo lived with her sister, Lorene.

House on South Broadway

Lt. Charles Knoblock – Lt. Thomas Skinner – George
July 1942 – George's 1941 Oldsmobile on left

Planes at the Pittsburg Airport

Lt. Calloway – Lt. Laird – George

The flight school at Pittsburg was also known as the school for Flying Sergeants. In addition to training pilots for glider school, the airfield also trained pilots for reconnaissance and medical evacuation missions. The Army had retained Marvin Reed, a civilian private pilot instructor, to train the pilots. Glider instruction included killing the engine of the plane and landing without power.

Lt. Laird had learned to fly during his civilian life prior to the outbreak of WWII, although he was in the reserves. He had been in Special Forces in the 1st Cavalry and had been stationed in El Paso, Texas, patrolling the Mexican/U.S. border on horseback. He was transferred to Camp Claiborne, Louisiana, about the same time as George before signing with the Army Air Force to become a pilot. Lt. Laird was taking glider training because the pay was good.

"I did it for the money," he said. "It was the best pay in the Army!"

Cleo and Lorene were attending summer school at Kansas State Teachers College in Pittsburg. George hadn't met Cleo when he returned to Tulsa the weekend of July 18, where he had a date with Olga and visited some friends of the Frederick family.

21st AAF Glider Training Det
Pittsburg, Kansas
July 22, 1942

Dear Mother:

15

Sorry I haven't answered your letter sooner but it seemed every time I sat down to write, someone wanted to go somewhere. I am writing this at the flying field as I just finished my turn in the air and have nothing to do until it's time to go back.

I have about 4 ½ hours flying in here now. These ships are light Aeroncos and are very slow compared to the others. We do the same stuff that we did in the others so it isn't all new to me.

I got sick in the air today for the first time and lost my hat & glasses out the window of the cabin.

As for the telegram from Dad & the uniform, I haven't seen or heard of either yet. Of course, if they were sent to the other address, they will probably be delayed a week more. If I don't get them by the end of the week, I'll let Dad know.

I'm sorry to hear Ruth Reiner isn't well. I told her in the last letter she should take things easy, but you know how girls are.

We live at a private home, that is, Lt. Laird & myself. We only pay $5 a week and she supplies everything. As a matter of fact, she has even done some mending for me. We eat at the college cafeteria and it only costs 35 cents a meal, so we are living rather cheaply. In fact, all the prices here are cheap.

We go to ground school at the Kansas State Teachers College, but fly from the Municipal Airport. Our physical training is at the stadium, so we really have a nice time as far as school work goes.

There isn't too much to do here at night. There is only one movie in town that is nice, but all the pictures that come here I've seen either in Tulsa or Houston.

Last weekend, Lt. Laird, another officer and his wife, and I went to Tulsa. I had a date with Olga and also went to Sunday School and church Sunday morning with Ralph Stodghill and then visited them for a while in the afternoon. We are going to go whenever we can, because Tulsa is about the only place you can buy any military goods in the vicinity.

We may take a trip to Kansas City, Mo. some weekend because it is only 125 miles from here and we have never been there.

I'm glad to hear Dad may get a promotion. He deserves it.

I hadn't heard any details of the wedding, but I assumed Ruth's husband would be an usher or something because of course he is a member of the family now.

Well, I'll close now because I want to write Eleanor a letter and I haven't any other news anyway.

Lots of love & kisses,

George

My mother, Cleo was born July 12, 1916, in a farmhouse west of Highway 7 a few miles south of Girard, Kansas. She was the second child of Perry and Letha (Hewett) Campbell. Her brother, Orville, was a year older. Her sister, Lorene, was a year younger, followed by Chester, and baby sister, Lavon. Shortly after Cleo was born, they moved to a farm three miles north of Farlington, Kansas. Perry and Letha bought the farm from the estate of her mother, who had bought the farm from the Frisco Railroad in the 1800s.

The children had one horse they shared. Sometimes they rode it to Johnson Elementary School, located one mile east of the farm. Orville rode in front to steer the horse. Cleo, being the next oldest, sat in back, holding Chester, with Lorene in front of Chester, holding Lavon. One of their games was to run the horse out of the barn to see who could do a somersault out of the hayloft and land on it. Cleo, being the most agile, usually won that game.

One time, Orville took the horse under a clothesline and yelled, "Duck!" Everyone ducked except Cleo, who was then swept off the back of the horse.

Hepler High School was a few miles closer to the farm, but Letha didn't like it and insisted that the children attend Girard High School, ten miles to the south. Orville became a mechanic after high school and worked at the Boeing plant in Wichita during World War II. Because of an eye problem, Cleo was held back a grade, which meant that she and Lorene were in the same class.

In fall 1935, Lorene and Cleo both attended Kansas State Teachers College in Pittsburg and received three-year teaching certificates. To obtain a lifetime teaching certificate in Kansas, it was necessary to obtain an additional thirty hours of credit within three years. Spring semester at the college started in March and the elementary schools let out in April. Cleo and Lorene attended spring semester, making up the first five weeks of classes, then attended the summer session before they started teaching the next fall.

After getting her teaching certificate, Cleo taught her first year at Myers School, earning $25 a month. Myers School was located in a Lutheran community near St. Paul and Brazilton, southeast of Girard. While there she attended a Lutheran church, in which the men sat on one side and the women on the other. One of her female students didn't speak English, but spoke Low German. Before the school year ended, that girl was reading and writing English. It was one of Cleo's proudest accomplishments.

The next year, Cleo went back to Myers School. She requested an increase in her salary to $55 a month, but the school board wouldn't give it to her. However, Liberty School, south of Girard, would. She started at Liberty, but they only had four students, so their school board decided to graduate two of the students and send the other two to another school. Meanwhile, Myers School had hired a teacher they didn't like, and Cleo went back to Myers after they had fired the other teacher—at $55 a month.

Cleo taught the 1940 school year at Johnson School and the following year at Petersburg School, east of Ft. Scott, close to Uniontown and Redfield. She had twenty-eight students, grades one through eight.

On the day of infamy, December 7, 1941, Cleo had gone out to a field to get a Christmas tree for the Petersburg School. She came back to the house where she was renting a room to find everyone gathered around the radio, listening to news of the attack on Pearl Harbor. The next day, her rent was raised another five dollars.

"Prices escalated instantly and money became more available," she later recalled. "One farmer even said that he hoped the war would last long enough for him to pay off his farm."

Home for Christmas, the Hewett and Campbell families congregated for the holidays. Chester and Dean Hewett had joined the Navy, since they didn't want to be in the Army. Don Hewett also tried to join the Navy, but was rejected, since he had shot his fingers off in a hunting accident. Clifford Hewett was exempted since he'd been farming. Since farmers were exempted, some avoided the armed services by instantly becoming farmers. One father in the community sold his farm to his son, hoping he'd be exempted, but the neighbors painted his barn with a large yellow stripe.

As was the custom whenever the Hewetts and the Campbells gathered, they had a hearty debate concerning political matters, the news, and now the war.

Letha, disgusted with the war and the stupidity of world leaders, commented, "We should just put all the world leaders on an island and let them arrive at a settlement among themselves—and not let them leave until they do!"

In 1942, Cleo and Lorene were again attending summer school in Pittsburg, when, on the last weekend of July, she met George and an intense whirlwind romance began.

Cleo and Lorene lived in a house on the west side of Broadway, across from the college's Russ Hall. The house had an L-shaped porch, and adjacent to the house was another house with an L-shaped porch. The porches faced each other. Lorene was on the porch next door. She and Rosalie Likely were talking with George, Lt. Laird, Lt. Evans, and Lt. Frank Walls. Apparently they were talking about tennis, and George and Rosalie made a date to play tennis the next morning. George had an 8mm movie camera with him and took movies of the group. When he saw Cleo coming across the street, from Russ Hall, he started taking her picture.

"Lorene," he asked, "do you know that blonde girl?"

Lorene told him, "Yes, she's my sister," and called for Cleo to come to the porch, where she introduced her to George.

Cleo was embarrassed, since she was wearing a feed sack dress when she first met George. She had gone to town with her father when he'd bought feed so she could pick out feed sacks to sew into a dress.

The next morning, when George returned from his tennis date with Rosalie, Cleo had washed her hair and was sitting on the porch. Rosalie jumped out of the car and George called for Cleo to come out to the car.

"We just sat in the car, getting acquainted," Cleo later recalled. "I was embarrassed again, since my hair was wet and I was wearing another old dress. All of a sudden, he just started talking about what he wanted from a wife and that he'd been married before. I just told him, 'Someday you'll meet that girl!'"

That same Saturday evening, July 29, as George drove his '41 Olds south on Broadway past the house, he saw Rosalie, Lorene, and Cleo sitting on the porch. He slammed on the brakes, backed up, and walked up to the porch. Rosalie was ready to go out and was upset because her date was late. George said that he'd go find him. He came back later and told her she didn't want to go out with that man, because "he was stinko!" from drinking all afternoon. George had been on his way to Tulsa for a date, but by then it was too late, so he called and cancelled. That evening, George, Cleo, Rosalie, and Lorene went to dinner at a supper club, where they danced the night away.

After that evening, George spent all his free time with Cleo, but there always seemed to be a group along. When the semester ended in early August, Cleo and Lorene went back to the farm, thirty miles northwest of Pittsburg.

Flight students, learning where the farm was located, were always flying over the farm. The farmhouse sat on a hill, overlooking a valley to the south toward Farlington Hill, three miles away. Lt. Frank Walls, another glider student, was serious with Lorene, George was serious with Cleo, and 21-year-old blonde Lavon had her share of suitors as well. At the time, Cleo's younger brother, Chester, and their cousin, Dean Hewett, were also in flight training.

Perry had three attractive eligible daughters, and one day when Lavon received a dozen letters from soldiers, he remarked, "By the time this war is over, I'll have my own army!"

One time, Chester and Dean saw Perry threshing in the field and buzzed so low that Perry had to jump off the threshing machine, laughing and swearing, his fist in the air as he jumped. George tied notes to a rock with a handkerchief and dropped them from the plane to let Cleo know when she could expect to see him next. Lt. Laird landed in the flat pasture just north of the farmhouse, came in without knocking, went to the refrigerator, and got a piece of chicken.

He came out and remarked, "I was hungry."

Without another word, he went back to the plane with his chicken and flew off.ᵛ

George Kimberling, a recluse bachelor farmer, lived in a ramshackle house two miles away. His outbuildings were merely shacks and his barn was decrepit. He rarely went to town, and when he did, he'd stop his 20-year-old Ford at the top of a hill on the farm and get water for his radiator. A few weeks after all the planes began flying around the neighborhood, Kimberling painted his house and all the outbuildings a camouflage brown and green. From the air, the students saw what he'd done and started calling him "Crazy George!"

The weekend of August 15, George and Cleo went to Wichita, and on the last weekend of August, they went to Kansas City.

When Lavon saw George come barreling over Farlington Hill south of the farm, she'd announce to Cleo, "Here comes George Frederick Ditto!"

Cleo would get mad, but Lavon would defend herself by telling Cleo that it was easier than saying, "Here comes George Frederick Frederick!"

One evening, George showed up at the farm while Cleo was at a farm a half-mile northwest, taking care of Frances Cloud, who had come down with poison oak. When Cleo got home, she went upstairs to get ready. Her mother brought a dishpan of water upstairs for her while George and Lavon sat in a swing on the back porch. The swing broke and they both fell down. Lavon noticed a lump in the side pocket of George's jacket. She went upstairs and told Cleo that she thought George was going to propose.

Cleo knew that George was the man she wanted to marry, but she was hesitant because of the war. He had so many qualities that Cleo admired. He didn't drink, smoke, or swear, and controlled his emotions. He was a Christian, but respected other people's beliefs and didn't try to influence others with his own.

Lt. Frank Walls of Tennessee had, in the meantime, proposed to Cleo's sister, Lorene. Lorene had accepted and they became engaged. But Lorene wouldn't marry him until he returned, stating she would rather lose a sweetheart than a husband.

Cleo responded with, "What's the difference?"

Cleo and George – August 1942

George wrote his mother about their Wichita date, alluding to his desire to marry Cleo, and in less than three weeks after meeting her, he proposed. George had eloped with Ruth Snuffin and had greatly disappointed his mother, so he didn't want to disappoint her again.

August 16, 1942

16 *Dear Mother:*

Just got back from Wichita, Kansas after spending an enjoyable weekend there with another officer, his wife, and a girl friend that I met here in Pittsburg. She is a very nice girl, only a year younger than I, and as you probably have guessed, she is a schoolteacher at one of the rural schools here, taking a summer course.

We stayed at her brother's house and the other officer that went stayed at his mother's home in Wichita. We went out together Saturday night and in fact were together for the weekend except that we didn't stay at the same place.

This morning, Cleo (that's her name) and I went to church in Wichita and surprising enough, they had a great pastor from Pittsburg, PA, there. That seemed funny to go all the way to Wichita and then hear a pastor from Pennsylvania speak. He was very good, though, and we enjoyed the service swell.

They have quite a defense area in Wichita. There are four aircraft factories there and together with the oil-refineries, they are quite busy. Cleo's brother works at the Boeing aircraft plant where they are making the gliders that we will fly. They are of plywood construction and hold 15 men, but that is about all I know about them.

We are nearly finished here. We have 2 more weeks and then go to Texas to finish up on gliders for two weeks. I have 39 hours to my credit now and over 18 hours of that is solo time. I've passed two checks so far and only have two more check flights to make, 10 hours of day flying and 5 hours of night flying before I am done.

We heard rumors that due to lack of gliders, we may get held here another week, but we will only have to fly ¹/₂ hour a day to keep in practice and no ground school if we stay until they find a place to send us.

That last letter you wrote sure surprised me. I thought Eleanor had typed it and if you hadn't have addressed the envelope in your handwrit-

ing, I would have really thought it was from Eleanor until I got to the end. Where did you learn to type so good?

Well, I guess Harry is all set now. I'm glad and if he keeps going at the rate he has in the last year, he will pass me on promotion. He can do it and it wouldn't make me mad at all, because I'm stuck for a while as a 1st Lieutenant until I can get through school and assigned to a permanent outfit.

Has Dad heard anything of his promotion yet? I sure hope he gets it and then another one. He deserves it. Imagine Davidson is a Lt. Col. and he doesn't know half what Dad knows about the Army. Oh well, that's Frederick luck, as usual.

Tell Harry to send me his address so I can write to him, in case I move soon. He told me not to write until I got his new address so I have not answered his last letter.

I guess Dad told you I got the uniform OK and it fit perfectly. I guess I haven't changed any in two years because that is the last measurements I had at Simpson. Everybody here admires it and I have the only khaki blouse in town, so I guess I am showing off a little bit, entirely unintentional.

I'm glad everything is settled now with Ruth, and I agree with you about dropping the whole thing. Anyhow, I am not sure yet, but I think I may have found the right girl at last. Don't worry about me doing anything foolish like getting married again or anything like that, but what I mean is who I may get serious enough with to want to come back to when this war is all settled.

Well, I guess that's all the news. Hope Eleanor gets my telegram OK for her birthday. I wrote her a letter Friday.

Lots of love and kisses,

George

August 25, 1942

Dear Mother:

Have a few moments before going to supper, so I'll write, even though I have no decent paper.

Dad wrote and told me Eleanor has gone to housekeeping. I'm sure it was best, but yet I hate to think of you being alone. I hope Dad remains in Philadelphia so he can be near you.

I guess you got my last letter by now. I was pleasantly surprised when I received yours and a funny coincidence in your letter and mine crossing in the mail was that I should happen to mention about meeting Cleo here and you mentioned in your letter that you prayed I would someday meet a fine Christian girl who would really be a real wife to me. I think this girl meets all the qualifications, but don't worry about me doing like I did before. When I get married this time, it will be a real church wedding and for good.

We had a swell time in Wichita, and last Sunday had a really fine time at Farlington Lake, about 20 miles from here.

Cleo stayed in town last weekend and went to Sunday school and church with me Sunday. Then another couple and 2 other fellows and the two of us went to Farlington. It is about a mile from her Dad's farm and she got some of his fresh corn from the field and fresh tomatoes and some of their own beefsteak that they keep frozen and we roasted the corn and had grilled steak. Boy, it sure was good.

We went fishing & swimming also, but I didn't catch any fish. We sure had a lot of fun.

Well, I'm nearly done here now. Have 47 hours flying in, 25 of it solo time. Only have to get 3 more hours day and 3 hours night before leaving.

Last night I flew for first time at night and was up 1 hour & 2 minutes solo after only 15 minutes instruction. The usual length of time is 45 minutes dual before solo so I feel pretty good about it. We were helped by a full moon, however, so it wasn't as bad as it could be. We use no lights at all and the ground sure looks dark and comes up fast when you consider we land at 60 MPH.

Well, I guess that's all the news.

Nearly forgot. Just received my physical examination paper back on an examination I took two weeks ago and I am in better shape than I've ever been. Even gained my weight back now and have a deep coat of tan, so guess it was the air & sunshine here.

Well, now that's all. I'll send my new address when I move but you can keep using this until I do.

All my love & kisses,

George

Postcard dated 8/29/42 – The Plaza – Kansas City

Dear Dad:

Was here for the weekend. Had swell time. Love, George

U.S. Army
Sept. 1, 1942

Dear Dad:

Well, I did it! Passed my final army check yesterday, so now all I have to do is wait for new orders sending me to Texas for a final two weeks on gliders before getting my "wings" as a glider pilot.

My ground school surprised me. I didn't have much meteorology at Spartan, so didn't figure I'd do as well with it here as I did with some of the other subjects which I had at Spartan. However, I managed a 96 in my final exam and that gave me a final grade of 92 compared to a 97 in navigation which I already had at Tulsa, so that wasn't so bad.

Received a letter from Eleanor at her new address. She seems to like it very well. I'm glad she does.

Last weekend I had a swell time in Kansas City. If you got my card, you already know I was there. I was surprised that the city was so hilly & full of bridges. I always imagined it as being flat.

The town was full of soldiers, as there are 5 air corps schools there now and an armored division is somewhere nearby. It is the 9th Armored Div. from the marks on the shoulder patches.

I received a letter from 44th Div. Hq. last week in answer to one I sent them to find out my status, and they said I have already been transferred to the air corps, but they never notified me of the fact. So now none of us are in the 44th anymore, which is just as well, because they apparently aren't going to do anything except guard duty and form cadres of new organizations.

Well, I guess that's all the news. Hope you get your promotion soon.

Love,

George

U. S. Army
Sept. 2, 1942

19 *Dear Mother:*

*Well, at last I am finished here. Passed all my final examinations –
my marks were for a final average—92, Meteorology, 97—Navigation,
82—Maintenance. That wasn't so bad was it?*

*Monday, I had my final army check flight and passed that OK, so
all I do now is fly either $^1/2$ hour every day or 3 hours a week and wait
for new orders to send us to Texas for a final two weeks on gliders before
getting our "wings."*

*Tomorrow and until Monday, I expect to take a little vacation on
Cleo's (that's the girl I was telling you about) Dad's farm. It is only 25
miles from here, so I will be within easy call but I figure that now that
the pressure is off I could stand a rest and I figure the change in atmosphere will be good.*

*Did you get my card from Kansas City? I had a swell time there
and was really surprised that Kansas City was as large as it was, also
that it was so hilly and full of bridges. I always thought it was flat.*

*Saturday we visited Union Station, stockyards, Soldier's Memorial
and the park. Sunday we went to the park and zoo. It is called Swope
Park and was left to the city by a man back in 1906. It covers several
square miles and the city, according to the terms of his will, had to make
an improvement every year on it and they cannot charge anyone for
using it, so you can imagine how pretty it is.*

*As for Ruth marrying, I hope she is very happy. I felt a little bit sad
about it, but she seems more like a real good friend than a girlfriend.*

*This girl I met here is really swell and we get along fine. She would
really make a good wife but I am not getting married yet. Anyhow next
time I marry, I want a wedding where you can be there—you would
want that, wouldn't you?*

Dad is really getting a break if he gets sent to Florida for two weeks.

Maybe you could see Hufner's when you are there (if it's Miami, he is going to). They always ask about you in their letters. They write to me about once a month. Their new address is 4345 SW 13th St., Coral Gables, Florida, which is a suburb of Miami.

Well, that's about all the news I have now. I'll write when I move again but meantime this old address will do because they will forward my mail.

Lots of love and kisses,

George

The vacation George mentions in his letter wasn't very long, since by the following week, he was on his way to Lamesa, Texas, for further training. Lt. Laird, Lt. Calloway, Lt. Wall, and others that had taken the introductory course in glider training were also headed for Lamesa. Cleo's brother Chester and cousin Dean, however, went into the Navy.

SIX HUNDRED ROOMS EACH WITH BATH

TULSA

Sept 7, 1942

Dearest Mother:

20

    Well, I'm on my way again. This time I am going to Lamesa, Texas. My address will be 28th AAF Glider Trng Detachment, Lamesa, Texas.

    Stopped off last night here in Tulsa. Saw Olga and she wanted to be remembered to you. She also gave me the enclosed picture that she took of me when I was here last and thought you might like it. Also saw the Stodghills and they wanted to know how you were and to be remembered to you and Dad.

    I received a notice from Penn Mutual that my policy would lapse Aug. 10, but I didn't get it until last Friday, so I mentioned it to Mr. Stodghill and this morning he took me down to the Penn Mutual agent and I filled out a form and health certificate and gave him a check for $5 for the quarterly premium and also told him to have the notices sent home after this, so I can send you the money for the premium. In that way, they won't have to follow me all over the country every time I move and I won't have to keep sending them change of address.

    Well, I guess there isn't time—wait, I nearly forgot. Prepare for a shock (a mild one, though) and I hope you don't think I was foolish, but here's the whole story.

    I think Cleo is really the girl for me and she thinks the same of me, so we decided that we would become engaged, and I gave her an engagement ring before I left Pittsburg. However, we will not be married right away and in that way, since I won't see her for several months, probably, we will be able to tell if we are really in love and if we are, then we will get married. Is that sensible?

Well, gotta rush this off as the others just came for me.

Love & kisses,

George

SIX HUNDRED ROOMS EACH WITH BATH

TULSA

Sept 15, 1942

Dear Mother:

Well, today is the second anniversary of our induction into the Army. It doesn't seem that long, but time goes fast when you are busy. I can't say we are busy here, because we are not.

The usual Frederick luck is still with me. We were told today that starting with our class, we will have 30 hours of gliders instead of 17 and that means a month here after we start flying, which we won't until the end of next week. Then, before we get our wings, we must go one

71

month to an advanced school on the large 15 place gliders. That will also be in Texas, so instead of finishing this Saturday, which we would have according to the original schedule, it will be near the end of November. Oh well, that's the Army for you.

I sent Eleanor a picture of Cleo Campbell (that's her last name) her full name is Cleo Vista Campbell. I told Eleanor all the details of her and how we met and asked her to show the picture to you so I won't bother repeating them here. I know I really love her and I am sure she is the girl you always prayed I would meet because for once I am satisfied and feel happy about being engaged to her (and I really miss her lot). Also as you say if I really love her I will have no desire to go out with anyone else and I don't.

About that insurance, it must be the policy you pay because I don't have any other Penn Mutual policy, so maybe the notice was a mistake but nevertheless they do have my check for $5.00 so if maybe you called them up, they can straighten it out. I didn't have time to take a chance on anything going wrong. That's why I did what I told you about it.

Well, that's all the news. Hope you are well. Tell Dad I got his letter same day I mailed him one.

Lots of love & kisses,

George

Wilson Glider School
Lamesa, Texas

Sept. 25, 1942

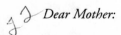 Dear Mother:

Received your letter today just as I was about to write you because I just got your letter that you wrote Labor Day and mailed to Kansas.

I wish you had attended Ruth's wedding because I am sure she would have wanted you to come. She probably figured you would come with Warren and Eleanor and as for people thinking you were mad because I didn't marry her why that wouldn't worry me because I'll admit now that Ruth seemed more like a real good friend than a sweetheart, although I admit for a while I thought different.

I did write Ruth because she wrote me and I merely answered her letters. She has always written me friendly letters and I answered them but I haven't written any since she got married. The picture she said I sent was one she asked for. It was one I took at Tulsa. You saw it when you were there. I intend taking some snaps when we start flying here, if I can, but we haven't started yet.

Today was supposed to be our last day in ground school but we are told now that we will get 30 more hours of it so maybe these marks I got today won't be my final grades. I got 91 in Military Courtesy, 97 in Meteorology and only 79 in Instruments, mainly because a lot of questions were asked on stuff we didn't have. No one in the class got even a 90. I believe the highest was 88 so I didn't do so bad, although that is the first mark I got here less than 91.

I'm glad you believe you will like Cleo, because I really am in love with her. When we made our plans about getting married Christmas, it was with the idea in mind that by then I would be thru training and know where I was going to be stationed as you suggest, so maybe I may have to change our plans if I'm not thru training by then.

I received the bulletin for Saturday but didn't see anything in it about Dad, Harry, and I. So do you have a clipping? If you do, send it to me and I will return it when I finish. I was surprised enough when I saw Dad's picture right on the front page! Some class!

I saw that write-up about the school in the New York Daily News and sent the clipping to Harry so he could see what we do. I wasn't there at the time it was taken. It must have been several weeks ago, because it men-

tioned that a Lt. Taylor was C.O. and he hasn't been here for three weeks.

Well, there really isn't any news except that I expect to take a trip to Carlsbad Caverns tomorrow. It is only 170 miles and I will go for the weekend. There may be another officer going with me, but if not, I will go alone because I would like to see the caverns.

Hope you are well.

Lots of love & kisses,

George

During training, the only place to get beer was fourteen miles away, at the County Line Beer Garden, and the nearest town of any size was Big Springs, Texas. Since George didn't drink, the other students liked George to go along so he could drive them home.

"He was a stabilizing influence on us," Lt. Laird remarked.

County Line Beer Garden

The following letter indicates that George was able to get leave and go back to New Jersey briefly. He asked Cleo to go with him, but she was teaching elementary school, just north of McCune, Kansas, and wasn't able to go. Cleo's sister, Lorene, was teaching in a school south of McCune, where they rented an apartment. Lorene bought an old Ford, drove Cleo to her school in the morning, and then drove south to her own school.

Wilson Glider School
Lamesa, Texas
Oct. 16, 1942

 Dear Mother:

Well, I got here OK, even if the train did pull in to St. Louis 4 hrs and 5 minutes late. We got in to Big Springs Texas at 10:15 Tuesday nite.

We are living out at the field as they just finished the barracks and since we are really getting plenty of flying they wanted us here so we could be called out at any time.

Was up 43 minutes yesterday in a sail-plane. Boy, they are really little. I could hardly fit into the cockpit and I felt as tho I was in a box-kite instead of a sail-plane.

If they continue to give us 3 hours a day and if the weather clears up, we should be thru here in two weeks, but the way it is today, we'll never get thru.

There isn't much new in the way of news because I haven't been back here long enough, but we are all "burnt up" because it costs us more to live out here than it did at the hotel—but that's the Army for you.

By the way, do you think I did the right thing by writing Sara down in Wadesboro and telling her as gently as I could that I was engaged? I didn't want to hurt her if I could help it, but figured I'd better let her know now so she'll get over it faster. She is a swell girl, but I

*felt she was too young for me—she was only 19 and I had enough of
that before—even tho Sara was different than Ruth S.*

*Incidentally, if you could spare a couple of dollars, I could use it as
I spent more than I figured due to fact we had to leave the hotel and
naturally paid up before we left, when we normally would have waited until the end of the month. I expected a check from the finance office
would be here when I got back, but it wasn't, so I guess I'll have to wait
until payday to get that.*

*Well, guess that's all. I am going to write to Mrs. Reiner now and
thank her for the Coke & candy. It was still good when I got it.*

Lots of love & kisses,

George

THE NAVAL BATTLES of the Coral Sea and Midway in May and June provided the balance of power enough for the Allies to consider an amphibious
engagement. The Japanese loss of five aircraft carriers, planes, and hundreds
of pilots tipped the scales, making the combating navies more evenly
matched. The navy battles gave the Allies an opening into the south Pacific.
It was obvious that the only force capable of containing the Japanese
advances was the United States. The Americans struggled to send enough
men and arms to protect Australia. The Japanese had, in the meantime, consolidated their gains in the south Pacific by building strong points throughout the islands containing navy ports and airfields, and manned with
infantry. The Japanese Southeastern Fleet was headquartered at Rabaul, New
Britain, with airfields and more than 100,000 troops.

Guadalcanal was an island ninety miles long and twenty-five miles wide,
containing forbidding terrain of mountains, dormant volcanoes, steep
ravines, deep streams, a hot humid climate, malaria-carrying mosquitoes,
and a coastline with no natural harbors. The only suitable invasion beach was

on the north central coast, since the south shores were protected by coral reefs. Guadalcanal was a most threatening position, since it could disrupt America's most direct route of supply to Australia.

In early August 1942, the Americans invaded Guadalcanal with the 1st Marine Division that had previously been shipped to New Zealand in June and July. A National Guard unit from Ohio had also been shipped to the Fiji Islands to form the 37th Infantry Division, and other troops had been shipped to Australia that had been destined for the Philippines following the attack on Pearl Harbor.

The Japanese defense of Guadalcanal consisted of 8,400 troops to hold the island and the airfield at Lunga Point. Fortified with many artillery positions in the adjoining hills, they held Mt. Austen, a prominent objective for anyone trying to hold or take the north coast. Their naval superiority in the area assured them of reinforcements from Rabaul or other positions in the islands. The Americans, however, were able to secure a beachhead six miles long and three miles wide and to gain control of the airfield. It's renamed Henderson Field and secured an aerial resupply line.

Henderson Field was regularly bombed and shelled by the Japanese, but American planes were still able to fly. Japanese efforts to build and maintain ground forces on Guadalcanal became very expensive in troops and materials. Both sides suffered casualties from disease, in addition to the casualties of battle.

What followed was a series of sea battles while each side attempted to supply their troops with reinforcements. The campaign featured two major battles between aircraft carriers that were more costly to the Americans than to the Japanese. The USS Saratoga was badly damaged, leaving only the USS Wasp operational. The area between Tulagi Island and Guadalcanal is named Iron Bottom Sound, for the number of ships lost from the opposing forces. Inside and just outside of Iron Bottom Sound, five significant surface battles and several skirmishes convincingly proved just how superior Japan's navy was in night gunfire and torpedo combat. The campaign's outcome was very much in doubt for nearly four months. In the first twelve days of November, the Japanese sent seventy missions of supplies and troops to Guadalcanal.

The Allies called it the Tokyo Express.

In New Guinea, the Japanese pushed the Australians back along the Kokoda Trail into the Owen Stanley Mountains, despite bombing along the trail by the 5th Army Air Force. The Kokoda Trail, a rarely used native trail, stretched through jungle terrain, bounded by deep ravines, rushing rivers and deep canyons. It led from a village on the north side of the Owen Stanley Mountains to Port Morseby on the south. The Japanese advanced to within thirty-six miles of Port Morseby before the Australians were able to force them back. General Vasey took over command of the 7th Australian Division from General Allen, who had been judged insufficiently forceful. Nevertheless, General Allen and elements of the Australian militia units and a 300-man Papuan infantry battalion engineered a sustained retreat that delayed the Japanese. The Japanese were better equipped, outnumbering the Australians five to one. As the Japanese advance continued, it became weaker as its supply line stretched, while the Australian units continued to gain strength as reinforcements were rushed to the front. Both sides suffered three times the number of casualties from disease and sickness as from battle. By the time the Australians retook Kokoda in early November more than 12,500 Japanese casualties were found along the trail.

While George was courting Cleo in August, General George Kenney had arrived in Australia to take charge of the Allied Air Forces in the South Pacific. He met with General Brett and found the lines of communication between General Brett and General MacArthur strained. Strained was an understatement. MacArthur was annoyed with Brett over his poor performance in the Philippines and for his rescue. Although Brett had recommended MacArthur to be Supreme Commander, he harbored resentment, since MacArthur had been a judge in the court-martial of Billy Mitchell.

General Brett had only met with MacArthur a few times, since General Sutherland, MacArthur's chief of staff, ran interference and had stated that he could personally do a better job running the Air Force than Brett. In their initial meeting, Kenney listened to MacArthur rant about the shortcomings of the Air Force: how they had promoted people they shouldn't have, how they overstated and bragged about their accomplishments, and how they had gone beyond being just antagonistic to his headquarters but being blatantly disloyal. MacArthur paced and continued to rant and complain. Kenney let him vent his frustration and responded that he'd been in hot water before, but he wasn't disloyal to his commander, and if his loyalty or that of any of his men was questioned, their bags would be packed and they'd be on the next plane home. Kenney said that he knew there were a lot of things wrong with the air show and he intended to fix them and get results.

MacArthur responded, "George, I think we're going to get along together all right."

First order of business for Kenney was to inspect the headquarters and the airdromes at Port Morseby and at Townsville, Australia. MacArthur had promised the 1st Marine Division support for the upcoming invasion of Tulagi and Guadalcanal. He had already provided a few cruisers and destroyers, but wanted to know what the Air Force could contribute.

Kenney thought the headquarters was overstaffed and that some of the officers would be more productive in battle. The organization was confusing to him, with personnel and supply records being kept in Melbourne a thousand miles away. Brett said that he couldn't communicate well with Sutherland, and only spoke to him by telephone when absolutely necessary. No wonder Brett needed to be replaced.

Kenney requested for General "Whitey" Whitehead, who had also recently been assigned to Australia at Kenney's request, along with Brigadier General Ken Walker, to accompany him on an inspection trip to New Guinea. The commander at Port Morseby, General Scanlon, had the authority to use any aircraft in New Guinea during an emergency or for targets of opportunity if they were in range. The authority was only exercised occasionally.

Bombardment missions were assigned at Brisbane, then passed to Townsville, where they were again passed to the 19th Bombardment group, stationed at Mareeba, another 200 miles north of Townsville. They would fly seven to ten bombers to Port Morseby, where they'd refuel and get weather conditions briefed from Australians as they were refueling. Kenney sat in on a briefing as the Aussie weatherman described rine clouds.

"What are rine clouds?" one of the pilots asked in the back of the room.

The copilot answered, "Probably the kind of clouds that have rime ice."

Other crews who had heard the conversation became anxious, since they didn't have deicing equipment. Kenney had to relieve their fears by explaining that the Aussie had been referring to rain clouds. Kenney told Whitey to have Americans present at all future briefings. They'd be lucky to get six bombers off on a raid, and they might or might not get together on their way to the target. They had no specifically assigned targets, except to bomb Rabaul. Rabaul was heavily defended, but no one expected to get that far anyway. Kenney ordered Whitey to be sure that bombing raids had definite primary, secondary, and tertiary targets assigned for every mission. If enemy planes were encountered, they would jettison their bombs and auxiliary fuel and return to base. It took more than an hour to get the bombers off the ground.

During Kenney's inspection, they had an air raid. The forty-plane fighter squadron stationed at Port Morseby didn't fare much better than the bombers. The squadron leader was proud of the fact he got ten planes off the ground just to intercept the enemy bombing mission. In case of a raid, the planes were to scramble and climb to 20,000 feet to intercept enemy planes. The squadron had less then five minutes' warning, so it couldn't be done. Most of the squadron's planes didn't work, anyway, since they were waiting for parts.

The bombing and fighter squadrons' inefficiency was compounded by the hostile environment. Food was inferior, the camps were poorly laid out, and they had the constant barrage of gigantic mosquitoes, biting insects, scorpions, flies, snakes, poisonous spiders, and lizards. Birds nested in the native huts, and malaria and dysentery were so bad that only two months of duty would send troops back to Australia. The natives also smelled so bad you didn't want to be within 100 yards downwind of them. One of the men bragged that the mosquitoes were so big that when one had landed at the end of the airstrip, they had poured 20 gallons of fuel in it before they realized it wasn't a P-38.

A few days later, General Scanlon requested a ten-day leave. Kenney told him to just pack all his things, since he was going home. Whitey would replace him. Kenney told Whitey that no matter what he accomplished, it would be an improvement, since the situation couldn't have been much worse at Port Morseby.

Returning to Townsville, General Kenney told General Royce, the commander, that another job awaited him in the states. Kenney assigned General Ken Walker the job at Townsville. He ordered Royce to brief Walker before he left and to show him around. Royce had an elaborate organization chart that resembled a can of worms. Kenney told Walker to tear up the chart and have no one issue orders except him. The only person who could answer any of Kenney's questions was a Captain Garing of the RAAF. He was familiar with New Guinea, New Britain, and the Bismarck archipelago. He knew of a landing strip that could be used north of Milne Bay and south of Buna called Wanigela Mission.

Kenney flew on to Mareeba, north of Townsville, to inspect the 19th Bombardment Group. The group had been pulled out of the Philippines with the Japanese invasion and the troops were homesick and due for a rest. They were equipped with thirty-two old B-17s, but only eighteen could fly, and those were in such bad shape that they would have been pulled if they'd been in another theater of the war. Planes were missing engines, wheels, gun turrets, and other parts. To get the eighteen B-17s into the air, they had salvaged parts from other planes. They had requisitioned parts that funneled through several channels before they landed at the supply depot at Tocumwal, 100 miles north of Melbourne. Most of the requisitions were returned a month later, with the notations not available or form improperly filled out. Kenney couldn't believe that, but the men made him eat his words when they gave him a handful of forms to take back with him.

Back in Brisbane, Kenney requested a report of the number of airplanes he had at his disposal. The number finally came in, totaling 517. The report didn't seem that bad, until he found that of 245 fighters, 170 were awaiting salvage or being overhauled, and the rest of the planes didn't fare well, either. Final analysis indicated that less than half of the planes were operable.

Kenney found General Lincoln, who was in charge of the supply depot and had a staff in Brisbane and another staff in Melbourne. He was very proud of his filing system and said that supplies were being received so fast that he couldn't keep up with the inventory. A colonel at Charters Towers complained about combat units not filling out the forms properly. The supply depot at Tocumwal was elaborate, with stocks of supplies. Kenney ordered the supply depot moved to Townsville, where they would perform maintenance and overhaul planes. He fired Lincoln and the paper shuffling colonel and placed a major in charge, explaining that their customers were combat units, "and the customer is always right!" He ordered supplies to be shipped to combat units as requested, oral or verbal, and regardless of whether the requisition form had been filled out correctly or not. Any officer that was considered deadwood was either shipped to Port Morseby for combat or sent home.

Kenney consolidated the bomber commands in Australia. He moved the 38th Bombardment Group to Charters Towers airfield, near Breddan and stopped all missions except reconnaissance flights in order to repair and make more planes operable. He requested the Air Force in Australia to be numbered for identification, and approval was officially granted for it to become the 5th Army Air Force, headquartered with General MacArthur in Brisbane. The Army Air Force in Australia consisted of remnants of the Far East Air Force, which had originally been stationed in the Philippines. On paper, it had already been designated the 5th Army Air Force in February 1942, but hadn't officially been transferred to Australia. The result, until General Kenney arrived, was an Allied Command dominated by Australian communications and intelligence. The official designation and recognition enabled the organization of the remnants into more efficient air units. Within a few weeks of arriving in New Guinea, Kenney was able to shake up the command enough to launch a major air attack on enemy bases in support of the Guadalcanal campaign.

The invasion of Guadalcanal was scheduled for the night of August 6. To protect the marine landing, Kenney directed all planes to attack Rabaul early August 7, to divert the Marines from being harassed by Japanese planes. A diversionary attack on Lae on August 6 would precede the morning attack the next day on Rabaul. Lt. Harl Pease, the boy who had landed at Del Monte to take MacArthur to Australia, was now a captain. Pease was assigned the early mission against Lae. Shortly after taking off from Port Morseby, an engine forced him to turn back, but there were no facilities at Port Morseby, so he nursed his plane 600 miles over open water to Townsville. There he looked for another bomber, but the only one remaining was a battered B-17 no longer suitable for combat. His crew worked on the plane, but if anyone had realized what was happening, Pease wouldn't be allowed to take off. However, Pease was determined that if he couldn't make the Lae show, he would make the attack on Rabaul.

Capt. Pease flew back to Port Morseby, arriving at 1 a.m. With only three hours rest, they took off again for Rabaul as another B-17 crashed on take-off, followed by two others that had to turn back because of engine problems. Before they reached their target, they were attacked by thirty enemy planes. They continued toward the target as their gunners, including Pease and his crew, shot down enemy planes and dropped their bombs over the target. As they were returning to base, they were again attacked. Pease's B-17 sustained major damage and began falling behind as they tried to hide in the clouds. The last that was seen of Capt. Pease and his B-17 was a burning bomb bay tank that had been jettisoned from the doomed plane. Capt. Pease was posthumously awarded the Medal of Honor.

An airstrip at Milne Bay, on the southeast cost of New Guinea, was held by the Allies, consisting of 9,500 troops, 7,500 of them Australians. The Japanese attempted to gain control of Milne Bay later in August. The fighters stationed at Milne Bay were able to destroy barges transporting Japanese troops headed for the attack on Milne Bay, stranding some on Goodenough Island off New Britain and along the coast north of the bay. Milne Bay was a miserable place, rarely seeing daylight, receiving over 200 inches of rain annually, and surrounded by rainforest and mountains. It did have a deep water harbor and its strategic location on the southern tip of New Guinea provided a launching pad for the Allies to harass Japanese shipping and bases in the Solomon Islands. Japanese troops, after trudging along the coast at night, were finally able to attack at the end of August, but having underestimated the Australian strength, they were driven back as they charged across an open airstrip.

A Japanese soldier recorded in his diary, "We were like rats in a bag and men were falling all around. I thought we were going to be wiped out, and then we were told to withdraw."

The Allies held Milne Bay.

GEORGE FINISHED HIS training in Lamesa and the group was transferred to South Plains AFB near Lubbock, Texas, for their final training in early November 1942. In his first letter home to his mother, he stated that the facilities there were nice and better than Ft. Dix, but in his second letter, he said they weren't as nice.

George wrote to Cleo nearly every day, and called her occasionally in McCune, Kansas. He wanted to get married as quickly as possible, but wanted the blessing of his mother, and sought her approval. Cleo also wanted to get married, but was hesitant, because she was obligated under her teaching contract. She would need to speak with the school board and either find a replacement or the students would need to attend another school. She was also hesitant because she had borrowed $90 from Earl Schefendecker at the Girard National Bank to attend summer school and wanted to pay it back before she got married.

UNITED STATES
ARMY AIR CORPS

Nov. 3, 1942

Dear Mother:

> *Well, we are now at Lubbock, Texas at the Advanced Flying School but when we will start to fly is another question. Class No. 1 has not*

gone thru yet and we are in class 22, so I don't believe we will fly for some time. At present, we are in the glider pool and tomorrow we will find out what they intend doing with us.

We are living in the bachelor officers' quarters at the field and they are really nice. We each have two rooms and they are nicer than the buildings at Fort Dix, although from the outside they look the same.

I am shipping one of the foot lockers home. It is the old blue one and it has all my summer uniforms in it as well as some junk of mine. You can leave it as is, if you want, because there is not any need to unpack it. Next time I come home I can sort out the stuff in it.

I have a very important question to ask you and I hope you realize that I really and truly know I am in love with Cleo because, honestly, I never even felt toward Ruth the way I do Cleo.

We had intended getting married on Christmas. I figured I would be finished by then and then get leave and come home and get married but now since I don't believe we will and the way things are so uncertain, I talked to Cleo and if you say OK we intend getting married here on Thanksgiving Day or the day following at the Post Chapel, if it can be arranged. Perhaps you could get here—but let me know because I don't want to disappoint you like I did before.

Another thing or reason why we figured we may as well get married now is that we could be saving our money because the married officers get so much more, especially now that I live at the BOQ and don't get rental allowance.

She can't get anyone to take her place till January but then she will resign and come with me.

I really love her but I am willing to do whatever you think best so let me know right away what you think.

Guess that's all the news. Hope you and Dad are well and enjoying your stay in Florida.

Love & kisses,

George

PS: My new address:
LAFS
Lubbock, Texas

UNITED STATES
ARMY AIR CORPS

Nov. 10, 1942

Dear Mother:

Possibly you didn't get my last letter because I sent it to Florida and I just got your card saying I better not mail anymore letters there because you were leaving.

In case you didn't get it, here is the big news. Cleo and I intend getting married the day after Thanksgiving in the chapel here at the post. I don't suppose there will be anyone here but her sister and the officer's and wives of those who know me here.

I have thought it over carefully and I am ready to settle down. I know I could never find a nicer girl or a better wife and I know you will like her too.

There are many reasons that prompted our getting married now. For one thing, I don't know how long we are going to be here, and I can get a 5-day leave at Thanksgiving where I probably will not be able to do so at Christmas. We had planned originally to get married on Christmas and get leave and come home, but that will not be possible.

Cleo is trying to get someone to take her job and when she does, she will come here with me and live.

Another reason is a financial reason. I figured that if we got married we could save more money because Cleo is making enough to live on and still saving and I would get $96 a month more if we get mar-

ried because I don't collect rental allowance now on this post, as we have quarters (although they are not half as nice as we had at Fort Dix).

So, all in all, and taking everything into consideration, we decided to get married now rather than wait and then we can be happy for a little while anyway, and if I should get sent overseas and not come back we would have had the little happiness we can have now together.

I hope you can see my point of view on this and please tell me you think I am doing the right thing because I really love Cleo. I always hoped that if I ever got married again you could be there to see it but if you can't make it, it is because of conditions being as they are.

As for my training here, we haven't even started yet and probably won't until next month, that's probably why no Christmas leave. There are 793 students ahead of us and none have finished yet.

Incidentally, I am going to tell Aunt Carrie that I am getting married but you can explain the reasons to her better over the phone.

Incidentally, mother, how about announcements of the wedding. Who sends them out and what? Will you tell me all I should do, because this time, both Cleo and I want to do things right. It is no sudden impulse and it will last forever this time, I know.

Well, guess that's all to say now. I am going to a football game tomorrow with the other officers as we have a half-holiday due to Armistice Day and a big game between LAFS and the "Gliderators" (glider pilots).

Can't think of anything else. Hope you and Dad had a safe trip back home and that Dad sends me a letter marked "Major."

Loads of love & kisses,

George

PS: Did I give my new address?
South Plains AAFS
Lubbock, Texas

George and Cleo were married November 27, 1942, at the post chapel of South Plains AAFB, just west of Lubbock, Texas. George's mother makes the trip from New Jersey to Texas to attend the wedding, but Cleo's parents are unable to leave the farm. Lorene is bridesmaid and Lt. Laird is best man. Lt. Evans uses George's 8mm movie camera and takes movies of the wedding. Lt. Walls throws a reception for George and Cleo.

At the reception, there are two punch bowls. Lt. Laird spiked one, unbeknownst to George's mother, but she keeps going back to the same punch bowl, saying, "That's the best punch!"

Lt. Wilbert Laird – Lorene Campbell – George – Cleo – Lt. Frank Walls

George had but a few days of leave, but Cleo and Lorene both needed to get back to Kansas to finish teaching. George took his mother to the station in Lubbock to catch a train back to Philadelphia. Little did George realize that it would be the last time he would see his mother.

George, Cleo, and Lorene took a later train back to Kansas.

At the Lubbock train station, Cleo and Lorene stopped at the restroom while George went ahead to get seats on the train. He sat down with another soldier where there were four seats facing each other.

As Cleo and Lorene walked by the window to board the train, the soldier remarked, "Wow, did you see that blonde walk by? I hope she gets on and sits by me!"

George knew they'd find him and sit with them, so he didn't say anything. When Cleo and Lorene sat down, George introduced Cleo as his wife. The soldier was apologetic and offered to buy them all dinner in the dining car.

Cleo was surprised by the remark and said, "Lorene is always the one who attracts the men."

Lorene exuded an aura that attracted men. She inherited the attractiveness of the Hewett and Dunn side of the family, who were tall and dark, whereas Cleo and her younger sister, Lavon, were blonde and fair like the Campbell family branch.

George's letter home told about their trip to Kansas and making the connection in Oklahoma City to Parsons, just west of McCune. Sunday was a very cold day, but they went to church in Farlington and had dinner at the farm. At church, they only had Sunday school. The minister was shared with the church in Girard and oftentimes when the weather was bad, the minister wouldn't make it to Farlington. The Sunday school had thirty-seven members huddled around a potbelly stove and Mrs. Pauline Townsend told George that he was "getting the pick of the litter."

UNITED STATES
ARMY AIR CORPS

Dec. 3, 1942

Dear Mother:

26

Well, how did you make out? I hope you were able to get a lower berth. I was sorry I couldn't wait until you found out, but I only had time to get gas and park the car and the train was already in the station.

We made swell connections going back, at Oklahoma City and arrived in Parsons at 3:45 AM Sunday. There was no bus out until 6:30 AM but a young man was at the station and he drove us to McCune because he didn't have anything else to do.

We slept until 8:00 AM and then went to Sunday school at Cleo's church in Farlington. I met the entire school (37). They are all nice folks. There was no church service as the minister was away. We had dinner at her mother's and then came back to McCune early because we were plenty tired. We were in bed at 7:30 and didn't wake up until 6:30 Monday morning.

Monday night a gang came around and "shivareed" us. That meant we had to pass out cigars and candy to all of them. It is a western custom that they do to all newly married couples.

Cleo spoke to her school board and they have made arrangements for the children to go to another school, so she will leave on the 22nd and be here on the 24th, so she can be with me for Christmas. I have already made arrangements for an apartment and so it will be all ready when she gets here and we can have Christmas together. I think that is swell and Cleo is anxious to be here with me. It is only 3 weeks away so that isn't so bad.

Incidentally, I wonder if you can take care of our Christmas shopping for all of you at home, and if you get it on a charge, I'll send you the money when you let me know what it is. Let me know if that's OK.

Hope you arrived safely and without too much trouble.

Incidentally Lorene and Cleo both said they didn't know what they would have done without you here to help. They told their mother that too.

Love & kisses,

George

The term shivaree was derived from the French word charivari and was passed down to the Midwest from French trappers and traders in Canada. Within several nights of a wedding, a group of relatives and friends would roust the newlyweds from bed by causing bedlam. They'd roll notched wooden spools up and down windows, shoot off guns, light firecrackers, and surround the house, to harass the newlyweds. When the newlyweds got up and came outside, they were "kidnapped" and taken away, usually with bells clanging or tin cans attached to a wagon or automobile. While the newlyweds were away, the women would prepare a feast and they'd party until morning. The groom was expected to supply cigars to the men and candy for the kids.

Dec. 6, 1942

Dear Mother:

I suppose you think I have a lot of time on my hands that I should be writing another letter so soon but it is going to be a short one.

I am enclosing 2 clippings. One was in the paper Thursday, Nov. 26 and the other in last Sunday's paper.

As to that picture I sent, it is only a proof and won't last long but nevertheless since it was an extra one, I thought maybe they could use it in the paper or maybe they can't use just a proof.

Did you get the snapshots developed yet? I was wondering if they turned out OK or not.

I guess we won't be flying for sometime because today it is snowing quite hard. I guess it is about 6 inches deep and drifting quite badly. That's another reason I have a chance to write. I'm staying in today.

Went to Church this morning at the Post Chapel and I was surprised that there was at least 50 present, even tho they had to wade through snow to get there. Tonite they are having a special service so I guess I'll go then also.

Did I tell you that Cleo will be here for Christmas? She is leaving the 22nd or 23rd and will be here on the 25th. I hope to have an apartment by then and have it all ready when she arrives.

I received the pictures from Harry. Does he want them back or are they extra prints? Let me know.

Well I guess I'll close as I have several more letters to write.

Lots of love & kisses,

George

LIEUT. FREDERICK WEDS KANSAS GIRL

Announcement has been made of the marriage of Lieut. George F. Frederick, of Beech avenue, Laurel Springs, and Miss Cleo Vista Campbell, of Farlington, Kans. The bridegroom is the son of Major and Mrs. George F. Frederick.

The ceremony took place in the post chapel at South Plains flying school, Lubbock, Texas, on Nov. 27. The Rev. Kenneth B. Combs, chaplain, officiated.

Lieutenant Frederick is a graduate of Haddon Heights High school and Peirce Business College. He is taking advanced glider training at the flying school. The bride is a former Kansas State Teachers College student and has been teaching at McCune, Kans.

SOUTH PLAINS ARMY FLYING SCHOOL

LUBBOCK, TEXAS

Dec. 14, 1942

28 *Dear Dad:*

Guess who arrived here today, also to take advanced glider train-ing—Lt. Arvin Northup & his wife. They were with us in North Carolina. Also if you remember Lt. Bob Gerant who also was with the 114th in NC, he is in or rather was in Ireland with the 1st Armored Div. and probably now in Africa.

As I told mother, I found a nice little furnished house to live in and will have it all ready by the time Cleo arrives. She will get here either the 23rd or 24th depending on the train connections.

We were told today that they are finally going to do something about all these officers waiting around for glider training, as they need experienced officers in the field and fast, so we could probably expect to be in Foreign Service within 6 months.

I still haven't had instruction in the big glider pictured in this let-ter but I have been getting time in on the Cubs. I flew $3^1/2$ hours Saturday and am scheduled again this Thursday. At any rate I wish they would do something.

As for promotions, I suppose some day I'll get one but at least next Feb. 7 I'll have 10 years service counting enlisted time in the National Guard and as I interpret that new pay act I get credit for that in longevity and also pay period so will go up to 3rd pay period anyway even if I don't get promoted. That plus flying pay is OK. In the mean-time, we sit and hope for assignment.

Well, guess that's all the news. Hope you are well and have mastered that new Vari-typer. It seems pretty tricky.

Love,

George

Dec. 14, 1942

29 | *Dear Mother:*

    I was sure glad to get your letter and learn that you arrived home safely, even if I didn't answer it promptly, because I didn't like the idea of leaving you at the station alone, yet it was all I could do.

    I'm glad you like Cleo. I am sure she is everything I could want and I know we'll be happy.

    I have rented a small 4 room house here in Lubbock. It is brand new and has all new furniture. There has only been one person live in it since it was built and that was the owner, so it was well taken care of. He went into the Army and I heard about it and got the place for only $45 a month plus utilities which are cheap here because they are owned by the city of Lubbock.

    In case you didn't put the wedding in the paper yet, Rev. Combs is in the 15th Troop Carrier Squadron—not me. Did you get the pictures back yet? I hope they were OK but maybe too small for use.

    Yes, I would still like a dark shirt for Christmas and the size is 15

- 35. Incidentally, when I asked you to get Christmas presents, I meant to get all but yours, because I would like to get it and send it to you, unless you already have bought something. I received a box from Eleanor & Warren for Christmas & you can tell her, in case she asks before I write, that I won't open it until Christmas.

I also received the gift from the Science Club and in case I don't get a chance to write, please thank them for me and also the Auxiliary of the Legion. It sure is a fine gift and is something I can use.

Well, guess that's all the news, so I'll close.

Lots of love & kisses,

George

PS : My address is just South Plains Army Flying School, not LAFS

SOUTH PLAINS ARMY FLYING SCHOOL

LUBBOCK, TEXAS

Dec. 16, 1942

30

Dear Mother:

Thanks a lot for the check for my birthday. I can sure use it at this time and I'll buy something with it for myself.

There really isn't much news since last letter, except they have finally decided to give us only 8 hours on the big gliders instead of 15 so we

*will get thru in half the time, when we finally start training—about the
end of February.*

> *Well, I just wanted to let you know I received the card & check &
thanks a lot and to Dad, too.*

Lots of love & kisses,

George

*PS: I opened this up again to tell you I mailed the wedding pictures. I
put a strip of title film around the one of the wedding indoors & I
thought that Bud Kingett, would, if he had time, put it on the roll of
film, & also cut all the blank spots out because you know I had to waste
some film when I switched from black to color. The other pictures on the
film are taken at Cleo's parents' home & show Cleo's sister Lavon, Lorene
& her Mother & Dad. There are also pictures of Cleo & her school &
her teaching the class. If Bud doesn't have a large reel, you could buy one
for him & I'll send you the money.*
George

Cleo arrived back in Lubbock on Christmas Eve. There had been a wedding shower for her and she'd taken all the gifts they had received back to the
farm to store until they had a permanent place to live. The school board
arranged for her students to attend another school, so she had fulfilled her
teaching contract. George had rented a small furnished house in Lubbock.
When they got to the house, Cleo was upset because there was no Christmas
tree. She tells George:

*When I was about 10, I bundled myself up and walked across the pasture to
Uncle Perry Dunn's house, a mile north of the farm. Uncle Perry had evergreen
trees in his front yard. He cut a small limb off one of the trees. I drug it back home*

over the pasture. Mom attached the limb in the corner of the front room. She popped popcorn, and we kids made popcorn streamers, plus cranberry and colorful paper chain streamers. We never had electricity, so the decorations were home created. Santa found our makeshift tree and we had gifts there the next morning. After that Christmas, we always had a tree. Our cousins, the Hewetts, would visit us on Christmas day and we always had a big dinner. After dinner, we would ice skate on the pond.

We always went to church on Christmas Eve. The folks had a 1916 Ford, so Mom would heat flat irons and place them on the floor between the seats and wrap us in blankets. Dad put a kerosene lantern on the front of the car so he could see to drive, and of course there was no traffic to deal with.

For the church program, the children said recitations and sang. When it was my turn to say my lines, I forgot part of it. I remember as far as "I am waiting for the reindeers," and didn't remember the next line. I stood there until the next line finally came to me. Guess what? The congregation thought I was waiting for the reindeers.

After the program, the congregation sang, "Jingle Bells" for Santa to come to church to hand out the Christmas gifts that were under a big tree in the corner of the church. They sang and sang, but no Santa. After awhile, in came Santa, shouting "Ho, Ho, Ho," and with a big bag of toys on his back, but no long beard. Dad was playing Santa, and when he put the Santa suit on he caught the beard on fire from the lantern. With a short burned beard, he went on stage, sang "Jingle Bells," and handed out bags of candy to the children."

The next morning, Cleo went to the living room and there was a tree, all decorated, with gifts strung out beneath it. It was a Frederick custom not to decorate for Christmas until Christmas day.

*UNITED STATES
ARMY AIR CORPS*

January 5, 1943

3

Dearest Mother:

I've been wondering what happened. I hadn't heard from you for so long and I suppose I haven't written either for some time.

Well, at last we are all settled down. Cleo got here the day before Christmas and we had a tree and I had left all our gifts to put under the tree, so it was a nice Christmas for both of us.

We have been busy (I mean Cleo has) cleaning up the house. I've helped her in the evening and it is all straightened up now.

I mailed Eleanor a letter the day before I received yours and Cleo had sent a card thanking them for the gift. She had been so busy cleaning up school work in Kansas that she waited until she got down here to send thank you notes on the wedding gifts. We received over $100 in money and she received a lot of things for the house from her friends in Kansas who gave her a shower before she left.

We received a beautiful tablecloth and napkin set from the Reiners. We have used up most of the money to buy things for the house. We have a Mixmaster, an electric waffle iron & grill, a toaster (Toastmaster) and Lorene is sending down an electric iron which we are buying out of the money we received. We couldn't get one here in Lubbock, but you can still get one in McCune. The demand isn't as great. As a matter of fact, that is where we bought the mixer because I couldn't get one in Lubbock.

I received the shirt Thursday and it fits perfectly, and I sure do like it. I really needed it. Thanks so much to you and Dad for getting it for me. Cleo said to tell you thanks also for the purse.

Cleo now—I took pen from Geo. I really do think that is a nice purse. I enjoyed Xmas very much with him. I hurried to get here, but made it. I like it here. This is all so will go give pen back to Geo & go back to bed. So goodnight.

I received the box from church and already sent them a letter of thanks. I have yet to write to the Service Club and Legion.

I am sending a check for $25.00. The difference between the $17.10 you paid for the gifts and the amount of check is for you to buy *something nice for yourself. I looked all over Lubbock for something for you but the stores here don't have a thing that I could take a chance on shipping back, so even tho it is after Christmas, get a Christmas present now.*

I notice you didn't list anything for Harry. I though you would get his too but if you didn't, let me know and I'll get him something now, even if it is late.

I wish I knew how to thank you for doing all that shopping because it must have been quite a job but I really don't know what I've have done if you hadn't done it for us.

The clock Eleanor & Warren sent us is really swell and is sure nice for traveling around.

As for our training here, it still hasn't started. I flew a light plane Saturday and nosed over on a landing and broke the propeller, but I didn't get hurt. In fact, I flew another ship right after that. The parachute slipped off the seat and jammed the control stick, so I couldn't level cut to land and I came in on my nose, but I had slowed up, so the ship didn't turn over completely.

Received a letter from Mrs. Lee today and Mr. Lee died the Tuesday before Christmas from a heart attack caused by high blood pressure. She is all broken up over it, of course, and it kind of made a sad Christmas for them.

Well, guess that's all so I'll say goodnight. Thanks again for the shirt and for the pictures and for doing my Xmas shopping.

Lots of love and kisses,

George

George continued in advanced glider training. One of the subjects was the ability to instantly identify enemy and friendly planes. George brought home flash cards and Cleo helped him memorize the silhouettes of the various planes. She flashed the cards and he named the planes. He got the highest score in his class. Cleo kept busy keeping the house straight and clean. One day, George came home with Lt. Evans. Cleo was on the floor in one of her old gunnysack homemade dresses, scrubbing the floor.

George said, "If I'd known you were going to do that, I would have gotten you some help."

One night, George asked Cleo if she wanted to go to the movies. She said sure, so she started to get ready, but George sat a movie projector up in the living room. The movie was of Cleo, coming across the street from Russ Hall at the college in Pittsburg. He finally showed her the 8mm movie he had taken of her before they'd even met.

The gliders used at South Plains were training gliders, and not the larger gliders used later in combat. The glider primarily used in combat was the Waco CG-4A, which could carry fifteen men and their equipment, a pilot and copilot, or a jeep or artillery, such as a 105mm howitzer. It had a wingspan of 84 feet and the fuselage was 48 feet long. It weighed 3,750 pounds. Each wing had 6' spoilers that were 10' long and when engaged in a sideslip, the pilot could land with no increase in airspeed, enabling fast, low-speed, short field landings. The glider was equipped with a minimum of instruments and controls.

Although a parachute was worn by trainees, they didn't use them in combat. If they were wearing parachutes, they'd need to run the gauntlet of the troops they were carrying to exit the glider at the rear of the plane. Not wearing a parachute was a "badge of honor." The glider was considered expendable, as were the glider pilots.

Initial training was in a light plane, where pilots, after some basic flight training, would ascend to several thousand feet and land without power. Bamboo poles would be erected at the end of the runway and pilots would be required to "deadhead" the plane over the poles and land within 100 feet. Later training in gliders consisted of clearing the poles and landing the glider on a white line. If they didn't land on the line, they'd have to manually drag the glider to the line, amid the jeers of their fellow students.

The traditions of the glider pilots horrified military officers who commanded the training bases. The men who volunteered for the new glider weapons were a real mixed bag. Response to the call for glider pilots, before production of the Waco CG-4A had been started, was overwhelming and astounded even the most jaded recruiting officers. It was filled with applicants from power-pilot training programs that had "washed out," wanting to prove that the Air Corps had been wrong. Others were attracted by the high flight pay and for the possibility of quick promotion. Some were too old for the Air Corps, pilots that had been trapped in desk jobs and wanted to fly, or "brawlers" who detested discipline and lived only for combat.

The pilots disdained saluting and their nonchalance about rules kept the company court-martial busy assessing fines and confinements to quarters. Booze, broads, and brawls were considered natural prerequisites of the flier and recruits felt they deserved to pursue them after a hard day of flying. One recruit stole a locomotive and drove it twenty-five miles before he could get it turned around and back to the starting point. While the state police were chasing him, his fellow recruits hid him until the excitement died down. Pilots had a love for flying, skill in the air, and a devil-may-care attitude toward everything else. One flier described his volunteering as a "temporary loss of sanity!"

Despite their nonchalance toward regulations, pilots quickly developed a professional competence in the air. They realized that they were responsible for the lives of the troops they carried and were alert to the dangers of the air and combat.

George in training glider

One night, Lt. Laird called and woke up George and Cleo. Lt. Laird was stinko, as George put it, and needed help getting back to base.

George said, "That just burns me up!" but drove out and got Lt. Laird back to base before curfew.

When Laird was in town and couldn't get back to base because he had drunk too much, he "usually just found a hotel and slept in the lobby. The curfew was midnight, and if you were caught out after curfew, you could spend some time in the brig. George took care of me when I drank too much. We looked out for one another. George was passive and I was aggressive."

Except for George, Lt. Laird had little respect for soldiers who were tee-totalers, since he felt they weren't aggressive. He told this story to penetrate his point:

When I was in Germany, a group of soldiers were taken prisoner by the Germans. The Germans had them surrounded and they were outnumbered four to one when the Germans asked them to surrender, promising them they could last out the war in a German POW camp and would be treated well. The lieutenant in charge of the group put the German ultimatum to a vote of the group and they surrendered.

I would have shot my way out and I had a similar experience. My glider was shot down behind enemy lines, we were surrounded, and we did shoot our way out. After the crash landing, we only had seven survivors. My copilot had a broken back and we left him in a ditch. I took the dog tags with me for later identification of those who didn't make it.

After 30 days of hiding, dodging enemy soldiers, and losing all but one other man, we were finally spotted by a French farmer in a field. We hid at one end of the field, determined to make a stand, but instead were approached by a group of young men, all wearing turtleneck sweaters. They were members of the French underground, who assisted us in eventually escaping back to England. When we finally got back to England, instead of being able to go home, I was given $500 and granted a 30-day leave to recover. I was really pissed off, since other pilots who got shot down were able to go home. I returned to duty and flew several more missions.

LUBBOCK, TEXAS

March 11, 1943

Dear Mother:

Well, I have definitely finished this time. We will graduate, Monday March 15 and as far as I know will leave here Tuesday for Ardmore, Okla. for further military training. I don't know how long that I will be there but I hope it isn't long because it isn't such a nice town or camp either.

As you know we were scheduled to graduate last Thursday but the course was extended to 15 hours. However, one advantage of it was that when we graduate now we are rated First Pilot, which means that we should not be assigned as a copilot but will be in charge of a glider when we start carrying troops.

I received a letter from Dad the same day I got yours and he also told me the good news about Eleanor. I admit I was surprised a little because since she just changed jobs I didn't think they had been thinking about it, but I'm glad and I know everything will be all right.

Did you enjoy the buffet supper and also the ball you were going to? Cleo and I went to a formal dance a week ago at the officers club and this Saturday nite they are having a big "Monte Carlo" nite, but I'm not sure we are going to it.

I sure am stiff and sore this morning. Since we finished flying, we have been taking 2 hours of physical training every day and I sure do feel it.

I guess that's all the news. Oh yes, Cleo's birthday is July 12.

Love and kisses,

George

Saturday night there was usually some activity at the officers club. One event was a formal dance. They went, and Cleo wore her wedding dress. They didn't attend the Monte Carlo night mentioned in the letter. George graduated with the class of 43-5 from South Plains Army Flying School on March 15, 1943. Cleo was able to pin the glider wings on George. The "G" on the wings stood for glider pilot, but the glider pilots said it stood for "Guts." Glider pilots were also described as "Suicide Pilots."

After graduation, the group was transferred to Ardmore, Oklahoma AAFB. George and Cleo went there in their 1941 Oldsmobile, stopping overnight in Wichita Falls, Texas. Ardmore Army Air Base had opened in August 1942 and operated until 1946. Initially, it was to be a glider training facility, under the command of the First Troop Carrier Command of the 2nd Air Force. It was short-lived, since the glider phase was transferred to Bowman Field, Kentucky, in April 1943.

MEANWHILE, IN WASHINGTON, D.C., General Kenney was scrambling for planes and pilots. On March 17, 1943, he met with President Roosevelt, who asked how he was doing on getting airplanes. Kenney responded that it wasn't good because of commitments elsewhere and that his chances of getting the planes and men he needed were remote. They discussed the war in the Pacific, and Kenney was surprised at how well the President knew the geography and the situation. The President told him that he'd look into the matter and see if he could find some planes somewhere to give him.

On March 22, General Arnold called Kenney into his office and told him he'd be shipping a new heavy-bombardment group, two and half medium groups, and three more fighter groups, equipped with P-47s and P-38s, but there was a shortage of pilots. Kenney responded that he'd find the pilots if he had to dissolve his own headquarters staff to fly them. General Kenney was amenable to anyone with flight experience. The meeting resulted in orders being issued immediately to George and a group of glider pilots at Ardmore.

WHEN GEORGE AND CLEO arrived at Ardmore, there were no camp facilities to house them, so most new arrivals were housed in hotels. The last week of March, George received his orders for overseas duty and only had a few days to prepare to leave. Cleo remembered him bounding up the stairs, excited that he'd be going overseas.

"I don't want anyone to think I was afraid to go into combat," he told her.

He had a loan on the 1941 Oldsmobile, so he paid it off. When he got back to the hotel, he told Cleo, "We're broke and maybe I should wire home for some money." He didn't, but added, "I'll pray on it tonight."

The next day, a friend that he'd loaned money to several months before paid him back. George had forgotten about it.

That evening, there was a party for all the men leaving for overseas. At dinner, Cleo couldn't keep her food down. She'd been having trouble for a week. She knew, or at least suspected, that she was pregnant. George told her to see a specialist when she got home. If she was pregnant, they both hoped for a boy.

The glider class was split. Lt. Laird and Lt. Walls were out on maneuvers when George, Lt. Calloway, and others received their overseas orders. George, Lt. Calloway and a contingent of glider pilots shipped out on a train from Gene Autry Station, south of Ardmore, on a special car bound for San Francisco before Lt. Laird and Lt. Walls even returned to base. Cleo stood next to Aalyce Calloway at the station. George was at the window, blowing her a kiss as the train pulled out. The next day, Cleo took Aalyce to Joplin, Missouri, with an overnight stop in Tulsa, as she drove the Oldsmobile back to Kansas.

I TROOP CARRIER COMMAND
"The Air Commandos"
ARMY AIR BASE
ARDMORE, OKLAHOMA

April 3, 1943

Dear Mother:

Well, I am on a train speeding along between nowhere in New Mexico. We are on our way to sunny California.

I left yesterday and we have a special Pullman car for the group that is going. It is pretty nice trip and so far everything is swell.

Cleo is driving the car home to Kansas along with all the junk &
household goods we have accumulated. She hopes to be able to come East
either late this month or in May before she is not in condition to travel.

I was a little disappointed in not getting the 12-day leave I had
because I wanted to get home and see you all & bring Cleo with me, but
this came up fast and of course I grabbed the opportunity to go.

There isn't much news and it is hard to write on this train so I
will close.

My address is Camp Stoneman, Pittsburgh, Calif. It is right out-
side San Francisco and I will send you my overseas address when I get
it.

This letter will have to do for Dad, Harry & Eleanor until later.

Lots of love & kisses,

George

Lt. Laird and Lt. Walls were transferred to Bowman Field, Kentucky,
where they were given more training in the Waco CG-4A, along with paratroopers who would ride in the gliders. The glider pilots were also given
infantry training, since they would undoubtedly be landing behind enemy
lines. They were required to run obstacle courses; to learn to set and neutralize booby traps; to qualify as marksmen with a Colt .45 automatic pistol, carbine, M-1 rifle, and Thompson submachine gun; and to master judo for
hand-to-hand combat. They also had to run at a Ranger's pace for twenty
miles with a full pack on a weekly basis. Both Laird and Walls were subsequently in the D-Day invasion at Normandy, where Walls was killed. My
Aunt Lorene, who had faithfully communicated with him was devastated
over losing her fiancé. After learning that he had been killed Lorene went to
Tennessee to visit his parents.

NEW GUINEA

George left Cleo at the train station in Oklahoma with an image of her trying to be brave memorialized in his mind. All he knew was that he was going to San Francisco, and that he'd be shipped out from there, and because it was San Francisco, he knew that he was headed for the war in the Pacific. Being the senior officer, he was placed in charge of fifty-two men and nurses. Were they going to the same place? Would they be assigned to the same unit or dispersed into other outfits?

Cleo's sisters, Lorene and Lavon, went to Wichita when their teaching year was over in April, to work in the Boeing plant producing bombers. Cleo returned to the farm to live with her parents. She went to Pittsburg and sought out Dr. Rush, a specialist, for her pregnancy, as George had requested.

George arrived in San Francisco, then to Sacramento, to get outfitted to ship out. He packed his trunk for shipment with items they weren't allowed to carry, and sent cards home, advising loved ones of his new address.

NOTICE OF CHANGE OF ADDRESS

(Post, camp, or station)

4/5/43

(Date)

This is to advise you that my correct address now is:

1st LT. Geo. F. FREDERICK   O-372630

(Grade)   (Name)   (Army Serial No.)

AC, APO 4090 C ℅ Postmaster, San Francisco, Calif.

(Organization)   (Name of P. O. or A. P. O. number)

Signature _____ George F. Frederick

This is for the convenience of the soldier in advising his correspondents of his
assignment to a unit or installation.   A maximum of three of these cards will be issued
to each soldier by his unit commander if he desires within 15 days of his arrival at his
new permanent station.

W.D., A. G. O. Form No. 204
October 1, 1941   16—24811-1   apo

In San Francisco, George wrote to his buddy, Lt. Laird, his mother, and
en route to the South Pacific, he sent a V-mail to his father.

Hotel Mark Hopkins
Nob Hill
San Francisco

April 11, 1943

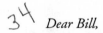

Dear Bill,

> *Thanks for the card. We received our orders to go to Camp
Stoneman near here about 2 days after you left and came on a special
car and really had a swell time.*
>
> *All this week was spent getting equipment—parachutes, emergency
jungle kits, helmets, goggles, earphones, mikes, etc., so now we are completely equipped. No idea where we are going, but India is rumored.
There are 18 nurses going with us and 26 glider mechanics that came
from Victorville, Calif.*

I am temporarily in command of the group of 52, as I am senior officer. What a job. I had a little trouble with Calloway, Mueller, Salisbury, Dunham & Williams when we went to Sacramento Air Depot for our equipment. They got "stinko" and we had to wait ? hour for them, so I restricted them to the post for 2 days. Calloway & Dunham said afterward I was 100% right in doing so, and it is all forgotten now. I was backed up 100% by post officers, because they must be strict here at the P. of E (Point of Embarkation).

We really have a swell set-up, but it ends next week because we ship away. Our baggage all ready is going. We were allowed a one foot locker, a bedding roll, and parachute bag so "B" equipment had to go in the hold. We take a muster bag and cross-country bag as personal luggage.

What a set-up at the field. We are the first glider pilots there and no flying officers around. We wear what uniforms we want and are the envy of all with our leather jackets. Another beautiful item, the barracks next to ours is the nurses quarters, so it is easy to have dates. We threw a party at the officers club Friday nite—it is in back of our barracks— could you think of a more beautiful set-up?

This being our last weekend in the U.S., probably. We all came to Frisco for a good time and we are getting it. Dunham, Holder, Handley & myself have a suite of rooms here and since all the bars and drinking places close at midnite, we each picked up a beautiful date and came up to our suite and finished the party here. Of course, they stayed all nite, each couple on a bed. We have 2 bedrooms and a living room. I am waiting now for the girls to return so we can all go to the beach this P.M. We have to be back at midnite and then we are on the "alert" or in other words, restricted till we leave.

Boy, this has really been a swell weekend, but it was due, I guess, as we are leaving and we figured one real good "binge" and hang the cost.

That's all of the news. Cleo has gone home to Kansas with the car and will stay there until (and if) I get back.

Gotta close, the girls just arrived. Mine is married to an Air Force Tech man at Chanute Field.

Write when you can.
Address:
1st Lt. – AC – 0-372630
APO 3899
TCC Glider Det
% Postmaster
San Francisco, Calif.

George

Over

Do me a favor and when you see Evans, tell him I wrote and will drop him a line. Hope his wife is OK and ask him how he likes my diaphragm gas mask. I have his. You can speak to him for this short message as I haven't time to write 2 letters. Thanks, George

George – third from right

George also wrote to his mother.

Hotel Mark Hopkins
Nob Hill
San Francisco

April 11, 1943

Dear Mother:

Well we had our last fling here in SF this weekend. I believe we will leave within a few days for an unknown destination.

I have been placed in command of the detachment temporarily, as I am the senior officer. There are 26 glider pilots & 26 glider mechanics, so it looks like we will form a new unit.

I just dropped this line to let you know I am still here and will leave soon. In case Cleo writes suggest to her she come east and visit. I'd like her to do it.

Well, guess this is the last letter until I arrive somewhere. Tell Helen thanks for the Easter card.

We had a swell time here and really saw the town. We were down at the beach today and also rode the famous cable cars. I couldn't take any pictures because my camera is already packed and shipped. It couldn't be taken on board any other way.

Tell Aunt Annie & Aunt Carrie I send my love and I'll write as soon as I can. I've arranged to have a safe arrival card sent to you, one to Aunt Carrie and one to Cleo so you will all know when I arrive at my destination. I figured Aunt Carrie would appreciate that.

Here's hoping it won't be long until we're home again. I'll close now with all my love & kisses to you and Dad.

Lots of love & kisses,

George

No. 746	Major Harry Frederick	Geo. F. Frederick
	601st AW Co Reg	1st Lt AC 0-372630
(V-MAIL)	PO Box 87	TCC Glider Det.
	Philadelphia, Penna.	APO 3899
(Censor Stamp)		% Postmaster
		San Francisco, CA
		April 21, 1943

3⁶ Dear Dad,

Well, at last I am on my way. Where, I have an idea, but of course, it is a military secret. I don't know what we will do when we arrive, but all I can say is, I am the senior officer in the detachment and so have all the worry of the trip.

I am writing this on the boat that is taking us, but that is all I am permitted to say.

I hope by the time you get this Cleo will have been able to make the trip east and that you like her as much as I do.

I started this letter last nite but ran out of ink so had to wait until today to get some from the PX on board.

This has been quite a trip and we are only about one third of the way to where we think we are going, so it is liable to get monotonous before we get there.

Guess that's all. Hope you are well and if you get your wish maybe we'll see each other in some foreign port.

Love,

George

GENERAL MACARTHUR had guessed the Japanese intentions correctly before arriving in Australia. The Japanese had already demanded Australia's surrender, but instead of an invasion, they decided to isolate the continent and force it into submission. The Japanese had struck at northern bases in Australia but hadn't landed troops to establish a beachhead. With the conquest of the Philippines, conquering Japanese troops could be released to strike elsewhere. They chose to land on the eastern side of Papua New Guinea, with bases at Buna and Gona. From there, they could proceed overland along the Kokoda Trail to attack Port Morseby from the east, combined with landing troops from the west. The Battle of the Coral Sea was considered a draw, but the Japanese foolishly withdrew their troop transports and didn't land. Meanwhile, the Japanese, from their staging area at Buna and Gona, had advanced to within a few miles of Port Morseby from the east on the Kokoda Trail, but determined Aussie militia held them off until MacArthur could reinforce them with the 7th Australian Infantry Battalion and the U.S. 32nd Division.

MacArthur faced the Japanese with untrained men and a shortage of supplies. Neither the Australians nor the United States had been adequately prepared for the Kokoda battle. The Japanese didn't think MacArthur would choose to make a stand in New Guinea. They felt that by taking control of New Guinea and other islands where they could establish air bases, they could take their time to invade Australia, and from navy and island air bases, Australia could be blockaded from receiving supplies and reinforcements.

Making a stand in New Guinea was a huge risk. Had the Japanese succeeded in landing troops at Port Morseby, New Guinea could very well have been lost, along with the troops, planes and assets the Allies had on the island. It could easily have been another Bataan. Few places in the world presented as many obstacles to warfare. New Guinea was as tough and tenuous an enemy as the Japanese. Covered with jungle, 13,000-foot mountains, a trackless jungle, swamps, insects, and swollen rivers made the few existing roads a muddy mess. The difficulty was further complicated by high humidity, sudden blinding rain storms, and heat that sapped the men's energy. All this was compounded by malaria, dengue fever, hookworm, ringworm, and scrub typhus. Disease was an unrelenting enemy and claimed triple the number of casualties than battle on both sides, and the natives, although normally siding with the Allies, weren't adverse to cannibalism.

In the fall of 1942, General Kenney proposed to airlift troops from Australia to New Guinea. MacArthur's staff protested violently.

"What's the difference between 180 pounds of freight and 180 pounds of infantry?" Kenney argued.

MacArthur allowed Kenney to experiment with a portion of the 32nd Division. A few troops were transported by plane, but when the planes returned, the rest of the regiment had already been shipped by boat and would arrive several days later. Kenney learned that the 128th Regiment was the next group scheduled to be shipped to Port Morseby. MacArthur's staff again protested, but MacArthur allowed Kenney to ship the regiment.

Kenney contacted Australian Air Minister Drakeford and conscripted a dozen civilian planes, as well as planes from all over Australia, for the maneuver. Combined with all available bombers, the 128th Regiment was transported to New Guinea and beat the first scheduled troops to Port Morseby, proving Kenney's theory. Kenney's vision encompassed transporting troops and equipment by air to forward bases in New Guinea. The terrain in New Guinea, consisting of deep ravines and rain forest jungle, demanded that they leapfrog over Japanese strongholds, starving or clearing them out with infantry. The Japanese could only survive by living off the land, and their ammunition, medical, and food supply would eventually be depleted, because Kenney would cut their supply line.

Viewed by many as having more confidence in the capability of air power than its potential, General Kenney forged ahead. He was a visionary, innovative and possessing knowledge of both air and engineering problems. He disdained red tape, and records weren't his forte. When officers higher in rank than second lieutenant were sent to him, he'd send them home if they didn't have experience, and he wasn't concerned about breaking the rules for promotion for officers that had proved their worth.

"Send me the WACS," he told General Arnold. "They'll free up some of my staff so they can fly airplanes!"

A reporter requested that Kenney write an article for his paper about an engagement. The article never arrived.

When asked about it, Kenney said, "We don't have time to look back. We look at the future."

Although he was in command of both the Allied Air Forces and the Fifth Army Air Force, his favorite was the Fifth. "Best damn air force in this or any other army," he was quoted as saying. His willingness to experiment, combined with his energy and confidence in his 'exaggerated' imagination of air power capability, inspired confidence in his men and in General MacArthur.

Led by the 7th Aussie Infantry Division after General Vasey took charge, the Japanese were forced back to Buna during the fall of 1942. Elements of the infantry were flown by Kenney to Milne Bay and a base was established at Wanigelia, near Collingwood Bay, south of Buna. While the 7th attacked the Japanese head-on, Kenney kept up a continual bombardment of Buna and targets of opportunity in the surrounding area, disrupting shipping and keeping Japanese planes at bay. The infantry flown to Wanigelia was able to push from the south, until the Japanese were forced to retreat north to the Huon Peninsula.

One of the bombing missions was described by Sgt. Don Harrison, a *Yank* magazine staff correspondent, on Feb. 10, 1943. His article was called "Zeros Ample," and tells how ten men in a flying fortress (B-17) fought a sky full of Jap planes, sank a Tojo ship, and got away.

"Somewhere in the New Guinea—Zeros ample, ack-ack limited."

When ribbed for his austere-like report of the ensuing Flying Fortress attack on a Japanese naval convoy, Cpl. Dick Hemphill, first radio operator, a former printer from Greer, South Carolina, explained with a grin, "At the time, I was kind of busy to do much sparkin' with headquarters."

In the last tottering days of the Buna-Gona butchering, Cpl. Hemphill and his nine mates took the lead in an attack on six Jap destroyers attempting to land reinforcements in New Guinea.

The weather was soupy, the ceiling low. Visibility at best ranged to 7,000 feet. It was a poor day to expect Zeros. And the Nips lived up to expectations.

The "Red Moose" squadron spotted their targets 50 miles off Rabaul. Battle stations were readied, bomb bays opened; Hemphill's bombardier plotted the course, calculated his sights for the opening attack.

"Zeros! Ten o'clock above." The power turret gunner's voice vibrated through the headsets, shattering the tenseness of the moment, yet adding to its intensity. The multiple guns of the upper turret sent a brief shudder through the ship. Then—the vibration ceased.

"My guns are jammed! They've knocked out my guns!" yelled gunner Bartlett as "Made in Japan" hail began rattling on the plane's exterior.

Kicking the rudder hard, the pilot dipped the right wing and brought the guns of the side well and ball turret within range of the oncoming attackers. The din of gunfire that followed could be heard above the throb of the four motors.

"Look at 'em come," explained Texas-born Cpl. Roy Schooley, manning his side-well guns.

Five at a time, 20 Zeros and two other unidentified aircraft kept up the relentless attack, droning like bees around a huge hive, their gunfire resembling blood-soaked stingers. And they did draw blood as more and more holes appeared like dry, festering sores on the metal hide of the tormented flying monster.

Hemphill had just logged his message when Pvt. Jimmie Wilson dragged a trail of blood through the small door leading aft to the tail gunner's pit. His face was marred with pain. He tried to speak, but his voice was muffled by the racket. Instead of words, only blood flowed past his lips. Leaping from the radio controls, Cpl. Hemphill broke open the first-aid kit and stripped the re-stained shirt from Wilson's body. Two holes stared like sightless eyes from the wounded man's breast where two bullets had gone through his body, puncturing one lung. A third bullet lodged in his shoulder.

Having administered what medical aid he could, Hemphill sat with Wilson's head eased in his lap and wiped away the red foam oozing through the gunner's clenched teeth.

Suddenly, an almost unrecognizable head appeared coming up from the ball turret. It had to be Cpl. Swanson, although his face was so covered with blood that it appeared as a solid red blot. His eyes stared wildly and he pawed the air with red stained hands. Shattering glass from the gun turret had mutilated his face, robbed him of his sight. "Dick, take care of Swanson," pleaded Wilson. "He's hurt bad."

Schooley, seeing Hemphill burdened with two casualties, dropped his guns to lead assistance.

As he bent over Wilson, the injured gunner shouted in his ear, "Get back to your station. We have only four guns working now."

Schooley returned to his guns—with a vengeance.

Still the Zeros attacked, getting more daring as they found resistance dwindling. As one came screaming down on the nose of the still-defiant Fortress, the copilot voiced the warning. "Zero at one o'clock. Zero at one o'clock above. Get 'em, Ritenour."

The flight engineer yelled back into his mike, "Dammit, I can't. My guns are out. They're...." His voice went dead as round of slugs tore into the ship, shattering the observation bay and scattering glass all around the bombardier's compartment. One burst exploded two oxygen tanks, between which Bill Ritenour sat frantically working to free his clogged machine guns. Another blast from the nearing Zero punctured a water canteen between his feet. A third severed the cord of his neck mike, silencing his prayers and curses.

As the Jap fighter pulled off, Ritenour thanked God he was still alive, wondered why he wasn't dead, and hoped that he might still see Virginia again. But his hopes seemed futile. Tracer bullets had hit a box of ammunition and set it ablaze. "Head for the ceiling. We're on fire!" thundered the bombardier through his mike as he helped fight the blazing box that threatened to explode and blow men and ship to pieces.

The plane climbed steeply and entered a protective layer of clouds. The engineer and bombardier heaved the burning gunpowder through the shattered bay of the pungent, smoke-laden compartment. With a sickly grin, Ritenour went back to work on his disabled guns and the bombardier again plotted the run over the target. Neither showed outward signs of nervousness, but both knew they were living on borrowed time. Both wondered just when the interest would fall due.

Following the bombardier's instructions, the pilot again nosed his plane down, through the clouds and leveled off at 3,500 feet.

"Circle wide and come in at six o'clock."

The plane banked, leveled off, and approached the fantail of one of the scattering destroyers. No heed was paid to the bursting shrapnel that threatened men and machine. "Stead-y-y. Hold 'er. Bombs gone! Let's get movin' the hell out of here," shouted the bombardier. The pilot needed no further encouragement, and he pulled the wheel into his middle, jammed the motors, and started aloft.

But before the huge plane could puncture the clouds overhead, two Zeros roared in from behind and below, fishtailing to get greater coverage as they sprayed the metal belly above them. It was their last bid for revenge for Tojo and the destroyer listing in a sea of its own burning oil.

"Hot lead whistled through our compartment like buckshot," related Cpl. Hemphill, "and reminded me of the time I got caught in a melon patch back home. One burst completely shattered the hydraulic system, and hydraulic fluid temporarily blinded the navigator and bombardier. I was instructed to radio the 'drome and tell them to get the basket ready. We were limping home with four men injured; four control cables shot away, the left aileron damaged, and the hydraulic system completely gone.

"Our pilot said he intended to land her on the crash runway, brakes or no brakes—and I prayed to heaven that if he couldn't have mechanical brakes at least give 'im a spiritual break. He got it and landed her intact, right side up."

"As we staggered out of the plane, the CO said something about Silver Stars. "But frankly," drawled the 29-year-old Southerner, "I was too damn busy thankin' my lucky stars to worry much about wearin' one."

Pushing the Japanese back to Buna and Gona and the battle in Guadalcanal were defensive efforts, fought mainly to stop the Japanese from capturing New Guinea and blockading Australia. MacArthur's principle objective was the reduction of Rabaul on New Britain. It was a central Japanese base from which strikes were staged, either directly or to outlying Japanese bases, and then onto Allied targets.

The JCS listed the elimination of Rabaul as sixth in priority, since the war in Europe came first. After the war in Europe had been won, concentration could be given to the war in the Pacific. War with Japan could last until the late

1940s. The objective was to hold the line in the Pacific at Midway, protect Hawaii, and keep communication open to Australia and New Zealand. The British resented and opposed shipment of troops and supplies to Australia, since it detracted from the war in Europe. Their position was to hold Japan off and to leave existing war-weary troops in Australia for protection.

An agreement between President Roosevelt and Prime Minister Churchill established just that—hold the line in the Pacific, make limited attacks on Japanese shipping, block Japanese attempts to isolate Australia, and keep the pressure on the Japanese by attacking Rabaul from the air. To accomplish that, defensive objective air bases were needed in eastern New Guinea on the Huon Peninsula, principally Lae and Nadzab, in the Markham and Ramu river valleys. Coordinated ground and air attacks against the Japanese by leapfrogging over geological obstacles were planned, using the perilous foothold in Guadalcanal to advance up the Solomon Islands and attack Rabaul from the south while General MacArthur kept pressure on the Japanese from the western front in New Guinea. Meanwhile, Admiral Nimitz would keep pressure on the Japanese from the northeast through the Gilbert and Marshall Islands.

In May 1943 Churchill had met again with President Roosevelt in Washington DC. Instead of going to Hyde Park, President Roosevelt took Churchill on a three hour drive through Frederick, Maryland to a place called Shangi-La, later called Camp David. As they drove into the mountains they passed the house of Barbara Fritchie, who was immortalized by the poet John Whittier for her defiant gesture during the Confederate invasion during the civil war. "Shoot, if you must, this old gray head, but spare your country's flag." Roosevelt or Hopkins quoted from the poem. Churchill proceeded to recite the entire poem, whether it was accurate or not - neither Roosevelt nor Hopkins would correct him.

As Churchill, Roosevelt, and Hopkins were celebrating news of the Axis defeat in Tunisia the combined Joint Chiefs of Staff were meeting in the countryside of Virginia. A Sunday afternoon meeting reinforced the British demand for resources to flow to Africa and for an impending invasion of Sicily and Italy later in the year. To the chagrin of Admiral King, only minimal resources were allocated to the Pacific.

The JCS suggested to MacArthur that he seize the Admiralty Islands to isolate the Japanese stronghold at Rabaul on New Britain Island, but he rejected the idea, since he didn't have adequate air cover for the seizure. He needed bases further north in New Guinea from which to launch an attack on the Admiralties. Besides, he wasn't prepared for an offensive action, because supplies and men had been stretched to the limit during the Guadalcanal and Papua New Guinea battles. The men were exhausted and suffering from diseases, and many would need to be shipped home. Of the nearly 11,000 casualties of the 15,000 troops of the 32nd Division in battle from October through February 1943, only 2,300 were from battle. The rest were from disease.

Organizational problems also plagued the Allies as the overlapping commands of Admiral Nimitz, pushing west into the Solomon Islands, and MacArthur, attacking north in the Solomons, resulted in conflicting orders. Admiral King, commanding the JCS, resisted MacArthur's request for naval power, because he didn't want a ground commander in charge of the Navy. Admiral Nimitz, commander in chief of the Pacific Fleet, wanted the Navy to be in a "fluid state," since he didn't know where the Japanese might attack next.

The JCS issued the following directive: "Units of the Pacific Ocean (not assigned by the JCS) will remain under control of the Commander in Chief Pacific Ocean areas." That directive gave MacArthur limited control over naval units assigned to him. Operation of the Navy remained with Nimitz, even for Navy commanders assigned to MacArthur.

In the spring of 1943, General Kenney had at his disposal slightly more than 700 planes of all types, but that number was deceiving. Of those, more than half were fighters and approximately one hundred were heavy bombers, with an equal number of light and medium bombers. The planes weren't new and he was losing double the amount of replacement aircraft from battle alone. The planes were old, battle weary, torn from rough and bumpy runways, stressed from lack of lubrication from the elements, and at any one time, more than half of his planes were in depots, needing repair. Kenney thought that if radar failed, the Japanese could wipe him out and he'd be out of business—and there were holes in the radar. Estimates of Japanese strength, on the other hand, included some 800 planes in good repair, or were new. Japan had prepared for the war. In addition, more than a 1,000 planes could be shipped in from other nearby operations.

The 8th Army Air Force, stationed in England, kept a minimum of 1,200 heavy bombers for their air assault against Germany. General Eaker, commanding the 8th AAF, wrote General Arnold, "I hope you will not let that fellow Kenney steal any of our heavy bombers." Nevertheless, General Arnold allocated one heavy and one medium bomb group to the South Pacific that had been initially scheduled for Eaker. The attrition of planes and troops in the South Pacific warranted the reallocation. General Kenney wasn't particular, either about the planes or the men he could get, but he preferred lower rank individuals, since many under his command deserved promotion because of their experience. He also promoted those with proven abilities over those with more seniority, simply because he felt they could do the job better. General Kenney didn't follow rules or protocol to more efficiently complete his mission of defeating the Japanese.

Major William Benn, commander of the 63rd Bomb Squadron, wasn't satisfied with results of the "glide bombing" that had been employed for bombing ships. He felt that better results would be obtained by skipping bombs along the water into ships. With the approval of General Kenney, he experimented to obtain the best altitudes and speeds.

A B-25 was modified, placing eight .50-caliber machine guns to fire forward. From experimenting with the concept, they determined that an attack, coming in with machine guns blazing, on a convoy from 200 to 300 feet and a skip bomb release from 200 to 350 feet achieved the best results. However, it was too dangerous to attack in daylight, so they could only attack at night, early dawn, or evening, against the light, in a surprise attack. Using spotter planes, they were able to disrupt Japanese shipping in the Bismarck Sea.

After returning from Washington, General Kenney reported to MacArthur in April 1943 that while they'd be pinched for aircraft for a few more months, it looked as though by August they'd be ready to take offensive action. MacArthur, relieved by the success of the Buna campaign, was more relaxed.

Kenney found his commander in Dobodura, Col. Freddy Smith, exhausted from his stint in the advanced base and decided to send him home for a few months before returning to New Guinea. He also sent General Whitehead to Australia for a month of rest the middle of April.

The War Department praised all Army units in Papua for crushing the Japanese invasion on April 29, 1943:

The Papuan Forces, United States Army, Southwest Pacific Area, are cited for outstanding performance of duty in action during the period July 23, 1942, to January 23, 1943. When a bold and aggressive enemy invaded Papua in strength, the combined action of ground and air units of these forces, in association with Allied units, checked the hostile advance, drove the enemy back to the sea coast and in a series of actions against a highly organized defensive zone utterly destroyed him.

Ground combat forces, operating over roadless jungle-covered mountains and swamps, demonstrated their courage and resourcefulness in closing with an enemy who took every advantage of the nearly impassable terrain. Air forces, by repeatedly attacking the enemy ground forces and installations, by destroying his convoys attempting reinforcement and supply, and by transporting ground forces and supplies to areas for which land routes were nonexistent and sea routes slow and hazardous, made possible the success of the ground operations.

Service units, operating far forward of their normal positions and at times in advance of ground combat elements, built landing fields in the jungle, established and operated supply points and provided for the hospitalization and evacuation of the wounded and sick. The courage, spirit and devotion to duty of all elements of the command made possible the complete victory attained.

GEORGE ARRIVED near Sydney, Australia, in late April and was stationed in a replacement depot while awaiting assignment. It gave him an opportunity to see the sights of Sydney. In the meantime, Cleo returned to Kansas and then went back east to New Jersey, in accordance with George's wish for her to meet the rest of his family and to see where he lived. She rode on a troop train to Philadelphia. When she arrived, "Pappy" Frederick, as she called George's father, met her at the station.

He came up to her and asked, "Are you Cleo?"

In New Jersey, Cleo met Eleanor, Aunt Carrie and Aunt Annie, and a cousin, Helen McKinney, as well as friends of the family. She also attended George's church. Eleanor and Cleo went to Philadelphia to the theatre and attended the play, Oklahoma. After the play, Eleanor suggested that they go to a bar and have a drink.

As Eleanor ordered a drink and lit a cigarette, she said, "Every family needs a black sheep, and in our family, I'm it. George doesn't approve of it, but he never says anything. I know he loves me and doesn't condemn me for my bad habits. He's like that—I guess he figures it's my own business, even though he doesn't like it."

Somewhere in Australia
May 12, 1943
Dearest Mother:

Gee, it sure was good to hear from you. I received four of your letters in the last 2 days.

I'm afraid you were a little optimistic in one of your letters, the one dated April 23. You said you hadn't received my safe arrival card yet. There may a good reason for that, because we didn't arrive until a few days ago. You probably have it now as well as our new address, which is on this envelope. By the way, keep sending your letters V- Mail because they are faster coming over although Air Mail is faster from this end, due to fact there is plenty of room in the planes returning to the U.S., but not much room coming over.

The Japs would really have a tough job if the think they can take this place. There is much more equipment & supplies over here than anyone realizes and I don't think the Japs will try anything here.

I guess the war in Europe will be over soon now. I see by the paper today that the final remnants of the German Army in Africa is getting cleaned up.

I received an Easter Card from Mrs. Townsend the day I arrived. I must answer her and thank her for it.

I have not been assigned to a unit yet but am still at the Replacement Depot. I expect we will be assigned today or tomorrow, although apparently they are not going to use us yet, as they are having a little trouble flying them over here. I don't know what kind of a job we will have to do but I hope it is something to keep us busy, because we sure have not been yet.

I am managing to see quite a few of the sites in this city and have taken a few pictures. Film is easier to buy here than at home, so are a lot of other things.

Well, guess that's about all, except I am sending a list of the fellows that came over with me, so in case anything should happen to any of us, you can get in touch with the others. We are all doing the same so every family will have a list. [Apparently, the list wasn't allowed to be sent by the censors.]

I hope Cleo made her visit OK and that she enjoyed being home. Did she meet everyone that I know? I hope she did and that she managed to get to go to church and meet Mrs. Townsend, Mrs. Orr, and the others.

Keep writing.

Loads of love & kisses,

George

IN JANUARY 1943, ten officers trained in air support were sent to General Kenney. Of the ten, four were sent home due to having too much rank.

Kenney stated, "The theory of an Air Support Command doesn't fit the picture in this theater. Whenever the necessity arrives, all or an appropriate part of the striking power of the Air Force is assigned to the task of supporting the ground troops."

He did realize that specially qualified liaison officers and communications personnel were needed to transmit information to air control headquarters, so he placed the support officers in the A-3 (operations) section. Two of the officers were sent to RAAF school of operations so that concepts of Australian and US air support could be coordinated. The school was necessary, since it was anticipated that most of the support would be given to Australian troops. The six remaining officers were re-enforced by eight other officers and they formed the 5th Tactical Air Communications Squadron. In July 1943, the whole section was reenforced by George and the contingent of glider pilots and moved to Port Morseby. In July, George wrote home, indicating that he had a desk job that he didn't like and would rather be flying.

From Port Morseby, the 5th AAF supported ground action in the advance to push the Japanese back to the east and north along the coast of New Guinea. In May, the new 345th Bomber Group (medium) arrived with fifty-seven new B-25s, under the command of Col. Jared Crabb, and another eighty-five B-25s arrived as replacements for the other groups. Also in May, Col. David "Photo" Hutchison arrived to command a new photo-reconnaissance group. General Walter Kruger, commander of the 6th Army, also arrived with his contingent of the 1st Cavalry Division in the middle of 1943.

In the spring of 1943 (which was actually fall in New Guinea), Kenney attacked Japanese positions from an advanced air base at Dobodura. Bombers from Port Morseby could land, refuel, and receive fighter cover, and by June, it was a bustling base, consisting of two fighter squadrons and light and medium bomb squadrons. Kenney, faced with red tape from Washington, bypassed some of the problems by not officially naming some of his commanders in their official functions. In March, he created the 1st Air Task Force and placed Col. Frederick Smith in charge at Dobodura. The group was never officially recognized and Col. Smith continued to be listed as Deputy Chief of Staff under General Kenney. All men assigned to the 1st

Air Task Force were also listed in other capacities. The task force's responsibility was to "rob" from other combat units when necessary for emergency operations, such as support of ground activity, and interception of enemy convoys, while remaining as fluid as necessary.

Another base was established at Wau, northeast of Port Morseby. In July, Captain Spencer Shropshire, with whom George would subsequently work, was stationed at Wau. Captain Shropshire was one of the ten air liaison officers that had been sent to General Kenney in January. Whether George was stationed at Wau, Dobodura, or Port Morseby during July and August isn't known, but he did write that he'd gotten some flying in and had also flown as an observer on some bombing missions.

The Australian Infantry Divisions, supported by air cover from Dobodura, continued to push the Japanese north along the coast toward

Salamaua, Lae, and into the Ramu and Markham river valleys. Kenney decided he needed an air base closer to the retreating positions. Reconnaissance discovered a small air strip at Marilinan, but it wasn't adequate, except for fighters and transports. Further north, another abandoned air strip was spotted at Bena-Bena. Kenney bribed the natives by telling them he was going to play a big joke on the "Jap Man." The natives built fires and grass huts at Bena-Bena in order to divert the Japanese. The ruse worked. The Japanese targeted Bena-Bena for their bombing, and the natives jumped for joy when they saw the big joke they'd pulled.

While the Japanese were concentrating on Bena-Bena, Kenney was busy flying supplies to Marilinan, including trucks that he ordered cut in half and welded back together when they reached their destination. Using an abandoned cargo plane, they performed time studies to determine the fastest method of loading and unloading supplies. The studies resulted in the ability to load and unload a jeep in less than two minutes. MacArthur remarked that if Kenney had been ordered to move New York City to the West Coast by air, he would have figured out a way to do it. The jeeps and trucks were necessary, since six miles from Marilinan another base was being built on more suitable ground. It was called Tsili-Tsili (pronounced silly silly).

Air operations shack – July 1943

Camp area – July 1943

Jungle trip – July 1943

Cpl. Irwin, Sgt. Gottlieb, and George examine carbine –
near Port Morseby, August 1943

No. 75132

(V-MAIL)

(Censor's Stamp)

Mrs. Harry Frederick
Box 285
Laurel Springs
New Jersey

Lt. Geo. F. Frederick
Hq 5AAF APO 925
% Postmaster
San Francisco, CA
15 July 1943

New Guinea

Dear Mother:

This being one of those days that you like to sit in bed and read, and since I can't do that, I am sitting at the desk writing. I haven't had any mail for about four days, but I'll probably receive a bunch of it *tomorrow. That's the way it usually is.*

There isn't a lot of news. I haven't been very busy as far as work goes, except to be here on duty about 12 hours a day, just in case anything comes up, and when it does, I am really busy.

Have you any news as to whether Bob Schaffer took part in the glider landings at Sicily? If you hear anything, let me know, as we are all interested in that. Hope you are well.

Lots of love & kisses,

George

No. 346247	*Mrs. Harry Frederick*	*Lt. Geo. F. Frederick*
	Box 285	*Hq 5AAF APO 925*
(V-MAIL)	*Laurel Springs*	*% Postmaster*
	New Jersey	*San Francisco, CA*
(Censor's Stamp)		*18 July 1943*

-8-
New Guinea

Dearest Mother:

Received your July 2nd letter yesterday and I still cannot under-stand why you or Dad haven't received any letters from me. I admit I probably haven't written as often as I should but I think I have written only a couple of days ago and it turns out to be a couple of weeks. Time seems to go fast here and yet I don't know why it should because it seems like nothing ever happens. I will number my letters from now on so you can follow them. This is number 8.

I was sorry to hear of Mrs. Reynolds' death. It will sure hit Eleanor hard, because I think she was closer to her mother than the other two girls. Don't feel too hard about us all being away, because some day we'll all be home and then it won't be as bad as when we are thousands of miles away. I love you very much.

Love & kisses,

George

No. 346251	*Mrs. Harry Frederick*	*Lt. Geo. F. Frederick*
	Box 285	*Hq 5AAF APO 925*
(V-MAIL)	*Laurel Springs*	*% Postmaster*
	New Jersey	*San Francisco, CA*
(Censor's Stamp)		*21 July 1943*

9

New Guinea

 Dearest Mother:

Having a chance to write today, I thought I would write a few lines even if there is no news.

Had a letter from Harry and he said they had a fine trip. I was telling him that after the war, if we are able to leave our baby that long, Cleo and I will have to take a honeymoon trip. We have never had a real honeymoon, although I like to think of those three months in Texas as one, because we sure were happy together.

Still on the same job—a desk job that I don't like and no nearer promotion than I was 2 yrs ago, in fact I guess this time 2 yrs ago I was nearer promotion then I am now, but that is the penalty for transferring my allegiance from the infantry to the air corps.

Hope you and Dad are well.

Lots of love & kisses,

George

No. 627227	*Mrs. Harry Frederick*	*Lt. Geo. F. Frederick*
	Box 285	*Hq 5AAF APO 929*
(V-MAIL)	*Laurel Springs*	*% Postmaster*
	New Jersey	*San Francisco, CA*
		27 July 1943

(Censor's Stamp)

10
New Guinea

Dearest Mother:

Received your letter of July 5th, that was sure good service. I had Harry's letter telling me of his good fortune in getting to go to adjutant general's school. That is always good to have a school to your credit. Maybe he will get a promotion soon. After all, the job he is on deserves higher rank, which is more than I can say for my job.

I have changed again, still with the same outfit, but I'm doing intelligence work now, because that was what I had done at one time in the infantry.

I have managed to get a few flying missions to my credit. I was observer on 3 of them, which were bombing missions and I completed a [censored] ferry mission today.

That was good news about Mussolini, wasn't it? Hope you are well.

Love & kisses,

George

11
New Guinea
1 Aug 1943

Dearest Mother:

It is now Sunday evening and I have just come back from a USO camp show at the Red Cross. It was fairly good, but I've seen better.

Thanks for the picture of the gliders. I was interested to see the formation flying with the [censored] ships. Some of the fellows who also graduated from Lubbock are here and they were interested in it also.

I hope you are getting my letters. I can't figure out why you shouldn't. I know Cleo enjoyed her visit and she sure likes all the family. I really do love her and I know she is the kind of girl I've always wanted and is a really swell wife.

Haven't seen a ballgame for so long I wonder what one looks like. I manage to play volleyball about an hour a day so as to get my exercise in. I should have quite a tan, but it seems that even tho the sun comes down regularly & strong, the atmosphere is moist and most persons don't tan easily around here.

Your garden really is sprouting. Cleo said they were canning vegetables from their garden also. I imagine they have quite a big one. She told me they now have 7 new calves and 18 more on the way, so you can get an idea of the size herd they have...the [much censored]...I see they used them in Sicily also.

I hope by the time you get this, Italy will be out of the war. That will make it that much quicker that we finish this whole affair and get back home.

Guess that's all the news from here. I better stop and get this in the mail bag or it won't leave until Tuesday.

Hope you and Dad are both well and are getting my letters.

Loads of love & kisses,

George

*12
New Guinea
4 Aug 1943*

Dearest Mother:

Received your 2 part letter of July 19, yesterday. I'm glad you are finally receiving my letters, but can't figure out what happened to the first ones.

As for Mr. Bramhall reading part of my letter, it isn't that I mind him reading it, but I didn't want him telling the amount I gave, because I don't want any credit for it. As long as others want to give money to that purpose because I am giving, it is OK, but to reveal the amount would be interpreted by some as trying to brag about how much I am giving.

You know I have always worked for the Lord and my church, but even at that, out here you get closer to God than you can in the States, and you get a better understanding of how great He is, and that what a much better world it would be if everyone in it were Christians. That was my purpose in giving to the missionary fund.

I believe I will take your suggestion and write to Mr. Nodor and enclose a little gift for the East Baptist Mission Fund. I like to give something each month, and it is just as well to alternate occasionally. I sent some to Cleo to give to her church one other month.

I would rather send money to the church the same as if I was home, that is a little each week. It always seems like a lot when a lump sum, but it can't be helped. Actually it is not much more than I normally gave, but I figure since I am getting more I should give more, because the Lord has been so good to me.

I haven't received any packages of photos yet, but they will get here eventually, so don't worry. Incidentally, don't forget this is another new address.

Speaking of ice cream, we have actually received an ice cream freezer within the last two days. We will run it off of our generator, so looks like we are getting civilized.

I write to Helen frequently, but don't get her letters very fast because she sends them air mail. I did get one yesterday, however, dated July 4.

Received a letter from Charley Irvins yesterday. That's the first he has ever written me. He says Milt is in North Africa and is a Lt. Col. now. He has another addition to the family, 22 months old, so you see it really was a long time since I had heard from him.

As for my writing to the Snuffins, you asked me not to last November and I haven't. In fact, in December, I received a letter from Mrs. Snuffin, but didn't answer it, which I didn't like to do, but since I had told you I wouldn't write, I didn't. The only exception was in June, when I sent Cliff a note congratulating him on his graduation from high school.

Mrs. Helms, however, writes me regularly and I answer all of them, because I think she is very nice and has always treated me swell, as well as Al's family has in NC. So I don't see anything wrong with that, do you? Al has recovered, although he lost quite a few pounds.

Well guess that's all the news. I'll write Dad tomorrow, when I may have some more news.

Hope you and Dad are well.

Loads of love & kisses,

George

From August to November 1943, George wrote ten other letters home, since his numbering sequence jumped from 12 to 22, but those letters were missing. Apparently, my grandmother either hadn't received them or had lost them. My grandfather had been transferred to Florida and she had been able to go with him. My grandfather had also transferred to the Army Air Corps and requested service in the South Pacific, with the hope of being with or near his son. The move to Florida didn't last very long until he was transferred back north.

THE JAPANESE finally discovered Kenney's deception at Bena-Bena and the air base at Marilinan the end of July. By that time, Marilinan had been equipped with radar and a squadron of P-39s had been flown in. The Japanese attacked with a dozen bombers, escorted by twenty-four fighters the next day. A P-39 squadron drove them off, but not until the chaplain and several men were killed during the bombing.

Using reconnaissance flights and photos of enemy air bases, the 5th AAF kept up a continual bombardment of Japanese shipping and air bases. Barges and shipping became a hunting game, and increasingly more difficult to locate, since the Japanese hid the barges and shipping began to decrease with the loss of barges.

One flight, led by Lt. Col. Don Hall, a big-nosed blond boy, made a low-level raid on the Japanese air base at Borum, on the east coast of New Guinea. Just as he came over at treetop level, Hall spotted sixty bombers lined up on one side with their engines running, ready for take off, and on the other side were some fifty Japanese fighters. One bomber was moving down the runway when Lt. Col. Hall fired, and it came crashing down, blocking the runway. The remaining Japanese planes suffered the rain of 200 .50-caliber machine guns as the rest of the B-25 squadron came over, dropping a thousand parafrag bombs. The Japanese defenses were devastated as their bomb-laden planes blew up, igniting nearby fuel tanks and killing and wounding ground personnel. Two other Japanese airdromes suffered similar destruction of planes and equipment on the same day. The Japanese referred to it as the "Black Day of August."

Another attack on Dagua was led by Major Ralph Cheli, of the 38th group. He was attacked by several Japanese fighters as they concentrated on his plane. With his plane damaged and on fire, he continued to lead his squadron toward the target at minimum altitude instead of gaining altitude in order to parachute to safety. Reaching the target, they were able to wipe out all the planes on the field. He instructed his next in command to take the rest of the formation home while he attempted to ditch at sea, but his plane disintegrated before he could land. He was posthumously awarded the Congressional Medal of Honor.

In August, the 2nd Air Task Force was activated at Marilinan and Tsili-Tsili. It was also known as the 309th Bombardment Wing. As with the 1st Air Task Force, also known as the Buna Task Force, and 308th Bombardment Wing, operational control rested with the commanders at their respective bases, Tsili-Tsili and Dobodura. The operational control was necessary at the outlying bases because communication lines from Port Morseby weren't dependable. George was assigned to the 309th Bombardment Wing and was part of the 2nd Air Task Force. He became an air liaison officer, in charge of the 6th Air Liaison Party (ALP), also known as a Supporting Air Party (SAP), with duties of close air support to aid ground troops.

Prior to WWII, aviation in support of ground forces hadn't been developed. The only guide for close air support until after World War I was Field Manual 31-35. Although practiced in North Africa, it had so far met with disastrous results. Early communications called for three radio circuits, one for Air Force HQ, one for planes, and one for liaison with ground forces. It was used in the campaign against Buna and Gona, but again without good results. The problems included target identification, communication, and a lack of detailed maps.

When used, a liaison was confined to the highest echelon of command and assigned to headquarters. An officer at air headquarters was to be notified when air support was necessary. Lt. General Robert L. Eichelberger, recognizing that air support would be of benefit, offered to house an air liaison officer in his quarters if General Kenney would send one. His reasons were to prevent the bombing and strafing of friendly troops, but nothing was done until later.

The communication channel was a coded message from a battle commander on the field, through ground force channels, to division headquarters. Division would decide which messages to forward. Then they went to the air operations section and on to headquarters, the 5th AAF at Port Morseby. Crews would be briefed if the mission was approved. The system was slow, targets would change, and they used map coordinates to identify targets.

Ground troops tried using panels to identify friendly troops, but they drew fire from the Japanese. Then they tried using reflective items, canteens, mess kits, and mirrors, but that also drew fire. In both cases, the pilots didn't always see the markers, since they were flying at high speeds and altitudes. Radio communications didn't work because of a shortage of frequencies and the Japanese would jam frequencies when they found them. Codes were considered more of a hindrance than a help, The infantry also felt that air liaison officers needed to be "ground minded."

On Guadalcanal, no liaison system existed, so one had to be improvised. The Marines used a pilot that had a day off to assist the ground troops. The radios used by ground troops weren't adequate, since they didn't have the required range. G-2 (Intelligence) supplied gridded photo-mosaic maps to identify targets, and in combat the infantry used smoke signals to identify friendly troops. Both of those tactics resulted in some success. Another tactic called for bombers to make "dummy runs," as if they were going to bomb and strafe enemy troops. This also met with some success. The bombers signaled friendly troops by rocking their wings, and ground troops charged the enemy while the bombers were making their dummy bombing and strafing runs.

On Guadalcanal, it was learned that the use of coordinates on maps were impractical, that photo-mosaic maps were the best, and that elaborate codes were an impediment. It also helped that on Guadalcanal, the air base was close to the battlefield.

The 5th Tactical Air Communication Squadron that was to form the ALPs began receiving replacements and enlisted personnel in July and August. Using the experience gained from the Buna campaign and from Guadalcanal, replacements were trained in cryptography, radio maintenance, and code practice. An ALP could be only a few men or as many as twenty-five, and it was only a coincidence if any two ALPs had the same personnel structure. The ALPs were equipped with Signal Corp Radio (SCR) radios and receivers. An SCR-193 radio was mounted in a chest on the back of a jeep and the batteries were placed under the chest. A 12-volt generator was mounted on a fender and powered by a long fan belt from the jeep's motor, which charged the batteries. A whip antenna was mounted on the back of the jeep. One or more ALPs would be assigned to the ground troops.

Lines of communication were also improved. The ALP was linked to the air support section headquarters. A request from any ground unit commander was transmitted through ground communication channels. Each request included a designation of the target, location of friendly troops, and time limits. The HQ ground commander would evaluate the request, with the advice of the ALP, and it would be forwarded to advance headquarters at Dobodura or Tsili-Tsili. During the mission, the ALP would have direct contact with the planes. After the mission, the ground commander was required to report the results to AAF headquarters.

Jeep – Tsili-Tsili – August 1943

To identify potential targets, the 5th AAF resorted to slow, low-flying airplanes to take pictures of terrain. The oblique photos revealed the terrain, elevation differences, and the locations of enemy pockets. The photos were gridded with coordinates and potential targets were numbered. Both pilots and the ALP were supplied with duplicate photos. The ALP could give a pilot the number of a target and the pilot, using the photo, could easily locate that target.

The big show in September was the taking of Nadzab and Lae from the Japanese. It was to be a coordinated effort of the 5th AAF, the Navy, the 7th Australian Infantry Division, under General Vasey, and the 9th Australian Infantry Division, led by General Wooten. Vasey and Wooten had bet twenty cases of whiskey on who'd enter Lae first.

The 9th would be transported by the Navy to Hopoi Beach, a beach-head east of Lae, while the 7th would march to Lae after taking Nadzab from the west. The 7th was transported by air, and men and supplies were to be dropped by parachute. General Kenney insisted on going into the battle, but

General MacArthur resisted, since he didn't want to lose his Air Force commander, but Kenney persisted, and finally MacArthur said that Kenney was right, and that he would go also.

Now it was Kenney who protested, "Why, after living all these years and getting to be the head general of the show, is it necessary for you to risk having some five-dollar-a-month Jap aviator shoot a hole through you?"

MacArthur replied, "I'm not worried about getting shot. Honestly, the only thing that disturbs me is the possibility that when we hit the rough air over the mountains, my stomach might get upset. I'd hate to get sick and disgrace myself in front of the kids."

Kenney arranged for a "brass hat" flight of three B-17s to fly just above and to one side of the troop carriers as they came into Nadzab for the big parachute jump on September 5—MacArthur in one plane, Kenney in another, and a third for protection, in case they were attacked, which carried General Blamey, the Australian commander.

Ed Gammill, of the 43rd Bomb Group, was stationed at Jackson Drome in Port Moresby when the Nadzab show started. His revetment had a good view of the runway from what they called the "The Vultures Roost."

Almost 100 C-47 aircraft flew into Jackson, lining one side of the runway. They almost reached the full length of the runway and were in perfect alignment waiting for their cargo. With the arrival of a parachute regiment, we realized that the first airborne operation in the Southwest Pacific was to be initiated.

Each man was loaded down with so much equipment that walking was difficult. I noticed a "Mutt and Jeff" couple that were obviously good buddies. One a very large man, standing about 6'6", and his buddy, about 5'6", were assisting each other to the airplanes. The big one pushed the little guy up the steps and into the plane. The little guy turned around and pulled the big one in and they disappeared along with all the others.

All of the C-47s were buttoned up, the engines started, and one by one they turned and taxied on to the runway. There were at least four airplanes in the process of taking off on the runway at one time. The steam of take-off was continuous until all were up and formed into "V's" of three airplanes. The formation passed over the field, heading for Nadzab. I wondered if those two came through the action okay.

Staff Sergeant Bill Elrod was a member of a crack B-17 air crew, considered the best in the 5th AAF. General Kenney also knew Elrod's father, Col. Elrod, an Army chaplain. Elrod was long overdue to be returned home. General Kenney had called and instructed three of the best B-17s crews to be on alert. Elrod realized something important was going to happen, but had no idea what it was. S/Sgt Elrod wrote a letter to Capt. Carl Hustad, recounting the events of the day:

A truck took us to the plane, B-17F #24537 (Talisman), at 6:00 AM the next morning and in just a few minutes a staff car brought Lt. Col. H.J. Hawthorne and Brig. Gen. R.M. Ramey. Hawthorne was our first pilot and Ramey was copilot. As they went about the pre-flight, a line of staff cars was coming down through the dispersal area and the one leading the line had a flag with four stars on it. Then I began to understand why the hush-hush. Before the first car stopped in front of our plane, the second car had a three star flag and Kenney hit the ground running before the first car got stopped. "Elrod! Elrod!" He was yelling. I ran to him. Out of breath, he gasped, "The Old Man knew I would have a crack crew for this morning so he ranked me out of it." All I could do was stand there with my mouth open trying to take all of this in. "The Old Man?" I asked. "Yes," said Kenney, "the Old Man MacArthur. You're going to be carrying him this morning and I'll be flying on your right wing. C'mon. I want to introduce you to him."

We went to MacArthur's car and Kenney introduced us. It must have been comical. We went through a routine you wouldn't believe, all because I couldn't decide whether or not I was to shake hands first and then salute or the other way around. Then he, the Great Man said, "Now Elrod, I want to meet the rest of the crew and have pictures taken with them." It was then I realized that flash bulbs were going off like mad the whole time. We were surrounded by photographers and newsreel cameramen. I looked back at the plane and almost laughed because everybody looked as stupid as I must have, their eyes bugged out and mouths hanging open.

I took him over and introduced each man (he already knew Gen. Ramey) and told him the position each man was flying. With each one he posed for a picture that was to be sent to their hometown newspapers. When we finished that he told us he would be back after while, that now he had to go and have his picture taken with the paratroopers. I looked down toward the runway and there sat about ninety C-47s angled by the runway almost its full length. So MacArthur left us. Finally word came to taxi down toward the apron and we did. After we had been sitting there for about a half hour, a staff car came up and it was Col. Morhouse, MacArthur's personal aide. He handed me a three-legged milking stool and asked that I help the General in and out of the plane.

When MacArthur did get back to the plane, we finally got airborne at 7:50 AM. The flight lasted until 12:20 PM and it was something to remember. But first, I'll give you the names of the personnel as they appeared on the Form 1. (Lt. Col. H.J. Hawthorne, Pilot, Brig. Gen. R.M. Ramey, Copilot, 1st Lt. H.A. Wilson, Navigator, 2nd Lt. J.E. Bordeaux, Bombardier, Sgt. J.F. Standlee, T/Sgt. L.J. Calitri, 2nd Lt. T.J. Evans, Sgt. W.W. Elrod, Cpl. A.C. Parent, the tail-gunner. Passengers were Gen. Douglas MacArthur, Col. L. Diller, Lt. Col. C. Morhouse, and E. Wildis, a war correspondent.)

I don't know if you will remember any of these names, but I think most of them had come into the squadron before you all left. The main thing is, I felt they made up as good a crew as we could put in the air that day.

Once airborne, we picked up a squadron of P-38s for top cover as we flew top cover for the C-47s. Our 'target' was Nadzab Strip, up the Markham River valley from Lae. Over the target, we picked up squadrons of P-40s to add to our cover. Col. Morhouse told me that our three 17s were the only 17s allowed to be flying and the order was that they must not be touched. After all, MacArthur was in the lead ship, Kenney on the right wing, and Blamey, the Australian commander, on the left.

Over the target, we watched the B-25s with eight .50-caliber guns in their noses strafe the runway area thoroughly. They were followed by the A-20s who laid a triangular smoke screen around the runway. Then the C-47s split up and dropped the paratroopers alongside the smoke screen.

Lt. Evans had never flown in the ball, so we traded places and I went to the waist. I was hanging out the waist port watching when someone tapped me on the shoulder. It was Morhouse and he wanted to know if the gun could be removed from the mount so the General could have a good view. I assured him it could and took it out and laid it on the floor. In a minute or two, someone else tapped my shoulder and I TURNED TO BE CONFRONTED WITH MacArthur. He pointed out the waist, gesticulated, and talked with me "very importantly." The only problem was I could not hear a word he said. Cautiously, I leaned toward him and informed him so. He never let on, just shook his head and continued. Finally, I leaned close to his ear, "I can't hear a word the General is saying, sir!" He leaned toward me, with something of a twinkle in his eye and said, "I'm not saying anything, sergeant, this for the newsreels." I straightened up and turned around to find the newsreel camera right in my face. I got out of there in a hurry.

His staff handled the publicity angle well. Later, the film was in the town in Kentucky, where my mother was living, and at the request of the air corps, a special showing was held for my mother, my three younger sisters, and some of the local dignitaries. I never did learn if my dad had ever seen the film wherever he was at the time. I often hoped he had a chance to see MacArthur "conferring" with me.

When we got back to Jackson (Morseby), we had to go through the routine of another round of pictures; all the while, Kenney was standing off to the side. As soon as MacArthur and his staff left, Kenny came over. "I'm a man of my word, Bill," he said and took out his pen and piece of paper. Right there under the wing of the plane, he wrote out my orders to go home as well as a one step promotion. "It wouldn't do for you to return in lower grade than you had when you came over. Give them to your 1st Sergeant. He'll know what to do with them." He smiled, shook my hand, and added, "Your father has been a good man and a good friend to me. I'll remember you as being just as good as he was. He'll be proud of you, and it's been a real pleasure having you serve under my command. Goodbye and good luck." He saluted and walked away, leaving me confused and a bit choked up, and I remember thinking, "Gee whiz, I wish it had been our original crew."

Bill Elrod returned home and became a minister, following in his father's footsteps. After the mission, Kenney wrote General Arnold:

You already know by this time the news on the preliminary moves to take out Lae, but I will tell you about the show on the 5th September, when we took Nadzab with 1700 paratroops and with General MacArthur in a B-17 over the area watching the show and jumping up and down like a kid. I was flying number two in the same flight with him and the operation really was a magnificent spectacle. I truly don't believe that another air force in the world today could have put this over as perfectly as the 5th Army Air Force did.

Three hundred and two airplanes in all, taking off from eight different fields in the Moresby and Dobodura areas, made a rendezvous right on the nose over Marilinan, flying through clouds, passes in the mountains, and over the top. Not a single squadron did any circling or stalling around but all slid into place like clockwork and proceeded on the final flight down the Watut Valley, turned to the right down the Markham, and went directly to the target. Going north down the valley of the Watut into Marilinan, this was the picture: Heading the parade at one thousand feet were six squadrons of B-25 strafers, with the eight .50-caliber guns in the nose and sixty frag bombs in each bomb bay; immediately behind and about five hundred feet above were six A-20s, flying in pairs—three pairs abreast —to lay smoke as the last frag bomb exploded.

At about two thousand feet and directly behind the A-20s came ninety-six C-47s carrying paratroops, supplies, and some artillery. The C-47s flew in three columns of three-plane elements, each column carrying a battalion set up for a particular battalion dropping ground. On each side along the column of transports and about one thousand feet above them were the close-cover fighters. Another group of fighters sat at seven thousand feet and, up in the sun, staggered from fifteen to twenty thousand, was still another group. Following the transports came five B-17s racks loaded with 300-pound packages with parachutes, to be dropped to the paratroopers on call by panel signals as they needed them. This mobile supply unit stayed over Nadzab practically all day, serving the paratroops below, dropping a total of fifteen tons of supplies in this matter.

Following the echelon to the right and just behind the five supply B-17s was group of twenty-four B-24s and four B-17s, which left the column just before the junction of the Watut and Markham to take out the Jap defensive position at Heath's Plantation, about halfway between Nadzab and Lae. Five weather ships were used prior to and during the show along the route and over the passes, to keep the units straight on weather to be encountered during their flights to the rendezvous. The brass-hat flight of three B-17s above the center of the transport column completed the set-up.

The strafers checked in on the target at exactly the time set, just prior to take-off. They strafed and frag-bombed the whole area in which the jumps were to be made, and then as the last bombs exploded the smoke layers went to work. As the steams of smoke were built up, the three columns of transports slid into place and in one minute and ten seconds from the time the first parachute opened the last of 1700 paratroopers had dropped. During the operation, including the bombing of Heath's, a total of ninety-two tons of high-explosive bombs were dropped, thirty-two tons of fragmentation bombs and 42,580 rounds of .50-caliber and 5,180 rounds of .30-caliber ammunition were expended. At the same time, nine B-25s and sixteen P-38s attacked the Jap refueling airdrome at Cape Gloucester. One medium bomber and one fighter on the ground were burned and three medium bombers and one fighter destroyed in combat. Two ack-ack positions were put out of action and several supply and fuel dumps set on fire. Between five and a half six tons of parafrags were dropped and 19,000 rounds of .50-caliber ammunition fired. Simultaneously also, ten Beauforts, five A-20s and seven P-40s from the R.A.A.F. put the Jap refueling field at Gasmata out of action. No air interception was made by the Japs on any of the three missions. Our only losses were two Beauforts shot down by ack-ack at Gasmata.

The paratroopers and advanced ground troops found that the Japanese had evacuated Nadzab. The following day, September 6, Kenney transported General Vasey and the rest of the 7th Infantry Division to Nadzab for their ground assault on Lae. George was in charge of the 6th ALP. Their C-47 crash-landed at Nadzab, but apparently no one was injured. George had his 8mm movie camera with him and took movies of them loading the jeep at Tsili-Tsili, the flight, and the crash-landing at Nadzab. It took three hours to unload the jammed jeep after it landed at Nadzab and another two hours to get the radio to work. After getting their radio working, they were on the air for twenty-eight straight hours without rest.

The 5th AAF also bombed Lae with more than 140 tons of bombs and expended another 75,000 rounds of ammunition in support of the attacking Australian infantry divisions. The bombing of Lae continued until September 16, when General Vasey, advancing from Nadzab radioed: "Only the Fifth Army Air Force bombers are preventing me from entering Lae, Vasey." The bombing stopped and General Vasey marched into Lae, followed two hours later by General Wooten and the 9th Infantry Division. General Wooten accused General Kenney of having a bet on Vasey, since he lifted the bombing on the west side of Lae.

General Kenney responded, "You are two grand commanders of two grand fighting divisions."

Meet P.I.B. — Native soldiers — August 1943

Cub I Flew – New Guinea – August 6, 1943

Japanese defensive position – September 1943
(Notice how hard it is to see)

Camp area – September 7, 1943 – Nadzab – Day after C-47 crash-landing

Lae – After the Air Force got through with it – September 1943

George's crew – Trip around Lae – September 1943

George – Jap Zero – Lae – September 1943

The Japanese responded by developing Hollandia, twenty-five miles up the New Guinea coast, into a major air base. They also activated a whole division from the Madang-Bogadjim area to attack the advancing 7th Australian Infantry Division of 20,000 troops that were moving up the Markham and Ramu river valleys from Nadzab and Lae. The Markham River flowed south toward Lae, whereas the Ramu flowed north. The 7th advanced quickly up the Markham Valley. Meanwhile, the 9th advanced along the coast toward Finschhafen.

Reconnaissance flights kept an eye on an advancing Japanese division coming down the road from Bogadjim and destroyed bridges across the Ramu to hold up the Japanese advance, but the Japanese engineers had an uncanny ability to repair bridges as fast as they were destroyed. A bombing mission of eight B-24s at the end of September on the largest bridge across the Ramu was thought to be a disaster since they missed their target and hit the side of a mountain instead. However, it turned out to be of benefit, since the bombs caused a landslide that dammed the river for a few days. When the dam finally broke, it washed out several miles of the road and held up the Japanese advance.

In October, General Vasey set up his headquarters at Dumpu, thirty-five miles north of Gusap and about fifty miles south of Madang, near the head-waters of the Ramu, and the 49th Fighter Group was moved to the Gusap-Dumpu base. The Japanese staged an air attack on the base on November 6, as well as on Nadzab, but the attack caused little damage.

With the advance to Gusap and Dumpu, General Kenney set up the 3rd Air Task Force. As with both the 1st Air Task Force at Dobodura and the 2nd Air Task Force at Tsili-Tsili, the command was necessary because of the distance and communication barriers. Kenney placed Col. Don "Fighter" Hutchinson in charge of the 3rd Air Task Force. Col. Hutchinson was a short, slight, brown-eyed, bald-headed veteran of nine years' service. His nickname, according to General Kenney, really fit him, but was also used to distinguish him from Col. David "Photo" Hutchison of the SATF at Tsili-Tsili.

IN THE FALL OF 1943, George is promoted to Captain. George's record in the battles of the Ramu and Markham valleys was recorded by General

Hq 7 Aust Div.
6 Feb 44

Subject: Record of Service, Capt George F.
Frederick, Air Liaison Party Officer.

The Commanding General, Advance Echelon, Fifth Air Force, APO 929.

1. The following record of Capt. George F. Frederick, recently relieved as Air Liaison Party Officer with this division is forwarded for any action deemed desirable.

2. Capt Frederick (then Lt) while assigned as Air Liaison Party Officer, materially assisted this division by voluntarily flying a Piper Cub on numerous missions for the benefit of this headquarters, in addition to his other duties.

3. Capt Frederick flew over 75 missions while this division was advancing up the MARKHAM and RAMU VALLEYS. These missions consisted of flying an unarmed and highly vulnerable light Cub aircraft on reconnaissance missions, locating and surveying from the air proposed routes for signal lines and reconnaissance to locate proposed routes for Jeep tracks and locating bivouac sites. These flights carried Capt Frederick within range of enemy ground fire and in several cases were over enemy territory. Several of the missions consisted of evacuating wounded and sick personnel from an extremely small field cut out of Kunai in the KESAWI AREA when that area was the most advanced of our forward bases. The use of this field presented a most difficult hazard and Capt Frederick deserves a great deal of credit for so willingly and without regard for personal safety performing these missions.

4. Capt Frederick was also instrumental in assisting the Air Engineer in locating a suitable field at DUMPU prior to the arrival of the division in that area and landing there in the Cub while that area was only held by a small patrol.

5. Capt Frederick also landed the officer and equipment necessary to construct the strip at FAITA. This necessitated two trips and two landings on the soft and unprepared ground and was accomplished without mishap. Thses missions involved flights over 30 miles in a light, unarmed Cub over territory then in possession of the enemy.

6. In addition to the above flights Capt Frederick flew the Commanding General, various Staff Officers, and officers of units under this command on liaison flights and reconnaissance missions over enemy territory in advance of the movement of the division up the RAMU VALLEY.

A CERTIFIED TRUE COPY:

CLAUDE W. SHENKEL,
1st Lt., Air Corps,

GEORGE VASEY,
Major General,
Commanding.

- 1 -

Vasey to the Commanding General, Advance Echelon, Fifth Army Air Force on the 6th of February 1944:

George – Near Shaggy Ridge

Little close support was needed by the 7th until it reached Shaggy Ridge. Prior to that, nearly 450 ground support strikes were flown, but they were directed against enemy communications along the Bogadjim Road. More valuable to the ground troops in their day-to-day fighting were the slow Boomerangs of the RAAF army cooperation squadrons. Those planes were mainly occupied with reconnaissance and spotting for artillery, but on occasion used their .30-caliber machine guns for emergency close support attacks.

A virtual stalemate occurred when the Australians attempted to advance, since the terrain prevented them from advancing. A major obstacle was Shaggy Ridge, where the Japanese had honeycombed the area with booby traps, machine-gun nests, and foxholes. The ridge itself was but a few feet wide, with drops of 300 to 500 feet on either side. It was the only approach north and seemed to stretch indefinitely. The infantry, supported by artillery, hadn't been successful in advancing. In December, an unprecedented procedure, combining air power with infantry, was tried. As an experiment, the RAAF, with slow Australian planes, guided P-40s to targets not more than 150 yards from the advancing Australian Infantry. The dive-bombing and strafing from low altitude proved to be the key to a successful advance up the valley. Air/ground communication, communication to headquarters, marking of targets by smoke bombs, and an arrow pointing to the target were new highs in close air support.

Meanwhile, General Wooten and the 9th Australian Infantry Division took Finschhafen, on the tip of Huon Peninsula, against stiff enemy resistance, culminating in the final battles being conducted in hand-to-hand combat. Although some Japanese continued to retreat to bases north or into the jungle, sometimes they would stay close to the base and hide in the battle wreckage. Several weeks after taking Lae, for example, several Japanese were found that were healthier looking than the Japanese troops who had been killed, proving they had not only been able to hide in the wrecks, but also had done a good job of foraging for food amid the advancing Allies.

14

7 Oct. 43

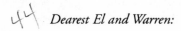 *Dearest El and Warren:*

This is to both of you, with my most brotherly congratulations on making me an uncle. Our prayers have been answered and I am really very, very happy about it. You sure picked a pretty name—Mary Ann Mackara. I know she will be as pretty as my "kid" sister is.

Funny thing about how I found out about it. Our mail has been none too regular out here in the woods and day before yesterday, I received letters from Aunt Carrie and Dad, and both told me about the good news. I happened to open Dad's first and he said he was now a granddad, so that's how I know. Boy, are he and mother proud and happy. I can't say as I blame him, because I think that is the moment he has been waiting for all his life. As for mother, I know she is really thrilled too because I think all mothers are closer to their daughter's children—it is just natural because girls must be together. Cleo is home with her mother as I think she should be and you were with mother or vice versa, but anyway it is swell.

By the way, El, received your letter of Sept. 13. Let me see, that was two days before your happy event.

Boy, am I wet right now. I've been flying a Cub around the past few days and last nite I had to stay all nite at the plane where I landed due to engine trouble. I luckily had my haversack or rather a makeshift one, and I borrowed a blanket off one of the control men at the field and slept on a wooden bed that the boys made out of some jungle plants.

I've really been kept busy, but I like it better than sitting around waiting for things to happen and then being busy for a few hours like mad.

Well, gotta stop now so I can write Harry and then I am going to bed as I am chilled to the bone from this "beautiful" heavy dew.

Congratulations again to a swell sister and brother-in-law. Thanks a lot, Warren, for that nice letter, but I'm sure I didn't deserve it. I'll sure keep it among my cherished treasures.

Lots of love & kisses,

George

22
1 Nov. 43

Dear Mother:

45

Well, how do you like Florida by this time? I believe you will like it very much and as you get to know the people there, it will probably be that much better.

Received a letter from Aunt Carrie and she said the baby is very sweet. I'll sure be glad when I get a picture of her because I bet she is pretty.

It won't be long now and you'll be a grandma again. You are running parallel to Cleo's mother. Her brother & wife expect an addition in December, so she will be a grandmother also twice within 2 months.

It would be odd if our baby was born on our wedding anniversary. According to the doctor, it will be about 2 days before, but sometimes they are wrong.

I forgot to put in Dad's letter that I had a letter from Cleo saying she owed Dad a letter and she was going to write it after she finished the one to me. He sure made a good impression on Cleo because she really thinks he is swell and said she doesn't think of you & Dad as in-laws because you are so nice to her. I'm sure glad, but I knew she would love you both because you are the swellest parents in the world. It'll be nice when we can all be home together again.

Well, there isn't any other news, I guess, so I better close or I won't have room in the envelope for all these pages and the pictures.

When you see the Hufners, tell them I said "Hello" and hope they are well.

Loads of love & kisses,

George

I WAS BORN November 24, 1943, while my father was fighting in the battle of Shaggy Ridge in New Guinea. It was also only three days before my parent's first year anniversary. On Christmas Day 1943, Cleo took me to Mt. Carmel Hospital in Pittsburg. I hadn't been able to keep food down and my weight dropped to less than my birth weight. The diagnosis was pyloric stenosis, a fairly common condition of first-born males. Dr. Rush performed an operation and I recovered.

26 Dec 43

46

Dearest El,

Well, I guess you have the news about George Clinton now, but in case you don't have the details, he weighed 6# 9 oz. at birth and was 20 inches long. Cleo said he has long arms—looks like he is taking after his old man.

Cleo said the nurses think he has a very beautiful shaped head. He has dark hair and dark blue eyes—they'll probably turn brown.

Cleo is able to nurse him and that suits her fine. Just in case she wasn't able, the doctor said there wouldn't be any trouble anyway because they have 12 milk cows. That's one advantage of a farm.

I bet Mary Anne is cute now. I'd sure like to see her as well as my own son. Seems like everything is turning out fine, both of us wanted a boy and we got one. It will be nice that the two will grow up together, just like Helen and I. Aunt Carrie used to take us everywhere together and it was very nice.

We had a nice Christmas Day, considering we are in New Guinea. It would have been perfect if I had been home, even tho it was like a mid-summer day.

We had a very nice church service in the morning and in the afternoon played volleyball and then served a turkey dinner to the men. At

7:00 PM, we had our turkey dinner, followed by the usual toasts—the first to the King, and then to the 5 of us Americans with them. It was pretty good homemade black currant wine.

Well, looks like Dad is getting transferred again, guess he'll be glad when he's settled again.

Tell Ruth & Walt I said hello and hope they are both fine. Guess I've run out of news so I'll close. Hope you all are well and that you had a nice Christmas.

Thanks so much for the birthday card. It was very nice and thoughtful of you to remember.

Lots of love & kisses,

George

EARLY IN JANUARY 1944, General Kenney made another trip to Washington, D.C. While there, he was able to obtain the 13th AAF under his command, as well as two new heavy bomber groups and additional planes. On his return trip, he attended a conference in Hawaii about taking the Admiralty Islands.

Meanwhile, to obtain bases further north on the New Guinea coast and to control the Vitiaz Strait between New Britain and New Guinea, inroads were made in the cooperation between naval, air, and ground forces, and attacks were made on strategic locations in the western shores of New Britain and at Saidor on the New Guinea coast. Kenney wanted bases further north in New Guinea, and resisted claims by the Navy for air bases on New Britain. Nevertheless, some bases were established in western New Britain. The plan was to neutralize the Japanese stronghold at Rabaul, with its numerous air bases, harbors, troops, and six-month supply of rations and ammunition. Weather permitting, combined attacks from Admiral Halsey and of General Kenney's land-based bombers were conducted on Rabaul harbors and air bases.

(V-MAIL)

(Censor's Stamp)

Major Harry Frederick
PO Box 196
Charleston, SC

Capt. Geo. F. Frederick
6 ALP % Hq. Adv. Ech
5AAF
APO 929
% Postmaster
San Francisco, CA
24 Jan 44

2

47 Dear Dad:

Just wrote you a letter on the 22nd but neglected to wish you a happy birthday. Time goes so quickly here that the 23rd popped up so quickly I didn't realize it.

Well, things are really going good here. The Aussies are throwing back the Japs and just completed a maneuver that actually looked impossible. After I get home, I'll show you the pictures of the country and you'd never believe they could outflank the Japs—and I guess old Nip thought the same—but they did, and in good strength. We captured one 75mm gun while it was still firing, which is an example of the surprise we accomplished.

Well, again, Happy Birthday and I hope next year I'll be with you again.

Love,

George

(V-MAIL)	*Mr. & Mrs. Warren*	*Capt. Geo. F. Frederick*
	Mackara	*6 ALP % Hq. Adv. Ech*
PM 2/15/1944	*207 Garfield Ave.*	*5AAF*
	Clementon, NJ	*APO 929 % Postmaster*
(Censor's Stamp)		*San Francisco, CA*
		2 Feb 1944

+8

Dearest El:

Was glad to receive your Jan. 7 letter today. Glad to hear Warren likes the Navy, but sure sorry to learn he's in the hospital. Sounds almost as if he had malaria. Do you know what it was? I hope he gets out soon so he can finish his "boot" training.

Cleo probably wrote you about Clinton's operation. I was wondering why he didn't seem to be able to keep his food down and here all the time it was a restriction in his esophagus. (I think that's right.)

Mother said she sent the money to you for the watch & I told Cleo to send it, so I guess you can straighten it out. The major likes the watch very much and is sure proud of it. I sure thank Mr. Mackara for getting it.

Loads of love,

George

(V-MAIL)

PM 2/22/1944

(Censor's Stamp)
#2460

3

49 Dearest El:

This will be a quickie, I think, because there is a movie on tonite and I don't want to miss it.

I received your Jan 17 letter a few days after I wrote last, but the reason I am writing so soon again is to tell you abut a package I sent to Walt (that's Warren's little brother, isn't it?) I thought he would like a little something from New Guinea to show the kids, so I got a native arrow and shipped it to him.

It has to be put together. I took it apart to make it easier shipping, but the end I have marked with red crayon goes into the open end of the shaft.

It is not a large gift, but as I couldn't get a Jap souvenir small enough to send home, I thought he would like this arrow. It was made by the Karaki tribe in the Ramu Valley of New Guinea, where I've been for the past 5 months. I was relieved two days ago and am now back here at headquarters. I'll know tomorrow whether I'm to get leave or not. Sure hope I do, even it only means to Sydney and not home.

Hope Warren is enjoying the Navy now. He ought to be about finished his "boot" training now. I'll be anxious to hear what kind of a job he will be given.

Well, El, this was short, but I'll write soon again and let you know if I get to Sydney.

Hope Walt likes the arrow OK. It shouldn't be too long coming as I sent it first class mail.

Mr. & Mrs. Warren Mackara
207 Garfield Ave.
Clementon, NJ

Capt. Geo. F. Frederick
0-372630
6 % Hq. Adv. Ech
5AAF
APO 929 % Postmaster
San Francisco, CA
9 Feb 44

Give Mary Anne a big kiss for me and tell her I think she is a very pretty baby. You're going to have to watch her when she grows up – she'll be the beauty of the town, I bet.

Loads of love & kisses,

George

(V-MAIL)	*Mrs. Harry Frederick*	*Capt. Geo. F. Frederick*
	15 – 7th Ave	*Hq 309th Bomb Wing*
(Censor's Stamp)	*Wagner Terrace*	*6 % Hq. Adv. Ech*
	Charleston, SC.	*5AAF*
		APO 216, Unit 1
		% Postmaster
		San Francisco, CA
		9 Feb 44

Dearest Mother:

Seems like I owe you some letters. I have two of yours I didn't answer yet, but I've been real busy. Got relieved of my duty with the Aussies and could go on leave, but when I got back to Hq. they had another more important job so here I am at this Hq. as coordinator of air liaison parties that are working with the various units. My official title is Ass't A-3 and it is a very important job, but I miss flying and just manage to get my required hours in per month. I'd much rather be with the troop carrier, flying transports as the others are doing, but they won't release me as they say my experience in the field is too valuable to waste.

Admittedly, if I stay on this job a year, I'd probably get another promotion if I did a good job, whereas if I go to flying I wouldn't, but I still like to fly. To get my time in, I just ferried a Cub over 170 miles, but it still didn't satisfy me. Haven't received the films yet, but all the other things arrived OK. The candy was certainly good and I am enjoying the magazines, as are the other fellows here. Hope you are all better now and that Dad is OK.

Lots of love & kisses,

George

THE BISMARCK ARCHIPELAGO consists of the large island of New Ireland on the east, New Britain in the middle, and New Guinea on the west. North of New Britain and the Huon Peninsula are the Admiralty Islands, nearly 400 miles across the Bismarck Sea and was the gateway for Japan to provide supplies, planes, and reinforcements to their Rabaul base on the eastern shore of New Britain.

Admiral Nimitz was pressuring the Japanese at Rabaul from the east, the South Pacific forces were within 250 miles in their push through the Solomon Islands in the south, and the 5th AAF and Australian troops were on the eastern coast of New Guinea. The Navy wanted to establish air bases on the western shores of New Britain, but General Kenney resisted, since he thought they were not needed to protect shipping in the Vitiaz Strait, a block of the ocean some sixty-five miles wide between New Britain and New Guinea. The Navy persisted and, using ALPs with the recovered and replenished Marines from Guadalcanal and the 112th Cavalry, invaded Cape Gloucester, a formidable Japanese satellite air base. They also attacked the islands of Arawe, south of New Britain, and at Saidor, north of Finschhafen on the east coast of New Guinea.

The Japanese, anticipating an invasion of western New Britain, attempted to stop it at the source. They staged an air raid on Oro Bay, an advance air base of the Allied forces, and reinforced their troops in western New Britain. The Japanese suffered heavy losses of air power during the Allied defense at Oro Bay.

Plans for the invasion of western New Britain and for amphibious landings up the eastern coast of New Guinea had been conceived in September 1943. The plan was called Operation DEXTERITY. Before it was implemented in the spring of 1944, it had undergone several revisions, including landing target changes, troops involved, and the function of the ALPs. General Kenney promised the Marines they would be able to go ashore at Cape Gloucester with their rifles on their shoulders. Consequently, he ordered a massive bombing of Cape Gloucester before the landing. The 1,600 bombing sorties prior to D-Day were so successful that subsequent saturation bombing missions were referred to as "Glousterizations."

One incident, however, marred the landing on D-Day, when the Japanese staged an air attack on the destroyers in the bay at the same time the 345th Bombardment Group came over for a bombing run, and two of the group's B-25s were shot down by friendly fire from the destroyers. Four ALPs were assigned to go ashore with the landing ground troops at Cape Gloucester and were instrumental in subsequent battles in pushing the Japanese back by calling for air support on artillery installations, and to within 500 yards in front of the advancing Marines. The invasion of the Arawe Islands, preceding the Cape Gloucester invasion, was accomplished with an ALP remaining on the command ship. For two days, the only communication with the ground troops was through the ALP.

Col. "Photo" Hutchison had, for more than a year, been performing photo reconnaissance of potential targets and landing sites in New Britain, New Guinea, and the Admiralty Islands. From the success of using oblique photographs from slow, low-flying planes to identify potential targets by number, the photo missions were stepped up and were occurring on a daily basis.

The specific role George played in the spring of 1944 isn't known, but there were hints in his letters. He indicated that he was with the bombardier group identifying targets, and also that he was performing coordination of air liaison parties. He also stated that he was barely able to get his flying hours in (for more pay) because of a desk job that he didn't like. They told him his field experience was too valuable. Whether he flew on bombing missions or flew low-flying aircraft for pictures is also unknown, although movies he took indicate that he did. Because of his infantry training prior to joining the Air Corps, he was ideally suited for air liaison duties.

Gradually, the Allies wore down the Japanese and started pushing them back toward Japan. Throughout 1943, the Allies supplied men, planes, and supplies, but it wasn't until November that General Kenney felt that air strength was more balanced. The Japanese had more strategically located bases, but Allied bombing had destroyed many of their planes and had sapped their air might. In January 1944, Allied air power controlled the skies.

On February 15, General Kenney was in his office when his intelligence officer, Col. Cain, brought in Master Sergeant Gordon Manuel. Manuel had been the bombardier on a mission over Rabaul on May 21, 1943, when their plane was shot down. Manuel and the copilot managed to jump before the plane exploded. The copilot made it to shore and lay exhausted on a road until the Japanese found him and executed him. Manuel hid in the brush with a broken leg near a stream and ate snails for subsistence. He was able to hobble down a path until some natives found him and hid him in their village until he was able to look after himself. He learned their language and made friends with them, and the natives built him a special hut, furnished it, and even gave him an orderly that Manuel called Robin. Robin would go to Rabaul and get supplies, including cigarettes, medicine, and alcohol. He organized the natives to watch for aviators when they crashed or parachuted and guide them to safety. Manuel passed the aviators off to Australian spotters and a submarine would come and take them to safety. Although he had several chances to escape, Manuel spent eight months helping other downed aviators and used the natives to gather information on Japanese installations. He wanted to go back to the natives with arms and ammunition and, with their help and that of the Allies, he felt that they could take Rabaul.

General Kenney told him they weren't that interested in Rabaul anymore, since they were going to bypass it and go on to the Philippines. Instead, he gave Manuel a commission as a second lieutenant and then sent him home to Maine, telling him that he'd have a job for him when he returned to New Guinea. Manuel went home and was stationed in the United States. In spite of his continual applications to be sent back to New

Guinea, he wasn't allowed to return because of continual attacks of malaria.

From lessons learned concerning close air support in New Guinea and the amphibious assaults in December and January, a memorandum concerning air support was issued February 8, 1944:

In order that requests for direct air support from all army forces can be properly evaluated, planned and executed; and in order to reduce signal communications lag to a minimum, the following system has been revised and is published for the guidance of all concerned.

General: All requests for cooperative strike missions, reconnaissance flights or sorties, fighter cover, artillery adjustment observation, aerial photographs, emergency air supply, and the like, originating at allied ground force headquarters engaged in combat will be coordinated through Air Liaison Party channels, except where otherwise specifically directed by existing Operations Orders and Signal Operations Instructions.

Headquarters, Advance Echelon, Fifth Army Air Force will provide appropriate ground headquarters with an Air Liaison Party. The officer in charge of this party is an Assistant, A-3, of this Headquarters and will represent the Deputy Commander, Advance Echelon, Fifth Army Air Force. His duties will be, as is implied by official designation, liaison in its broadest sense.

The Air Liaison Party Net is the communications link between all ground forces in the field and the Advance Echelon, Fifth Army Air Force. Also it is a communications link between the Ground Forces and all Air Task Forces. It will also be available for the transmission of emergency traffic such as air raid information and flash intelligence.

a. Air Liaison Party: Normally an Air Liaison Party will consist of two officers and eight to ten enlisted men, all of whom are Air Corps personnel. The senior officer is known as the Air Liaison Party Officer (ALPO) and is responsible for the proper liaison between air force Headquarters and the organization to which his Air Liaison Party is attached. He is also responsible for all matters pertaining to the administration of the party. The assistant party officer will assist in this respect and have other attendant duties. The enlisted personnel will consist of radio operators and mechanics, cryptographers, and one or two basics or drivers.

b. Equipment: An Air Liaison Party is equipped with two or more radio sets mounted in vehicles. The nature of the operation that it is to participate in controls in this regard as a party is equipped to meet the exigencies of a particular situation. When necessary an Air Liaison Party can be completely airborne.

c. Administration: An Air Liaison Party is self-contained in that its personnel, equipment, clothing, weapons, etc., are supplied by its parent Air Corps organization. (To wit: Air Support Control Squadron). However, when an Air Liaison Party is attached to a ground force headquarters, it is expected that the party will be quartered and messed with that ground organization.

In February, plans were being laid to invade Kavieng in New Ireland, Madang and Wewak further up the New Guinea coast, and an Admiralty Island invasion on April 1, 1944. Plans for the Admiralty Island invasion involved more than 45,000 troops and all members of the 1st Cavalry. Admiral Nimitz was to furnish aircraft carriers, battleships, and destroyers. Taking the islands would seal the fate of the troops remaining at Rabaul. Although George didn't know it then, he would play a major role in the Admiralty Island invasion—and before April 1944.

ADMIRALTY ISLANDS

Saturday, February 26, 1944; Nadzab, New Guinea, 1100 hours

A t 1100 hours on Saturday, Feb. 26, 1944, George was alerted of the impending invasion of the Admiralty Islands. He was ordered to proceed from Nadzab to Dobodura. The order was the final confirmation of General MacArthur's decision to stage an invasion of the Admiralty Islands.

While operation DEXTERITY had been under way, operation BREWER, the battle plan for invasion of the Admiralty Islands, was being completed. Both DEXTERITY and BREWER were specific battle plans, under an overall operation code-named CARTWHEEL, designed to secure the Bismarck Archipelago and to eliminate the threat of the Japanese base at Rabaul. Reconnaissance planes were photographing the islands and Allied bombing had been pounding enemy installations in the islands since January. One mission had been flown in a Stinson L-5, a light Piper Cublike plane, under cover of some B-25s, and received minimal opposition. Other B-25s flew over for an hour at treetop level and received either no fire or only small arms fire.

By February 26, they had dropped 645 tons of bombs and had peppered the islands with nearly 340,000 rounds of .30 and .50-caliber bullets. The last real engagement had been on February 24th, when 38 B-25s attacked shipping and harbor installations on Manus Island, destroying a squadron of Japanese planes. A ninety-minute flight at treetop level over Los Negros found no clothes hanging out to dry, and a heap of dirt from a bomb dropped two days before in front of a field hospital that hadn't been cleared.[vi] There were no vehicles spotted, and the airfield at Momote was overgrown with grass. The airfield had been pitted by bombs, but hadn't been repaired. The flights over Los Negros and the Momote airfield hadn't even received small arms fire. It appeared as if the Japanese had withdrawn.[vii]

General Whitehead received the reconnaissance reports with glee. He wanted to get the Admiralties out of the way soon, so he could concentrate on bombing the Japanese airfields at Wewak and Hollandia, further up the New Guinea coast.[viii] The elaborate plans that had been drawn up in January and early February for the April 1st show had called for a land-based reconnaissance by the Alamo force scouts, an invading force of 45,110 men, including the full division of 15,000 troops from the 1st Cavalry as assault troops, with the 6th Army held in reserve. They were to be supported by ships and aircraft carriers from Admiral Nimitz's thrust through the Central Pacific.[ix]

The war in the Pacific had been divided into two theaters. General Douglas MacArthur had been named Commander in Chief of the Southwest Pacific Area, encompassing Australia, the Solomon Islands, the Bismarck Archipelago, New Guinea, the Netherlands East Indies, and the Philippines. Admiral Nimitz was named Commander in Chief of the Pacific Ocean Areas, or the remaining Pacific areas.[x] The invasion plan was to attack from the north through Seeadler Harbor. Seeadler Harbor was considered as one of the finest natural anchorages in the South Pacific. An initial conference had been held on February 19th with representatives of air, ground, and naval units to coordinate the operation. Armed with the reconnaissance reports that showed the Admiralties as being only lightly defended, a second conference that had been scheduled for the 25th was drastically revised.[xi]

General Whitehead had arrived in Australia just before General Kenney arrived in August 1942 to take command of General MacArthur's Allied Air Force. Kenney had known Whitey for more than twenty years. Whitey had

his own ideas about how the air force should be used. His innovati
with others in his command, included skip-bombing, parafrag bombs, putting nose cannons in medium bombers, and the use of transport planes for
mass troop transport.[xii] Kenney had the same concept, and when he arrived
in Australia, he placed Whitey in charge of the air forces in New Guinea,[xiii]
and named him as his deputy commander. Although Kenney was in charge
of the 5th Army Air Force, for all tactical purposes, it was commanded by
Whitehead.[xiv] Kenney recognized Whitey as an outstanding tactician and
planner and a good combat commander who engendered respect rather than
admiration among his subordinates. He was also seen by some in the Air
Force hierarchy as too attached to Kenney and MacArthur, too political, too
outspoken, and too tactically focused.

On the evening of the 24th, Whitey radioed his report to Kenney in
Brisbane: "The whole area looks completely washed out. Los Negros is ripe
for the plucking."[xv] Kenney had spent the day shuffling papers, primarily
concerning the resources of men and equipment allocated to his command.
The British/American JCS had established a policy of "Germany first," followed by Japan. Consequently, only enough resources were sent to the Pacific
to hold the Japanese advance, using limited offense. The JCS felt that
Germany could be defeated as early as 1944, but that it might take until
1948 to defeat Japan. However, Admiral Nimitz was advancing rapidly and
getting the lion's share of resources allocated to the Pacific[xvi] as he pushed
through the Gilbert and Marshall Islands. Since planes designated for
Kenney had to pass through the central Pacific, they were often "hijacked"
by Nimitz for "emergency purposes." At the rate Nimitz was advancing, it
was possible that he would get to the Philippines before MacArthur. The
news from Whitey was music to his ears, since he felt that he could convince
MacArthur to immediately invade Los Negros. Kenney agreed with Whitey
that they should also make a ground reconnaissance of the area to confirm
the aerial reports.

Armed with the reconnaissance reports and proposed plans, Kenney
hurried upstairs to General MacArthur. MacArthur had been brooding over
criticism of his slow advance in New Guinea and failure to break the Japanese

stronghold at Rabaul. In addition to their planes and ships, more than 100,000 Japanese troops manned the Rabaul fortress. A Washington strategist in the JCS[xvii] Joint War Plans Committee had previously suggested isolating Rabaul. The JCS felt that Rabaul was so heavily defended that Iwo Jima, Okinawa, and Tarawa would fade to pink in comparison with the blood that would be spilled if an attempt was made to attack Rabaul.

MacArthur had initially opposed bypassing Rabaul, since he felt that he needed it for a naval base to secure his right flank. Also, he wanted air bases on the coast of New Guinea for air cover if he was to invade the Admiralty Islands. Rabaul was the ultimate objective of his CARTWHEEL campaign.[xviii] When Kenney relayed the news to MacArthur, Brigadier General Charles Willoughby, MacArthur's Chief of Intelligence, and other staff members were called in.

Kenney pitched his case to strike Los Negros as soon as possible. He argued that by taking the air strip at Momote, they would be able to control all the Japanese activity south of the Admiralties and that taking the base would allow deep reconnaissance to the north and would enable a base to strike the northern coast of New Guinea. It would provide a launching pad to organize the invasion of the Philippines. They could starve out the Japanese garrison in Rabaul, making it a nonfactor. CARTWHEEL's objective of taking Rabaul would be completed, and the JCS would also like the action, since they had considered bypassing Rabaul, thinking that Seeadler Harbor was an ideal navy port.

Kenney argued that a quick seizure of the islands would catch the Japanese off guard before any Japanese reinforcements could be made and would kickstart the BREWER[xix] operation. It could likely be "the most important operation ever conducted" in the battle for the Bismarck Sea.[xx] The 100,000-plus Japanese forces in New Britain, New Ireland, and Bougainville would be isolated and left to "die on the vine."

Willoughby argued vehemently that his intelligence and also that of ULTRA[xxi] (an acronym given to the code breaking of Japanese and German intercepted communications) indicated that there were at least 4,000 Japanese on the islands and that they had to be hiding. Willoughby thought

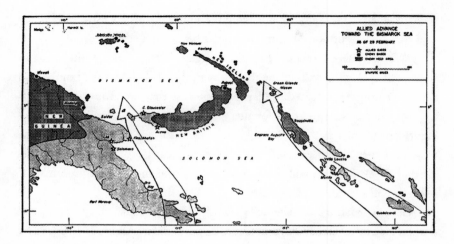

that conducting an invasion a month before it was scheduled[xxii] would lead to disaster and could be a huge setback in the advance.

"Besides, many of the sailors from the ships needed are on leave in Brisbane. Lt. General Krueger[xxiii] isn't here, and he will only have a few days to do the planning," Willoughby argued.

MacArthur had a lot of respect for Willoughby's opinion. His intelligence was always on target and made MacArthur look good.

General Kenney responded, "We can load a couple hundred of General Swift's crack 1st Cavalry Division on destroyers, run up there during the night, unload, and seize the place by daybreak. I can have fighters overhead and bombers to knock out the Japanese if they do try to stop us from stealing Los Negros from under their nose. If the weather stops me from supporting the show, it will also prevent the Jap air force from interfering. We need not take any real chances. If the Nips do too much shooting, we can always call it an armed reconnaissance and back out. If we do go ashore and stick, we can forget all about Kavieng and Hansa Bay. That coral strip [referring to the Momote airstrip] on Los Negros is the most important piece of real estate in the whole theater."[xxiv]

General MacArthur questioned Kenney about Japanese air strength at Wewak, Kavieng, and Rabaul, since they were the principal Jap airdromes and if the Japanese did strike, it would likely be from those bases. Kenney said that his recent bombing missions had been quite effective.

"We used a new tactic," Kenney bragged. "At Wewak, Whitey sent in fifty-eight B-24s, forty B-25s with P-40s, P-38s, and P-47s. We bombed all but one runway and forced the Jap planes to use that one runway for refueling. When they had to go in for fuel, we strafed them. We estimate we got eighty enemy planes.[xxv] At Rabaul, we have consistently bombed their runways and they are so cratered with holes they can't get any planes off the ground.[xxvi] Besides, we will provide air cover, and if the weather prevents our show, it will stop the Japanese also."

General MacArthur listened patiently. Finally, he started pacing back and forth, puffing on his corncob pipe. Capture of the Admiralties would be a strategic gain of the greatest importance, he reasoned. It was not only near the center of the great semicircle formed by the main Japanese defenses on New Guinea, but was also on the Japanese side of the crescent. Developed as an offensive base for Allied air and naval operations, they would control the western approaches to the Bismarck Sea, flank Japanese strongholds on New Guinea, and protect the Allied advance into the Philippines. He questioned the preliminary plans for the invasion and asked if any big guns had been spotted from the air.

Kenney responded that reconnaissance flights over Hyane Harbor area hadn't spotted any guns, and their bombing had knocked out what they had found. If there were any, they had to be well camouflaged. He suggested that the invasion be performed at Hyane Harbor, since he suspected that if the Japanese were strongly defending the islands, they would probably expect a Navy attack through the more navigable Seeadler Harbor.[xxvii] Hyane Harbor couldn't handle larger ships and had a narrow passage. Except for the airstrip, the landing area was a mass of tangled mangroves and brush. It wasn't an obvious place for a landing. Even on the south shore of Los Negros, there were more obvious places to land an invading force, and sailing troops from Oro Bay meant the ships would come in from the south and not have to circle around the islands, where they might be spotted. Control of Momote was the key, since they could fly in troops and supplies.

The marines were pushing north of Guadalcanal through the Solomon Islands and had reached Vella Lavello. The Japanese held Bougainville, the Green Islands and New Ireland to the north as well as New Britain. The Bismarck Sea was shaped like a bottle with the Admiralty Islands several hundred miles to the north guarding the neck to the bottle. Control of the Admiralty Islands would also control the supply chain to Japanese troops 400 miles to the south and to all the islands surrounding the Bismarck Sea. The risk of losing troops by transporting them through the narrow Vitiaz Straight from Oro Bay was minimized since they held both the western edge of New Britain and the eastern tip of New Guinea. With that exception the Japanese held the rest of the territory surrounding the body of the bottle.

Finally, MacArthur stopped pacing, turned, and said, "That will put the cork in the bottle![xxviii] Let's get Brigadier General Chamberlin (MacArthur's operations officer) and Vice Admiral Thomas C. Kinkaid (Commander of the 7th Fleet under Admiral William "Bull" Halsey) up here."[xxix]

Admiral Kinkaid said he would provide four destroyers as escorts to the unarmed troop-carrying transports. MacArthur responded, encouraging Kinkaid to supply more destroyer escorts.

"This operation is a gamble and we need more destroyer protection for our troops," MacArthur argued, "and especially if we need to pull our troops out."

Kinkaid countered, saying that it was a Navy operation and that he felt confident four destroyers would be more than adequate. Finally, MacArthur stated that he was going along to observe the invasion for himself and invited Kinkaid to go also. MacArthur said that his G-2 intelligence (Willoughby) was probably right, but that he liked the bold plan Kenney had presented. MacArthur said that he'd make the decision either to stay or to pull out. Kinkaid then added the cruisers Phoenix and Nashville and four more destroyers. The cruisers were necessary for MacArthur's accommodations and communications.[xxx]

After General Kenney had "sold" the idea of a reconnaissance in force, he dispatched a courier with a letter to General Whitehead:

The plan is that about the 28th or 29th February six destroyers, accompanied by three APDs [xxxi] *and carrying the equivalent of a battalion of 1st Cavalry with a battery of mountain artillery and a battery of .50-caliber ack-ack machine guns, will make a reconnaissance in force of the Momote airdrome area. The destroyers will open fire on possible shore installations and if they draw no return fire, will land troops to take over the Momote area. Two minesweepers will leave Finschhafen the afternoon before, timing their arrival at Hyane Harbor with that of the raiding force. As soon as they have swept the harbor entrance clear, the destroyers are to steam in and discharge their cargoes and probably remain there the day.*

You will have to provide a flight of fighters over the minesweepers during the afternoon preceding the landing at Los Negros, and I have told the Navy that the landing should not be made before 8:15 in order that we have a chance to deluge any possible opposition around Momote and Hyane Harbor by attacks with the heavies and strafers. I do not believe there is much possibility of any Jap air opposition to the show but you had better use P-38s to afford fighter cover for the landing operation and during at least the morning the raid takes place. To further insure the safety of the landing, I would clean out any gun positions that may be located in the Momote area, and in addition, comb over the four Wewak dromes with strafers the afternoon before and the morning of the landing operations on Los Negros.

With their regular equipment the troops will carry some shovels to fill up enough holes on Momote strip so that our transports can land there. As soon as this is possible, we will fly up some airborne engineers to put the strip in shape for transport operations for the purpose of bringing in supplies or reinforcing troops in an emergency. This probably will not be necessary as the Navy seems willing to consider the Bismarck Sea their own private lake and Admiral Kinkaid is perfectly willing to send APDs or destroyers from Finschfafen to Los Negros at any time after the Hyane Harbor is cleared out by the minesweepers. Following the landing of this cavalry expedition a CB battalion has been ordered to get ready for movement into Momote about March 3rd. They will take over construction of the strip in order for us to base two or three squadrons of fighters there. Better get in touch with the RAAF and warn them that they may have to move in soon after that date." [xxxii]

On February 25, in Brisbane, trucks patrolled the streets with sirens and bullhorns, blaring a code word meaning, "All Navy personnel of the Phoenix—report to base immediately!"[xxxiii]

Sailors from Kinkaid's flagship Phoenix were on leave. General MacArthur and Admiral Kinkaid were to oversee the attack from the Phoenix. In less than two hours from the announcement in the streets of Brisbane, the Phoenix was underway. Only twenty-two sailors of the 300 on leave didn't make it back to base in time to make it on board before the Phoenix left port. Several of the men who didn't make it back in time jumped in small boats and as they caught up with the Phoenix, started waving frantically. Some of the men were taken aboard. Those that didn't make it in time were flown to Milne Bay, where they boarded the Phoenix.

Rear Admiral William Fletcher, of the Navy's Amphibious Force, was ordered to command the actual attack group. His command consisted of eight destroyers and three destroyer transports (APDs). The APDs were required, since they were the only ones with enough speed to reach the Admiralty Islands in the necessary time. The APDs were old destroyers that had been converted to carry troops. Their guns had been removed. About half of the invading troops were to ride in the APDs, while the destroyers would transport the remaining troops and act as escorts.

Lt. General Walter Krueger wore two hats. He was the commanding general of the 6th Army, but had also formed and personally commanded the Alamo Scouts. The commanding general of the 1st Cavalry, Major General Innis P. Swift,[xxxiv] and his staff were stationed with General Krueger in Finschfafen, although the division itself was at Camp Borio, near Oro Bay, training intensively for its first combat duty of the war.

General Swift had been included in the conferences at Alamo Force Headquarters regarding the BREWER operation.[xxxv] Kenny had suggested to MacArthur that the Admiralty invasion could be accomplished with just a few hundred troops, but MacArthur ordered Krueger to use at least 800.

Another order followed, instructing Krueger to increase the number of troops to 1,000, followed by a third order to prepare a support force of 1,500 ground combat troops and 428 Seabees, to land on D-Day plus two, if the reconnaissance force stayed. As was customary in MacArthur's area, his head-quarters prepared general plans that assigned forces, missions, and target dates. Operational plans were prepared by ground, air, and naval command-ers and their staffs. To Lt. Gen. Walter Krueger, commanding the U.S. Sixth Army and Alamo Force,[xxxvi] MacArthur gave the responsibility for coordina-tion of the planning. Krueger's responsibility gave him a preeminent posi-tion; he was primus inter pares.[xxxvii]

Krueger mulled over the conflicting intelligence reports. Kenney claimed his aerial reconnaissance indicated only a few hundred Japanese, but Willoughby estimated slightly more than 4,000. Krueger's own intelli-gence unit estimated closer to 5,000 Japanese defending the islands. Whitehead had also suggested that a ground reconnaissance be conducted, as they all knew how easy it was to fool aerial reconnaissance. Consequently, General Krueger ordered two separate actions. First, he ordered General Swift (commanding general of the 15,000-force 1st Cavalry Division, and also for BREWER) to form a reinforced battalion element to conduct the reconnaissance in force on the 29th, landing on the east side of the island at Hyane Harbor.

"We will come in the back door," Krueger said.

Second, Krueger directed the Alamo Scouts to conduct reconnaissance of the south coast of Los Negros and of the 5,000-foot runway at Momote Airdrome, beginning on the 26th.

General Chase of the 1st Brigade was assigned to organize the 1,000 "reconnaissance in force" invading troops. He picked three rifle troops of the 2nd squadron, 5th Cavalry Regiment, who were in training exercises when the order was received. The 800 members of the rifle troops stopped train-ing and prepared for battle overnight. They were reinforced by a platoon from the 99th Field Artillery Battalion, eighty men from the 673rd Antiaircraft (Machine-Gun) Battery (Airborne), a detachment of 592nd Engineer Boat and Shore Regiment, a platoon from A Troop, 8th Engineer

Squadron, and thirty-five members of the 30th Portable Surgical Hospital. Also landing would be the headquarters troop, with a platoon to furnish communications and reconnaissance, George and his 12th ALP, a Navy liaison, and an ANGAU (Australian New Guinea Administration Unit) detachment to interface with the natives. If the reconnaissance landing was successful, Col. Hoffman would follow with the rest of the 5th Cavalry.

In February 1943, the 1st Cavalry had been alerted to an overseas assignment. Consequently, their previous assignment of patrolling the Mexican/American border on horseback was dissolved and the troops were "dismounted." The horses were sold at public auction, slacks were substituted for riding breeches, shoes and leggings for boots and spurs, and packs for saddlebags. Although dismounted, they retained the same structure as if they were mounted. A platoon of thirty-seven soldiers, broken into four squads, with four or five platoons assigned to form a troop. The 5th Cavalry, for

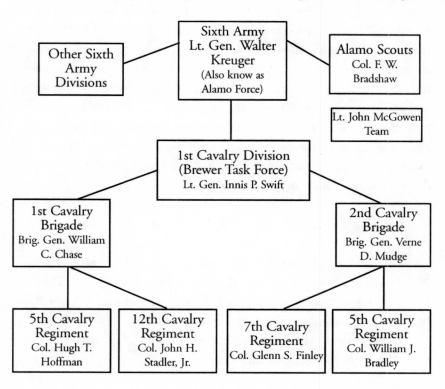

example, had Troops A through H, plus headquarters, service, weapons troops and a medical detachment.

The fifty member Alamo Scouts were a separate command reporting directly to General Krueger. They were organized into small teams, designed to operate deep behind enemy lines. They were charged with intelligence gathering and performing reconnaissance in advance of major battle offensives. The all-volunteer Alamo Scouts, although highly trained, were untested in actual battle. This would be their first test. Based on the original plans, Krueger's chief of staff, in a handwritten note as late as Feb. 21, said, "this should be a good test for the Scouts and should prove of value to them,"[xxxviii] but those plans would change.

Initially, the Alamo Scouts were to go ashore on the western edge of Manus Island from a submarine, remain on the island for a few weeks, and work east, maintaining contact with headquarters by radio. As finely tuned as the original plans were, they were scrapped just as they were ready to leave. In the early morning darkness of the 26th and undercover of B-25s to keep the Japanese occupied, they were to land near Los Negros Island and row to shore in a rubber raft. The six man team,[xxxix] headed by Lt. John McGowen, with their weapons of choice and two days' rations, dressed in camouflage and soft hats, they took off in a Catalina flying boat (PBY) in the middle of the night. Bombs were dropping and the team was ready, but the PBY pilot refused to land because of "bad weather." The team returned to the USS Halfmoon, a seaplane tender that was home for the PBY. The mission was delayed twenty-four hours, until the 27th.

Sunday, February 27, 1944; USS Halfmoon

The McGowen team didn't get as early a start as they had on February 26th, and it was dawn by the time they reached the landing zone. The same PBY pilot realized that he could be seen from shore and wouldn't slow down for the Alamo Scouts to unload their rubber boat.

"I was so damn mad about the plane not slowing down," McGowen said later, "I couldn't focus on anything else."[xl]

Fortunately, it wasn't storming, but on the other hand, the bombers were late and didn't cover their landing. No sooner had the McGowen team unloaded the rubber boat when the pilot gunned the PBY and took off. It took about a half hour to reach the shore. Pvt. Gomez jumped out and pulled the boat to shore.[xli] The Scouts deflated the boat and buried it near a tree that would be easy to find later. They landed west of the planned invasion area, but didn't need to know that and hadn't been informed. All the recon team needed to know was their mission: "to make an assessment of the number of enemies on the island and report back." The landing site had been picked by design. By landing west of the invasion site it could fool the Japanese into thinking an invasion would come from that spot. The most obvious place for an invasion of the Admiralty Islands, however, was still Seeadler Harbor on the other side of the island.

With Lt. McGowen leading the way, the team moved off the beach and headed toward their objective, the Momote airdrome. They used a compass to determine the direction of Momote, since they found few landmarks. After three hours of following their compass, setting through the jungle, they came across some vines that had been strung from tree to tree. The vines had been cut so they were about five feet off the ground. The Scouts concluded the vines had been used by the Japanese to keep from straying off the trail at night.

Suddenly, the earth exploded! The bombing raid had started. Thirty B-25s, modified with .50-caliber machine-guns in the nose, were attacking to cover the McGowen landing.[xlii] Four squadrons of the 38th Bomber Group unleashed thirty-eight tons of 500-pounders and peppered the ground with more than 60,000 .50-caliber rounds of ammunition. McGowen and his team froze, since the strafing gunfire was spurting all around them! There was no return fire from the ground by Japanese troops. After the bombing had ended and guided by their compass, the team continued toward Momote.

Soon after the raid, the scouts stumbled on newly dug trenches, running northwest and southeast. The trenches were camouflaged with green leaves and branches. Vines ran parallel to the trenches. The Scouts believed they were for marking the trenches. There were about 200 yards of trenches, two feet deep and two feet wide. Within the trenches, they identified at least three machine-gun positions.

Just as the scouts moved past the line of trenches, they heard a painful scream, followed by a voice. Apparently, the voice was trying to quiet whoever was in pain. The team froze for several minutes and then continued when they heard nothing further. McGowen was walking on point when suddenly he spotted a Japanese soldier pass in front of them. He gave the "freeze!" signal and the Scouts froze standing up. Fifteen or more Japanese soldiers, all carrying shovels, passed right by the still frozen Scouts. As the Japanese solders passed, the Scouts noticed a well-camouflaged shack nearby and the insignia of the Japanese soldiers.

Lt. McGowen in camouflage

Shortly past noon, they came to a wide creek near the Momote airstrip that they were unable to cross because of its size. They felt as if they had come as far as they could, so they decided to turn back. Sgt. Ramirez and Pvt. Gomez became separated from the rest of the Scouts when Japanese soldiers walked along the trail between them, but by evening, the Scouts were all together again. They set up an all-around security for the night.

As the McGowen team was landing in the early dawn, Generals MacArthur and Kenney were leaving Brisbane for HQ Fifth Army Air Force Advance Echelon in Nadzab, New Guinea. The generals wanted to review any last minute changes to the plans resulting from Japanese activity and the weather with General Whitehead. After meeting briefly with Whitey and his staff, MacArthur continued on to Milne Bay to board the cruiser Phoenix with Admiral Kincaid. Kenney stayed behind to review the details with Whitey.

Whitey's planning had covered every detail. He even had eight old B-17s fixed up to drop supplies by parachute. Those planes, stationed in Finschhafen, were to be at General Kruger's disposal in case of an emergency. Some members of Whitey's staff were worried that MacArthur and Kenney had bitten off more than they could chew, but Kenney was able to reassure them that such wasn't the case.[xliii] Kenney especially felt that there were only a few Japanese troops on Los Negros. Although Whitey had supplied the estimate of not more than 300 Japanese troops on Los Negros, he was more reserved and said that he was anxiously awaiting a report from the Alamo Scouts.

Colonel Merian C. Cooper was particularly worried, but both Whitey and Kenney knew that Cooper was a constant worrier. Cooper had previously served as General Chennault's chief of staff in China, where he had contracted dysentery. Kenney said that although Cooper was a constant worrier and chain smoker, "he had more ideas in an hour than most people get in a month." The conflicting reports concerning the number of Japanese troops they'd face was a matter of concern, but Kenney felt that the planning done by Whitey and his staff would overcome any obstacles the Japanese could throw at them.

The plans for air support of the invasion had been hastily put together as a result of the acceleration of the invasion date. The 1st Cavalry Division was ordered to make a reconnaissance in force and to remain on Los Negros only if it appeared feasible, but the plans were generous in providing air support. Three squadrons of heavy bombers were to strike Los Negros twenty minutes before the landing, four squadrons of B-25s were to attack upon orders from the flagship, or an hour past H-Hour (landing time) if no orders were issued. It was contemplated that the air attacks would stop when the first landing crafts reached the shore. An air alert of three B-25 squadrons, one squadron on duty at a time for an hour, was to be ready to support the operation for the first four hours. Three B-25s were prepared to lay smoke over the area from H-Hour until H-plus-6 (hours).

Communications were essential. A stripped-down Supporting Air Party[xliv] (SAP) was assigned to the 12th Air Liaison Party (ALP), command-ed by George and assisted by Lt. James C. King and five enlisted men—S/Sgt. Martin W. James, Sgt. Mark D. Kohn, Sgt. Hugh H. Bement, Sgt. Roy H. Clark, and T/5th Gr. Gordon R. Rule. They were scheduled to go ashore with the first wave. Plans called for them to have an FM-12 radio and one SCR-193 radio with them. Until noon on D-Day, the ALP was to con-cern itself solely with air/ground communications. At noon, they were to enter the radio net, which included the three 5th AAF Bombardment Wings, the Advanced Echelon 5th AAF, and the Sixth Army. To ensure contact, a B-24 was to take a position between Los Negros and Dobodura to serve as a relay station if it was needed. Command for all planes entering the area would remain with the headquarters ship until it could be established with George on shore. The communications for the air support can best be illus-trated by a diagram.[xlv]

The entire bomber force stationed in New Guinea was ordered to be uti-lized, supplemented by troop carrier forces as required and supported by

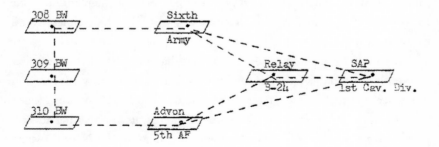

three fighter squadrons. The Bomber Force was to attack enemy installations in northern New Ireland and along the north coast of New Guinea, as well as in the Admiralties. George was to report to the Commanding General, 1st Cavalry Division at Oro Bay, on D-minus-3, the day before, but George didn't leave until 1600 hours on the 27th after meeting with Generals Whitehead and Kenney. He took the plans of the air operations, maps, and photos with him. More than 500 duplicate photos were prepared, identifying targets by number with coordinates and distributed to pilots for easy identification.

At 1800 hours, George reported to G-3[xlvi] (Operations), 1st Cavalry Brigade at Oro Bay, as instructed. An hour and half later, he reported to the USS Reid, which was serving as the headquarters ship.[xlvii] There he conferred and gave the plans of the air support to G-3 of the 1st Cavalry Brigade. George left the headquarters ship at 2330 and arrived aboard the USS Sands, an APD, and reported to the Task Force Commander. Meanwhile, General MacArthur and Admiral Kinkaid had arrived in Milne Bay, on the southern tip of New Guinea, and boarded the cruiser Phoenix that afternoon. They were to rendezvous with the attack group at sea, north of Oro Bay.

The Admiralties are located 200 miles northeast of New Guinea and 260 miles west of the tip of New Ireland. The Admiralty Islands had been discovered in 1615 by William Cornelius Schouten, but weren't given their name until 1767 by Rear Admiral Philip Carteret, in honor of the British Admiralty. European nations neglected the islands until 1884, when Germans established plantations. They became part of Australia in 1921, after an Australian naval and expeditionary force occupied the islands. In 1942, the Australians withdrew when the Japanese invaded the islands. Japanese shipping to Truk, Kavieng, and Rabaul passed through or near the islands from Japan.

Manus, the largest island, is separated from Los Negros by a shallow creeklike strait. Los Negros extends in a rough horseshoe curve to form a natural breakwater for Seeadler Harbor on the north side of Los Negros and was the most extensive of several anchorages. As expected, and according to air reconnaissance, it appeared that the Japanese were defending Seeadler

Harbor more than other parts of the island. Seeadler Harbor itself was six miles wide and more than twenty miles long. Depths ranged to 120 feet. The adjacent large Momote airfield was the most important part of the islands.[xlviii] The Japanese had guessed correctly that an invasion of the Admiralties would be centered on Seeadler Harbor, which was the original plan, but plans are subject to change, and change, they did! New plans were drawn up in only a few days and the previous elaborate plan was scrapped. Consequently, coordination of air, ground, and naval support was nearly nonexistent.

D-Day-1, Monday, February 28, 1944; Los Negros Island

The next morning, the McGowen team was up early and made radio contact with Barnes, their contact on the PBY. McGowen sent a short message that the area was "lousy with Japs," in case they didn't make it back. They pumped up their rubber boat and started rowing out to where the plane was to land. No sooner had they loaded into the boat and started rowing out to sea when the coast exploded with a B-24 dropping bombs and two P-38s strafing the coast. The PBY was close behind and started his landing approach at the designated spot, but the same pilot was flying and again wouldn't stop to let the patrol board. Sgt. Roberts managed to grab a strut, and as the plane was dragging their rubber boat along, the rest of the crew managed to climb on. Roberts told McGowen to jump on board, but as he did, the propeller knocked McGowen into the water. Roberts grabbed his hand and helped him back into the boat. Eventually, both Roberts and McGowen made it onto the PBY and with their legs dangling the plane took off with a roar, leaving the rubber boat behind.[xlix]

At 0645, the destroyer-transports of the attack group, the Humphreys, Brooks, and Sands, moved out, escorted by destroyers Reid, Stockton, and Stevenson. The second half of the invasion force followed at 0819 on the other converted destroyers, the Flusser, Mahan, Drayton, Smith, Bush, and Welles. Allied control of the air over the invasion area was counted on to protect the invading troops, but they were exposed to Japanese attack from neighboring islands, particularly New Guinea, New Britain, and New Ireland. Some 10–18 enemy submarines were also reported in the area.[l] The destroyers would need to protect the invasion force from submarine attack. Three squadrons of B-24s and four A-20s struck enemy positions in Hollandia and the Hansa Bay airfield. Poor weather had prevented "flattening" the Admiralties, but the diversion of the bombing effort to the New Guinea airdromes cut down potential Japanese aerial opposition to the landing of the invasion force.[li]

At 0900, George met with his assistant, Lt. James C. King, and the five men of his 12th Air Liaison Party.[lii] They checked and double-checked the equipment they were taking with them. They had a generator and the SCR-193 radio. In addition to their other gear, rifles, ammunition, shovels, maps, and photos, they had yet to be issued enough rations to last them until reinforcements or plane supply drops could be coordinated. They'd have to wait until the rations were issued before they loaded their equipment onto the Landing Craft Personnel Ramped (LCPR).

Arriving back at the USS Halfmoon at 0930, McGowen repeated his findings to G-2 (Intelligence) that Los Negros was "lousy with Japs." He told of the Japanese patrol that had passed within a few feet of them on the trail.

He said, "I never wanted to hit the ground so bad in my life, but I didn't dare."[liii]

Major Franklin M. Rawolle of the G-2 staff, realizing the importance of the mission, immediately arranged for a PT boat to escort him and McGowen to meet the 1st Cavalry commanders that were on their way to Los Negros.

At 1000 hours, George met with General Chase and his staff and received the ground plan. At 1300 hours, their rations were issued and they loaded their equipment onto the LCPR. At 1326, they had caught up with Admiral Kinkaid and General MacArthur aboard the Phoenix and the rest of the attack group, consisting of the cruiser Nashville and destroyers Daly, Hutchins, Beale, and Bache.

General Kenney, who had convinced MacArthur to advance the date for the Admiralty invasion, discounted the report.

"Twenty-five Jap soldiers in the woods at night don't make for the island to be lousy with Japs!" he remarked.

Nevertheless, General Chase, not one to risk failure, continued to arrange for all the firepower he could get. If the G-2 reports were correct and there were 4,000–5,000 Japanese troops on Los Negros, the 1,000 man reconnaissance force could be overrun and wiped out.

"Besides," he said, "Krueger has always been skeptical of the bomber reconnaissance. Even at twenty feet off the ground, the Japanese can camouflage their emplacements."[liv] Then he added, referring to the intelligence opinion of the 25th, "This suggests that at the moment in the Admiralties enemy ground strength is not heavy and that what there is of it is being conserved. Air strength appears to be nonexistent."

Operation BREWER was a bold stoke, undertaken when information about the enemy was far from satisfactory. Although there were reasons to believe that the enemy had evacuated most of its forces, there was no definite evidence to show that had happened. When the decision was made to advance the date to February 29, commanders of the BREWER Task Force knew practically nothing about the enemy's defensive preparations, or even if any had been made. Nevertheless, General MacArthur seemed to be fully aware of the gamble. When General Kenney sold him on the idea of striking quickly, he sensed a temporary confusion and weakness of the enemy that they could capitalize on. The situation presented an ideal opportunity for a coup de main, which, if successful, would advance the Allied timetable in the Pacific by several months and save thousands of Allied lives. An invasion of a reconnaissance in force, accompanied by additional troops, if successful, would be a huge step forward. However, if they had to retreat, he could save face by claiming that it was only a reconnaissance mission. Using destroyers for troop transport instead of the slower troop carrier ships, they could advance quickly, achieve the element of surprise, and also make a speedy withdrawal if unforeseen enemy strength was encountered.

For a week preceding D-Day, reports from bomber sorties over the Admiralties added to the growing belief that the main strength of the Japanese had evacuated the islands. On the 28th, a day before D-Day, crews, now familiar with the area and becoming more and more alert to small details, were able to find signs of activity. Once sightings began, they started to pour in, and extensive trench and earthwork systems, pillboxes, coastal guns, and motor launches in temporary blocked-up frames were spotted.

General Chase, upon hearing the reports, called for a meeting with his subordinate officers. George, his airborne liaison, was called to the meeting, along with the Navy commanders. At the meeting, General Chase arranged for more naval gunfire, specifically targeted along the route of the Alamo Scouts' reconnaissance and concentrated at the point where they had landed. Targeting the Alamo Scouts landing spot could fool the Japanese into believing the invasion would occur at that location rather than Hyane Harbor.

D-Day, Tuesday, February 29, 1944; Hyane Harbor, Los Negros Island

In Nadzab, New Guinea, a sleepy GI woke Bill Dunn from a deep slumber on his air mattress. At four in the morning, they drove the two miles to a tiny grass shack with a dirt floor, where a youthful captain stood in front of a large map tacked on an improvised board. Two dozen youngsters were crouched around him; a lone light bulb illuminated the grass shack.

"Bill Dunn?" the captain asked.

"That's right!"

"Okay, the colonel called me last night. Be with you in a moment," the captain said as he returned to his map. "The weather really isn't good anywhere along the route, as near as we can learn. There's been no word from the naval force, and there won't be until after the landing, so you'll have to keep your eyes open. When you reach the target, keep in tight formation and circle until you hear from the command ship or the ground station if they've been able to set one up, GANGWAY (code name for the 12th Air Liaison Party). Be particularly careful approaching any naval vessel if the weather is bad, because it will be hard to identify you and their ack-ack is good. You all have maps of your primary targets. Keep them handy, but stay away from those targets until you hear from GANGWAY. If they give you an objective, go in as low as possible and strafe it good before you drop the bombs. Remember now—tight formation. You don't know how many enemy aircraft will be in the area, so keep in close. Any questions?"

"How long are we to circle before we leave the target?"

"That will depend on your gasoline supply. If you don't hear from the command ship or beachhead, you'll probably have enough gas for an hour. By that time, there'll be someone to relieve you."

"How high do we hit the secondary target?"

"Treetops, strafing as you go in. Anything else?"

"Who will we have for fighter cover?"

"The 348th Fighter Group will cover preliminary naval bombardment and the 475th is to cover the landing. The bomber squadrons will be leaving at one hour intervals, and all groups will have fighter cover. The 90th Bomber Group will stage a diversionary attack up the coast. The 43rd and 38th Groups will precede you to cover preinvasion and the landing."

"What frequency do we use to contact the GANGWAY ground station?"

"It should be the 'VJ2' on 'Q' net."

"How crowded will it be, and are there some other groups that will be up there?"

"The 43rd Group should have three squadrons in the area, but they should be out of there, and the 38th Group should have launched four squadrons, but they should also be gone. By the time you arrive, it'll be just you, the 499th Squadron, and the fighter cover."

Their questions answered, the men started to leave for their mission.

The captain turned to Bill Dunn, hand extended, and said, "I'm Captain Hiller and this is Lt. Boden, who will be your pilot. He'll give you a good ride. Good luck, and I hope you have a good story to tell." Then he turned to Lt. Boden and added, "Bill Dunn is a war correspondent, with CBS News."

Alvin Boden, a farm boy from Adams, Nebraska, was a tall, angular youngster who didn't look old enough to vote. A pair of green coveralls covered his splinter-like frame, and a huge Adam's apple thrust its way through the open collar. The gold bar of a second lieutenant was pinned to his open collar and another one to his mechanics-type cap. He looked as though he might be on his way to do the morning's milking. It was still pitch dark as he led Dunn to a waiting truck loaded with the other pilots and crew, all dressed the same, cracking jokes, and laughing.

As they drove through the night, someone started singing "I've Been Working on the Railroad" and the others joined in, making a feeble attempt to harmonize. It was quite a distance to the airstrip, and by the time they arrived, they had placed a half dozen pilots "in the kitchen with Dinah." Dunn thought that if there was any tension in the air, it was confined to the correspondent perched next to the quiet pilot from Nebraska, who was no doubt thinking about the bad weather, the naval fire power, treetop levels, the reported enemy air reinforcements in Hollandia, and a few dozen other subjects that seemed important at the moment.

Bill Dunn had known something was up when MacArthur left Australia. He had first joined MacArthur in 1941 in the Philippines, before the bombing of Pearl Harbor. His original 90-day assignment at CBS had turned into more than three years. Knowing MacArthur, he could sense that something was imminent, and he had guessed right. A successful invasion of the Admiralty Islands would secure MacArthur's right flank and destroy enemy hopes of reinforcing or relieving 100,000 Japanese troops that were scattered throughout the islands south of the Admiralties.

He had pumped one of MacArthur's aides and learned that if he was to accompany the landing force, he'd have to leave his microphone behind. If he was to accompany the invasion fleet, he wouldn't be able to report the events for a couple of weeks, but if he was able to go with a bomber group, he'd only be gone for two or three days. The operation was veiled in more secrecy than normal, and he learned that there was almost unanimous opposition from MacArthur's staff, who thought the general was courting disaster.

At the last minute, Dunn was able to secure a seat with the 345th Bomber Group and the 498th Squadron, under the command of Colonel Jared Crabb. The operation in the Admiralties for bomber and fighter groups was still undefined. Dunn wondered if one of the P-38s would be piloted by Captain Dick Bong, who had made the P-38 famous.

Captain Bong had recently returned to active duty after a savings bond promotion tour at home. Dunn didn't know if Bong was assigned to the 475th Fighter group or not. It was rumored that he'd been assigned to headquarters and allowed to freelance. It would be a real thrill if Dunn could see Bong in action.

Finally, the shadowy form of a plane roared out of the graying morning twilight and several flashlights picked it up.

"What plane's this?" someone asked.

"Thirty," came the reply.

"Best damn plane in the air force," someone shouted, and a half dozen men piled out to loud cheers.

Several numbers and cheers later, a voice called from the darkness, "Sixty-three."

"That's us," Boden said as he swung over the side.

Dunn followed. The B-25 stood waiting, its bomb bay doors open and a half dozen ground crewmen moving quietly about, making their final checks.

Lt. Boden's personality changed completely. Gone was the reticent, gangling country boy and in its place was a combat aircraft commander, a man in full control, whose every mannerism inspired confidence. He introduced Dunn to his copilot and the other members of the crew, then excused himself to check the bomb bay load and to confer with his crew chief. When he returned he asked Dunn if he'd ever made a bombing mission in a B-25.

"Have not," Dunn replied.

"You'll ride up front with me and the copilot, Gwyl Davis. You can sit in the navigator's seat. He has the day off, since the squadron leader navigates today and we follow. In case of a crash-landing, Davis will open the hatch directly overhead, and he'll be the first out, to open the rubber boat. You'll follow and I'll be last. The gunners and crew chief will use the rear hatch. Of course, we don't expect to crash-land, but it's always good to know the procedures. You'll find a parachute inside the plane, but there's no need to wear it unless there's an emergency, in which case, I'll warn you. Sergeant Dreibilbies will fit you with a Mae West and give you headphones and a throat microphone. I'll tell you more when we get going."

Another officer appeared to check the crew list, and everyone climbed aboard. In the distance, Dunn heard the roar of others warming up, and the dawn began to break just as Boden started his own engines. Boden was second in line as they rolled down the taxi-strip and waited as the lead plane roared down the runway, spraying Boden's plane with sand and pebbles. At 0705, the six planes of the 498th took off, followed ten minutes later by six B-25s of the 499th. They made a slow turn over the Huon Gulf while the other planes joined up.

The sergeant clamped headphones over Dunn's ears and buttoned a microphone around his throat. A few minutes later, Boden was pointing out Finschfafen on their left and Rooke Island just ahead. Almost immediately, they ran into the first of the promised bad weather and dropped down to less than a hundred feet above the choppy waters of the Bismarck Sea. All of Dunn's instincts craved more altitude, but the crew chief wasn't worried. He produced a comic book from somewhere and settled back to enjoy a real adventure, as experienced by Captain Marvel.

Boden and Davis began studying maps and pictures of the target area while Dunn watched the other two planes in immediate formation to their left. No other planes were visible, but these two were so close that Dunn could see the facial expression of the top turret gunner in the lead plane.

Suddenly, Dunn's earphones crackled as Boden warned him, "There'll be plenty of noise when we let loose with all guns, and you'll probably jump a couple of feet. Don't let it bother you—we all do the same. I'll warn you in advance."

The B-25s were equipped with eight .50-caliber guns in the nose instead of the one .30-caliber gun, as originally mounted by the manufacturer. Kenney called these planes his "Commerce Destroyers." The guns had been installed over the designing engineers' protests that the project was impossible. The innovation had proved itself in the Battle of the Bismarck Sea, however, and modification of the B-25s immediately became one of the favorite weapons of the Far East air forces, particularly the 345th Bomb Group.

Originally designed to drop its bomb load from 6,000 feet above anti-aircraft fire, the pilots found it safer to fly as low as possible, at treetop level. The main danger was not from anti-aircraft fire but from clipping trees. The

Japanese were baffled by the attacks, because they didn't have time to see them, let alone track them. The bombardier was displaced and became a navigator on these flights, since a bomb sight didn't work well at 50 feet, so the copilot would release the bombs over the target as the machine-guns were chattering away.

WHITE BEACH, the designated landing area, was barely visible through the overcast skies to those on board the USS Sands, 5,000 yards offshore. The invading troops could see no sign of Japanese activity, but knew they

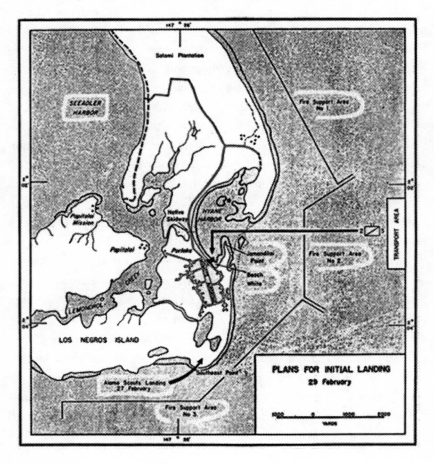

were there. The morning had started with a low ceiling. Air cover for the landing would be difficult, if possible at all. Navy destroyers encircled Hyane Harbor in three designated fire areas.

At 0723, the signal "Deploy" was given. Twelve LCPRs were swung outward on davits and lowered to the sea. George and his men climbed down the nets on the side of the USS Sands to their LCPR. As soon as they were boarded, the helmsman signaled that they were loaded and with a roar, they took off through the choppy water toward their objective, White Beach, in Hyane Harbor on Los Negros. The first wave would use four LCPRs, with thirty-seven troops in each boat. The second wave would follow, using the next four, followed by the third wave.

Meanwhile, the USS Bush and other destroyers were firing at designated targets, as recorded in the ship's log:

0721—Manus Island, Admiralty Group, bearing 270°T, sky entirely overcast, visibility approximately 10 miles.

0724—Deployed from main group (TG 76.1) in company with USS Welles astern at 1,000 yards and stood in to bombard Los Negros Island.

0736—U.S. aircraft observed bombing beach on Negros Island.

0740—Commenced bombarding targets #10 and #12 on beach on Los Negros Island bearing 292°T, range 28,000 yards, all cruisers of TG 74.2 and destroyers of TG 74.2 and TG 76.1 firing.

0750—Army troops aboard USS Humphreys, USS Brooks, USS Sands, disembarked for beach.

0751—Misfire on gun #3, cooled with fire hose.

0756—Ceased firing, having expended 384 rounds of 5"/38 AA Common ammunition of mi d lots.

0759—Cleared jam on gun #3.

W. A. Kozumplik, Lt.(jg), USNR.

There were supposed to be forty B-24s from two squadrons of the 43rd Bomb Group bombing the shore, but only seven made it through the storms raging in the Bismarck Sea. The seven bombers unloaded on the shore at 0737. The LCPRs carrying assault troops started firing on the bombers as they shelled the two points flanking Hyane Harbor.[lv] Someone had forgotten to tell the Navy that the Air Force would be bombing the shore. As the bombers left the area, the destroyers opened fire on their assigned targets at 0740. Meanwhile, the LCPRs weaved and bobbed in the surf, attempting to dodge the machine-gun and artillery fire that had opened up from the beach after the bombing.

Flashes from the southeast point of the island resulted in three and four-inch shells landing perilously close to the Flusser and Mahan. Enemy artillery on shore was firing at the Phoenix. General MacArthur was watching the action through binoculars from the bridge of the Phoenix with Admiral Kinkaid and his aides. MacArthur's aides tried to get him to take cover, but he wouldn't move. The salvo from shore landed on the other side of the ship. Before the Japanese manning the guns could find the range, the guns of the Phoenix found their mark and silenced the enemy guns, but machine-gun fire was bouncing off the sides coming from the southeast point of Hyane Harbor. The Phoenix attempted to silence them, but was falling short of the target. Admiral Fletcher ordered the destroyers to maneuver closer to the target, saying that if one of them got grounded in the uncharted waters, he'd take full responsibility. The destroyer Mahan shifted its fire and, combined with the cruiser fire, soon found the target. At 0755, the destroyers were to stop their firing, but the air cover wasn't visible, and no communication established with the scheduled four squadrons of B-25s that were to follow the forty B-24s. The naval bombardment continued until 0810.

Star shells were fired, signaling for air cover to begin, but as the star fire ended, only four B-25s of the scheduled four squadrons from the 38th

Group appeared beneath the cloud cover and began strafing and bombing the landing area at low level. The 38th had been beset with difficulties from the start. The pilots had flown by instruments through darkness and heavy storms and had gotten separated before they reached Vitiaz Strait. They missed their appointed rendezvous, but three planes from the 822nd Squadron, led by Col. Clarence Tauberg, gathered three other planes fifty miles south of the target and cruised sixty miles, both east and west, for two hours in an effort to find a way over, under, around, or through the storm over the Admiralties. Finally breaking through, they circled for another thirty minutes, waiting for orders to attack, but radio communications failed. Finally, they saw the star shells from the bomber command ship signaling them to the attack, so their mission hadn't been wasted.

At 0817, and only two minutes behind schedule, the four LCPRs of the first wave reached the beach. The first boat was led by 1st Lt. Marvin J. Henshaw, of Company G of the 5th Cavalry, followed closely by Sgt. John Faulkenberry and Sgt. Troy A. McGill. A Japanese machine-gun crew had been set up on the beach and was firing at the LCPRs as they made their way to the beach in the choppy waters. Two .30-caliber machine-guns, mounted on the front of the LCPRs, were peppering the beach as the thirty-seven men, led by Henshaw, unloaded.

The enemy machine-gun crew made a hasty retreat. Henshaw and his men rushed across the beach and took cover at the edge of a coconut plantation behind some fallen trees in the kunai grass. Japanese troops had started to flee the area, some as far away as the other side of Momote airstrip. Lt. Henshaw shot one fleeing Japanese with a long distance shot, and other members of the platoon killed more as they were retreating. They formed a fifty-yard semi-circle on the beach next to the logs and grass.

Close behind Henshaw, Faulkenberry, and McGill, George waded in the surf with his men, towing the generator, the SCR-193 radio, and their other supplies. Under small arms and machine-gun fire, George and his men set up the radio inside Troop G's Command Post (CP). George entered in his morning report: "0815L29—Landed first wave at Beach White at Los Negros Island in the Admiralties. Heavy Mg and Art fire encountered Hazac Sbr."

A LEGACY OF LETTERS

The Japanese troops were retreating across the Momote airfield and enemy machine-gun fire was being received from the north and south arms of the harbor entrance. The points were about 750 yards apart. The firing had stopped during the naval and B-25 bombing, but had started again. The four LCPRs of the second wave were attempting to enter the harbor. Enemy machine-gun fire had caught their landing craft in a cross fire. The Japanese had apparently been hiding in their dugouts. The beach was a safer place to be than the landing craft, and they were forced to turn back.

William B. Dickinson, a United Press war corresponded, reported landing with the first wave:

The firing from enemy guns started when the first wave of landing boats, in one of which I was riding, reached a point about a mile from the entrance to Hyane Harbor.

The first shell landed about 30 yards to our left and the next one kicked up a fountain 50 yards ahead. The third one whined directly overhead, sounding very close and splashed in the water behind our last boat. I had been standing erect in the stern of the landing boat, because it was so crowded. But when the shells began falling, I suddenly found there was plenty of room in the bottom of the boat.

The naval barrage from U.S. warships off shore still was going full blast and apparently scored a hit on an enemy gun, because no more shells fell nearby. At 8:10 AM we reached the entrance and started between the headlands. We passed safely through without a shot being fired and the boats then simultaneously swung left, heading toward the beach.

At 8:12, a red flare suddenly blossomed in the sky, signaling for the end of the bombardment and the naval guns fell silent.

As the barges ground on the beaches, the men came down the front ramp, running full speed. I was the last off, splashing through the water, thigh-deep and bent beneath a pack and typewriter. A few rifle shots came from 100 yards in the jungle and I dropped my burden and burrowed into deep grass and shrubs.

After the first wave reached the edge of the airstrip, the second wave came in and took the left flank, the third rolling in five minutes later on the right flank, all advancing clear to the strip.

Suddenly heavy machine-gun fire opened on the right flank and tracers zipped overhead. The direction of the Japanese fire changed and I looked back toward the landing boats bringing in the fourth wave.

The boats had cleared the harbor entrance and turned for the 300-yard run toward the beach. But the Japanese fire was so heavy they were forced to turn back, racing back to their ships while machine-gun fire tore up the water around them.

The boats made it from the harbor safely, although we learned later that one gunner had his head literally blown off and two soldiers were wounded.

Then the Japanese gunners concentrated their fire on the positions taken up by the first, second and third assault waves. Bullets ricocheted from coconut palms, whining off into space as the troops belly-flopped, dug in and answered the fire the best they could.

Anxious moments ticked off while we lay face down, expecting a Japanese counter-attack any instant and worrying whether the other forces had given up in the attempt to send in more men.

Then suddenly the naval barrage opened up again, concentrating exactly on the positions from which the Japanese fire was coming. Thirty minutes later, a squadron of B-25s roared in and bombed and strafed the enemy position on the right flank.

Then came the most welcome sight of the day — troop-filled barges again entering the harbor, they drew some fire from the shore and a couple of men were wounded. But this time they reached the beach. It was an hour and 15 minutes after the first wave landed.

There were only a few minor casualties on the whole beachhead, all of which merely were nicks. A few men had been killed aboard the landing craft and several wounded. At least 14 Japanese were killed by the U.S. troops ashore, in addition to others killed by the bombardment.

Cpl. Bill Alcine, a *Yank* magazine correspondent riding in the second wave, reported:

As we neared the channel, the Navy men in the bow hollered to us to keep our heads down or we'd get them blown off. We crouched lower, swearing a lot, and waited.

It came with a crack: machine-gun fire over our heads. Our light landing craft shuddered as the Navy gunners hammered back and answered with the .30-calibers mounted on both sides of the barge.

As we made the turn for the beach, something solid plugged into us. "They got one of our guns or something," one GI said. There was a splinter the size of a half dollar on the pack of the man in front of me.

Up front, a hole gaped in the middle of the landing ramp and there were no men where there had been four. Our barge headed back toward the destroyer that had carried us to the Admiralties.

White splashes of water were plunging through the 6-inch gap in the wooden gate. William Siediebda, S1/c, of Wheeling, W. Va., ducked from his position at the starboard gun and slammed his hip against the hole to plug it. He was firing a tommy gun at the shore as fast as wounded soldiers could pass him loaded clips. The water sloshed around him, running down his legs and washing the blood of the wounded into a pink frappe. Two soldiers and the coxswain died. The other man of the four was uninjured.

Ted Majusick and Joe Chartrand,[lvi] both from the troop transport USS Humphreys (APD-12), participated in the landings on Los Negros in the Admiralty Group that began on February 29, 1944. Both would have contact with the USS Bush during the landings. In addition to several troop transports, the destroyers also carried Army personnel. The USS Bush carried about seventy soldiers who would participate in the landing on Los Negros. Both Ted and Joe were part of boat crews that helped to land men from the U.S. Army's 1st Cavalry Division. As the landings began, Ted acted as engineer and port machine-gunner on the USS Humphreys Boat #3 and Joe was the bow-hook and a machine-gunner on Boat #2.

Joseph Chartrand

Just prior to the landings, Joe had switched places with another man, Albert Pinto, so that he could ride in Boat #2 with his good friend, Walter Bretz. Albert took Joe's spot in a different boat and was killed during the landings. Just as Boat #2 was about to land, a sniper shot Joe in the chest.

Recalled Joe, "A Japanese sniper fired from the trees and struck me in the chest. I was losing blood, but managed to get the ramp lowered so the 1st Cavalry could hit the beach, then passed out."

Boat #2's orders were to head for the USS Bush after the initial landing and to pick up any soldiers that may still be aboard.

Joe said, "I was transferred to the Bush for care, and came to about the time I was placed in a bunk aboard ship. I was conscious and aware of all that was happening to me after that. There I was treated by an excellent doctor named Johnson (Lt. George Johnson, the USS Bush Medical Officer)."

Joe was the first casualty treated by the medical team aboard ship. The USS Bush deck log for February 29, 1944 reads: "0834—Took aboard wounded crewman Chartrand, J. C., 610-21-23, Slc, USNR, gunshot wound in upper left chest."

When wounded, Joe was 17 years old. His mother had signed for him so that he could join the Navy. Because Joe had switched places with Albert Pinto, and due to the nature of Pinto's injuries, Joe was mistakenly identified as killed during the landings instead of Pinto.

Noted Joe, "My mother received a telegram telling her that I had been killed in action on February 29, 1944, but figured out that there must have been an error when she received a letter from me dated March 5, 1944."

Ted Majusick

Ted Majusick was on Boat #3 from the USS Humphreys. States Ted, "That morning arrived gray and rainy with heavy swells....In addition to 36 troops we had a quantity of ammunition, 30 caliber, carbine, hand grenades and a small field gun. The swells gave us a heck of a ride. First higher than the ship, and then almost under the ship, made loading troops a hairy business.

On one such bounce the boat banged against the side and dislodged my 30 cal. air-cooled machine gun, and it ended up in Davey Jone's locker. We hit the beach in the second wave, shells flying over, some crashing all about our frail craft. At one point I giggled because my being there seemed so insane. My mother had sent me a box of Oreo cookies which I passed out to the G.I.'s and the rest of my crew. There we were eating cookies, while all hell was breaking loose around us. I didn't think there was any advantage to save them for another time."

Once on the beach, Ted was transferred to Boat #4 and beach duty, while Boat #3 was slated to remain at the landing site, transferring wounded and running other errands. After spending the night on Los Negros, Ted and Boat #4 helped transfer wounded soldiers for medical treatment to the USS Bush.

Ted recalled that after one run, Boat #3 took a shell, killing several GIs and wounding a sailor that had taken Ted's place.

Noted Ted, "Around noon, we evacuated some wounded GIs to the destroyer Bush, which was patrolling offshore. It was chow time and the crew invited us to lunch. They took us to the head of the line and treated us like heroes. I gave them some battlefield souvenirs, Jap ammo and such. We grabbed a quick lunch because the ship couldn't stay in one position too long. We had brought the real heroes as I discovered when I looked down on the deck of our boat. It was red with blood and not from our crew. I washed the decks with pails of sea water and the bilge pump dumped the gore overboard. We repeated the process twice."

The USS Bush deck log for D-Day +1 (March 1, 1944) indicated that wounded Army personnel were delivered to the ship at 1029 hours (five soldiers), 1227 hours (three soldiers), and 1617 hours (two soldiers). Ted spent a second sleepless night with the Army on Los Negros. After finally falling asleep in some shade, he awoke as LSTs arrived with more troops and supplies. But his boat and the USS Humphreys had departed. It would take a couple of weeks for him to catch up to his ship.

OBSERVERS FROM THE DESTROYER Mayhan saw the machine-gun fire coming from the north and south arms of the harbor entrance. In a matter of three minutes, the Mayhan was able to silence the guns on the southern point with its 20 and 40mm guns. It couldn't fire on the northern point because the landing crafts were in the way. When the machine-gun fire was silenced on the southern point, the second wave landed with machine-guns firing on the beach at the southern and northern arms where the Japanese had their machine-guns. The gunner on one landing craft was killed, but S/Sgt. Bobbie K. Horton of Alpine, Texas, jumped from behind the ramp, manned the machine-gun, and covered the enemy fire effectively enough to permit the unloading of his platoon onto the beach. At H + 8 minutes, the second wave rushed the beach, moved swiftly past the troops of the first wave, and took up a position 100 yards past the first wave.

The plan had been for the second and third waves to land at five and ten-minute intervals after the first wave landed. Returning to the ships was necessary, since the twelve LCPRs were the only ones available to pick up the remaining troops. Between the first three waves and the next three waves, forty-five minutes were to elapse while the LCPRs returned to the ships. After another forty-five minutes, the last three waves were to land. If all had gone according to plan, the whole reconnaissance force would have been landed by 1035 hours, but the persistent Japanese disrupted the plan with their firepower.

Twenty minutes after landing at 0835, George had the SCR-193 running and had made contact with the control ship, "JUMBO." Four squadrons of B-25s were scheduled to contact JUMBO (USS Reid), at H − 18 minutes, and to circle over Pak Island on station for one hour. At the end of that time, they were to contact JUMBO and notify the air control officer that they were commencing attack and returning to base upon completion. From H hour, four squadrons of the 345th Bomb Group were to stagger every hour, one squadron over the target area on air alert for four hours. They were to hit predesignated targets on call from task force commanders at either JUMBO or GANGWAY. The weather was lousy and getting worse, with rain squalls and a low ceiling, and wasn't conducive to locating targets.

The third wave landed at 0845, established a line of defense just short of the airstrip and moved south, taking two-thirds of the eastern dispersal area around the airstrip. At 0900, the 1st Cavalry had established a line of defense 300 yards inland. Although the enemy situation hadn't been determined, the command post was moved 500 yards inland fifteen minutes later. The only enemy contact was from some patrols that had been operating in that area.

BILL DUNN'S EARPHONES CRACKLED. Lt. Boden was flying only fifty feet above the sea in tight formation.

"When we go in over the target, we'll be very close to the treetops, but don't get scared. It's a perfectly normal procedure. We're right on schedule."

"Just forget me and fly your airplane," Dunn responded.

The 498th had flown down the Markham Valley to Lae, turned north to Umboi Island, and toward the Admiralties through soupy weather. The 499th, leaving ten minutes later, headed up the Markham and Ramu valleys to Bogadjim, and north to the Admiralties. After flanking several thunderstorms, the 499th flew through a seventy-mile front that extended from 900–15,000 feet. The navigator took the squadron through a small hole in the weather at 0915 near Pak Island, one minute after the specified time.

A B-24 Liberator from the 43rd Bomb Group met them flying south— it was uncomfortably close. A few minutes later, Boden pointed out, under the clouds, the first of scores of atolls in the Admiralties group. The planes were flying so low that they had to pull up to clear the trees on a couple of the islands, but they had to continue for several minutes before a welcome break in the clouds revealed Manus and Los Negros on their left.

On the blueberry-colored waters before them stretched the invasion fleet, reaching as far as the eye could penetrate through the heavy weather. Occasional pinpoints of light sparking from the beaches indicated gunfire; otherwise the scene was reassuringly peaceful. They began making long sweeping circles over an area northeast of the landing area while other mission planes came into view, first from behind and then from almost dead ahead as they continued to circle. The 499th had beaten them to the Admiralties, although they had left ten minutes later.

The B-25s of the 499th circled for twenty-three minutes while rain squalls swept across Los Negros. Then JUMBO ordered the squadron to attack the "Native Skidway" area on the west side of Hyane Harbor. The skidway was merely a narrow native trail connecting the north side of Los Negros Island at Seeadler Harbor to the south side at Hyane Harbor. At 0942, the landings craft were entering the mouth of Hyane Harbor. The six B-25s turned in over Momote airdrome for their first bombing and strafing run. The landing crafts were about halfway across the harbor upon completion of the second run, and on the third pass, the boats were too close to permit still another run, as called for by JUMBO.

In the nine-minute attack, the B-25s dropped seventeen 500-pound bombs and expended more than 12,000 rounds strafing the targets. As the planes turned back toward base, pilots saw twelve P-38s coming down through the overcast, heard the 12th Air liaison party's station, GANGWAY, broadcasting from the beach, and saw the 498th circling over Pak Island. The P-47s of the 348th Fighter Group hadn't gotten through and had lost four planes because of weather conditions.

Dunn heard his earphones crackle again, and the pilot said, "Apparently the landing is going well. They have a ground station set up and they tell me we're no longer needed."

Dunn settled back, looking out, but not seeing anything because of the overcast. Suddenly, the eight .50-caliber machine-guns came to life and the plane zoomed upward with green treetops flashing by the window. They had been forced so low that instead of diving on the target as expected, they'd had to climb to clear it. In a split second, they had sprayed the area with 3,700 rounds and dropped twenty-four 500-pound bombs, and they were now on their way home for a breakfast of bully beef and some unidentifiable canned vegetables. An hour later, at 1142, the 500th Squadron would unload their bombs and spray Lou Island.

By 0950, troops were moving freely around the Momote airfield. It was overgrown with weeds and littered with rusting fuselages. Pools of water had filled the many bomb craters that covered the field. With the 12th Air Liaison Party was also a Navy liaison to relay or assist in directing the shelling. George obtained the targets from the field, relayed the messages to his radio operator, and then either planes or destroyers shelled the beach.

General MacArthur and Admiral Kinkaid had observed the landing and naval shelling from aboard the Phoenix. MacArthur was in awe of the accuracy and power of the Navy shelling. The silencing of the guns on the southern point and the destruction of the bunkers and gun emplacements was impressive.

Looking through his binoculars, MacArthur cheered, "That's the way to hit them!" when a salvo scored a direct hit on an enemy machine-gun. Turning to Admiral Kinkaid, he asked, "Is the Navy always this accurate?"

Admiral Kinkaid felt that he should downplay the display by the Navy, since he didn't want MacArthur to think it would always be that good.

"Not all shelling by the Navy is as effective as it's been today, sir," he responded.

At 1100 hours, George was ordered to move his station closer to the squadron's command post, 100 yards from the perimeter. George was with a colonel when three Japanese were spotted in the brush. They were ordered to surrender. Earlier, pamphlets had been dropped, saying in both Japanese and English:

The bearer of this pass is voluntarily surrendering and

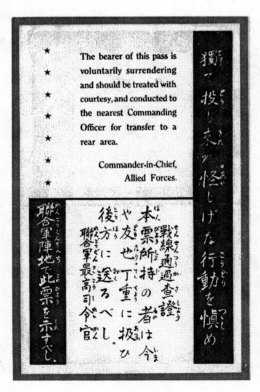

The bearer of this pass is voluntarily surrendering and should be treated with courtesy, and conducted to the nearest Commanding Officer for transfer to a rear area.

Commander-in-Chief, Allied Forces.

should be treated with courtesy, and conducted to the nearest Commanding Officer for transfer to a rear area. Commander-in-Chief, Allied Forces

The Japanese refused to surrender, and George killed two of them as they fled. He took their rifles as souvenirs of the occasion. One was new, but the other had fourteen notches carved in the stock.

Inspection of the airstrip found it to be pitted from the bombings of the previous two months. It had been built in 1942 by the Japanese, but apparently hadn't been used for some time, since it was overgrown with brush and weeds. Rusting plane fuselages dotted the airstrip, along with a rotting truck and a sorry-looking Japanese bulldozer. However, with a few graders, the airstrip could be made serviceable.

The beachhead continued to be safer than the harbor entrance. By the time the LCPRs of the third wave had returned, four of them were out of commission. The destroyers continued to bombard the Japanese gun emplacements. A spotting plane from the Phoenix ran into light antiaircraft fire and observed 25mm guns at the entrance. He divebombed, strafed the gun emplacements, and got one with a direct bomb hit. Since the four landing crafts had been put out of commission, the troops that had already landed couldn't be evacuated if they were overrun by the enemy.

At H+4 hours, 35 minutes (12:50 hours), the unloading of the reconnaissance troops was complete. Increasing rain during the past three hours had made the threat from enemy fire negligible. It had also prevented any effective participation by the Air Force, which had made its chief contribution by pointing out opportunities. The troops were moving freely about the airstrip, with only occasional sniper fire. They had advanced across the Momote airfield, their original objective, and 1,300 yards to the southwest point and 500 yards northeast of the airdrome. It looked as if the real estate was theirs, and all that was required would be the restoration of the airfield by the Seabees and mopping up of the island when reinforcements arrived.

Patrols were sent out to assess the enemy situation. One patrol went as far as 1,000 yards past the airdrome until they reached Lemondrol Creek, without contact. A patrol that went about a mile south found a bivouac area and the vacated quarters of a high-ranking officer, and fired at a Japanese officer as he was fleeing the area. The patrol also found three large kitchens and a warehouse of food. They obtained documents that revealed that some 200 antiaircraft Japanese had been encamped in the area.

At 1301, General Kenney wired a message to Col. Cain, A-2, in Brisbane: "The dice made the point easily. Quit worrying."

William B. Dickinson writing for the *El Paso Herald Post*, reported on General MacArthur's landing on Los Negros:

"We were waiting on a jetty when a Higgins boat brought in General MacArthur. As he stepped from the barge, he smiled and remarked:

"I see the press is present."

After an hour's detailed inspection of almost the entire beach, I asked MacArthur how he found the positions.

"Splendid," he replied. "Just fine."

At the dock, MacArthur congratulated Brig. Gen. William C. Chase, commander of the landing forces.

"My heartiest felicitations to you and your men," the general said. "You have performed magnificently. Hold what you have taken no matter against what odds. You have your teeth in him now. Don't let go."

At 1400 hours, George saw General MacArthur walking toward the airstrip with General Chase, Admiral Kinkaid, and their aides. Lt. Colonel William E. Lobit, commander of the 2nd Squadron, Fifth Cavalry, was acting as tour guide for MacArthur. They were followed by a bevy of war correspondents and photographers. Lobit was telling MacArthur that the area wasn't safe.

He motioned in George's direction and said, "Two Japs were shot over there not that long ago! We still have sporadic sniper fire."

"He won't do it," Lt. Commander Samuel Nixdroff, Kinkaid's operations officer from Schenectady, New York, responded. "I tried to get him to stand down on the barge on the way over here, but he insisted on standing up the whole way. Most of our wounded so far have been on the barge trip over here."

MacArthur ignored them. Instead of the green fatigue uniform that was standard for invading troops, he was wearing a khaki gabardine trench coat and his famed gold-braided hat. He strolled the entire length of the airstrip, stopping occasionally to congratulate the troops on their landing. The rain had let up and troops were milling around the airstrip, thrilled that the head man himself would come ashore.

As he passed Sgt. Faulkenberry, MacArthur said, "That's the way I like to see them."

The sergeant was standing by some dead Japanese that had been laid out by the corpsmen.

General MacArthur found Lt. Marvin Henshaw of Alice, Texas, as he was returning to the beach. MacArthur congratulated him on being the first man on the beach and for having killed the first Japanese.

As he pinned the Distinguished Service Cross on Henshaw, he said, "Share this with your unit. It's symbolic of a job well done. You and your men have earned it."

As reports from patrols trickled in, General Chase suspected that the Japanese would counterattack during the night. He also suspected that the higher estimate of Japanese troops might be more accurate. He ordered a con-solidation of the troops by pulling back to east of the airstrip and establishing a defensive position 1,500 yards long that angled at 90 degrees. That defen-sive perimeter position allowed an unobstructed view of half the airstrip.

General Chase set up his command post in the center of the triangular defensive area. Lt. Col. Lobit set up his post in an abandoned Japanese dugout with a triple log cover and dry floors. Chase ordered George to pull back from his advance position and to set up closer to the command post. They found an abandoned revetment and started setting up their tents and digging in. They covered their revetment with logs and sandbags. The revet-ments were steep banks of earth, reaching some fifteen feet high at one end, with two smaller embankments flanking it to form a pattern that from the air looked like cleats on the sole of a football shoe. On top of the tallest bank, they dug a foxhole they could use as an observation area. From there, they could observe the bombing and drops of supplies. The revetments were used to shield airplanes in the dispersal area around the airstrip. Telephone lines were then strung between all officers and defensive positions.

General MacArthur and Admiral Kinkaid returned to the Phoenix, having ignored sniper fire, but were wet and covered with mud. By radio, MacArthur ordered more troops, supplies, and equipment at the "earliest possible convenience." By 1729 hours, the Phoenix was underway, leaving only the destroyers Bush and Stockton to support the troops on Los Negros. The returning destroyers were low on ammunition, having expended more than 2,000 rounds of heavy artillery.

General Chase, by consolidating the toehold on White Beach, couldn't use the 75mm howitzers because the beachhead they held was too small. He turned artillery men into riflemen. Then he radioed General Krueger: "The estimate of enemy strength is much greater than what Kenny thinks."

He requested supplies of barbed wire, mortars, and more ammunition, and told George to have supply drops made on the north side of the airstrip. He positioned the .50-caliber antiaircraft guns along their front lines and scattered troops outside the defensive line to confuse any counterattack, but those troops would need to pull back. Abandoned revetments and bomb craters were used for protection. Foxholes were also dug, but it was backbreaking work, since picks had to be used to break through the hard ground and coral.

Bill Alcine, a *Yank* Magazine correspondent, saw Major Everett King setting up a hammock between two palm trees next to an abandoned Japanese pillbox, close to the command post.

"Nothing like comfort," King said with a smile.

He felt safe, since he was close to the command post. Any attack by the Japanese would first be centered on the defensive line, well over 100 yards from his foxhole. He had come ashore from the flagship to aid George and the 12th ALP.

As the sun began to set in the west, the Japanese attacked, firing on the outlying troops. The Japanese had the advantage with the sun setting behind them, causing American troops to stare into the setting sun. Placing troops in the outlying positions foiled the Japanese attack, however, since they thought that was the main defensive line. The remainder of their attack was uncoordinated and out of control. George killed the generator powering their radio. They couldn't risk drawing attention to their revetment with the generator running.

After the initial attack, it became strangely quiet. As the night progressed, the only way the Japanese could be seen was from the glare of hand grenades or when they were silhouetted against the dark sky. There was occasional rifle fire, machine-gun fire, and hand grenade explosions during the night as groups of 7–15 Japanese troops advanced, throwing hand grenades at any rifle fire they saw. Cloud cover made the night pitch black, adding to the 1st Cavalry troop's anxiety and raindrops sounded like footsteps. They thought they heard the enemy, everywhere—behind, in front, and all around them. With no chance of rescue, it was a nerve-wracking night, wondering if their meager 1,000-man force was greatly outnumbered by the Japanese. Were they like condemned men, waiting for several thousand Japanese troops to overtake their position? They knew the Japanese would attack in force—they just weren't sure when.

Despite sporadic rifle and machine-gun fire, some men drifted off to sleep. The Japanese indeed were infiltrating the defensive line in the dark, and managed to cut the communication lines. The 3rd Platoon of Company E, guarding the southern sector, was completely cut off where the attack was the heaviest. Japanese, with life preservers, came in from the sea and hid in the brush and kunai grass. Without communication, Company E had to fight it out alone against heavy attack. Communications weren't needed anyway, since the best defense was to stay in your foxhole and fire at anything that moved. It was extremely dangerous to leave your foxhole. Most of the wounded had to stay in their foxholes until morning, but some didn't make it and bled to death.

Several acts of extraordinary courage occurred during that night. Pvt. George L. Sumpter of Mt. Holly, North Carolina, was at his post on the perimeter when he saw his buddy in a foxhole near him being stalked by three Japanese, one of them an officer. At the same time, he saw that he was also being stalked by another of the enemy. He jumped out of his foxhole, killed his buddy's attackers, then turned and killed his own attacker.

Pvt. Walter E. Hawks of Wylie, Texas, was also in a foxhole on the perimeter. He saw eight enemy soldiers setting up a machine-gun. He waited until they had all assembled in a small area and then killed them all with his automatic rifle. Seeing his position, a group of twenty Japanese charged, throwing hand grenades. Hawks was able to avoid the hand grenades and enemy fire and killed all twenty within fifteen feet of his foxhole.

Major Julio Chiaramonte, S-2, of the task force, saw two Japanese soldiers enter the perimeter of the command post within fifteen feet of General Chase. Unable to identify the men in the dark, he didn't fire. They took out hand grenades and started chattering in a low monotone, as if they were planning their attack. Chiaramonte opened fire with his tommy gun, killing both of them.

Alertness was the best defense. A stealthy Japanese soldier found Major King asleep in his hammock and killed him with a sword in the early morning. Ten Japanese soldiers were found and killed by the troops in a pillbox next to him the following morning.

George recorded in his morning report for March 1: "0400—Enemy attacked entire perimeter. Up all night. We held."

Major Reed, who had come ashore with the original invasion, was in a foxhole not far from George and his men. In the early morning light, the Japanese were retreating into the brush. The Japanese threw a hand grenade into Major Reed's foxhole. He jumped out in time, and after the hand grenade went off, he jumped back into his foxhole. A few minutes later, another grenade landed in his foxhole and he had to jump out again. The grenade exploded, and Major Reed jumped back in his foxhole. After a third grenade was thrown into the foxhole, troops spotted the Jap and opened fire, killing him. Once more, Major Reed jumped back into his foxhole after the grenade had exploded. During the close contact within the perimeter, the primary arms were hand grenades.

D + 1, Wednesday, March 1, 1944; Los Negros Island

Sunrise on the morning of March 1st gave promise of a clear day as it began to cast its brilliant colors through the clouds on the Bismarck Sea. Except for dead Japanese soldiers lying on the ground where they'd been shot, there was no sign of the enemy. They had either retreated or were hiding in the brush or unoccupied pillboxes they'd previously constructed.

The erratic rifle fire within the perimeter in the early morning light had confirmed the suspicion that the Japanese had indeed crept through their defenses. Those snipers would need to be cleared out before it was safe to move about. The snipers gave their positions away by firing at Allied troops.

Medics operated on former Japanese mess tables in the makeshift hospital that had been set up in a revetment in the center of the compound. Troops helped the wounded to the hospital through the early morning light. Medics had worked with the aid of flashlights or lanterns during the night on the few wounded who had made it to their station.

At 0730, the divisional wire chief, Capt. Joseph Q. Tuck of Winterville, Georgia, was shot as he was making his way to the command post. Wounded in the groin and chest and lying in mud six feet from the tip of a V-shaped dugout, Capt. Tuck pointed to the pillbox. Pfc. Allan M. Holliday, of Miami, Florida, and Cpl. James E. Stumfoll, of Pittsburg, Kansas, who were coming up the track when the captain was shot, ducked behind some palms and began firing at the pillbox. Meanwhile, Capt. Tuck was being pulled to safety by Lt. Col. John R. Hall, Jr., of El Paso, Texas, the ranking medical corps officer, when a grenade was thrown by the enemy and landed on Tuck, who grabbed the grenade and threw it back. However, Lt. Col. Hall was also slightly injured now from a grenade. A signal corps photographer, who was trying to get movies of the action, was shot through the stomach. Nearby corpsmen saw the commotion and quickly evacuated the wounded to the hospital.

When four Japanese ran out the other entrance, they were cut down by a squad on that side. Holliday and Stumfoll crept up and tossed grenades into the opening near them. The Japanese threw out two of the grenades, but the others exploded inside the hole. Silence then engulfed the pillbox, so Holliday, Stumfoll, and a handful of other cavalrymen circled to the other entrance and started to pull the palm fronds away from the hole. Inside, a

215

Japanese was sitting up, drawing a bead with a rifle. Some twenty carbines and tommy guns sawed him in half as he folded over like a man in prayer. The troops, hearing more noise inside, tossed TNT in it, and that was the end of the pillbox.

General Chase sent patrols north of the perimeter toward the native skidway and west of the airstrip to determine enemy strength. Documents recovered from dead Japanese during the first day's attack revealed various stockpiles of supplies and ammunition and the location of Japanese defen-

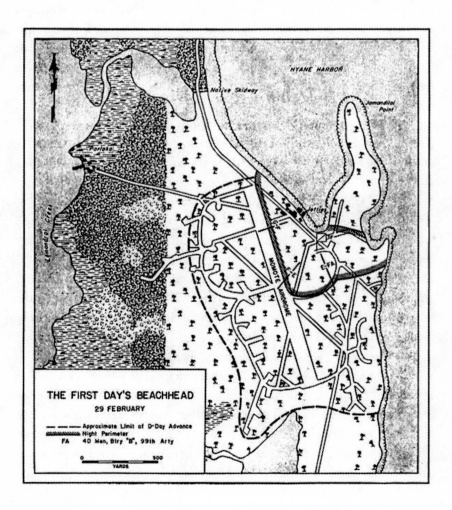

THE FIRST DAY'S BEACHHEAD
29 FEBRUARY

— — — Approximate Limit of D-Day Advance
Night Perimeter
FA   40 Men, Btry "B", 99th Arty

0   500
YARDS

sive positions. The maps were sent to the destroyers so targets could be determined and coordinated.

At 0830, the first of the supplies were dropped by three B-25s of the 38th Group. Ten minutes later, the Yankee Diddler began the first of three supply runs it would make. It was a converted B-17, previously with the 65th Squadron of the 43rd Bomb Group, but was now with the 39th Troop Carrier Group. It dropped three tons of supplies, including plasma, grenades, ammunition, and mortar shells.

The YANKEE DIDDLER had been converted for use as a troop and supply carrier in November 1943. The bomb rack had been replaced with special bins containing static lines for releasing parachutes. Although the belly guns had been removed, the nose, tail, and waist-gun positions were retained. It was the first of the "armed transports" in the South Pacific, providing close air support to ground troops and dropping time-critical supplies.

The YANKEE DIDDLER gained its fame among the troops when it flew from New Guinea to Sydney, ostensibly for supplies, but in reality, as a beer run for the enlisted men. Arriving in Sydney, the Aussie women manning the control tower made them park out of public view behind a hanger because of the nose art.

After each run, the B-17s made a strafing pass along the west edge of the runway to cover troops retrieving supplies and dodging enemy machine-gun fire. The YANKEE DIDDLER returned at 1500 to drop barbed wire,[lvii] anti-personnel mines, grenades, and ammunition. Again it strafed Japanese positions after completing its drops. The strafing was so heavy that 100 terrorized Japanese ran out into the open, yelling, "Banzai! Banzai!" but a withering barrage of ground machine-gun fire cut them down. It wasn't an attack, but an attempt to escape the strafing.

Four B-17s of the 41st, 56th, and 69th Troop Carrier Groups also dropped supplies and made strafing passes. The strafing protected troops as they retrieved supplies dropped outside the perimeter. One drop that landed in enemy territory was destroyed by strafing. Medical and breakable items were dropped by parachute, while ammunition and other supplies were simply dropped.

Troops of the 1st Cavalry that weren't out on patrol were kept busy in the morning making sure that all Japanese inside the perimeter were actually dead. They also cleared any pillboxes that the Japanese had reoccupied. Using the supplies that were dropped, they tightened their perimeter and fortified their position. Later that morning, the Japanese dead within the perimeter were gathered and counted. There were eighty-five dead, as opposed to seven American casualties and fifteen wounded. The most critical were evacuated to the destroyers.

Based on the documents that had been captured from the Japanese, the Bush and the Stockton moved into position to shell the southern coast of Hyane Harbor. The documents revealed several enemy machine-gun, field artillery, and mortar emplacements. Also dispersed in the southern area were ammunition and food dumps. The 99th Field Artillery was able to move its howitzers to the front lines and bombarded the southern tip with fifty rounds. The destroyers moved about, bombarding north of the native skidway, the road back of Hyane Beach, the eastern tip of Manus Island, Porlaka, and Papitalai. The patrol that had been sent north of the airstrip had gone only about 400 yards when they had to turn back because of enemy resistance.

Squadrons on bombing and strafing missions to the Admiralties after D-Day were briefed on both primary and secondary targets before taking off. On occasion, they were assigned secondary targets only, which were to be attacked in case the 12th ALP failed to assign a target. At other times, squadrons of mediums were ordered to circle over an outlying island on air alert and attack as directed, and if no direction was received from the 12th ALP, to proceed to their secondary target. The 38th group had six B-25s at a time over Lou Island starting at 0845 and circled until 0945 before it went on to bomb and strafe Lombrum Point and Papitalai Mission. The 822nd stuck Lombrum Point an hour later. The 405th was unable to contact GANGWAY and attacked Lorengau Township at 1132.

From the documents recovered and from patrols sent out, it was learned that the Japanese were assembling at Lorengau for a counterattack. The information was received in time for three squadrons from the 43rd Bomb Group to respond to a call from GANGWAY. Three hours later, they dropped more than forty tons of bombs on the area. The 71st, from the 38th, had been circling over Lou Island and after the 43rd had bombed Lorengau, they also strafed and dropped their bombs.

The 499th, after circling on alert, was the last mission of the day. A call from GANGWAY requested them to attack a plantation and wooded area 500 yards west of and parallel to Momote strip. Two destroyers were shelling targets in the same area, but ceased fire when the B-25s came over for their two runs and resumed after the 499th had left the area, indicating how closely naval and air bombardment were coordinated. The 499th let loose with twenty-two 500-pound bombs and strafed with more than 14,000 rounds of machine-gun fire. The pilots couldn't observe the results of the bombing because of heavy foliage, but GANGWAY reported excellent results.

A few enemy aircraft appeared, but didn't put up a successful defense. Eight enemy fighters were destroyed in air combat over Momote, including one shot down by a B-17 dropping supplies. Eighteen enemy fighters intercepted twelve B-25s shortly after noon, thirty miles south of Momote. One B-25 was lost and one enemy fighter destroyed.

SECRET

12 AIR LIAISON PARTY

FEBRUARY

1. 1100L/26 - Alerted and moved to Dobodure.

2. 1600L/27 - Capt. Frederick left Nadzab for Dobodura to take charge of 12th ALP, with plans of operation, photos.

3. 1800L/27 - Reported to G-3, 1st Cav Brig at Oro Bay.

4. 1930L/27 - Arrived on Hq Ship USS Reid. Conferred and gave plans to G-3 1st Cav Brig.

5. 2330L/27 - Arrived aboard USS Sands on APD and reported to Task Force Commander.

6. 0900L/28 - Aboard USS Sands. Check party and equipment. Have Lt. King and five men.

7. 1000L/28 - Discussed entire plan with CO and Staff and received ground plan.

8. 1300L/28 - Rations issued and loaded equipment on boat.

9. 0615L/29 - Landed first wave on Beach White at Los Negros Island in the Admiralties. Heavy MG and Art fire encountered Hazac Sbr.

10. 0835L/29 - Station set up on beach in 20 minutes and in contact with control ship.

11. 1100L/29 - Capt. Frederick killed first two Japs on Los Negros. Moved station to location of Squadron CP, 100 yds from perimeter fo defence. Set up all around the tents and dug in.

12. 1400L/29 - Radio Log being kept of messages on CW. Working with W2 on "Q" net. Only station we could contact. Using a 193 set.

MARCH

13. 0400L/1 - Enemy attacked entire perimeter. Up all night. We held. 1 Squadron arrived as reenforcement.

March 1st - Received several dropping and support missions. Had set tuned in all day on 4475KC & talked to planes directing them over target and having droppers (B-17) strafe several areas. Communications excellent and planes understood targets OK. At 4:00P, after the bombing and strafing the western side of the strip while we held the eastern side. The Japs attacked and ran out into the open as a result of the bombing and strafing. They were mowed down by MG fire. We killed about 400 during the day & evening. Japs set up MG 10 ft from our dugout and we were under cross fire of enemy; friendly guns. Several shots in our dugout.

RESTRICTED

Morning report – page 1[lviii]

An enemy patrol almost succeeded in their mission when they were discovered at 1600 in the secondary brush, thirty-five yards from the command post. Their mission was to kill or capture General Chase. It was led by Captain Baba, the commander of the battalion that had made the major attack the night before. Cavalry troops had been confident that they'd mopped up all the infiltrators from the night before, but had failed to detect the enemy patrol. A single sniper started firing at the command post. Major Chiaramonte set out with four men to get the sniper. Colonel Thompson, with hand signals, directed the major and his men right or left, depending upon movement in the underbrush. Whenever they detected movement, they fired into the brush. When they were finally able to enter the area of the sniper, they heard a click, followed by a grenade explosion. Three of the Japanese had committed suicide. Another had rolled over on his back and used his sword to commit hara-kiri. When the disruption was over, fifteen dead Japanese officers and sergeants were counted, including Captain Baba. One document found on Baba contained orders:

Tonight your battalion will annihilate the enemy who has landed. This is not a delaying action. Be resolute to sacrifice your life for the Emperor and commit suicide in case capture is imminent. We must carry out our mission with the present strength and annihilate the enemy on the spot. I am highly indignant about the enemy's arrogant attitude. Remember to kill or capture all ranking enemy officers for our intelligence purposes.

The order was signed by Colonel Yoshio Ezaki as Commander of the Admiralty Islands Garrison. It was surmised by the officers in the command post that the attack orders were for the previous night. However, an attack later in the night could be expected, since the Japanese hadn't succeeded the night before.

At 1700, the Japanese attacked. The attack wasn't expected until after dark. The intensity of the attack wasn't as severe as the night before, in part due to the remaining daylight that made targets visible and to the tightening of the perimeter that increased the effectiveness of the cavalry's firepower. In addition, some of the Japanese enthusiasm was gone, since they'd lost their leader and his staff. The attack ended at 2000 hours, but the night was not over.

It was another dark night, interspersed with sporadic gunfire. It was obvious that the Japanese were infiltrating Allied positions with small groups. When one group approached Pvt. Andrew R. Barnabei, of Philadelphia, Pennsylvania, he moved from his shelter and laid a grenade outside his fox-hole, which killed five of the enemy. His action drew enemy fire, but he escaped. S/Sgt. Gilbert Newman, of Mt. Enterprise, Texas, saw an officer from his troop seriously wounded in front of a strong enemy emplacement. Newman rescued the officer as the Japanese fired and threw grenades at him. Anyone moving out of their foxholes would be fired upon. It was another scary, sleepless night.

HEADLINES ACROSS THE NATION and around the world heralded the Admiralty Island Invasion on March 1st. Papers in Texas were particularly proud of the Texas-based 1st Cavalry.

The *El Paso Times* front page stated: "First Cavalry Troops Invade Vital Nippon Base in Admiralties—Gen. Inns P. Swift Commands Soldiers In Brilliant Maneuver Against Enemy."

The *Washington Post* headline read: "Invasion Troops Seize Admiralty Island Airfield—MacArthur Watches Landing Unopposed by Jap Forces."

The *Brisbane Telegraph* described the landing on an inside story, saying, "The element of risk was not small in this stroke, which relied largely on the audacity and speed of its conception and execution for success" and covered their entire front page with another story taking up nearly a half page with the headline, "Admiralties Invaded—Sudden Landing Outflanks Japs."

In reporting the invasion, the *London Daily Mirror* stated, "We had spent 24 hours at sea steaming parallel with the coast of the mysterious Los Negros Island. Japanese lookouts must by then have seen the imposing cavalcade of warships steaming into action, but there was no sign of stir on shore...the war-ships opened their bombardment and for half an hour the air reverberated with noise resembling some primeval warning of a jungle cataclysm."

Many papers included a map depicting the location of the Admiralties, with arrows pointing the way to the Philippine Islands and Japanese holdings in the surrounding islands and New Guinea, but the battle for the Admiralties had yet to be won.

D + 2, Thursday, March 2, 1944; Los Negros Island

George, his men, and the troops of the 2nd Squadron of the Fifth Cavalry were anxiously awaiting the arrival of reinforcements. The 1st Squadron of the Fifth was due to arrive with support troops, adding another 1,500 troops for defense of their toehold on Los Negros. The additional troops would be a welcome relief, since they'd gone forty-eight hours with little sleep or rest.

General Chase ordered an expansion of their beachhead to include the airstrip and the surrounding roads so repairs could be started in order to land planes as soon as possible. They would also clear out Jamandilai Point, move the 2nd Squadron Companies F and G to defend attacks from the Native Skidway and Porlaka on the right and the newly arrived 1st Squadron Companies B and C on the left. Artillery would be placed in the middle. They planned to cover their expansion with air and naval bombardment.

The evening before the 1,500 remaining ground troops, under the command of Colonel Hoffman arrived, the rest of the 99th Field Artillery Battalion, 428 Seabees of the 40th Naval Construction Battalion and equal number of the 2nd Engineer Special Brigade loaded at Oro Bay and Cape Cretin on Landing Ship Transports (LSTs) towing LCMs (Landing Craft Mechanized). Also on board were a machine-gun and antiaircraft battery, which would increase the firepower in defense of the perimeter. The LSTs and LCMs were escorted by both Australian and American destroyers. Australian minesweepers, under the command of Capt. E.F.V. Dechaineux, also accompanied the convoy. At 0800, the destroyer Bush met the convoy and escorted it to Hyane Harbor. The minesweepers and one destroyer were then dispatched to Seeadler Harbor.

Captain Dechaineux, his minesweepers, and destroyer escort steamed

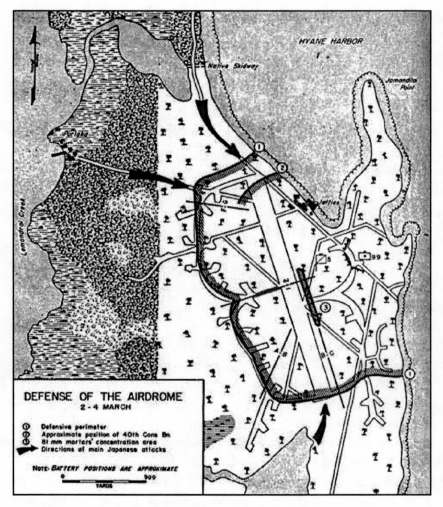

DEFENSE OF THE AIRDROME
2 - 4 MARCH

① Defensive perimeter
② Approximate position of 40th Cons Bn
③ 81 mm mortars' concentration area
➤ Directions of main Japanese attacks

NOTE: *BATTERY POSITIONS ARE APPROXIMATE*

0   300
            YARDS

around the northern tip of Los Negros to clear the 1,500 yard-wide entrance to Seeadler Harbor. As they were rounding the tip, they encountered heavy fire from enemy positions on the outlying islands of Hauwei and Ndrilo. He called the convoy for help, and three more destroyers were dispatched to aid his entrance. When the destroyers came to the rescue, they also received intense heavy fire and had to retreat. The minesweeping would have to wait another day until the islands could be bombed and cleared of enemy gun emplacements.

Meanwhile, at 0926, LSTs and an LCM were maneuvered through the entrance of Hyane Harbor to the beachhead. As the landing crafts trudged through the harbor entrance, they received light, ineffective enemy mortar and machine-gun fire from north of the skidway. The LSTs opened up with their 20mm, 40mm, and 3-inch guns and silenced the fire.

Fifteen hundred reinforcements stormed the beach as the large landing crafts came to a stop at 1000 hours. Bulldozers followed and construction started immediately on ramps to unload supplies and other vehicles. The men were surprised to see B-25s bombing and strafing all around them, since they had heard the area was safe. The Seabees, 428 men strong, were assigned the task of taking out the sniper fire that was being received from across the airstrip. Led by Navy Commander I.S. Rusmusson, the Seabees unloaded a ditch digger that only one man had the patience to operate. With Seabees guarding him with Browning Automatic Rifles (BARs), he was able to dig a trench 300 yards long. By that time, the battalion's truck, with a 20mm gun mounted on top, had been unloaded. They set the truck up behind the trench and fired across the airstrip where the sniper fire had been coming from.

By noon, the construction battalion had gone to work clearing and grading the taxiway. They also started to bury the enemy dead and cleared firing areas for field artillery and mortars. They demolished enemy dugouts and fortifications within the perimeter. The beach was becoming crowded with all the supplies being unloaded.

Air action on March 2nd again started with a supply drop from the Yankee Diddler at 0830, dropping wire, plasma, ammunition, and grenades on the east edge of the strip. After the supply drop, it made seven strafing runs west of the air strip to cover the troops retrieving the bundles. The 38th arrived nearly at the same time to be on air alert with twenty-three B-25s. At 0935, GANGWAY relayed a request for an attack against the west side of the Momote strip. The 71st Squadron didn't hear the orders, and bombed Lorengau instead. The leader finally heard GANGWAY calling to bomb Momote, but only had two bombs left, so he strafed the area and dropped his remaining bombs. The lead flight of the 822nd turned back to base because of fuel shortage, but two pilots thought Lorengau was the target. Only one pilot interpreted GANGWAY's message correctly and bombed the proper target. The 405th saved the mission from disaster. On orders from GANGWAY, six B-25s separated into single elements and made excellent bombing and strafing runs through a light rain under a 600-foot ceiling.

Another air drop of machine-gun barrels, grenades, ammunition, and rations was made by two B-17s of the 69th Troop Carrier Squadron at 1105. As they were leaving, they were jumped by four enemy fighters, but were able to shoot one down. They escaped and returned to their base in New Guinea.

The afternoon cavalry attack to expand the perimeter was scheduled for 1500 hours. All four squadrons of the 345th were ordered to leave Nadzab to attack 1,000 yards west of the Momote strip, but were to contact GANG-WAY before bombing. George changed the target to both sides of Porharmenemen Creek, southwest of the strip. All four squadrons of the 345th were circling on air alert at 1225 when they were attacked by fifteen enemy fighters. Eight fighters of the 341st Fighter Squadron intercepted the enemy and were able to shoot down eight with four probable, but not before the enemy fighters had inflicted some damage. The 499th was flying last in the formation at about 8,000 feet, fifteen miles from Lou Island, when two of the "Tonys" shot the top half off a vertical fin and knocked out the turret on Jayhawk, piloted by 1st Lt. Carl L. Cessna. The gunner, S/Sgt. Christopher S. Bartzokas, refused to leave the damaged turret, even though he was badly wounded in the back and legs by shrapnel from a 20mm cannon round. 1st Lt. Louis E. Higgins, the navigator, was looking out the astrodome for enemy fighters when a row of machine-gun bullets punctured the fuselage a few inches from his head, but he received only a minor scratch. T/Sgt. Fredrick R. Mitchell, the radio operator, was also wounded in the back and legs by shrapnel. The Japanese fighters were only able to complete one pass before P-47 escorts were able to drive them away.

The 500th Squadron was the first to drop its bombs. They were seen to burst east of the airstrip about halfway up the runway and across the strip into the northwest dispersal area, missing the specified target entirely.

GANGWAY kept broadcasting the proper target and ordered them to cease bombing. The 501st Squadron dropped its bombs on the new target, but then heard "a voice on the radio saying that bombs were falling among friendly troops and to cease the attack and return to base."

A mission report filed by one pilot of the 501st stated, "It is considered likely that this was an attempt by the enemy to upset the attack with false radio orders, as intelligence reports received from Blue Landing Force after the attack reported bombing excellent."

Except for the bombing of the 501st "Black Panthers" and the 498th "Falcons," the bombing was far from excellent and the Japanese weren't again accused of playing games with the radio. The 498th dropped its bombs on the proper target, but returned to base with eight bombs when they heard the order to cease bombing. That order was actually prompted by the 500th "Rough Riders," who had dropped their bombs on friendly troops. The 499th "Bats Out of Hell" received the order to cease bombing only twenty seconds before it was ready to release its bombs. Two of the planes didn't receive the order, one (the Jayhawk) because its radio had been shot out, and the other because the pilot had switched to the interphone for final corrections. They dropped their bombs on the west dispersal area. Two men were killed and three were wounded before George at GANGWAY could stop the bombing. In all fairness, Company E, which sustained the casualties, had advanced further than their assigned position.

The not-so-excellent bomb results were blamed on poor radio communications, the sudden change in target, and a bad error by one squadron. The 13th and the 90th saved the day with their A-20s when they hit the marshy area along Porharmenemen Creek. The radio calls from GANGWAY were weak, but a fighter control station (SAUCEPAN) picked up the signal and relayed it to the two bomb groups. They made dry runs first, in order to locate the target, and then unloaded with seventy 500-pound bombs and 20,000 rounds of strafing.

The day's aerial activity wasn't over. Eight P-47s from the 340th Fighter Squadron strafed the coast northeast of Momote at 1530, followed by sixteen P-38s from the 433rd Fighter Squadron, strafing enemy gun positions along Hyane Harbor. The bombing on Momote for the day totaled more than sixty tons and some 60,000 rounds of ammunition were expended.

Within an hour after starting their attack, the 5th Cavalry had secured the expanded perimeter. They started digging in, with aid of bulldozers and the trenching machine. Graders started grading the topsoil from the airstrip. To block possible enemy landings from across Hyane Harbor, two antiaircraft batteries and Company E of the 592nd Boat and Shore Regiment defended the shore. The Seabees formed an inner defense line to the west and northwest of the brigade command post. The north and northwest sectors, considered critical by General Chase, were manned by Lt. Henshaw, of Company G and F of the 2nd Squadron, under Col. Lobit. Their positions were secured by interlocking bands of machine-gun fire while the 1st Squadron, commanded by Col. Hoffman, dug in on their left flank.

As planned, the field artillery positions were placed some 500 yards to the rear, south of the jetties and shielded by revetments. The battalion front formed a half moon, enabling one battery to cover each flank of the beachhead and all three batteries to fire in front of the central sector and at vital points and expected enemy attack routes. The three batteries were placed so that each, without changing position, was able to cover not only its own sector but also the sectors on both sides. General Chase assigned the Seabees the defense of the west and north flank toward the Native Skidway behind Companies F and G. With their trencher, they dug six trenches. Ten men were stationed in each trench as an inner line of defense. The 99th Field Artillery was placed some 500 yards south of the command post at the entrance to Jamandilai Point, although the point had been cleared.

At 1700, the LSTs were ready to return to New Guinea. General Chase called for a naval bombardment on the north point of Hyane Harbor and the Skidway area. The destroyers Warramunga, Mullaney, Ammen, and Bush moved into the area and fired fifty rounds each on the enemy positions, but the LSTs still received heavy machine-gun fire when they started to leave. Since their guns were located on the front of their ships, they backed out of their beachhead with their guns blazing.

Based on captured documents, the 5th Cavalry expected a severe counterattack the night of March 2nd. At 2100, the counterattack happened, but it wasn't as severe as expected and was repelled. Despite the elaborate defensive measures they had taken, the troops could still expect the Japanese to infiltrate the perimeter. The brush and undergrowth made that impossible to prevent. The snipers would need to be cleared again in the morning.

The men who had landed on Feb. 29th were exhausted. They'd had no rest and little if any sleep for nearly eighty hours. If they weren't alert, they could easily be killed. Throughout the night, the troops were kept awake by occasional rifle fire and, once in awhile, the clatter of machine-gun fire. They could tell the difference between American fire and that of the Japanese. Japanese rifle and machine-gun fire had a high pitch, sort of like a soprano.

IN KANSAS, Cleo went to the mailbox daily to look for letters from George and to read the Girard Press and Pittsburg Sun newspapers. George wrote almost daily. Sometimes it would be just a short note, and other times the censors had cut a lot from his letters. All his letters said "Somewhere in New Guinea," since he couldn't tell where he was located. An unknown author from the New York Times commented on the Admiralty Island invasion in an article:

The Admiralty Islands

In another one of those daring surprise moves made possible by American superiority in the southwest Pacific and the virtual blinding of Japanese reconnaissance, American forces, under the personal supervision of General MacArthur, have leaped forward more than 250 miles and landed on the Admiralty Islands. This new thrust comes on top of the conquest of the Marshalls, the blows against Truk and the Marianas, and the continuous pounding of most Japanese bases in that region. In the present stage of operations, the American task is made easier because the Navy and the Air Force dominate both the sea and sky lanes along which they move almost at will, if not without risk. And since they dominate the roads, they are able to convert the innumerable islands that were to serve Japan as impregnable fortresses and unsinkable aircraft carriers into death traps for the Japanese garrisons.

The Admiralty Islands are of particular importance because they are like a cork whose possession enables General MacArthur to seal the whole Bismarck Sea and trap all Japanese south of them by cutting their supply lines. Though there is evidence that the Japanese command had begun to evacuate some of the endangered troops, the Japanese remaining in the trap are still estimated at more than 70,000. They may still be able to sneak in some supplies by submarine, and some may be able to sneak away, but the great majority would seem to be doomed. And in that trap lies the main Japanese base of the southwest Pacific—Rabaul.

But possession of the Admiralty Islands provides even greater strategic advantages. The islands are only 610 miles from Truk, which in turn is only 700 miles from Eniwetok. This suggests the prospect that the Japanese "Pearl Harbor" will be soon in the midst of an aerial pincer offensive. The islands also dominate the sea approaches to the main Japanese bases on the north shore of New Guinea, Wewak and Madang, a fact which should greatly facilitate their capture by the Australian and American forces now moving against them. Their elimination would carry General MacArthur well along on the road toward the Philippines.

At the same time it is necessary to keep in mind that we are still fighting only at the outposts of Japanese power, and that we still have to engage the bulk of the Japanese land and naval forces. Japan appears to be ready to sacrifice the outposts because her great shipping losses make it difficult to supply them. But the closer we advance to Japan, the shorter become her communication lines, and the longer become our own. And there is still the Japanese fleet, weakened perhaps, but still powerful. It would be dangerous to take it lightly, or to assume that it will always hide. The tricky Japanese mind works along jujitsu principles, seeking to take advantage of the opponent's very strength and weight to overcome him. There can be little doubt that Japanese land and naval forces are in wait somewhere, trying to catch us off our guard. But Pearl Harbor has taught us a costly lesson, and in Washington, General Vandergrift gives assurance that our commanders understand the Japanese mentality and do not intend to be fooled.

D + 3, Friday, March 3, 1944; Los Negros Island

The entire cavalry regiment jumped to life just before daylight from the ack-ack of machine-guns and a barrage of rifle fire, followed by the unleashing of 300 rounds of artillery fire. The firing on the south beach stopped as daylight approached. About fifty Japanese had crossed the harbor using inflated life belts.

As the sun crept higher in the east, the cavalry troops started looking for snipers. They sprayed the trees with their BARs and tommy guns. They threw grenades into empty pillboxes and fired into brush where infiltrators might have hidden. The beach and surf was littered with 147 more dead Japanese, and many that had been killed earlier had yet to be buried. The smell of death permeated the island, but the cavalry troops didn't smell much better, since they were caked in body odor from wearing the same mud-crusted fatigues since they had landed.

While the cavalry troops were busy clearing the perimeter of infiltrators and snipers, the Seabees started their work. The Seabees were mostly older, middle-aged construction workers. They could perform miracles with bull-dozers, graders, trenchers, and were masters at construction. They donned gas masks and went to work on the airstrip. They pulled dead Japanese from the brush and bulldozed pillboxes inside the perimeter, but work on the airstrip was the number one priority. While one Seabee was grading the airstrip, repeated sniper fire bounced off his grader.

"I'm sure glad my mother let me come this time," he was heard to remark with a smile. "She wouldn't let me go to the other war."

The Seabees gained their name from the initials for "Construction Battalion." Their official motto is "Construimus Batuimus" ("We Build, We Fight"). After the bombing of Pearl Harbor, the need for military construction crews to rebuild Navy bases became evident. Civilian labor couldn't be used, because if they were captured by the enemy, they'd be considered guerrillas and could be executed. In 1942, a call went out for recruits, emphasizing construction experience and skill. In order to attract men with the necessary skills, qualifications and physical standards were relaxed. All applicants had to do was adapt their construction skills to military needs. Although the age range for enlistment was 18–50, several men past 60 had managed to join. During the early days of the war, the average age was 37. The first recruits were men who had worked on Boulder Dam, national highways, and skyscrapers. Others had built shipyards, docks, wharfs, ocean liners, and aircraft carriers.

New enemy documents suggested that the Japanese were delaying their attack while they brought in additional troops from outlying islands. Those who had floated ashore wearing life jackets were infantry men, whereas the attackers from the first day were marines. General Chase estimated that the regiment could be attacked by a force of 4,000 experienced Japanese. Although they'd be outnumbered, the delay worked to their advantage, as it gave them time to further strengthen their defensive perimeter. The 2nd Squadron of the 7th Cavalry, of General Custer fame, was scheduled to arrive on March 4, which would be a day late for the impending attack.

Bad weather interfered with the air program on March 3. Three squadrons of B-24s from the 43rd Group took off from Dobodura to bomb the road leading to Salami Plantation. Since individual planes were ordered not to leave the formation as they attempted to get through the front, the heavies turned off to bomb Alexishafen. At 1600, nine A-20s of the 13th Bombardment Squadron bombed and strafed the north peninsula of Hyane Harbor with good results. One enemy fighter that came through the clouds was driven off by destroyer fire. Two minutes later, six B-25s of the 499th Squadron dropped fifty-six white phosphorous bombs from 500 feet onto enemy troop areas north of the harbor and strafed with more than 10,000 rounds. Captain Richard Bong scored two enemy bombers on his mission to Los Negros over New Guinea. With those and future victories, he would become the number one ace of WWII in his P-38, named Marge.

General Swift sent a message to all members of the 5th Cavalry on March 3. Formed exactly eighty-nine years earlier, on March 3, 1855, their first leader had been then Lt. Col. Robert E. Lee. The message was dropped from an airplane in form of a leaflet.

Soldiers of the 5th Cavalry:

On the 89th anniversary of the 5th Regiment, U.S. Cavalry, the 1st Cavalry Division is proud of its oldest regiment. Your courageous, victorious conquest of the Japanese-held Momote Air Field adds a luminous page to the regimental history. You have earned an honored seat beside your illustrious predecessors.

This anniversary is not a celebration; rather let each of us make a prayer to Almighty God to care for our comrades who gave their lives to achieve this victory.

Your country, your Army, and your Division are proud of you, as am I—God bless you.

INNS P. SWIFT, Major General, U.S. Army, Commanding

Receiving that message revived the vigor of the 5th Cavalry. The coincidence was timely, since a severe counterattack was expected.

General Chase ordered George and his men to move closer to his Task Force Headquarters and loaned him an SCR-299 radio set belonging to the 5th Cavalry. He was also furnished with a jeep, where he placed the SCR-193 radio. They were housed in a large dugout covered with logs and sandbags.

During the previous several nights, the greatest danger had been from infiltration. Cavalrymen attached C-ration cans to wires, which were then strung about ten inches off the ground. They put coral inside the cans so they would rattle when Japs tripped over the wire. Both squadrons used all of their rifle platoons with no reserves. The platoons were placed so they could lay down crossfire in the area in front of their positions. They again placed men in the outlying area, with orders to withdraw by nightfall. Machine-guns were placed on both flanks, protected by dugouts and the abandoned revetments. Near the crest of the revetments, foxholes were dug and two .30-caliber machine guns were mounted to allow crossfire near their positions.

They placed 81mm mortars near the center of their perimeter and moved their 60mm mortars closer to the front. The .50-caliber antiaircraft guns were placed nearer the command post, in abandoned revetments, except for one that was placed at the north end, close to the skidway. Patrols had run into the greatest opposition in the north. Troop G protected that perimeter at nearly a 90-degree angle from the beach to the west, where Troop F had dug in, with Troop E on their left. Continuing south, the 1st Squadron dug in, strategically reinforcing the same positions they'd occupied the day before. Seabees cleared enough space to allow two artillery batteries to cover most of the perimeter, with the remaining 3rd Battery overlapping part of the defensive line.

At 1600 hours, cavalry patrolling north of the skidway spotted barges, concealed by vegetation, unloading Japanese troops. The Navy dispersed 2,000 rounds into the positions that sank the barges with the artillery, firing more than 12,000 rounds. They also scored direct hits on a 75mm gun emplacement and two antiaircraft guns.

At 1800 hours, Japanese troops were spotted inland, northeast and northwest of the skidway, toward Porlaka. Navy destroyers shelled the enemy in the tree-covered area with seventy-two rounds. Even with the shelling by the Navy, the cavalry was still receiving machine-gun fire from that area an hour later.

At 2020, with the sun setting behind them, the Japanese tested the defense of the cavalry. The Japanese looked like shadows moving about. They fired harassingly and their machine-guns opened up on any fire they saw from defensive positions. The American troops knew it was only a test. A strong attack could be expected soon.

At 2100, a Japanese plane flew over the area and dropped eight bombs. The bombs managed to cut the telephone lines of the 1st Squadron, and their communication was cut off, except for radios, for the rest of the night.

No sooner had the plane departed when two 20mm flares were fired by the Japanese from Porlaka in front of Troop B in the southwest sector of the perimeter. Immediately an attack was launched against the 1st Squadron. Lt. Colonel Brady radioed that it appeared to be two platoons left over from Capt. Baba's infantry. The enemy moved close to the defense, under cover of the jungle growth, and again the cavalry's greatest danger was infiltration. The cavalry's automatic weapons were of little value, due to the closeness of the Japanese, so they fired the weapons from their hip.

Meanwhile, the Japanese moved machine-guns in front of the cavalry, depending on the darkness to conceal them, but their chattering gave their positions away, so the cavalry fired at the noise. Mortar fire was ordered by radio and blanketed the area 20–50 yards in front of the defensive line. Still, the Japanese were able to infiltrate to the south end of the airstrip, where they hid in the brush and climbed trees to wait until morning.

The flares also signaled the enemy to attack the 2nd Squadron in the northwest sector. Loudspeakers were set up by the Japanese, broadcasting "Home Sweet Home" and statements such as, "Roosevelt is making a fool of you! You'll never see San Francisco! If you want to see your wife and babies, you'd better retreat! Get out, Yanks! We're only 600 miles from San Francisco and we're going to get you!"

The troops were tired, having been under constant attack or sniper fire since they'd landed the morning of February 29. Their only advantage was that they were now experienced and hardened troops. The propaganda over the crude public address system was more of a joke than a nuisance to the American troops.

The northwest sector was the hardest hit. Japanese troops moved about in front of the lines, drawing fire from machine-guns. Snipers in trees fired tracers into the machine-gun positions, enabling Japanese artillery to spot the positions and fire their mortars. With guns blazing from both sides, Japanese troops ran through the interlocking machine-gun fire and overran the cavalry's defensive position.

At 2230, a lone plane appeared, landing lights on, dropping flares. The command post ordered antiaircraft batteries to hold fire until the plane could be identified. After the plane made a fourth pass over the perimeter and no radio contact had been made, the antiaircraft batteries opened up on the plane. The plane headed north, dropping bombs on Japanese troops.

The attacking Jap strength was estimated at a battalion against a very narrow width of Troop G and part of Troop F. The platoon leaders, 1st Lieutenants Marvin J. Henshaw, Winn M. Jackson, and Jack P. Gilligan, ordered their troops to stay in their foxholes and fire at anything that moved. Their machine-guns kept up a constant barrage, and riflemen protected their flank, but the attack kept coming. Japanese infiltrated the lines as far as the mortar positions and the command post, and managed to cut and tap into the telephone lines of forward positions.

They had somehow learned the names of platoon leaders and used that to issue conflicting orders, such as, "Retreat, Thorne, the whole regiment is falling back."

This fake Japanese order caused a mortar platoon to leave their positions. Three artillerymen were killed and the platoon was no longer able to direct fire the rest of the night. In other areas, the conflicting orders over telephone lines reported the success of the Japanese attack.

A clear voice, in perfect English called, "For God's sake, lift your fire! You're hitting your own troops!"

They attempted to order cavalry troops to retreat, but with the exception of the artillery position changing their command post, the attempts were foiled, since troops could recognize their commanders' voices.

Five Japanese infiltrators climbed on top of Colonel Lobit's command post and started setting up a knee mortar, but Colonel Lobit heard them and motioned for the men in his revetment to be quiet. They sweated out several anxious moments, until Captain Bruce Merritt, in a nearby foxhole, spotted the enemy and cut them down.

At midnight, the artillery and antiaircraft positions came under another heavy attack. Japanese had loaded onto barges and were coming toward shore. The artillery opened up with their 90mm and 40mm guns, stopping the barges before they made it to shore. The attack from the north and northwest sectors caused the antiaircraft positions there to fall back. Surviving crewmembers withdrew to the remaining antiaircraft positions, where they kept firing until they redirected their fire north of the skidway to support Troop G. The artillery, firing on the same attacking troops, pulled their fire in as close as they could to the defensive line.

S/Sgt. Clarence D. Sparks of Dallas, Texas, from his forward position, fired on the barges until his machine-gun burned up. Disregarding the enemy fire spurting all around him, he crawled to the rear, grabbed another gun and crawled back to his original position. His fire was so accurate that when enemy troops jumped off the barges and started to wade ashore, they were mowed down like weeds in a field.

Meanwhile, the enemy battalion attack from the Porlaka and skidway area concentrated against Troop G and the right flank of Troop F continued, intending to break the cavalry defense so they could occupy the north end of the airstrip. The Japanese threw hand grenades in their attack, but luckily, the grenades fell short. Mortars kept up a constant barrage, blanketing the area in front of the defensive line. The Japanese ran into the booby traps that had been set, antipersonnel mines exploded, wire tripped the attackers, C-ration cans rattled while the cavalrymen rained bullets on them with constant fire from rifles, machine-guns and tommy guns. Although the earlier attacks had been stealthy, these were in the open, and Japanese climbed over the dead bodies in front of them as they made their attack, and snipers still managed to crawl through the lines. The attacks on the north were fierce and over-whelming, in both size and frequency.

Shortly before dawn, Japanese using knives and grenades, broke through to Troop G's positions, but S/Sgt Terry of Troop H was able to stop the attacks against Jackson and Gilligan's platoons, which saved the forward positions from being completely overrun. Captain Frank G. Mayfield was able to organize a counterattack and drove the Japanese out. The position was restored, but only a few minutes later, another strong frontal attack was launched.

Suddenly, over the noise of the battle, the troops heard "Deep in the Heart of Texas" being broadcast over the loudspeakers as fanatical Japanese troops charged, singing and giving the impression that they were having a good time. However, the song hit home with the Texas cavalry troops, since they had been stationed in Texas.

As the Jap fanatics came forward, Cpl. James R. Renfro, of Kentucky, yelled, "Let's get 'em! Those guys don't even know the right words!"

S/Sgt. Troy A. McGill,[lix] of Troop G, in a revetment with eight men, was ordered to fall back with his men as they were charged by 200 drunken, crazed Japanese troops, but McGill, who'd served twenty-one years with the 1st Cavalry, heard the broadcast and yelled back, "No yellow-bellied Jap is going to sing about Texas! I'm from Texas!"

Sgt. Faulkenberry, in a foxhole behind him, kept yelling at him to fall back. McGill was covered by crossfire from his own troops on both flanks, but could get no support from Faulkenberry and his own troops behind him. When all his men but one had been killed, McGill ordered the other man to fall back while he kept firing. When he ran out of ammo, he charged from his foxhole, using his rifle as a club against the attacking troops in hand-to-hand combat, until he fell from a dozen bayonet wounds. He was given credit for killing 135 of the enemy in the battle. McGill was taken to the hospital, where he lived for two days.

Cpl. John E. Walkney, of Pittsburgh, Pennsylvania, also performed one of many valiant feats during the battle. His platoon retreated to their secondary defensive position but Walkney returned to the original position and his abandoned machine-gun. He reassembled the gun and fired continuously until he ran out of ammunition. He was found the next morning, stooped over his machine-gun, with many dead enemy soldiers in front of his position.

When Troops G and F ran out of ammunition, they pulled back to the Seabees' secondary defensive position while the Japanese kept up a furious attack, particularly against the left flank. As their ammo ran low, cavalrymen and Seabees became separated from their stock at the other end of the line. At first, Seabees at the other end tried to throw ammo boxes to their comrades from foxhole to foxhole, but that proved too slow, so Cpl. Clarence W. Johnson, of Bay City, Wisconsin, ran fifty yards, with every gun in the perimeter still firing and the enemy attacking, and delivered the ammunition.

The cavalry was able to surround a group of 100 Japanese, but they wouldn't surrender and kept fighting. After thirty of them had been killed, the remaining seventy, realizing their situation was hopeless, killed themselves with hand grenades.

General Chase commented, "That saves a lot of ammunition."

Cpl. Bill Alcine, a Yank staff correspondent, told the following story:

The dead Japs were big men, Imperial Marines, and fresh troops. All were in good condition and well-equipped, cool, tough, and smart. A large number of

them could evidently speak English. Cpl. Joe Hodonski, of Chicago, Illinois, heard
a noise outside his foxhole. Joe stuck his head up and saw a Jap setting up a
machine gun about a yard away. The Nip said, 'How you doin' Joe?' Joe was
doing o.k.—he killed the Jap with an automatic.

Just at daybreak, when only a couple of cavalry guns were left firing, the
Seabees on the north of their line moved up to defend the now hard-pressed
right wing. They arrived as the attacks subsided, but killed a Japanese soldier
who had taken over one of the cavalry's .50-caliber guns. Other Seabees,
ordered to cover the beach, ran into a Japanese party attacking another .50-
caliber gun position with grenades and rifles. The Seabees arrived too late to
save some of the gun crew, but did kill the Japanese on the beach.

At daybreak, the attack quit, except for shrapnel that continued to fall
until 0730. A Japanese officer came out of the brush, followed by 12 of his
men. He pulled a grenade out and pulled the pin. He tapped the grenade on
his helmet than held it to his stomach while his men watched. When the
grenade exploded, his men in unison followed suit. The Japanese continued
to fire mortars into the perimeter, but the close fighting had stopped.

AN ASSOCIATED PRESS article on March 3, reporting on the situation in
the Admiralties, also mentioned the Japanese propaganda. Within ten minutes of each other, different radio broadcasts from Tokyo were made to China
and North America.

Troops on Los Negros Reinforced;
Invasion Began as Reconnaissance

ALLIED HEADQUARTERS IN THE SOUTHWEST PACIFIC, Friday,
March 3—Heavy reinforcements have been landed on Los Negros Island, in the
Admiralties, turning the surprise American thrust against the Japanese from
reconnaissance in force into a campaign for complete occupation.

Gen. Douglas MacArthur's communiqué today said that the original landing by the Fifth Cavalry Regiment Tuesday caught the numerically superior Japanese force so completely by surprise that it was "outmaneuvered into dispersed positions" and the reconnaissance was "immediately developed into a penetration which is being exploited into complete occupation."

The reinforcements were landed yesterday and were reported ready to push beyond the original beachhead after the first invasion troops had withstood repeated Japanese infiltration and mortar attacks Wednesday night. The enemy attacks were against the thinly held American perimeter around Momote airfield, the 5,000-foot long airstrip that was captured shortly after the Tuesday landing at the seaward edge of the airfield.

Fighting with their backs to the beachhead, the cavalrymen beat off all attacks until morning brought boatloads of men and equipment. With the perimeter defenses firmly established, restoration work immediately commenced on the airfield, which was pitted by bombs unloaded on it during the pre-landing bombardment.

Latest reports from Los Negros Island described the American beachhead as based upon a coral-fringed beach at the south end of Hyane Harbor, extending about a mile north and south and three-quarters of a mile inland. A few thousand Japanese still hold the rest of the island, which extends seven miles westward and about eight miles northward of the American-held Momote airfield, which with the adjacent Hyane Harbor is the strategic key to the island.

Allied bombers not only hit Japanese positions around Momote, but also ranged westward to adjacent Manus Island to strike at sources of reinforcement for the enemy troops on Los Negros.

CONTRADICTING AN EARLIER Tokyo propaganda broadcast to China, the Japanese Domei agency said yesterday in an English-language dispatch to North America that the United States force that invaded Los Negros Island in the Admiralty group Tuesday had "reinforced its position" after its "successful" landing and declared that Japanese "garrisons are continuing their fierce counterattacks."

The Domei wireless dispatch, recorded by United States Government monitors, claimed that the "Americans" first landing attempt had been "repulsed" on the south shore of Hyane Harbor but that the second attempt, which it said, was made on the north side of the harbor, had succeeded because "only a small number of our troops were stationed" there.

The attack on the south shore of the harbor, according to the dispatch, was made "under cover of a bombardment from two cruisers and more than ten destroyers."

The dispatch claimed that "in the course of the counterattack" the Japanese force destroyed "many landing barges in addition to inflicting more than 200 casualties on the enemy."

The Domei English-language dispatch for North American consumption gave an entirely different picture of the situation from that of a Tokyo radio propaganda broadcast in China only ten minutes earlier, which claimed that the "enemy attempt to land in the Admiralty Islands was repulsed by the Japanese defenders" and that "the enemy force was entirely wiped out."

D + 4, Saturday, March 4th, 1944; Los Negros Island

In the mist of the dawning sunlight, dead Japanese troops were piled three and four deep in front of the cavalry revetments. Fearing that snipers had infiltrated during the night, cavalrymen fired their tommy guns and BARs into the trees and brush from their dugouts and foxholes. Continuous firing during the night had turned their gun barrels an orange color. Metal flakes fell off the barrels, but they kept firing.

Radio communications had been stopped during the night because the noise of the generators drew enemy fire, but they were started again early in the morning and General Chase sent a message, outlining the current situation and making new demands through code talkers, consisting of members of the Dakota Indian tribes, who had accompanied the 1st Cavalry since D-Day.

"We hold entire perimeter. Everything under control."

Also included in the message was a statement that enemy strength had been greater than previously estimated and a request for more ammunition. Nearly 10,000 rounds of ammunition had been expended in the previous night's defense, killing more than 750 Japanese. Some 160 Japanese were piled up in front of Company G alone.

Reconnoitering the area uncovered the mystery of "Deep in the Heart of Texas." A battered phonograph was found in the jungle along the Porlaka road, only a few hundred yards in front of the defensive perimeter.

Bodies were searched for information and souvenirs. Colorful battle flags and trinkets were found, and also found on nearly every body were 'quality' pornographic pictures.

"These would make Minsky's blush!" a tough top soldier remarked.

The souvenirs also indicated that the enemy troops were well seasoned and experienced, since coins from Hong Kong, Manila, and Singapore were found, as well as British and American trinkets.

Another group of ten enemy troops had committed suicide by holding hand grenades to their bellies and blowing themselves up. Seabee Chief Frank Newman, of Los Angeles, who stumbled upon the site, remarked that it was "the most horrible thing I've seen, and we've seen plenty since we landed at this joint!"

The promised landing of the 2nd Squadron of the 7th Cavalry from the 2nd Brigade was eagerly awaited by the tired, tried, but now battle-seasoned 5th Cavalry. The 5th would pull back while the 7th took over their position and pressed north, up the Native Skidway. Preceding their arrival, known enemy gun positions would need to be cleared.

The USS Swanson reported the events of its trip to the Admiralty Islands:

General Krueger requested Admiral Barbey to transport 1,250 troops to Hyane Harbor from Oro Bay to arrive at dawn on 4 March. Rear Admiral Barbey by visual dispatch dated 2 March at 0850 hours notified Swanson to transport 105 men of the 5th Cavalry Unit, as part of Task Group 76.1.3.

At 0700 hours the 5th Cavalry Unit came aboard the Swanson for transportation to Hyane Harbor, Los Negros Island, Admiralty Islands. Many of the Swanson seamen voluntarily gave up their bunks so the cavalrymen would be able to get a night's sleep prior to landing.

At 1120 hours the Swanson was underway to join Task Group 76.1.3 com-

posed of Destroyers: Drayton, Stevenson, Smith, HMAS Arunta, Wilkes, Flusser, Thorne, Nicholson, Swanson and four APDs. Each destroyer of Task Group 76.1.3 had on board about 100 troops and two tons of stores. Each unit of Task Group 76.1.2 was transporting about 170 troops and five tons of stores. This Task Group would be able to cover the 500 miles from Buna Roads to Los Negros Island easily in 20 hours.

On 4 March at 0745 hours the Swanson began to patrol eastward of Hyane Harbor to provide anti-submarine protection for convoy, which was making preparations for unloading troops. In combat information center continuous radar sweeps were being made to warn of any approach of enemy aircraft or surface ships.

The enemy was still firmly entrenched north of Native Skidway (just northwest of Momote airstrip) in target areas 7, 8, and 9. General Chase ordered a bombard of this area beginning at 0500 hours, which was carried out by destroyers Warramunga and Welles, to prevent the enemy from firing on our landing craft as they entered Hyane Harbor carrying troops. During the debarkation the first few waves met machine gun fire from North Point. Warramunga, assisted by Drayton, took the enemy machine-guns under fire and silenced them.

At 1305 hours Task Group 26.3 departed from the Admiralty Islands leaving the Swanson, Wilkes, Nicholson, and Smith as naval gunfire support vessels. Whose mission was: (a) Furnish fire support as called for by forces ashore, or at targets of opportunity. (b) Destruction of enemy barges. (c) Destruction of enemy surface forces attempting to support or reinforce Japanese troops ashore. The Swanson assumed Fighter Director duty.

At 1745 completed receiving 14 wounded Army personnel aboard and they were placed under the care of Lieut. Sidney Gaines, M.D., Chief Pharmacist Mate John Anderson, and Pharmacist Mate 2/c Edward Engberg.

At 1930 hours an unidentified plane passed directly overhead. At 2115 the Smith reported unidentified planes in the area.

In a reunion of Swanson crewmates, Bill Clancy remembered the trip to Los Negros and the condition of the ship:

Los Negros in the Admiralty Islands, an island no one knew. We had 100 dogfaces aboard for the invasion. We had fourteen wounded brought back within five hours. On the way back, Jap planes came and General Quarters was sounded. We had one GI with a bullet wound in his throat, who died within an hour after we secured from General Quarters. His body was transferred to the Army ashore. I have prayed for this GI for the last 45 years.

The Swanson was a new ship, sporting the latest in naval weapons, navigation and range finding equipment. Crew comfort was in step with the times. Berthing accommodations, messing spaces, and galley equipment had received the grand treatment. But before you get too comfortable with how nice it all was, let me tell you that you'd find about 60 sleeping in a space not much larger than your living room. Also, there were some things that had not changed from the days of John Paul Jones.

Swanson sailors reported on board ship with all their worldly goods stowed neatly in a sea bag. The sea bag neatly stowed with your gear and encased inside a neatly lashed mattress and hammock. Together this made a very handy and singularly heavy set of Navy luggage. Revolutionary War sailors would have been proud of every one of them.

Also, as in the days of yore, no air conditioning! So when the berthing space temperature got up to 110 degrees nobody complained a lot. There were no commodes or urinals in the head but simple troughs, with water gushing through them, of a type in use for nearly a hundred years.

Every sailor was assigned a tour of duty in galley or on the mess deck. While on this duty, he slept in his hammock over the mess tables. There he swayed to the rhythm of the sea. This was a tradition from ancient days. Another item from sailing ships, the crow's nest. A sailor stood watch on top of the mast, as there was no radar.

At 0850, unloading of the troops started as they boarded the landing craft to proceed to White Beach. The first few waves met with slight fire from the north point. The destroyers closed in and bombarded it from 1,200 yards. When that fire was silenced, the Warramunga moved inside the harbor to silence a machine-gun nest that had remained concealed in vegetation. The Warramunga fired at point-blank range while the Mullany delivered call fire from the ground troops. The enemy machine-gun positions were knocked out with a combined effort of destroyer fire and B-25s and P-38s that strafed and bombed north of the skidway and around the whole of Hyane Harbor and west of the airstrip. When the 7th came on shore, the front lines of the 5th Cavalry were pointed out to Lt. Col. Robert P. Kirk, the new squadron's commander, and the 5th dug in behind them for some well-deserved sleep.

GANGWAY directed A-20s from the 13th and 90th Bomb Squadrons and the 500th and 501st of the 345th in strikes west and north of the perimeter in a series of attacks in support of the landing, and the landing was made without casualties.

The response from GANGWAY to the squadrons was, "Very good—right on the target!"

General Chase decided to wait until the 12th Cavalry arrived to attack the Salami Plantation, which was the next objective. Patrols were sent out, and again the strongest resistance was from the skidway. They used the time to again strengthen their perimeter and to repair the damage from the previous night. The Native Skidway took a beating from aerial bombardment, destroyer shelling, and artillery.

All available bulldozers were put to work burying the dead and clearing fields of fire. Batteries from the 82nd Field Artillery were placed to support the 2nd Squadron of the 7th Cavalry in a central location northeast of the airstrip, equipped to place call fire in front of any sector. Ammunition was dropped by B-17s that also made strafing runs on call from GANGWAY. All the available ammunition was distributed along the front lines.

Defense to the north was again the chief concern. At 1600, two squads of cavalry acted as security for engineers who were putting in a double row of antipersonnel mines across the skidway area, 200 yards beyond the perimeter. Despite the beating from aerial bombardment, destroyer, and artillery shelling, halfway through the job, they were fired on by a lone Japanese from a concealed foxhole, but Sgt. John V. Todd advanced alone and killed him. Then Todd and the engineers continued to arm the mines until they were driven away by sniper fire, coming from the edge of a coconut grove. Todd, however, remained behind and continued to arm the mines.

During the night, groups of 10–15 enemy troops, led by officers, approached the perimeter, but were disorganized and routed by cavalry fire. Several did infiltrate the lines, but were wiped out after dawn. An enemy plane dropped three bombs, but caused no damage. The next morning, it was found that several antipersonnel mines had exploded, killing a dozen Japanese. A patrol sent to reconnoiter the Porlaka road found seventy-nine Japanese, in one close group that had committed suicide with hand grenades.

D + 5, Sunday, March 5th, 1944; Los Negros Island

Except for a one plane bombing attack at midnight and some harassing attacks and attempts at infiltration by the Japanese, the night of March 4th was relatively quiet compared to the nightmare of the previous nights. At 0745, B-17s made a supply drop and again did a good job strafing as directed from GANGWAY.

The destroyer Swanson, which had transported elements of the 5th Cavalry to Los Negros the day before, was ordered by GANGWAY to bombard target area 9—the west beaches inside Hyane Harbor. The Swanson hurled sixty-six rounds onto the target. At 0745, George directed B-17s dropping more supplies to strafe again along the Native Skidway and the western section of the defensive perimeter.

General Swift, scheduled to arrive that morning, would be assuming command. General Chase and members of his staff were escorted to the USS Bush, where they apprised General Swift of the present situation. From the destroyer Bush, Swift ordered the 7th Cavalry to advance their position up the skidway 500 yards at 1100 hours. Since the Bush was busy executing fire support for the ground troops, the generals stayed on board until 1600.

The 7th Cavalry was supported by a weapons company and artillery from the 5th Cavalry. The 5th was ordered to advance northwest toward Porlaka. The rest of the 1st Brigade and the 12th Cavalry Regiment were due to arrive on March 6th. The attack on the Salami Plantation would kick off after the 12th Cavalry arrived, so they could parallel their attack with that of the 7th Cavalry.

At 1100 hours, the Japanese started a series of harassing attacks against the cavalry, just as the 2nd Squadron of the 5th was moving up to relieve the 7th of their defensive positions so they could reorganize. The Japanese attack was accompanied by another strong attack from Porlaka, but it was repelled by mortar and artillery fire. During the attack, twenty-five Japanese were killed and twelve U.S. cavalrymen were wounded.

At GANGWAY, following the 5th again, George ordered the Swanson to fire at targets 7, 8, and 9 in the Native Skidway. The firing was reported from the Swanson's Commanding Officer's action report:

At 1345 the shore fire control party called for controlled fire against enemy positions in target areas 7, 8, and 9. Spots were made after each four-gun salvo and when the single salvos had been spotted on the target, three salvos of rapid fire were called for. This procedure was applied to five targets in all. Although the shoreline just in front of these targets was clearly visible, dense jungle foliage prevented observations of the results. However, at least two straddles were reported on each target and direct hits are believed to have been made on a machine gun nest and a Japanese barge loaded with troops hidden in the foliage. Altogether, this fire is believed to have been most effective in driving the Japanese from the strip of land west of Hyane Harbor. From 1345 to 1456 hours the Swanson fired 164 rounds of 5".38-cal. projectiles into enemy targets.

At 1630, thirty minutes after General Swift came ashore, the now-reorganized Lt. Col. Kirk's 7th moved out again. The progress was slow because of heavy mining placed to counter the enemy attacks of the previous nights, in addition to mining that had been placed by the Japanese guarding entrances to the Native Skidway. The mines caused a few casualties to cavalry troops before they were removed. A pungent odor of Japanese dead from the previous night's counterattacks pervaded the road and the entire skidway area. The 7th was forced to dig in after advancing only 500 yards.

General Swift, hearing of Sgt. McGill's heroic effort, went to the makeshift hospital the first chance he got. He had known Sgt. McGill since he'd joined the Army, and went to his bedside.

Before he died, Sgt. McGill told the general, "Don't worry about it, sir. I've been training in the Army for twenty-one years, looking for scraps like this—and after all, I can't think of a better way of going out than taking 135 Nips along with me."

On March 4th, General Kenney had ordered for Salami Plantation and Red Beach to be Gloucesterized—a term that had been adopted for saturation bombing—in preparation for the cavalry advance.

Specifically, his order to General Whitehead was: "Get bombing line from Sixth Army and Gloucesterize Los Negros. Liquidation of Jap forces there essential at once."

General Whitehead responded, "Will give them the works tomorrow."

Other targets included the Mokorang Peninsula that formed Seeadler Harbor. Weather obstructed the Gloucesterization ordered for March 5th, although some bombing missions did get through between 1100–1300. George was able to direct mediums (B-25s of the 345th Bomb Group) to the opposite beach of Hyane Harbor, and heavies (B-24s of the 43rd Bomb Group) to the Salami Plantation. Thirty-five planes of the scheduled fifty-five from the 43rd were turned back because of the weather, but the bombers still dumped nearly 100 tons on enemy installations and 38,000 rounds of ammunition were expended. One salvo from the bombing runs landed 300 yards from one of the destroyers patrolling in the bay.

The mission for one crew of the 500th Squadron became a close call. The forward hatch in the bottom of the fuselage blew off the plane piloted by 1st Lt. George C. Mitchell about fifteen minutes before he reached the target area. No stranger to danger, Mitchell had previously had his plane riddled with more than a hundred bullets on December 26th, had a landing gear collapse after a previous bombing mission to Momote in January, and had made an emergency landing at Finschhafen after his plane was severely damaged from an enemy ship they sank on February 21st. Mitchell continued the diving bomb run, but a hydraulic line burst when the bomb bay doors opened and the pink fluid splattered across the windshield, complely obscuring it. He continued his treetop-level attack using instruments, placing all his bombs in the target area. When they returned to base, the navigator, 1st Lt. George J. Hurt, stood on the edge of the open hatch for thirty minutes, trying to crank the landing gear down by hand. Only the nose wheel would lock into place, so Mitchell brought the plane in for a belly landing, with no injuries to the crew.

Although there was little enemy activity during the night, the new troops holding the area were trigger happy, doing a lot of firing. Two cavalrymen were killed during the night, but Japanese casualties were impossible to estimate because of the dead from previous action. At 2105, Japanese planes dropped bombs in the vicinity of the Momote airdrome. One bomb, a 100-kilo "Daisy Cutter," landed within fifteen feet of George and his men in their dugout.

He said, "It shook us up a bit, but no one was hurt. The Lord was with us."

The Swanson didn't fire on the planes because they couldn't see them.

March 5th ended the toehold phase of the 1st Cavalry's seizure of the Admiralty Islands. The next operation would be expansion to the Salami Plantation and Seeadler Harbor, and clearing of the Mokorang Peninsula and Papitalai Harbor.

D + 6, Monday, March 6th, 1944; Los Negros Island

Sunday night, March 5th was relatively quiet compared to the previous two nights. There were the usual air raid warnings, rifle fire from the skidway area, and consistent explosions from their own mortar fire. The BREWER Task Force had accomplished their initial objective of securing a beachhead in the Admiralties. The next objective was control of Seeadler Harbor, formed by the Mokorang Peninsula and the airdrome at Lorengau. It would necessitate moving troops north and west toward Manus Island and neutralizing enemy artillery positions on the Koruniat, Ndrilo, Hauwei, and Pityilu islands, north of Seeadler Harbor.

The Navy had an added incentive for the landing at Salami Plantation, since Seeadler Harbor was destined to be a major naval base. On March 2,

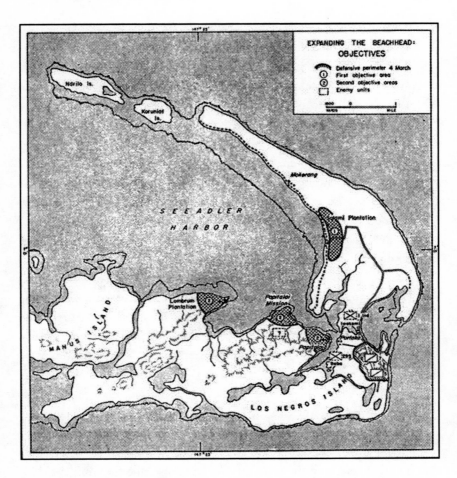

the Mullany had accompanied two minesweepers within the harbor and had received intense, accurate fire from Hauwei Island. The Mullany had asked the Warramunga, Bush, and Ammen to knock out the batteries, and each had fired seventy rounds from their five-inch guns. Although the effectiveness of their fire had been hindered by rain squalls, it was assumed that the enemy defenses had been silenced.

On March 3rd, the Mullany had accompanied the minesweeper again, but was driven off by an estimated five four-inch guns that were so well emplaced that they seemed unaffected by the Mullany's return fire. The

Mullany and the Ammen returned for a third time to bombard the shore battery, but again were met by fire that straddled the ships. This time, it seemed as if the Japanese had even stronger defenses than previously encountered, since their guns opened up from positions that had been unobserved before. However, the enemy was evidently conserving ammunition, since they wouldn't fire when the destroyers were some 10,000 yards away, so the two destroyers stationed themselves beyond that range and bombarded the enemy positions.

On March 4th, cruisers from Task Force 74 bombarded positions on Hauwei Island with undetermined results. On March 5th, the Nicholson approached the same positions in an attempt to draw fire, but the Japanese waited until the Nicholson was 850 yards off the island. Then they registered one hit that rendered a 5-inch gun useless, killed three men, and wounded two others. Nevertheless, the Nicholson reported that she silenced the gun that had fired on her. Subsequently, the Nicholson was credited with destroying two enemy guns and determining Japanese shore strength and gun positions, thus making possible the selection of suitable landing points in Seeadler Harbor out of range of hostile gunfire.

Seizure and control of Red Beach at Seeadler Harbor would enable the landing of Brig. General Verne D. Mudge and his 2nd Cavalry Brigade, scheduled for March 9th. The landing would nearly complete the move of the 15,000-troop contingent of the 1st Cavalry and their supporting units to the Admiralty Islands.

Returning to Hyane Harbor on March 6, the USS Nicholson tested enemy defenses before the ships carrying the 12th Cavalry arrived. General Swift's plans were for the 12th to assist the 7th in their advance up the Salami road. The 271st Field Artillery unit was to cover the southeast corner of the airstrip. They brought with them three light tanks and five amphibian tanks, also known as buffaloes or LVTs (Landing Vehicles, Tracked). By this time, a makeshift harbor had been erected, consisting of ramps with rollers on which supplies could easily be moved to hasten the unloading process. At 0820, Col. John H. Stadler, Jr. started unloading his 12th Cavalry, consisting of 2,837 men and the 271st Field Artillery.

At 1030, the 2nd Squadron of the 7th moved out, followed by a bulldozer, an engineering platoon, tanks, and the rest of the troops. The 12th, having come up to aid the 7th to an assembly area, caused a mass of confusion and congestion. The stench from dead and decaying Japanese bodies, combined with mud, mire, and body odor, was unbearable. Seabees, most wearing gas masks, were busy identifying and salvaging papers from dead Japanese before they were buried. It became obvious that the Japanese were running low on ammunition, since many of them were armed with bayonets attached to five-foot poles. Their support troops had also been pressed into the night attack. It was also obvious that the Japanese intended to fight to the death, since most had bands on their arms at pressure points. The bands acted as a tourniquet and gave them the ability to keep fighting, even after they'd lost the lower portion of their arms.

The road to Salami Plantation, if you could call it a road, was little more than a path through the jungle. The caravan proceeded single file, but was soon bogged down in the mud. Bulldozers were used to pull other bulldozers when they weren't being used to pull tanks, trucks, and jeeps through the mud.

The first obstacle was an unexploded 500-pound bomb that needed to be neutralized before the caravan could proceed. Engineers exploded the bomb, creating a crater that necessitated a detour through the jungle. Japanese booby traps were sidestepped by the advance guard while the engineering platoon followed, clearing the obstacles. No sooner would a four-foot ditch, covered with canvas and coral sand, be cleared before the caravan would get mired down again where bomb craters had ruined the road.

Lt. Col. Kirk was leading the way with his assistants when PFC Floyd H. Lewis, of his headquarters staff, broke through the brush in front and was jumped by two Japanese troops, armed with knifes. As other troops sloshed through the brush to aid Lewis, they saw him in hand-to-hand combat with the enemy. By the time the other troops reached him, Lewis had killed both of them.

Lt. Col. Kirk rushed up to the badly shaking Lewis and said, "Lewis, you stay with me and let someone else take the lead."

Dave Gutterman, an Army medic with the 7th Cavalry, told of his experience:

*I was from the Bronx, and it was getting kind of lonely after the war start-
ed, since most of my friends had already left for the service. I was ready to go, but
I was still in high school. I got drafted into the Army right out of high school, and
I had basic at Fort McClellan in Alabama, which was quite a change for a boy
from the big city.*

*After basic training, our commanding officer lined us up and said, "Well,
you guys did pretty good, and from here you'll be going off to hell's kitchen." And
that's just about what happened. We piled onto a troop train, and one morning
we woke up in Fort Bliss, Texas. We see guys in boots and breeches, and horses, so
we said, "What the hell is going on?"*

*I found myself in the First Cavalry Division, Seventh Regiment. That was
Custer's old command—his last, as it happened. They started right away teaching us to ride horses, since we were a cavalry outfit. They took us out to corrals,
and we were trained how to ride horses. I really enjoyed it, but the first time I got
on a horse I was wondering if I was going to stay on or get knocked off—one or
the other. Being a city boy from the Bronx, it took me a while to learn how to ride
a horse, but I liked it.*

*I ended up as a medical corpsman, an aid man. The way this happened was
that one day they lined us up and said, "Any volunteers?" And then they said,
"You, you, and you." And that's how I ended up as a medic. It wasn't bad, but in
combat it got kind of rough at times, because you have to go out there and get the
wounded. We did carry side arms, but when you are out there under fire you're
ducking, and you aren't thinking about using a side arm. You're just trying to get
the wounded guy out as fast as possible.*

*We finally got shipped out to Australia and landed in Brisbane. We got there
in June or July of 1943, which was winter there in Australia, and it was cold!
We were in a camp outside of town and got jungle training there. Australia was
a very nice country, and I enjoyed it there. We'd get leave and go to town, and
that's where we first tasted Australian beer. And holy cow, the goddamned beer
was warm! But once I got to drinking it, I liked it. I think you got drunk faster
on that warm beer. There were a couple of dances we went to, and the Australians
were very personable. I think the Australians liked us. We had no problems. And
in combat, those Australians were tough. We stayed there for a while, and then*

they shipped us to New Guinea.

We landed at Oro Bay in New Guinea. This wasn't a combat landing, night training in the jungle, and we were there for about another month. Then we went into our first combat in the Admiralty Islands, just north of New Guinea. We went down the cargo nets and into the landing craft. They were bobbing and weaving, and I was kind of scared getting over into those goddamned landing crafts. You wonder if you are going to make it or not. I know that there were a few broken legs, where guys slipped and fell off those cargo nets. But you have a job to do, and you have to get down with the rest of the guys. You don't want to chicken out, but you're still scared. You just try not to show it.

So that was our first combat landing, and you think, "This is the real thing, buddy!" Actually, that first landing was fairly safe, they weren't shooting back much there, not like later. Our objective was the Momote airfield. Some other troops ahead of us took the airfield, so we moved inland, but we started to get a couple of guys knocked off. Then you know that this is the real thing, and that's when you start worrying and sweating it out, and you're scared. We were advancing on a muddy road, and every so often you would see wounded guys getting carried back from action ahead of us. Those troops had their own aid men, so I wasn't involved yet in picking up wounded. We were going up the road in a double column, and every so often the column stopped when there'd be mortar fire or something.

At this point you don't really know if you're going to chicken out; you don't know that until you actually get called to go after a wounded guy. So we started to get hit, and they were calling for an aid man, and just for a moment you hesitate, geez, do you want to go out there and risk getting hit yourself? Out you go, and you just kind of dodge up to where the guy is, and you're scared as hell. I was just hoping I wasn't going to get clobbered too. You try to talk to the guy and tell him he's okay and it's not too bad, just relax, and maybe give the guy a cigarette. If he was in pain you'd shoot him with a morphine Syrette, which was like a quarter grain of morphine, or something like that. If he was bleeding you'd try and tie him off. You'd open that big package of gauze compresses and patch him up. Sometimes you'd go out alone, and sometimes the stretcher-bearers would follow. If they didn't follow you but you needed them, you'd holler for stretcher-bearers, and soon a couple of guys would come running out with the stretchers.

By noon, the 7th had advanced only $2^1/2$ miles when it was ordered to cover the northwest flank of the 12th as it proceeded around the 7th on the west. The 12th made better progress, encountering the enemy in occasional pillboxes occupied by one or two Japanese. Generally when the Japanese were encountered, they retreated toward the Salami Plantation. The pillboxes were concealed and it was necessary for cavalrymen to fire tracers into the slits of the pillboxes so the tank gunners could fire into them.

Also at noon, the three squadrons from the 345th were on air alert over Momote. George had them hit Lombrum Point and targets 1, 11, and 14 in support of the ground troops. The heavies, referring to the 43rd Bomb Group, targeted Lombrum Point and Papitalai Mission.

Meanwhile, the 5th Cavalry was assigned to advance toward Papitalai and southwest to Porharmenemen Creek. The advance to Papitalai was up the Porlaka Road to the Porlaka Peninsula, where they stopped at Lemondrol Creek. From there, the command post reported that they could see no enemy activity across the creek toward Papitalai. Their only opposition in advancing toward the creeks had been from enemy snipers. The retreating Japanese left a mass of papers and supplies that were salvaged by the cavalry. A store of lemon pop was found and shared by the troops, and even General Chase had some. Stores of sake and beer were also found. The troops disposed of the beer rather quickly, but the sake wasn't palatable, at least to the cavalry, and was disposed of "by other means."

Three tanks and advance elements of the three squadrons broke into Salami Plantation at 1630. The rest of the troops and vehicles were mired in mud on the skidway. Large amounts of equipment, ammunition, gasoline, radios, charts, and other items were salvaged from the hastily retreating Japanese. The captured equipment belonged to the Japanese Iwakami Battalion, which had defended the skidway area. Bodies from the bombing and strafing attacks and from the vicious Japanese attacks on March 3rd and 4th still littered the road as the cavalry advanced toward Red Beach. The Seabees had the unsavory duty of burying the decaying enemy bodies. The remaining Japanese retreated across the harbor to Papitalai Mission. Natives told the cavalrymen that the Japanese had retreated so fast that some didn't even wait to take paddles for the canoes they had 'appropriated' for their escape.

Momote was getting crowded with a mass of vehicles and supplies from the ships that had arrived that morning. The Seabees were working on the airstrip and had it in shape for limited use by P-40s and C-47 transports, and they'd started constructing a control tower. Artillery spotter planes had also started using the airfield. The more seriously wounded troops had been moved from the overworked medical staff to the destroyers, and the 58th Evacuation Hospital, which had landed that morning, had set up under tents in a reinforced revetment in the center of the compound.

By March 6th, 204 effective bomber sorties had been flown by the 5th Army Air Force. They had dropped 291 tons of bombs and dispensed 198,000 rounds of ammunition strafing Japanese emplacements. In spite of bad weather, much assistance had been given to the ground troops, enabling minimal casualties on the cavalry, compared to the damage inflicted on the enemy.

The events of March 2–6 were reported by George in his morning report:

SECRET

March 2nd — Japs kept up continuous attack all around our perimeter making two very determined and desperate attacks. These were infantry and some had life jackets on, opposition first day was Marines. At 900L, the enemy, was piled two and three foot deep in front of our guns. We suffered several casualties. 1570 Capt Bobba & Inf'men of Jap Bn Hq were killed 70 ft from our revetment, they had been hiding in undergrowth. More reenforcements arrived including about 300 Sea Bees to work on the Air Field. They began work even though Japs held the western dispersal areas. Still several snipers in the area.

March 3rd — Up all last night again due to enemy infiltration. Moved in morning back near beach by Task Force Hq on General Chase's orders. Now have a 193 in command car operating, belonging to 5th Cav. Dug in large dugout covered with logs and sand bags. Received bombing attack on 900P, but most bombs on their troops. Up every two hours on guard.

March 4th — Had first breakdown in communications last evening when we could not contact anyone due to Radar interference. Had Brigade pass message but they failed also as none of us can operate at night due to closeness of Japs and snipers. Sent message in clear and voice via fighter sectors, requesting air support today. Two squadrons strafers came over at 1300L in answer to message and we gave them target over air. We now have a 299 set on CW net "Q" and keeping 193 in command car on 4475 to direct aircraft on targets and dropping missions. All droppers are straffing when requested. Closed down again at night and stayed in dugout. Japs did not attack. Also had contact with an Aussie station (Tripod). A cruiser task force and used 3000KC as air emergency channel. Had to have task force message center decode as we did not hold code.

March 5th — On air again at 0745 and contacted droppers who again did good job and straffed. Also gave us a recco report. Having air strikes due, but probably will not get, due to rain. Heavy air strikes partially thru and successful. Directed them on opposite beach over Hyane Harbor. Some turned back due to weather. One string, 300 yds from our destroyer.

March 6th — Had heavies hit Lombrum Point and Popitalei Mission. 3 Squadrons mediums on air alert over target at 1145. Called and had them hit Lombrum, and targets 1, 11, & 14. Droppers as usual - no straffing. Balance of Brigade arrived and perimeter extended to include western dispersal area and part of native skid way. Had air raid during evening. One 100 Kilo daisy cutter hit 15 ft from dugout. Felt concussion. One direct hit on Zada plane also strafed causing casualties in artillery outfit. Brigade moved off LST's and seized Porlaka and good landing beach at Salomai Plantation west coast. Perimeter around beach in evening - no contact with them at night. Japs still hold ground in between during night.

- 2 - SECRET

257

Although similar to a diary, the morning report was an official and required record of daily activities. Normally, men couldn't keep diaries. In fact, an enlisted man or officer caught keeping a diary would face a court-martial, and several men spent time in the brig for doing it.

"Loose lips sink ships," had been drilled into both enlisted men and officers. Some of the men of the 43rd Bomb Wing who had come over in early 1942 joked about it. They had boarded the Queen Mary in Boston, gone to Rio de Janeiro, and then crossed the Atlantic to Cape Town, South Africa, before landing in Perth, Australia. It had been reported that the Queen Mary had been sunk five times before they'd even reached their first stop in Rio de Janeiro.

One soldier, speaking in an Arkansas accent, thought they were going to be sunk in the harbor at Rio de Janeiro, saying, "Brazil, you know, was a neutral country. There were over 10,000 troops on board and it was reported there was a German submarine in the harbor. Well, that skipper poured it to the Mary and it sped out of that harbor like a speedboat. It was so fast that it could outrun the enemy. We didn't even have an escort, except in the harbor areas."

D + 7, Tuesday, March 7th, 1944; Los Negros Island

After a week of nights filled with gunfire, artillery shelling, air raid warnings, bombs, enemy attacks, and infiltrators, the troops who had landed on D-Day finally got their first good night's sleep. The Navy had contributed to that sleep, as if in sympathy for the battered troops, by sending enough fresh hot beef ashore for every man in the compound, since they'd been surviving on canned rations for a week. Noise from artillery and rifle fire heard from the front two miles away didn't bother them, since they'd grown accustomed to it.

George noted in his morning report: "Brigade moved off LSTs and seized Porlaka and good landing beach at Salami Plantation west coast. Perimeter around beach in evening—no contact with enemy at night. Japanese still hold ground in between during night."

In the rush to leave Oro Bay, the cavalry took only the essential items they'd need for battle. It was possible that the 1,000-man force would only be there a day or two and would return, so one of the items they left behind was clean fatigues. For a week, the troops had been in battle, wearing the same set of green fatigues as they had sloshed and crawled through the mud and grime of the island. High humidity and sweat soaked their fatigues, and if they didn't get a change of clothes soon, they'd start developing various tropical skin diseases. When their fatigues dried, they were stiff as tree trunks.

The cavalry had pushed the Japanese into the jungle when Chaplin Charles Trent, from Topeka, Kansas, found a patrol from Troop H of the 5th Cavalry that had stopped by a clear stream to wash their clothes and get cleaned up. They had hung their fatigues on nearby brush to dry as other troops stood guard wearing only a carbine.

"Smitty," from Ft. Worth, Texas, remarked, "Chaplin, I'm not a praying man, but the other night I really prayed."

Trent knew that in battle, soldiers experienced every emotion known to man—fear, terror, horror, grief, anger, sympathy, love, and devotion—intensely and in rapid succession.

"Why is it that the cleanest, bravest, and finest soldiers are the ones that don't make it?" someone asked.

"Yeah, like Snuffy Williams (Pvt. Everett l. Williams KIA March 3rd, 1944) and Bill Simpson (Pvt. William O. Simpson KIA March 4th, 1944). They don't come any better than that," someone replied.

Chaplin Trent suggested to the sergeant that they have a church service.

"Hell, yes!" the sergeant replied. "All you bloody troopers who want to attend church, gather round."

Except for the naked guards holding their carbines, the rest attended church service in their "Sunday Best Birthday Suits." Chaplin Trent called it his Naked Congregation and "my finest hour."

During the night, the USS Swanson moved to the north side of the island into Seeadler Harbor. At 0915, according to the Commanding Officer's action report, the shore party called for bombardment of Papitalai Mission. The mission was clearly visible, and within an hour, they had poured seventy-nine rounds onto the target. The fire appeared to be extremely accurate, since holes could be observed in the mission house.

The 12th Cavalry foothold, established at Salami Beach the day before, needed to be expanded. By mid-morning, the 7th finally broke through on Salami Road and reached Seeadler Harbor and the rest of the 12th caught up with their advance party. The 7th was then assigned to go over water and secure Lombrum Point, while the 12th was assigned to clear out Mokerang Peninsula and reconnoiter Ndrilo and Koruniat islands. A second assignment was to attack Papitalai Mission by water from the northwest while the 5th advanced across Lemondrol Creek to attack Papitalai from the east. Three light tanks were sent to reconnoiter Mokerang Point. The patrol killed a few Japanese and saw a number of pillboxes in the Mokerang area, but encountered no enemy in strength.

George received a call by voice for urgent supplies at Salami for the 7th and 12th to complete their missions. The droppers from Dobodura were from the 39th Troop Carrier Squadron called "The Flying Covered Wagons." In addition to their C-47s, B-17s had been converted for dropping supplies, but hadn't had their guns removed, so they could also do strafing as requested from ground forces. The Yankee Diddler had already flown many missions into the Admiralty Islands, had strafed as called from GANGWAY and had made duplicate missions to the Admiralties the same day. Like the linemen on a football team, they were the unsung heroes of WWII. George also had contact with an Aussie cruiser, and directed them to shower Hauwei Island, which guarded the entrance to Seeadler Harbor. Supplies were dropped by air, but not enough to complete all the planned missions.

The 43rd Bomb Group dropped nearly thirty tons of bombs on Ndrilo and Hauwei islands at noon while the 345th strafed Papitalai Mission, in anticipation of a 12th Cavalry landing later in the day. One B-24 from the 43rd received credit for a direct hit on gun emplacements on Hauwei, killing seventy-five of the enemy. One plane, the HELL'S BELLES, carrying Lee Van Atta, an International News war correspondent, and Lt. Col. Henry J. Clagett, was damaged in the strafing of Papitalai Mission and made an emergency landing at Momote at noon as the ground troops cheered its arrival. Van Atta described the landing:

...landed our 30,000-pound aircraft on the bare, 2,000-foot cratered, ruptured and gutted runway. Barnum and Bailey would have been proud of our hazardous arrival on the bomb-blasted strip. Before we came to a standstill we knew we had arrived in the midst of a first-class war, and our impression was confirmed immediately when an artillery barrage backed by 14 batteries let loose as our engines stopped. Our forces were opening a new attack and the big shells whistled over our heads with a whistling swoosh followed by a distant blast. ...Bloated Jap dead can be found in nearly every cluster fringing the strip. American troops are burying the Japs as fast as possible, but the airdrome takes first priority...

Meanwhile, patrols from the 5th Cavalry's 1st Squadron had moved their forward positions south and southwest along Porharmenemen Creek. They captured medical supplies, ammunition, and documents. Their main opposition was four snipers who had been left behind in a suicide attempt to delay the advance. The lack of opposition further reinforced the notion that the enemy had hastily retreated from the eastern side of Los Negros Island to the western side of Lemondrol Creek.

A patrol from Troop F of the 5th Cavalry had simultaneously moved to the northwest shore of Lemondrol Creek on the Porlaka Peninsula. The patrol increased the count of enemy dead and retrieved abandoned equipment, as had the 12th Cavalry that moved into the Salami Plantation. The patrol reached the shore with little opposition. They called for protection from Troop H, which sent an antitank platoon and a mortar platoon. With protection from those platoons, Troop H established a bridgehead, and a command post was established at the point. It had a view across Lemondrol Creek, north toward Papitalai Mission, and out to Seeadler Harbor. Although they could report no enemy fire from their observation point, they expected opposition when they crossed Lemondrol Creek. They suspected that the Japanese had retreated to the mission and the surrounding area.

Using canvas, pneumatic, and rubber boats, Capt. William C. Cornelius, the regiment's intelligence officer, asked for a reconnaissance patrol of forty volunteers from Troop B to cross the creek. While the volunteers were loading and preparing to cross, the mortar and artillery platoons shelled the opposing shoreline for fifteen minutes. Heavy machine and antitank guns stood by while Troop F readied their boats, which included a salvaged Japanese barge, for the crossing. They were to follow forty-five minutes after Capt. Cornelius and his volunteers had landed on the opposite shore.

Upon reaching the shore Capt. Cornelius and his volunteers were met by fifty frantic Japanese in a heated clash. Capt. Cornelius charged ahead of his troops, firing his rifle and throwing grenades. The volunteers trudging behind their captain, yelled for him to hold back so they could catch him, but he moved on, some fifty yards in front of them. They watched as he single-handedly killed at least four of the enemy before he fell from his wounds.[lx]

Establishing a defensive perimeter, the volunteers held their position while Troop F crossed Lemondrol Creek. Medics were attending to Capt. Cornelius but were not giving him much hope. A lone enemy artillery position was still shelling their area while the second wave landed with the mortar and antitank guns. Well-placed mortar fire soon took out the enemy artillery. Four officers, including Capt. Cornelius, and another enlisted man wounded in the attack were evacuated back to the hospital at Momote. As nightfall came, the Japanese made futile counterattacks, but the cavalry held their position. The troops spent a restless night avoiding enemy rifle and mortar fire.

While Troop F was attacking the Papitalai area across Lemondrol Creek, the Seabees salvaged buffaloes from the supply dump, loaded them with ammunition and other supplies, and then motored to Salami, arriving at 1300 hours. Even with those additional supplies and those that had been dropped that morning, the 7th Cavalry still wasn't sufficiently equipped to attack Lombrum Plantation as planned. General Swift ordered the 7th to wait a day for additional supplies, but ordered the 12th to attack Papitalai Mission to relieve pressure on the 5th, which was attacking across Lemondrol Creek.

Shortly after the Seabees arrived with supplies at Salami, Lt. Alfred W. Prentice led Troop G of the 2nd Squadron of the 12th Cavalry onto three of the buffaloes. As they were loading, the 345th was bombing Papitalai

Mission, followed by the 271st Field Artillery Battalion shelling the mission for a half hour after the air strikes. The bombing and artillery fire was watched from Salami, a mile away.

On schedule at 1400 hours, the attack by the 12th Cavalry got underway. The buffaloes had to shuttle back and forth over the one-mile stretch of water to get the 2nd Squadron across. Lt. Prentice and the first wave landed under a barrage of enemy fire from mortars, machine-guns, rifles and a 75mm howitzer. The fire was coming from bunkers and native shacks. Lt. Prentice, wounded just after landing, ordered the platoon to move in on a shack twenty-five yards from the beach.

S/Sgt. Frank W. Rye took up the charge, eliminated an enemy machine-gun crew, and repulsed a strong counterattack. He was such a commanding figure that he drew concentrated fire from the enemy and was killed. The platoon, however, was able to reach the shack. One enemy soldier was killed in the doorway, and Prentice, although wounded, went inside and killed seven more. He rejoined his platoon and redeployed their fire as twenty-five Japanese attacked, but the cavalry repulsed the attackers, killing a dozen of them. Lt. Prentice maintained the toehold for forty-five minutes until the second wave arrived.

By nightfall, the troops held a beachhead fifty yards inland and 150 yards wide. An artillery liaison officer accompanying Troop G of the 12th Cavalry was able to direct artillery fire just beyond their defensive perimeter. The artillery barrage broke up three determined counterattacks the Japanese waged during the night.

In 1988, Chester Hill of the USS Swanson remembered the events of that day:

That bombardment on the Hyane Harbor beaches in the afternoon of 5 March let those foot-slogging cavalrymen loose to take over the place! The next morning a hospital ship arrived offshore, and we transferred, via landing barge, the wounded we had taken on board the afternoon of our arrival on the 4th over to them, after another half hour bombardment at our troop's request. This was on the Papitalai Mission area, which they had targeted for the next morning, while part of their force was already sweeping northward toward Salami Plantation. The next day it was a lot more of the same, with three separate bombardments towards the west—this time in direct support of our advancing troops. Late that evening we and the Wilkes departed from the eastern part of the area en route for a new sort of duty around to the north, escorting old friends of the First Cavalry. A little after dawn the next morning we sighted the destroyer minesweeps (old WWI "four pipers") Hamilton and Long coming up behind us from the east. Within about an hour we had formed a column with the sweepers leading and Wilkes and Swanson escorting the LCVPs behind.

As we headed south into Seeadler Harbor, I could not but wonder if that magnificent anchorage had not been used as a refuge by Count Felix von Luckner in his Imperial German raider of the same name in World War I. I never did find out! We gave the island to the east of the entrance a good going over with our guns as we entered, because it was there that the Nicholson had drawn damaging fire the day before.

We detached the landing craft, who proceeded to support the seizure of Papitalai Mission, which was already in progress. Wilkes and we followed in close covering support of the minesweeping operation. These were about a dozen magnetic mines that our planes had laid several weeks earlier, so locating them was not too difficult. They were exploded by long electrically-charged cables towed astern on the surface, and the resulting explosions were indeed spectacular. I nearly wore out my thumb pressing the control buttons of our degaussing (demagnetizing) equipment, as the settings had to be changed with every appreciable change of course. Just as we were leaving the harbor—mission accomplished—I spotted an apparently nearly spherical object awash in our port bow wave, and nearly froze in terror of the imminent blast. Daring to look again, I saw it was waterlogged kapok life preserver, not of our design at all, with something still laced in it. We randomly firehosed Hauwei Island on the western side of the harbor entrance with our 40mm as the formation departed.

The next day we went back into Seeadler Harbor two times—once to escort six LSTs in for a landing in support of the Salami Plantation captured three days before, and then back in about a half hour later to cover the minesweeper Long while she finished mopping up the sweeping of the previous day. Nothing much happened except putting a few rounds into an enemy barge alongside a jetty over near Lorengau, just to keep her inactive. That afternoon we sent our Assistant Gunnery Officer Ensign John Lindsay ashore for temporary duty as a naval gunfire spotter for the troopers.

USS Swanson

At Momote, George reviewed the bomb line with Lt. Col. Clagett. That night, the Officers of the 499th "Bats Outta Hell" Squadron was able to celebrate the successful emergency landing of the HELL'S BELLES and their first night on Momote with a loud party. To the strains of "Bless Them All," they did the "Bats Outta Hell" victory yell. The more they drank, the louder it got.

Kill them all—Kill them all
From Wewak right down to Rabaul.
Kill all the slant-eyes and set their suns,
Hold down the trigger till yellow blood runs,
'Cause the 499th's on the ball,
We'll strafe till we see them all fall.
There'll be no more Zeros or Japanese heroes
The Bats Outta Hell killed them all!

During the merrymaking, Maj. Julian B. Baird's tent exploded and the highly inebriated officers struggled across a dark ravine to form a bucket brigade to fight the fire. The tent burned to the ground, but somehow the highly inflammable officers avoided being consumed by the flames. I am confident my father was there, but he wrote in his morning report that it had been a quiet night.

D + 8, Wednesday, March 8th, 1944; Los Negros Island

March 8th saw more heavy air strikes on Hauwei, Ndrilo, and Pityilu islands and the Lorengau airdrome on Manus Island. The strikes, performed by both the 345th and 43rd Bomb Groups, dropped some thirty-five tons of bombs and expended nearly 39,000 rounds of ammunition strafing suspected enemy positions. At noon, Lt. Kent, of Air Tech Intelligence, and others arrived in two B-25s, making a successful landing on the newly developed Momote airstrip. Despite the repairs, the runway was never level, causing several accidents. A slight hump in the middle gave a sensation of taking off in the middle of the runway, causing inexperienced pilots to think they had sufficient air speed to become airborne. There were no subsequent enemy air strikes on Los Negros, although Capt. Masajiro Kawato,[lxi] a Japanese ace pilot, flew reconnaissance flights over the airdrome.

The USS Swanson sighted the Long and the Hamilton and proceeded to join them in removing eleven magnetic mines that were known to have been laid by American aircraft and other Japanese mines that had been laid in the harbor. They formed a column, along with the USS Wilkes, and at 0945, entered Seeadler Harbor. The mission of the Wilkes and the Swanson was to protect the minesweepers as they cleared the channel of mines and to protect the landing barges as they proceeded to the newly won beach on the west shore of Salami Plantation. The destroyers also bombarded Koruniat and Ndrilo islands, to be sure the 2nd Brigade would land safely at Salami. However, it was still undetermined whether the enemy gun emplacements on the islands had been displaced.

The 12th Cavalry moved up the Mokerang Peninsula to protect the landing of the 2nd Brigade scheduled for the next day. Their advance, led by three light tanks, met little resistance, but did free sixty-nine Sikh soldiers who had been captured by the Japanese in India and used as slave laborers.

The rest of the 12th reinforced Lt. Prentice and attacked Papitalai Mission. The enemy put up more fight at Papitalai Mission than at Salami or Porlaka, but the 12th obtained their objective by noon, after having had seven men killed and twenty-seven more wounded. The 12th recovered messages that Col. Ezaki had sent to his superiors at 8th Area Army Headquarters. His account, in a series of messages:

Fresh enemy troops initiated a landing at Sabukaleo (Papitalai Mission) by amphibious trucks under cover of terrific gunfire. Enemy strength is approximately 1,000 at present and is increasing. The Garrison Unit and the Sabukateo Sector Unit are at present engaged in a terrific battle and the count of dead up to 1700 hours has been 100. However, morale is high. We are attacking with the spirit of fighting to the last man.

The Sabukaleo Sector Unit carried out a night attack and did considerable damage, but the enemy successfully increased his strength with support of terrific bombardment and shelling; moreover, they have established a gun position by the water's edge at Papitalai and are advancing. Tonight the 8th, the Garrison Unit, together with the Sabukaleo Sector Unit, as well as a platoon of infantry, will carry out a night attack against the enemy at Papitalai and Sabukaleo.

Those night attacks never developed. The perimeters at Papitalai and Papitalai Mission were undisturbed during the night and, significantly, the record of Ezaki's messages to his headquarters ended.

The 7th Cavalry received supplies, some air dropped and some trucked up the nearly impassible Salami road from Momote. Other supplies were shipped around the Mokerang Peninsula by buffaloes. After being resupplied, the 7th loaded onto buffaloes and attacked Lombrum Point, under cover of a courier B-25 from the 345th and fire from the USS Swanson. The Swanson reported the event:

At 1317, this vessel fired 165 rounds 5" .38 ammunition at Lombrum Point. This fire, which was continued until 1344, was requested by shore fire control party to precede assault by our ground forces at 1400. Since the target was clearly visible and the range short almost every shot burst within the area and it is believed that enemy forces were completely cleared before the arrival of our troops. At 1600 Wilkes, Long, and Hamilton departed for the Hyane Harbor area, leaving the Swanson to patrol off the entrance to Seeadler Harbor in order to prevent the laying of mines in the newly swept entrance.

With the capture of Papitalai Mission and Lombrum Point, enemy resistance on Los Negros Island was virtually nil. During the course of taking Los Negros, many enemy documents were recovered. The documents revealed that the landing on February 29th had taken the Japanese by surprise.

After the cavalry attack, the Japanese had been unable to concentrate their forces against the beachhead. Faulty intelligence reports and lack of coordination between units were partially responsible. The enemy had felt that the main Allied landing would be at Seeadler Harbor, since it had been better defended, including beach obstacles and heavy guns, in the outlying islands surrounding Seeadler Harbor. Apparently, Lorengau airdrome was also considered an invasion objective point, since it was also protected by beach obstacles not found at Hyane Harbor. Although antiaircraft units were stationed near the Momote airstrip, only a few heavy guns were used against the landing forces and were mostly defended only by infantry weapons.

A document entitled "Emergency Defensive Plan," dated July 1, 1943 and drawn up for the force defending the Hyane sector, gave directions based on the supposition that Lorengau would be the point of the Allied invasion. Los Negros was designated as the place for a last-ditch resistance. Troops bivouacked near Lorengau were to withdraw to Momote. Papitalai and Porlaka were "to be held firmly." The preinvasion reconnaissance by the Alamo Scouts on the south coast of Los Negros had also deceived the enemy as to the direction of the actual landing.

Messages from Colonel Yoshio Ezaki, the Commander of the Admiralty Islands Garrison, to his commander at the 8th Area Army Headquarters,

described the enemy position. Colonel Ezaki was also the commanding officer of the 51st Transportation Regiment, which was referred to as the Manus
Garrison Unit. The 1st Battalion, 229th Infantry Regiment (called the Baba
Force after its commander, Captain Baba) was assigned to defend Momote
strip and the Hyane Harbor area. That force didn't react against the beachhead until the night of the 29th.

Colonel Ezaki had reported a different story to the 8th Area Army
than what actually happened. He'd either been misinformed or was deliberately coloring the situation for his superiors. According to his report, the
landing began at 0400 on the 29th, and was checked by the Baba Force
with the aid of naval guns. Later the same day, Ezaki admitted that the
strength on the beachhead was increasing but also reported a false story
that American forces had landed "around the north point of Hyane Harbor
and Salami Plantation."

Colonel Ezaki had kept his other large combat element stationed on Los
Negros, the 2nd (Iwakami) Battalion of the 1st Independent Infantry
Regiment, at Salami instead of sending it to aid the Baba Battalion against
the cavalrymen at Momote. Ezaki apparently thought the landing at Hyane
Harbor was a "feinting" action and still anticipated the main attack to be
made at Seeadler Harbor. Even when the cavalry had advanced to Seeadler,
they found the guns defending the position still pointing toward the sea.

The first night attack on February 29 was made with 200 men, consisting of two platoons of the 229th Infantry and one platoon of Marines.
Ezaki's account of the outcome was false, since he reported on March 1st that
they had defeated the Americans and were engaged in mopping-up operations. The situation around Momote wasn't described as serious. Ezaki's chief
concern was the Allied bombardment of his own headquarters at Papitalai.

By March 2, Colonel Ezaki was beginning to take a more realistic view
of the situation. He admitted to his superiors at the 8th Area Army that the
Americans had occupied the principal parts of the airstrip. Orders were sent
out to the garrison units on Rambutyo, Peli, Pak, and Pityilu islands to concentrate at Lorengau. To remedy the admittedly bad situation, Colonel Ezaki
promised an attack at 2000. Elements of the Iwakami Battalion at Salami

would attack the perimeter from along the Salami-Hyane road, while another company of infantry would come from western Los Negros across Porlaka Channel to hit the airstrip from the west. He also asked for air support to aid the hard-pressed Baba Force south of Momote and for an operation planned for dawn, which was referred to as a "land battle."

The planned forces couldn't be assembled by nightfall, so the attack was postponed until the 3rd. Ezaki promised on March 3 that, "Even though communication and liaison becomes difficult because of the terrific bombardment, the officers and men will accomplish their mission."

Colonel Ezaki reported that the night attack of the 3rd "broke through the enemy's first line of defense but was unable to advance after attacking the second line. The Iwakami Battalion was led by the battalion commander in person and penetrated the northern sector of the airfield . . .these positions are held . . . To extend these positions a portion of the Garrison Unit shall attack tonight."

The proposed attack of March 4th never came off. During the day, Colonel Ezaki discovered the seriousness of the situation on Los Negros, which he admitted, with slight deviations from the truth, to headquarters of the 8th Area Army on March 5th:

On the night of the 3d the Iwakami Independent Mixed Infantry Battalion and the main strength of the Garrison Unit combined and attacked the enemy position and seized the southern half of the airfield. Casualties were high due to the severe bombing and shelling. The units were unable to hold because the ammunition ran out. We were defeated.

The former Hyane Sector Unit from the 229th Infantry Regiment suffered two-thirds casualties, is in the swamps west of Hyane and is engaging the enemy. One company of reserve infantry and the transport battalion of the Sabukaleo (Papitalai Mission) Sector Unit suffered few casualties and their strength was not affected. The night attacks will be discontinued and future attacks will be made by consolidating the units.

The enemy is continually bombing and reconnoitering by air and the enemy shelling is especially severe. Situation desperate.

A letter written by a Japanese executive officer of a guard unit on March 6th depicted the animosity and lack of cooperation between units. He was "indignant about the enemy's arrogant attitude," but also disrespectful of the Japanese units. He wrote:

The main force of the enemy which came to Hyane Harbor, north point area, landed successfully because Iwakami Battalion commander employed such conservative measures as to engage it at a rear position. Baba and Iwakami Battalions could not work together in close cooperation. Until 1 March, the battle was "fogged up."

Even though the attacks weren't well coordinated or well planned, it was some of the most ferocious fighting in the Pacific Theater. The count of Japanese killed, combined with the captured documents, relieved the fear of a coordinated enemy offensive on Los Negros. But the determination to resist to the last man and the number of Japanese remaining in the Admiralties meant that the 1st Cavalry would be faced with more hard fighting in the weeks ahead.

WHEN IT BECAME evident that the Admiralties would be secured ahead of schedule, plans for their use for air bases and a Navy shipyard had already been made. Allied air forces had decided to move the RAAF 73rd Wing into the Admiralties as soon as conditions permitted. Plans were also underway to establish heavy bomber and fighter groups quickly. Construction was already started. With the Japanese forces south of the Admiralties left to "die on the vine," the 13th AAF wouldn't have a battle commitment. General Kenney had proposed that it be placed under his command and moved to the Admiralties, and Generals Arnold and Marshall of the JCS had endorsed the idea.

In February, before MacArthur had made the decision to attack, Admiral Nimitz had proposed to Admirals King and Halsey that he be given the responsibility for developing and controlling the base in the Admiralties. General MacArthur, upon learning of the Nimitz proposal to the JCS, became so irate that he ordered work on the Admiralties "restricted to facilities for ships under his direct command—Halsey's Seventh Fleet and British units." Although Halsey was assigned to MacArthur, he was under the direct command of Admiral Nimitz. Politically it placed Halsey in a tenuous position as he was faced with conflicting directives from two vastly superior officers.

In early March, Halsey made a hurried trip to Brisbane to meet with MacArthur. MacArthur was angry over the Nimitz proposal and was formidable in his arguments.

As Halsey recorded the lively meeting: "Unlike myself, strong emotion didn't make him profane. He didn't need to be; profanity would have merely discolored his eloquence."

But Halsey, supported by Admirals Kinkaid and Carney, asked MacArthur to rescind his order, saying, "If you stick to this order of yours, you'll be hampering the war effort! The command of the Admiralties doesn't matter a whit to me. What does matter is the quick construction of the base. Kenney, or an Australian, or an enlisted cavalryman can boss it, for all I care, as long as it's ready to handle the fleet when we move up New Guinea and on toward the Philippines."

Finally, after two days of heated and unproductive discussion, Halsey told MacArthur that he had placed his personal honor before the welfare of the United States.

MacArthur responded, "My God, Bull. You can't really mean that. We can't have anything like that."

MacArthur rescinded his order and construction was started by the Seabees, under direction of Admiral Kinkaid. In the meantime, the JCS rejected Admiral Nimitz's proposal.

D + 9, Thursday, March 9th, 1944; Los Negros Island

George and his men went to Salami on March 9th to investigate parachutes that had been dropped in the trees on the east side of the beach. They were American parachutes, but any supplies or rations were gone. They also investigated several huts, dugouts, and a warehouse area and got several

Japanese souvenirs, including a new map case, a flag, a new Japanese radio, and several abandoned packs. The 2nd Brigade landed in the afternoon, bringing with them the 8th Air Liaison Party, and also arriving to provide liaison with the USS Swanson was Ensign John Lindsay.

Mid-morning, two squadrons, the 498th and 501st, bombed Lorengau and Bear Point on Manus Island. Their B-25s expended fourteen tons of 500-pound bombs and 30,000 rounds of ammunition in strafing their targets. Another B-25 escorted nine P-40 Kittyhawks of the 77th RAAF into Momote as Seabees worked feverishly, packing the runway with water absorbent coral sand to complete the airstrip and construct dispersal bays. With fighters and B-25s at Momote, air cover over the Admiralties wasn't dependent on the weather at New Guinea air bases.

Preparing for the 2nd Brigade's landing, the 12th drove their three tanks back to the Mokerang Peninsula, toward the southeastern shore. They encountered a small number of the enemy, killed two, and cut a telephone line. The lack of opposition, combined with the previous day's bombing and shelling of the outlying islands, indicated that the 2nd Brigade would have a safe landing. The rest of the 1st Brigade, at Salami, pulled back 200 yards to protect the right flank of the landing.

Since the outlying islands had been thoroughly bombed in the previous days, destroyers Wilkes and Swanson centered their activities on Manus Island, sweeping the area by Lorengau and firing at what appeared to be light gun emplacements.

At 1300 hours, 4,000 men of the 2nd Brigade disembarked from LSTs and the Liberty ship Etamin. The brigade, commanded by Brig. Gen. Verne D. Mudge, included the 8th Cavalry, the 1st Squadron of the 7th Cavalry, the 61st Artillery Battalion, two antiaircraft batteries, a troop of engineers, a medical squadron, and a surgical hospital, as well as ordnance, quartermaster, an Australian New Guinea Administration Detachment, and other support troops, including Capt. Eyman and his 8th Air Liaison Party. The 2nd Brigade faced little of the life and death risk that had faced the initial 1,000 troops on February 29th.

It didn't take long to unload the troops and vehicles, but what was most needed at the front was the engineering equipment that had been loaded in the rear. The vehicles that were unloaded first sloshed through the sea to reach the beach, but soon became bogged down in a sea of mud. According to a report from Troop C of the 8th Engineers:

> *It was practically impossible to get engineer equipment forward to the "bot-tlenecks" and many hours were wasted in hacking out new routes. At dark that night many vehicles were still mired in the mud, and work continued the follow-ing day clearing the roads. A route for a new road was selected, roped off, and work started, cutting corduroy. This proved to be a tedious, backbreaking job, as the only available materials were coconut logs, 8 to 12 inches in diameter, and too heavy to handle by manpower alone. But with the aid of winch trucks, bull-dozers, and manpower, logs were placed, sand hauled in with dump trucks and carryalls, and on 12 March traffic was moving in all areas.*

Shortly after arriving, the natives, who were overjoyed to see the arriving Americans (since the Japanese had stolen their furniture and canoes and had forced them to work with little compensation) pointed out a group of fifteen Japanese hiding in the jungle between Salami and Mokerang. A patrol from Troop F of the 8th Cavalry surrounded them and killed them, but lost one member and two others were wounded.

The new troops had been briefed about Japanese infiltrators and expect-ed a fight as they dug their foxholes. The experience of Troop F had triggered their expectations, and all during the night, grenades were tossed and palm trees were sprayed with small arms fire. The next morning, after the fierce battle, no dead Japanese were found, but several Americans had been wound-ed. George, however, in his morning report, stated that it had been another "quiet night."

Although pockets of the enemy still existed on Los Negros, the island was relatively secure. The possibility of any sizable resistance had been removed. The base at Seeadler Harbor was to be a launching pad for the next objective of Japanese holdings on Manus Island, principally Lorengau and its air base. To protect the invasion of Manus, gun emplacements on outlying islands protecting the proposed Lorengau invasion site needed to be cleared. The count of enemy dead through March 8th was 1,288, with no prisoners. The cost to Americans in obtaining Los Negros was 116 killed and 434 wounded.

MANUS ISLAND

Friday, March 10, 1944; Seeadler Harbor, Red Beach

Coming ashore with the 2nd Brigade was the 302nd Cavalry Reconnaissance Troop, consisting of eight officers and 177 men. Their mission was to "sneak and peak," to gain information about the enemy and to reconnoiter invasion sites. They were highly trained in being stealthy, the ability to conceal themselves, and mapping. They made their landings at night, hid their boats, concealed themselves along trails, reported enemy activities, and made corrections to existing maps. The troops befriended and quickly learned the language of the natives. When the Japanese left their villages and disappeared into the dense jungle, the natives reported their activities. Elements of the 302nd were in daily contact with the enemy from the day they landed until the end of the Admiralties campaign.

To get messages back to headquarters, the 302nd relied on carrier pigeons, native runners, radio code, and six Sioux Indians, who transmitted messages in their tribal language "in the clear and with impunity." Sometimes small patrols couldn't lug a radio with them, so native runners were used. Sometimes carrier pigeons also proved reliable, except in the frequent heavy rain squalls that visited the islands. It was necessary to carry the pigeons in a cage with a waterproof cover because if they got wet, they either couldn't or wouldn't fly.

While the 1st Brigade was left to mop up the estimated 150 to 200 Japanese on Los Negros, the 2nd Brigade was assigned to attack the estimated 2,700 Japanese troops that had retreated to Manus Island. The generals surmised that the Japanese would stage a last stand at Lorengau and the nearby airdrome. There were only four roads on Manus, all converging on Lorengau. The roads were made of red clay and would be difficult to transverse in wet weather with heavy equipment. Manus was the largest island in the Admiralty group, covered with dense jungle and swamps. The initial plan was to pin the enemy between the mountain range and the coast, since the interior mountain range provided strong defensive positions.

Although Lorengau and other suspected Japanese positions had been bombed and strafed since the initial landings on February 29, the results of the intermittent bombing and shelling weren't known. Also, the status of enemy artillery emplacements protecting Lorengau that might hamper the invasion was in doubt. The 302nd was assigned to reconnoiter Butjo Luo and Hauwei islands, and Bear Point, on Manus. Artillery officers were to go with them, to determine where artillery could be placed to support the Manus invasion.

At Momote, the Seabees had extended the runway to 4,000 feet. A dozen more P-40 Kittyhawks joined the 77th RAAF Fighter Squadron while their support crews arrived by boat as thirty-one bombers from the 43rd, 345th and 90th Bomb Groups unloaded more than seventy-five tons of 500 and 1,000-pound bombs on Manus targets. Even the heavies (B-24s) dropped down to treetop level, strafing some 25,000 rounds at Japanese positions. They were preinvasion bombings, in anticipation of D-Day on March 13.

General Chase requested George to accompany him to Salami to meet with 2nd Brigade General Mudge, who was finalizing plans for the Manus invasion. George ordered his 12th ALP to Salami, and they followed by barge as George met with cavalry generals and naval officers to work up a tentative air and fleet plan to support the Manus invasion.[lxii] George met Capt. Eyman of the 8th ALP and discussed plans for using both ALPs. The

12th and the 8th were combined, and George took charge in the evening.

George received a personal letter of commendation from General Whitehead:

```
                          HEADQUARTERS
                          ADVANCE ECHELON
                          FIFTH  AIR  FORCE
                          APO 713, UNIT 1


                                             9 March 1944


         Captain George F. Frederick,
         Air Liaison Party Officer,

         Dear Frederick:

                  Just a note to tell you what a swell job you have done at
         MOMOTE.  You got the information through to us promptly and it was
         always correct.

                  I have also had a report from General Swift regarding your
         gallantry in action and I want to congratulate you upon the fine manner
         in which you have upheld the best traditions of the Fifth Air Force.


                                  Sincerely,

                                  Ennis C Whitehead
                                  ENNIS C. WHITEHEAD,
                                  Major General, USA,
                                  Deputy Commander,
                                  Fifth Air Force.
```

After George received the letter, he requested General Whitehead to direct the letter to his men, since they were responsible for the job well done and deserved the credit. Whitehead sent the following letter:

HEADQUARTERS
ADVANCE ECHELON
FIFTH AIR FORCE
A.P.O. 713 UNIT 1.

11 March 1944.

AG 201 – Frederick, G.F. (O).

SUBJECT: Commendation.

TO   : Captain George F. Frederick, O-372630, A.C.
         Officer in Charge, 12th Air Liaison Party.

1. There is evidence to show that in the recent successful seizure of MANUS ISLAND the entire conduct and performance of your party were exemplary. The evidence further indicates that the role played by officers and men of your party contributed immeasurably to the success of the entire operation.

2. It is with greatest pleasure that I note such actions on the part of members of this command, and I hereby commend you for them. The work that you performed was an outstanding example of a job well done, and exemplary of the highest traditions of the Fifth Air Force.

3. A copy of this communication will be placed in your 201 file for attachment to your next efficiency report. You will notify each member of your party of the contents of this communication.

Ennis C. Whitehead

ENNIS C. WHITEHEAD,
Major General, USA,
Deputy Commander,
Fifth Air Force.

Saturday, March 11, 1944; Seeadler Harbor, Red Beach

At 0900, George met again with the generals on an LST to go over plans for the Lorengau attack on Manus Island. As the meeting was in progress, phosphorus bombs were dropped on Lugos Mission and forty-five were dropped on Lorengau. Although the air attack didn't come off as planned, the heavies again dropped to treetop level and strafed their targets.

Meanwhile, the first Japanese prisoner was captured. Lt. Joseph Curtin, while souvenir hunting (a fact that Lt. Curtin vehemently denied.), discovered a Japanese soldier in a bunker not more than 100 yards from the command post. Lt. Curtin persuaded him to surrender.

General Mudge had decided to land $2^1/2$ miles west of Lorengau, at Lugos Mission, on both sides of the Liei River. The west bank, designated Yellow Beach 1, was assigned to Troop C of the 8th Cavalry and the east bank, Yellow Beach 2, to Troop A. After the beachheads were secure, the 8th Engineer Squadron would construct a crossing to connect the two beaches. After Troop C crossed over, the 7th would arrive to protect the right flank and remain in reserve. When the rest of the 8th Cavalry had assembled, it would divide with the 1st Squadron, moving east along the coast on Road #3 toward Lorengau while the 2nd Squadron ventured south to Road #1. Securing Road #1 would cut off the majority of retreating Japanese from Lorengau and force them from occupying defensive positions in the mountains.

D-Day for the invasion was set at 0930 on March 13. George wrote up the air plan, requested that Major Shropshire come the next day to review the plan, and then sent Lt. King to Momote to review the tentative plans with the RAAF.

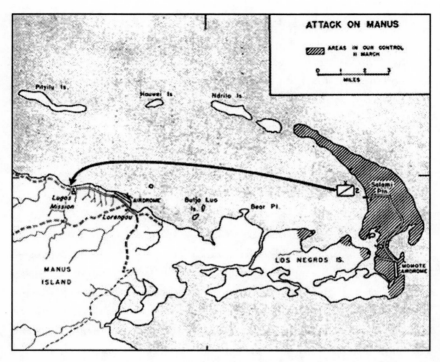

The 302nd Cavalry Reconnaissance Troop sent out three patrols, each accompanied by artillery officers. They found Butjo Luo Island deserted and suitable for artillery placement. The patrol at Bear Point on Manus Island found it deserted, but unsuitable for artillery.

The patrol sent to Hauwei Island landed on the west shore in an LCV, accompanied by a PT boat, and landed without opposition. Unknown to them, the Japanese had planned an ambush. Major Carter S. Vaden, the artillery officer, tossed a grenade into a camouflaged bunker he spotted not far from shore. The grenade triggered the ambush prematurely, and immediately a mortar struck behind the patrol and enemy machine-gun fire opened up from three sides. The patrol was able to hold off the attacking Japanese, thanks to the heroic efforts of Pfc. Warren Pruitt, from Huntington, Tennessee. Although wounded, Pruitt continued firing on a pillbox containing three machine-guns and drew their concentrated fire. Although Pruitt's efforts didn't succeed and he was killed, his actions allowed the rest of his squad to retreat. It took the men $2^1/2$ hours to reach their LCV, since the PT boat, with its wounded commanding officer, had deserted them and returned to its tender, the Oyster Bay. The coxswain of the LCV tried to get the men loaded onto the LCV, but only five made it on before a direct mortar shot hit the LCV and it sank offshore. As the remaining men swam out toward the sinking LCV, the only two men who hadn't been wounded helped the rest of the men with their life jackets. As the survivors struggled in the shark-infested sea, the Japanese set up a machine-gun on the beach and fired at the group of eighteen men drifting in the water. Three hours later, another PT boat rescued the survivors while a destroyer shelled the island. Major Vaden and seven men died in the nightmare, three were missing, and all the rest were wounded.

When news of the disaster reached the command post, another conference was held and the invasion of Lugos Mission was delayed until March 15. The Navy had lobbied to postpone the invasion anyway, since they wanted to ensure that the sea lanes were clear of mines. The 7th Cavalry was assigned to clear Hauwei Island.

Sunday, March 12, 1944; Hauwei Island

The 7th Cavalry's 2nd Squadron, assigned to occupy Hauwei Island, was moved from their position at Lombrum Point on Los Negros when the 12th Cavalry relieved them from that duty. In the afternoon, Troop F, with artillery personnel, moved to Butjo Luo, which was unoccupied. The 5th Army Air Force had scheduled most of its planes to other targets and the only bombing was by planes of the 345th, which dropped fifty-two 500-pound bombs on Lorengau and strafed with 18,000 rounds. George's attempts to get air cover for the landing on Hauwei that would happen later in the afternoon failed. At the last minute, he was able to arrange for six P-40 Kittyhawks from the RAAF 77th Fighter Squadron, stationed at Momote, to bomb and strafe before the landing.

George accompanied the 7th to their landing and transmitted instructions over their artillery net to Lt. King, who then relayed the messages to the planes. The system worked. Destroyers and artillery from the 61st Field Artillery Battalion, stationed at Mokerang Point, also shelled the island before the landing, but many of the cavalrymen reported the covering fire wasn't accurate, since missiles fell short, into the sea. During the shelling and bombing, the Japanese set up star shells, the American signal that bombs and shelling were falling on their own troops. The only problem with the ploy was that the Americans hadn't yet landed and weren't on the island, so the attempt at foolery didn't work.

At 1400 hours, Troop E attacked from the west shore near, where the reconnaissance patrol had landed the day before, while Troop G landed on the south beach. Both troops were pinned down by heavy fire, losing three men and having ten others wounded. Troop H landed shortly after Troop E and set up mortars, allowing the men to move east across the island about 300 yards, but still 1,000 yards from the eastern shore. Meanwhile, Troop G couldn't move forward due to the heavy enemy fire. Contact broke down between Troops E and G, so Col. Kirk pulled Troop E back and dug in for the night. After getting his report, General Mudge arrived at 1600 on Hauwei. He ordered Troop C to land at 1800 and take up a support position. He also arranged for a tank to dislodge the Japanese bunkers.

George returned to Salami and met with Maj. Shropshire, who approved the air plans George had worked up. Shropshire stayed overnight and planned to leave the next day to take the plans back to 5th Army Air Force for approval.

During the night, there was harassing enemy fire from Pityilu Island, but it caused no damage. The American 61st Field Artillery at Mokerang Point shelled 1,000 rounds onto the enemy positions, sometimes within 100 yards of their own line.

On March 12th the *New York Times* ran an article by Frank L. Kluckhohn, accompanied by a map depicting the location of Japan's areas of control. The location of battle areas from the north, near the end of the Alaska Aleutian Chain, China, Burma, and the Central Pacific at Wake were also on the map. In the south, the Allies controlled the southwest coast and a portion of New Guinea and the southern Solomon Islands. Japan controlled New Britain, the northern Solomon Islands, and east nearly to the Gilbert and Marshall islands. Allied control of Los Negros in the Admiralty Islands was illustrated as a spear in the belly of Japan's control, since Japan controlled the areas in the east, north, and west.

MacArthur Tightens the Net on Japanese in the South
At the Same Time He is Advancing Toward His Real Goal, the Philippines
By Frank L. Kluckhohn
By Wireless to the New York Times

ALLIED HEADQUARTERS IN THE SOUTHWEST PACIFIC, March 11—The American net this week stretched out steadily toward the Philippines, our next major objective on the way to the China coast and the defeat of Japan.

General MacArthur announced that, although the fighting is still proceeding, a base is already being constructed on Los Negros Island in the Admiralties for further forward moves. Naval vessels shelled into silence Japanese land batteries which had made the excellent harbor difficult to employ.

On the New Guinea coast completion of new forward air bases has made the Japanese withdraw most of their bombers and fighters from Wewak to Hollandia in Dutch New Guinea.

Long-embattled New Guinea has little romantic appeal and most of us forget it is more of a semi-continent than a typical Pacific Island. Thus the movement of elements of the Thirty-second American Division up the coast beyond Saidor, as may be the case with subsequent advances up this jungle shoreline, received relatively little notice. Yet from Manowkari, Dutch New Guinea, it is only 800 miles to Davao in the Philippines.

Brief Breathing Space

In the Central Pacific, where the Navy moved far more rapidly than anyone expected, there was a breathing space while supply lines were reorganized for fur-

ther moves, possibly in the direction of Guam, Ponape Island, only 400 miles from Truk, came in, however, for further bombing from the air, while some by-passed Japanese islands were also subjected to aerial pounding.

It seems obvious that, although our firm foothold assures complete control of the Admiralties within the next few days, thus flanking Rabaul and the Bismarck's and although the Navy is in possession of Eniwetok Atoll and is thus in position to move on Truk, more must be done to tighten the net around Truk in order either fully to neutralize or capture it.

In other words, if Truk could be struck regularly by planes and attacked by ships based on some such points as Ponape and the neighborhood of Rabaul, it could offer no threat as we move by it, or it could fall easier to a direct assault.

The Admiralties affair signaled a lesson that was overdue. While planes and ships cut off Japanese ground forces from new supplies these still must be reckoned with if we need the points they hold as sea and air bases for further advances. In the Admiralties we found shore guns in concrete emplacements, which put up strong opposition, even without aerial or naval support.

Truk Strongly Held

This is by way of saying that Truk is still strongly held and probably will be for months until the supplies dwindle or we tighten our net around it. This is also true to a lesser extent of Rabaul.

In the southwest and the south Pacific areas, the work of reducing and eventually eliminating the estimated 72,000 isolated Japanese has been quietly going on with great intensity. The Marine heroes of Guadalcanal who landed on Cape Gloucester on New Britain some weeks ago and who overcame opposition by killing a thousand Japanese then worked up the coast against dwindling opposition, and made an amphibious landing on Talasea Peninsula, 180 miles south of Rabaul.

Infantry and Bushmasters fanned out from Arawe on the south coast of New Britain toward Gasmata. Planes with heavy loads of bombs continually bombarded Rabaul and various installations on New Ireland and Bougainville. Warship shells and speedy motor torpedo boats—PT's—played havoc with enemy concentrations, installations and shipping wherever these could be found.

While our planes on numerous daily missions fly over hundreds of square miles of territory, the Nipponese now see none of their planes in the sky—a fact that must be discouraging to even the best of soldiers. There was one weak strike in the Admiralties by a handful of planes, which took advantage of bad weather to come from New Guinea.

In the Admiralties fighting alone, 3,000 to 4,000 Japanese have been killed or wounded in what amounts to a mass slaughter. Once again it was found that the Japanese react badly to the unexpected. It was perhaps significant that in the Admiralties again no capital ships or aircraft carriers were present.

Pointless in Appearance Only

During the next few weeks, in both the south and central Pacific, seemingly pointless fighting far behind our advance positions will continue. But it all fits into the pattern of eliminating enemy pockets of resistance that were left behind reorganizing supply lines—a nightmare of the Pacific war—and completing base airstrips and harbors for the next big moves.

Come hell or high water, General MacArthur is determined to get back to the Philippines as quickly as possible and cut the main Japanese supply lines southward as fast as he can.

Monday, March 13, 1944; Salami, Los Negros

At 0900, the medium tank General Mudge promised arrived at Hauwei. Troops C, E, and G attacked at 1000 hours, following the tank. The 302nd Reconnaissance Platoon provided additional support and the Navy shelled enemy bunkers along the beach. Advancing in a perpendicular line, the troops crossed the 1,300-yard by 400-yard Hauwei Island. The troops were caught in crossfire as the enemy fought furiously, using snipers hidden in bunkers and brush. Sniper fire was accurate, felling two troopers and wounding eight, all with shots directly to the head or chest. One bunker was so well constructed that it withstood four direct mortar hits before finally being knocked out with an additional four 75mm point-blank hits from the tank. Again the fighting was kill or be killed, and no quarter given. If the Japanese didn't accomplish their objectives, they committed suicide. The battle finally ended at noon, with eight cavalrymen killed, forty-six wounded, and forty-three Japanese Navy personnel killed, but, of course, no Japanese prisoners were taken. The Americans were able to salvage a 5-inch gun and a range finder from the captured equipment.

By mid-afternoon, the 61st and 271st Field Artillery Battalions were starting emplacements of their 105mm and mortar batteries on Hauwei Island. Combined with the artillery batteries of the 99th on Butjo Luo they would be able to give close support to the landing troops on March 15th.

Meanwhile, on Los Negros, the 1st Brigade's 5th Cavalry pushed west from Papitalai Point while the 12th pushed south and west from Papitalai Mission. The pressure on the estimated 200 Japanese remaining on Los Negros was an attempt to make them think they would be attacking west through Los Negros to Manus Island and to divert their attention from a possible landing. The 12th, being placed on reserve for the pending Manus attack, was limited to sending patrols to explore trails and to block the Japanese from escaping to Manus. The 5th could only advance 800 yards west until they were stopped. The Japanese were entrenched on a ridge running east to west containing hills, with the highest named Hill 260. The enemy pocket on Hill 260 would be delayed for another day.

Other elements of the 5th, stationed at Momote, were ordered to move south around Lemondrol Creek to attack the enemy concentration from the south. The wet, sticky clay, narrow trails, and dense brush plagued their progress, since supplies had to be brought forward manually.

George took Major Shropshire to Momote to catch a transport plane back to Nadzab. While waiting, they went over the air plan once again. In other words, they basically took the day off, although they were on duty. One plane from the 38th Bomb Group's 71st Squadron strafed Lorengau at 1015, while a dozen planes dropped fifty-seven bombs and strafed Lorengau and Manus with 38,000 rounds. Finally, at 1800 hours, twenty transports arrived, bringing men and equipment from the RAAF.

Tuesday, March 14, 1944; Salami, Los Negros

The artillery battalions on Hauwei and Butjo Luo adjusted and tested their artillery by firing at Manus. It was an artilleryman's dream. They had a clear view of the area, and could adjust their artillery with slight deviations to hit specific targets.

On Los Negros, the 5th started its attack on the ridges leading to Hill 260, the 12th sent Troop G along the coast toward Chaporowan Point, on an inlet between Papitalai Mission and Lombrum Point, and other patrols of the 12th pushed south toward the ridge. Troop G was to link up with another patrol at Chaporowan Point, but ran into heavy resistance 500 yards before they reached it. The Japanese were able to flank them, and they were trapped on the shore. With machine-guns blazing and mortar fire from Lombrum, they were able to break away and return to Papitalai Mission, suffering two killed and fifteen wounded. They left thirty-one dead Japanese behind.

The 5th Cavalry was to attack the ridges until 1500 hours, then stop for the night. Their attack included an air strike along the ridges at noon, followed by a heavy concentration of artillery fire, adjusted by forward observers 50–150 yards in advance of their front lines and by air observation. Four hills along the ridges were set as objectives for the attack, the last being Hill 260. The first objective was taken with ease, but the 5th ran into sniper, mortar, and machine-gun fire while attempting the 2nd hill. A rare open field in the dense jungle allowed a bazooka to make a direct hit from seventy-five yards on a pillbox, killing eight Japanese. Lt. Ralph L. Hill was killed leading Troop B by automatic weapon fire only fifteen yards from the enemy position. Lt. Wm. H. Swan, of Tucson, Arizona, with Troop D, was close behind. Swan, also wounded in the engagement, came forward and assumed command of both troops. The only machine-gun in action was a heavy water-cooled gun that was the target of the enemy. Cpl. Elmer L. Carlton, of Arkansas City, Kansas, disregarding the enemy concentration of fire, moved the machine-gun to a better position as enemy fire riddled his legs. With the assistance of another wounded crew member, he delivered fire on the enemy, enabling Swan and the rest of the troops to eliminate the enemy position.

By 1440, the second hill had been taken by three platoons. The enemy counterattacked at 1555, but artillery and mortar fire fought them off. They attacked again at 2100 hours, but the experienced 5th held, with rifle and machine-gun fire and help from the artillery that had been peppering the next objective.

George and his men spent the day preparing for the attack on Lugos Mission. He also received word that his air plan had been approved by 5th Army Air Force Headquarters. After dinner, they moved to the staging area. Church services were held in the moonlight with prayers for the troops to survive the events of the next morning. Two Australian guides, wearing short pants and floppy hats, left in native canoes to spread word to the natives to move out of the area because of the bombardment scheduled for the next morning.

George used the opportunity to write a V-Mail home.

Dear Mother and Dad:

This is honestly the first time I have had to write since Feb. 27, due to the fact that instead of going on leave, I took part in an operation on Feb 29. I didn't have my camera with me or I would have some really good war pictures. Someone stole it a few days before I left. I was all set to go down on leave when this came up and so out I went again. We were in the first bunch to land and a colonel and myself got credit for the first two Japs. I got both of them but he was with me so we made the official report that we got them. I guess the job I did was OK because I received a personal letter of commendation from General Whitehead, the C G Adv Ech 5th AAF. It was really due to the fact that I had a good crew again and another officer as assistant who really did a good job. Leaving tonite on another mission so will write more in a week or so. Hope you get this.

Lots of love,

George

George wrote Cleo daily, even if it was just a quick note. She didn't get too worried when she didn't get mail from him, since she'd sometimes receive two or more weeks worth of letters at once. Many of his letters were heavily censored, to the extent that they didn't make a lot of sense. Officers supposedly had the luxury of not having their letters censored, but censors would pick out officers letters to censor anyway.

In March, Cleo received letters that had Japanese writing on them, and she began to worry about George. Some of the letters had only one line – "I'm fine – Love George!" He had mentioned that he was on a mission, that he was probably furthest north of the troops in the South Pacific, and that she no doubt was reading about where he was in the papers.

Cleo spent a week in March 1944 in the hospital in Pittsburg, Kansas, under the care of Dr. Rush, having her appendix removed. I was four months old and recovering from my Christmas operation. My grandmother, Letha Campbell, and Aunt Lavon took care of me. Lavon had returned from Wichita to teach at the Mayview School, four miles from the farm. She rode her horse, Peggy, to and from school each day, as did several of her students. When she returned from school, her evening ritual was to ride Peggy to the pasture and drive the milk cows back to the barn for the evening milking. When I was old enough to sit in the saddle in front of her, I rode with her and pounded on the saddle horn as we went after the cows.

My mother took me to Miller's Studio in Pittsburg to have my picture taken, so she could send it to George. She also clipped a lock of my curly blond hair to send with the picture. While she was waiting for a traffic light at 5th and Broadway, near Baugh's Drug Store, she was approached by a couple of excited soldiers. One wanted to hold me. He'd just gotten news that his wife had given birth, and he wanted to hold a baby. He cried as he held me.

Wednesday, March 15, 1944; Lugos Mission, Manus

The slow-moving amphibious tanks (buffaloes), loaded with the 1st wave of the 8th Cavalry of the 2nd Brigade moved out at dawn, followed by twelve LCMs, seven LCVs, and an LST. The procession slogged across Seeadler Harbor as artillery fire, flying over them, showered the Lorengau airdrome, attempting to fool the Japanese into believing that the landing would be there instead of Lugos Mission. At the same time, four destroyers offshore hammered the Tingau River, east of Lugos Mission, to Lorengau. On schedule at 0900, after a three-hour flight from Nadzab, New Guinea, two squadrons from the 345th, coming in only forty feet above the ground, dropped twenty tons of bombs on both sides of the Lihei River and peppered the landing area with 44,000 rounds of ammunition. Ensign John Lindsay watched in awe with George and Lt. King from their landing craft as the planes accomplished their mission.

"How can any living thing survive that onslaught?" he exclaimed.

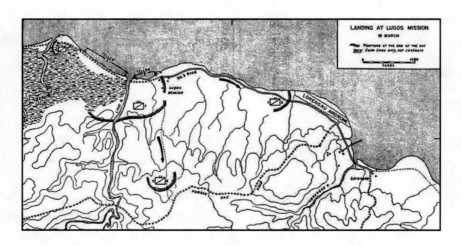

At 0930, the first wave of the 8th Cavalry, boasting more Congressional Medal of Honors than any other unit in the Army, unloaded from the landing crafts just as the 345th cleared the beach. It appeared as if they would land without opposition, but machine-gun fire from east of Yellow Beach 2 interrupted the landing. Two PT boats moved in and, combined with the machine-gun fire from the landing crafts, the enemy fire was silenced. Capt. Raymond Jennings, commanding Troop A with the first wave, rushed Lugos Mission. They quickly secured it, eliminating the few Japanese who had survived the bombing before they had time to react. They moved toward Road #3, leaving behind twenty dead enemy soldiers, while Troop C landed on Yellow Beach 1 on the western side. Troop C was able to obtain a ridge without opposition 800 yards inland.

George, with Ensign Lindsay and Lt. King, were in the first vehicle ashore at 0950. They waded ashore alongside the jeep, armed with carbines, and Ensign Lindsay carried his trusty .45-caliber pistol. Col. Bradley, coming ashore, set up a temporary command post and ordered the rest of the brigade to unload on Yellow Beach 2.

General Swift watched the landing from the deck of a PT boat. He noted the timing was off by $1^1/2$ minutes, blaming the delay on the rough sea. The split-second timing of the operation furthered the glory of the regiment. William Courtney, a correspondent with the *London Sunday Times*, called the landing "a brilliantly executed, daringly conceived operation."

The beach became congested with troops, vehicles, and tanks. George set up the SCR-193 radio on the beach and was in direct contact with the 345th and the RAAF Fighter Squadrons that were on air alert. GANGWAY gave orders for the next two squadrons of the 345th to hit Tingo Village in advance of the 2nd Squadron's drive toward Road #1. The 501st had been circling over Hauwei Island on air alert, waiting for instructions from GANGWAY, followed by the 498th, which took its turn after the 501st had left for Nadzab. They dropped twenty tons of "eggs" on Tingo Village and expended 17,000 rounds of ammunition. Ensign Lindsay noticed that the dead Japanese soldiers were not Japanese, but Koreans, who had been pressed into service. The congestion on the beach was complicated. Wounded men were carried back to landing crafts to be returned to the hospital at Salami. When the ships returned to Lugos Mission, they'd bring the rest of the 7th Cavalry.

As the 1st Squadron drove along the coast road, the 2nd Squadron moved toward Road #1 to prevent an escape into the mountains. In the meantime, George had moved into Lugos Mission, but radio reception wasn't good and he had to relay messages through the RAAF Fighter Sector on another station. The 1st Squadron ran into difficulty along the coast with the red clay that stuck like glue. By 1100 hours, they had moved only a mile along the road when they ran into three mutually supporting bunkers that blocked their progress. They couldn't go around them, because the beach was on one side and a dense swamp on the other. The only approach was head-on, so S/Sgt. D. H. Yancy, an experienced horse cavalry sergeant of the regular Army, rushed the bunkers without waiting for orders from Capt. Jennings or Major Moyer S. Shore, commanding the 1st Squadron. Sgt. Yancy was killed in his attack.

A forward artillery observer called on the 271st Field Artillery Battalion on Hauwei Island to fire on the bunkers as Troop A moved up through Troop B to attack. Troop B got within 100 yards from the bunkers, but shrapnel from the artillery barrage and fire from the bunkers pinned them to the ground. Tanks were called, but they didn't show, since they were stuck in the mud, so the troops called for another artillery barrage.

At brigade headquarters, George called in eight P-40s that had been on air alert since morning. He talked to troops on the front line on one radio and to Lt. King on another radio that had direct contact with the P-40s from their jeep radio. The P-40s, each carrying a 500-pound bomb, started their attack. The second two hit the target with direct hits, so he called off the last two as they were in their attack dive and directed them toward another target. When the enemy position had been silenced, Troop B was finally able to advance. Forty Japanese troops that had remained in the bunkers were pulverized. After clearing the bunker, a lone sniper, hidden in the dense jungle, again halted the advance. Pvt. Garvin O. Presslar, of Rogue River, Oregon, crawled along the beach in the water until he spotted the sniper and killed him.

At 1700 hours, the 1st Squadron occupied a ridge in a coconut grove overlooking the Lorengau Airdrome. Snipers in another coconut grove between the airdrome and the beach harassed the cavalrymen all night long. Two men were killed and eleven wounded on the advance up the coast road.

While the 1st Squadron was battling its way along the coast road, the 2nd Squadron, commanded by Maj. Haskett L. Connor, was trudging through the jungle with borrowed artillery tractors pulling their supplies and ammunition. Except for occasional sniper fire, they were unopposed and were able to reach Road #1 by 1500 hours. They found it was also protected by three bunkers and scattered mortar fire, coming from somewhere in the jungle. They decided to dig in, create a defensive perimeter, and called for artillery fire to be leveled at the bunkers throughout the night.

The landing crafts had returned to Salami and brought back the 7th Cavalry, commanded by Col. Glenn S. Finley. By 1635 hours, the 7th was unloaded and had established a defensive perimeter around Lugos Mission and the landing area. They found that they could wade across the waist-deep river on a sand dune at the river's mouth. Their assignment was to remain at Lugos Mission in case they were needed and to protect the flank from attack.

George was to determine targets for the 16th and needed to call them in to 5th AAF Headquarters, but couldn't send the request until 1900 hours, since the brigade commander didn't know where their troops were located.

George vented his frustration in his morning report, saying, "This brigade doesn't know the value of air support and will not take suggestions as to use of it."

The cavalrymen spent the night in their foxholes and dugouts. As with the landing of the 1st Brigade at Momote, the Americans stayed put as the Japanese tried to infiltrate the lines and kept up sniper fire to harass the cavalrymen. Ensign Lindsay and Lt. King, sharing a dugout, suspected at one point during the night that a sniper had infiltrated their area. They cocked their guns, expecting more movement and ready to jump in case a hand grenade was tossed in, but it proved to be unnecessary.

MacArthur's headquarters issued a communiqué on March 15, advising the public of the current position in the South Pacific.

ALLIED HEADQUARTERS IN THE SOUTHWEST PACIFIC
Wednesday, March 15 (AP) —A communiqué:

Northwestern Sector
Reconnaissance Only
Northeastern Sector

Admiralty Islands

Our ground forces have cleared Hauwei and Butjo Luo Islands of enemy opposition. Our medium air units bombed and strafed targets on Manus Island. Weak enemy air raids during the night were ineffectual.

New Ireland

Our air patrols bombed Kavieng, Namatanai, and Borpop. East of Cape St. George our Solomon's light naval units at night shot down an enemy float plane.

New Britain

Rabaul: Our escorted heavy, medium and fighter-bombers, following a night harassing raid, raided the enemy base at midday, causing severe damage. One hundred and twenty-one tons of bombs were dropped on the township, waterfront and Rapoppo airdrome, causing numerous fires and explosions. Fighters swept over the area, destroying five enemy planes and one other probable attempting interception. Three harbor craft were set afire. Two of our planes failed to return.

Talasea Area: Our ground patrols landed at Linga Linga in Eleonora Bay, killing fifty-five enemy stragglers.

Wide Bay: Our Solomon's air patrols bombed Tol Plantation and strafed barges near Adler Bay. At Jacquinot Bay our light naval units shot down an attacking enemy floatplane.

Cape Hoskins: Our air patrols strafed enemy installations at Commodore Bay and villages to the east.

New Guinea

Hollandia: Our night air patrols attacked an enemy convoy, destroying three 1,000-ton vessels. Two were sunk and the third driven ashore on a reef.

Wewak: In air combat on the 12th we shot down eighteen enemy planes with six probably, losing only two. We continued the assault the following day, our heavy, medium and attack planes dropping 210 tons of bombs on Brandi Plantation and gun positions at Wewak Point. Numerous fires and explosions were seen causing severe damage in building and supply areas. Escorting fighters shot down eight enemy aircraft and another probably, bringing the enemy's total to sixty-five planes shot out of action in three days. Our air patrols bombed Mushu Island and possibly destroyed a coastal vessel in Nightingale Bay. Our fighters and naval patrols destroyed five barges at Hansa Bay.

Madang Area: Our light bombers attacked enemy-held villages south and west of Madang and air patrols bombed targets on Karkar Island.

Green Island

Enemy planes ineffectively raided our positions at dawn.

Bougainville

Three enemy attacks on our Torokina perimeter were heavily repulsed. Enemy killed during the past three days exceeds 1,000. Our torpedo and dive-bombers dropped eighty tons of explosives on enemy positions.

Our air patrols attacked barges off the southwest coast and bombed targets at Ballale and in the Shortlands. Medium units struck Bika while fighters strafed targets to the southeast.

Choiseul

Our naval units and air patrols attacked enemy small craft off Milli Island.

Thursday, March 16, 1944; Manus Island

Early in the morning, Pvt. Webster J. Ough, an engineer operating a bulldozer, pulled a light tank and two medium tanks inland through the jungle as he cut down grades and cleared brush, dodging sniper and mortar fire that was falling around him. Sgt. Sammie C. Mandel, another engineer, was wounded by a sniper as he climbed on a tank to give the driver directions. The objective for the 2nd Squadron of the 8th for pushing south through the jungle was to connect with Road #1. After reaching the road, they turned northeast to pinch the enemy at Lorengau between them and the 1st Squadron moving along the beach. Road #1 was littered with camouflaged bunkers situated to enable fields of fire up and down the road. The only space for the cavalry to maneuver was in the heavy jungle, so they used the dense foliage to their advantage. Aided by a tank on the road, troopers slipped through the jungle and destroyed bunkers with hand grenades. By nightfall, the squadron was 1,000 yards short of the eastern end of Lorengau Village, where they holed up for the night. In their push up the road, they suffered seven casualties.

George was becoming more frustrated with the 2nd Brigade, because he couldn't get clearance from them for the air strikes that were scheduled for 0900. He was told to put it off until 0945, but to wait for clearance. He received a message at 0930, asking if it was OK at that time, but George didn't answer, since it was then too late and freeing them to hit their secondary targets. At 1010, he received confirmation that the planes wouldn't be over, just as another message came through that the target was now ready. He was able to get six P-40s from Momote to dive bomb the target. Two P-40s had previously been briefed to lead in the B-24s, but since they weren't available they led in the other six P-40s. In the meantime, General Chase commandeered the courier B-25 parked at Momote to strafe some hold-out Japanese troops.

As the 2nd Squadron was moving up Road #1, the 1st Squadron was trying to take the Lorengau airdrome. Before Major Shore, leading the 1st Squadron, could advance across the airstrip, he needed to clear the snipers in the coconut grove on the north side of the airstrip that had held them up the night before. He sent a platoon from Troop A along the beach, around the north end, to attack the snipers. At the same time, he ordered Capt. Winthrop B. Avery, commanding Troop C, to flank the enemy from the south. Troops B and D were to wait until the snipers were eliminated from the coconut grove before they advanced down the airstrip between Troops A and C. After clearing the snipers, Troop A was to proceed along the beach and secure the east end of the airdrome.

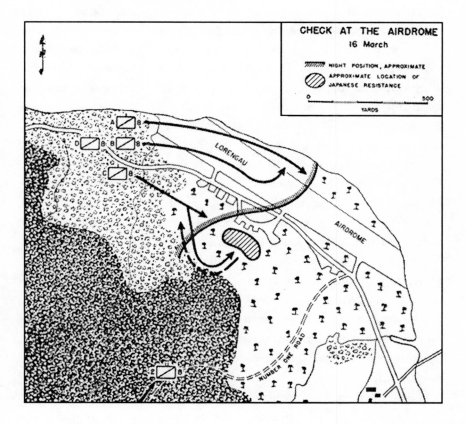

While Troop A was clearing the snipers, Capt. Avery advanced Troop C 2,100 yards over small ridges until it was stopped by machine-gun fire. He directed one platoon around the south of the emplacement, placed his own water-cooled machine-gun in place, and fired mortars at the enemy position.

Meanwhile, Troop A had cleared the snipers, so Major Shore ordered the rest of the squadron to attack at 1300 hours, in the open, up the air strip, but left the light tanks to support Troop C. The platoon leader of Troop C, who had been ordered to move south to flank the enemy, was injured. S/Sgt. Erwin M. Gauthreaux[lxiii] continued to lead the platoon, destroying two bunkers with hand grenades and forcing the Japanese into the open.

Troop B, which had moved down the strip, received fire from the Japanese position and started firing south to cover removal of their wounded. S/Sgt. Gauthreaux's platoon was caught in the fire from both friendly and unfriendly troops. The light tanks advancing down the strip realized Troop C was on the other side of the enemy and that their fire could land on them. They were firing diagonally across the strip with their machine-gun, but had stopped short of firing at a coral bunker where an enemy machine gun was nestled because of Troop C on the other side. The tanks, not having a two-way radio, couldn't call off Troop B's firing at Troop C.

Although Troop C had advanced to the main enemy position, Capt. Avery called them back because of the not-so-friendly fire from Troop B. Unable to contact Troop C, Pvt. John J. Kriger, of Santa Barbara, California, ran 200 yards through the crossfire to deliver a message for the troops to withdraw so artillery fire could be leveled on the enemy. Avery then called for artillery to break up the enemy stronghold while Troop B disengaged and moved to a coconut grove to their north. Troop C reformed after the artillery fire and again attacked the enemy position, but were again repelled by enemy fire. General Mudge, seeing his men exhausted from the attack and suffering nine men killed and nineteen wounded, called 7th Cavalry reserve troops from Lugos Mission to take over the attack for the 8th Cavalry. Their attack resulted in an additional five men killed and fifteen wounded before the unsuccessful charge was called off for the night.

The 1st Squadron dug in with the 7th, occupying the high ground south of the air strip with the 8th on their left, extending to the beach. The 2nd Squadron of the 7th defended their rear, while the balance of the 2nd Squadron was across the jungle to the south, guarding Road #1.

With the troops in their foxholes, artillery fire was directed at the enemy bunkers, along with fire from destroyers patrolling the bay. The USS Swanson received a request from Ensign Lindsay, with George and Lt. King, the Army Shore Fire Control Party. The targets were identified as 134 and 135, bearing 202 degrees, distance 11,800 yards. Fire commenced at 2116 hours and landed within fifty yards of the cavalrymen. The bombardment continued until 0538 the next morning.

Jack Sloan, a retired US Navy Lieutenant serving aboard the USS Swanson as the chief signalman remembered walking past port hole of the Combat Information Center and heard Ensign Lindsay calling in on the radio. The Fire Control Officer said, "If I give you rounds there I am going to be hitting all around you." John replied saying, "Fire, that's where they are!" A few seconds later he called in "Rapid Fire!" Jack stopped listening, but later met John as he boarded the ship, dirty and unshaven, and Jack asked him about the incident. John replied, "I'm here ain't I?"

Chester Hill, of the USS Swanson, remembered the event at their 1988 reunion:

That evening we lay a mile north of the entrance, patrolling almost casually, when we got a request from the troopers through the very fine spotter they were using to "keep 'em awake" in an area which they wanted to clean out early the next morning, over in the general vicinity of Lorengau. And so we did.

Without going to General Quarters, we just used the two five-inchers regularly manned during Condition III and lobbed a few sleep disturbers in at randomly selected intervals. According to our log, those intervals were 13, 33, 76—thought we'd let 'em get to sleep around midnight and then wake 'em up again—35, 50, 25, 30, and 13 minutes. Devilish.

Friday, March 17, 1944; Manus Island

Because the original objectives of March 16th hadn't been accomplished, General Mudge regrouped the night of March 16th for a coordinated attack the next day to push through the airstrip and join the squadrons together. The objective: get as far as the Lorengau River separating the heavily defended Lorengau Village and the airstrip. The plan called for artillery and mortar fire to precede the cavalry attack. Air cover wasn't planned or requested. Besides, the 5th AAF had plans to unleash 100 bombers on Wewak, southeast of the Admiralties on the New Guinea coast.

George left with an Australian guide lieutenant to reconnoiter Bowat Mission, located eight miles west of Lugos Mission. The trek crossed several creeks that dumped into the bay. They waded across them, through water up to their necks. They found signs that the Japanese had been in the area. Natives said the bombing had killed three, but the rest had left when the bombing started. They located a half-caste Chinese and five children and picked up some native souvenirs at Inum Point. They arrived back at Lugos Mission at 1830 hours.

While George and the lieutenant were trudging to and from Bowat Mission, a mortar barrage was laid down on the enemy bunkers that had stopped the 8th Cavalry advance the day before. Aided by two towed 37mm artillery and two light tanks that fired point-blank at the enemy pillboxes, the 1st Squadron of the 7th Cavalry faced their first battle with the Japanese under the command of Col. Glenn S. Finely. Troop D of the 8th Cavalry, commanded by Lt. Donald D. Taylor, spotted a bunker being worked on by the Japanese across the airstrip and macerated it with a direct mortar hit, killing fifteen of the enemy and putting several machine-guns out of commission. As the mortar fire lifted, the 7th jumped out with a battle cry of "Garry Owen" and rushed the bunkers. They fired flame throwers into the bunkers as retreating Japanese fled across the river, leaving behind, in their rush, poorly-concealed antitank and antipersonnel land mines.

By 1300 hours, the squadrons were in contact with each other. The 2nd Squadron had advanced up Road #1 facing little resistance in their final drive to link up with the 1st Squadron advancing across the airstrip, except for running into the first of the land mines that blew the track off a light tank. The final 1,500 yards to the Lorengau River made for slow going, while land mines were cleared.

Lorengau Village was nestled in a valley, bounded by 400 foot hills. General Mudge felt the village would be the most well-defended area in the

Admiralties. At 1500, the reconnaissance platoon ventured across the river, but was repelled by artillery fire from the hills around the village. The cavalrymen set up a defensive perimeter on the west bank of the Lorengau River, expecting a counterattack during the night, but the counterattack didn't develop.

A search of a dead Japanese officer resulted in a map depicting the enemy's defense of Lorengau and Road #2, leading south through Old Rossum and on to Rossum Village, a few miles further south. Old Rossum and Rossum were native place names. Old Rossum was merely a clearing in the forest, located on a small rise on the trail, while Rossum was a village of about twenty huts on a higher hill. The road was a narrow native trail of clay that could turn into a sticky mess, bounded by rain forests, making observation impossible. There were no maps showing elevation or contour levels to aid artillery barrages, making battle planning difficult.

ON LOS NEGROS ISLAND, the 5th Cavalry finally achieved their third objective on March 15th with no resistance. Troop B joined them and sent patrols toward Hill 260, their fourth objective. They returned, reporting that 100 Japanese were well entrenched on the hill. The attack was delayed while Troop C came in to relieve Troop A and bring supplies by hand through the jungle.

On the 16th, the 12th landed at Chaporowan Point, moving by barge across the inlet from Lombrum Point. Artillery from Lombrum protected their perimeter. The Japanese were taking advantage of the dense rain forest and their familiarity with the landscape and trails to hide and to reconnoiter the cavalry. Cavalry patrols were sent inland from Chaporowan to scout for Japanese in the hill country. A patrol, led by S/Sgt. Lindal L. Barrett, was ordered to reconnoiter a trail, but finding none of the enemy, the patrol returned. Another patrol, led by S/Sgt. Rex C. Clark, moved out on a different route and returned on the same trail that S/Sgt. Barrett had returned on just fifteen minutes before. However, Clark's patrol was ambushed and forced to withdraw. At 1330, Barrett's platoon was sent back down the trail and was also ambushed and completely surrounded. Barrett, despite being wounded, ordered his men to withdraw as he stood and fired, making their escape possible.

Saturday, March 18, 1944; Manus Island

Engineers had worked the short stretch of road from Lugos Mission with bulldozers since the 15th, and through the night of the 17th to move men and supplies to Lorengau airdrome. They also worked to clear the Lorengau beach of mines so they could receive deliveries directly from Salami. Remaining mines, although ineffective, did cause some minor damage. They had already cleared vast quantities of mines on the roads and on the eastern edge of the airdrome.

George recorded in his morning report that they were stuck in a "sea of mud," but received orders to move out at noon. At 1030, an officer came up and told them they were to move out at once.

George vented his frustration, writing: "as usual, the 2nd Brigade was all screwed up and not knowing what they were going to do. This bunch is sure not as aggressive as the 1st Brigade."

Engineers reported that the road was ready for traffic at 1100 hours, but stationed bulldozers at points that frequently became impassable. George reported that they were on the road at 1100 hours, but had to stop every quarter mile while trucks were pulled out of the mud. Twice, George cut off the road running through the ocean along the beach. The trip took five hours to drive the $2^1/2$ miles to Lorengau, where the 7th Cavalry had established their defensive perimeter.

At 1600 hours, George finally arrived. They set up shop along the beach by digging a hole and putting their hammocks in it. Major Smith, of the A-2 section, 5th Fighter Command, arrived to see what he could learn of their setup. On the ridge, they saw the front lines a half-mile away and the mortars firing on enemy positions. There were a few hundred men bathing in the river and the ocean, but the Japanese weren't firing on them. Perhaps George's frustration for the day was from not being at the front lines or because of the incompetence of his superior officers.

While George was slogging through the mud from Lugos Mission, artillery had been directed at Lorengau Village preceding the 8th Cavalry attack. Excellent mortar positions were set up on a ridge that overlooked the village, and even the most distant target was only 1,800 yards away. Their fire could be furnished in close support of the attacking cavalry. Captured maps depicted artillery targets for enemy defense positions at Lorengau, as well as along the road to Rossum, south of Lorengau. However, the enemy defense was more extensive than had originally been estimated.

Troops E, F, and G of the 8th Cavalry were assigned to the attack. The 302nd Reconnaissance Platoon led them out in a single file across the mouth of the Lorengau River on a sandbar. Strangely, the Japanese fired only occasionally at the advancing troops. Once in awhile, a trooper would be hit or sink in the waist deep water, but would be helped to shore by one of his buddies. The Reconnaissance Platoon, upon reaching the eastern shore, drove the defenders back and killed those who remained. The captured maps had shown explosives buried on the beach, connected to a master cable linked to a detonator. The Reconnaissance Platoon found the cable and cut it before the explosive could be detonated. Following the cable, they found a single Japanese soldier who had been killed by artillery fire, still clutching the detonator.

When the 8th Cavalry reached the shore, Troop E was ordered to drive a wedge into the enemy's center while Troop F protected the left flank, and G the right flank on high ground. With a coordinated effort and communication between troops and artillery, the enemy bunkers were eliminated, one by one. No sooner would the smoke clear from a mortar barrage when troopers were on the enemy bunkers with tommy guns and hand grenades.

Pvt. Codzy L. Curnutt, of Fruitvale, Texas, and Pfc. Duane C. Irvin, of San Francisco, both set up a machine-gun while under enemy fire and directed their fire at the enemy with such intensity and accuracy that the Japanese retreated. Sgt. Glen A. Prater, from White Pigeon, Minnesota, Pvt. Lee E. Wilkerson, of Lebanon, Tennessee, and Cpl. Vincent J. Zlotow, of Chicago, stormed an enemy strongpoint, rescued five wounded troops, and eliminated a concealed foxhole. Their actions and those of the other troops caused the Japanese to retreat south, down the Rossum road.

By afternoon, the enemy's Lorengau defense was broken, with the enemy suffering eighty-seven casualties, while the Americans lost only one trooper and sustained seven wounded. With Lorengau captured, patrols were

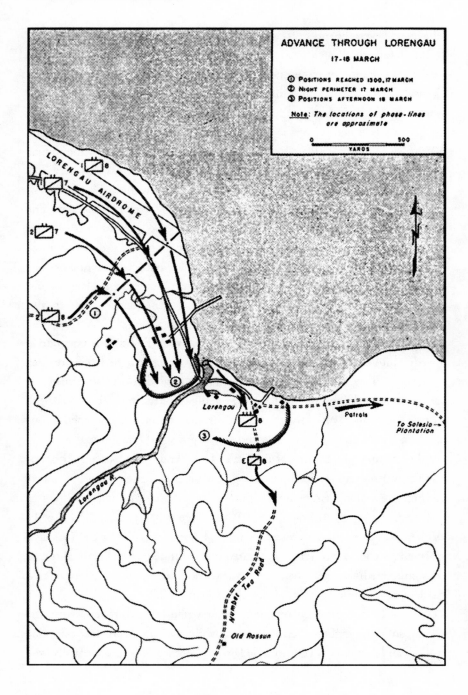

ADVANCE THROUGH LORENGAU
17-18 MARCH

① Positions reached 1300, 17 March
② Night perimeter 17 March
③ Positions afternoon 18 March

Note: The locations of phase-lines are approximate

0   500
YARDS

sent out to test the resistance on the road to Rossum and east along the beach to Salesia.

ENSIGN JOHN LINDSAY returned to the USS Swanson the evening of March 18th. According to the captain's log, George radioed the USS Swanson by voice and thanked them for the services of Ensign Lindsay and the excellent manner in which he had carried out his duty.

Commander Edward L. Robertson was the third commanding officer of the USS Swanson. He graduated from the U.S. Naval Academy in 1931 and was the commanding officer of the USS Swanson from December 1942 until May 1944. He didn't think he would attend the ship's 1987 reunion, and had prepared a letter that was recorded in the ship's Recollections.

E.L. ROBERTSON 1987

Recently I found in my files, the following letter which was prepared in 1987 but not mailed, when I did not think I could make the Boston reunion. I was able to attend after all, and it was my first SWANSON reunion.

Dear _____ :

As you know, I was the first Officer to report for duty in the Swanson, and was her first Engineering officer, her second Executive officer and third Commanding Officer. Altogether I served aboard for more than 3 years after commissioning, having been detached in June 1944, as I recall it in Lae, New Guinea. During that time we had considerable excitement.

I deeply regret being unable once again to attend the reunion; I'd love to see some of my old shipmates. The closest I've come lately was a visit at my marina here by Mann's married daughter, who bore greet-

ings from her father. It was good to talk to her and to tell her about the time her dad, dressed as a Brooklyn Navy Yard workman, came leaping out of Mount 2 as the ship was finally departing and yelled to the bridge to return to the dock and get him back ashore. Hundreds of other workmen lining the dock took up the hue and cry. The confusion was unbelievable, until Manni could no longer keep from laughing.

Since I can't be with you, perhaps you might enjoy a few anecdotes that couldn't be told at the time they happened, for reasons that will become obvious.

The first one concerns our most illustrious shipmate, John Lindsay. By the time the ship reached New Guinea in early 1944, he had been assistant Gunnery officer for quite some time. He was a good one, too, and impatient to become Gun Boss. About that time a dispatch to the whole 7th Fleet came out asking for Officers to volunteer for training as Beach Masters in the Seventh Amphibious Force. Next thing I knew, John was in my cabin with an official letter from himself to Commander 7th Fleet, via me, his C.O., volunteering to train as a Beachmaster.

"What do you want to do, get killed?" I asked him.

"Captain," he answered, "When I asked for destroyer duty, I thought I'd see some action, but we haven't had much. I'd like to see some."

"You'll get plenty before long right here, John."

"Yes, Captain, but I want to get into the real action. I feel as if I were caught in a backwater. The war is passing me by."

"John, I'll forward your request." I told him. "But in my endorsement I'll recommend disapproval, and I'll tell you why. You've spent over a year as a Gunnery Assistant, and in my opinion you're fully qualified to become Gunnery Officer of this or any similar destroyer. In fact, as you know, I've already reported you qualified, and any day you can expect orders. Now, what would happen if all the qualified destroyer Gunnery Officers suddenly became Amphibious Beachmasters? I'll tell you what would happen: a lot of good, well-trained officers would be

wasted. Now think it over for a while. I'll forward your request, but I'll recommend disapproval."

That same day John approached me on the bridge and told me he had reluctantly decided not to submit his request. I forgot about the matter, but it was not over, as you will see.

Meanwhile, in March 1944, the assault on the Admiralty Islands took place. As many of you remember, the assault was made by the First Cavalry Division, which had no artillery to speak of. B-24s supported them in the early stages but their bombing, which was high level only, appeared inaccurate. In fact, the Swanson took a near miss from them. You remember the assault troops were nearly driven into the ocean and that the Seabees building the airstrip had rifles in their hands and their backs to the beach.

While this was going on, the 4 destroyers, including the Swanson, which were naval gunfire support, were little used at first. Finally by necessity, the Army called on us for more and more support. As it became apparent how accurate our fire was, the First Cavalry Division Commander realized he needed a naval gunfire liaison Officer who could keep him briefed on our capabilities, limitations, procedures and so on. He asked for one, and the Swanson was designated to help.

Aha! I thought. John Lindsay wants a little experience in amphibious warfare, and is ideally qualified for the job. He's my man.

John was ecstatic when I told him. As the Swanson stood in toward the northern shore of Manus Island, he appeared on deck, wearing his helmet, with a Colt .45 strapped to his bandoleer of ammunition. His khaki shirt and trousers were immaculate. The ship slowed, the boat was lowered, and that was the last we saw of him for a week or so.

But we heard him often over the gunfire support circuit. He was on top on his job. Target coordinates were concisely given, together with firing orders, fire checking, spotting, and the like. As the days went by, it was apparent the First Cavalry Division was gaining confidence in the accuracy of our gunfire, to the point of calling for moving barrages as they advanced.

Finally Japanese resistance broke, except for isolated pockets, and the need for a naval gunfire liaison officer ceased. We had a message from General Swift thanking us for Ensign Lindsay's services and giving us a rendezvous for picking him up.

What we found out later was that John was not exactly living in style ashore. Most of the time, his headquarters was a foxhole in the jungle front lines, which he had to dig himself. There was usually six inches of water in it because of the frequent rain, and the mosquitoes tormented him twenty-four hours a day. He subsisted on 2 C-rations a day, and his two packs of Luckies were soon gone. Worst of all was the night—both sides fired at anything that moved, so he had to stay in the foxhole with his head down from 6 PM to 6 AM. And it was not equipped with a latrine. Thus it was not long before he began to miss his comfortable bunk and his three hearty wardroom meals aboard the Swanson.

I couldn't believe what my binoculars showed me as the boat bringing John back to the ship approached. He was slouched over in the stern with his helmet in his lap, his hair disheveled. He was covered with mud from head to foot, his clothing was torn, and he apparently hadn't shaved since leaving the ship. He was so weak that he needed help getting up the ladder we put over the side for him.

To my surprise, he came directly to the bridge, where I was.

"Captain", he said, "I apologize for coming on the bridge looking like this, but I just wanted to tell you that I don't want to be a Beachmaster!"

That evening he came down with malaria, but fortunately, he was on his feet in a few days.

I've seen John several times in the past thirty years, and we've both laughed about his tour with the Army.

Lt. Jack Sloan also remembered John Lindsay's incident ashore:

I recall answering one of John Lindsay's calls for fire as the Japs were advancing.

I was in the CIC (Combat Information Center) when I heard John's voice calling for a salvo and gave the coordinates and the Gunnery officer said to John: "If I give you a salvo in those coordinates it will land all around you!"

John's voice came back: "That's where the Japs are. Fire the salvo!"
Our guns fired.

I anxiously waited for a couple of minutes, and then John's voice came back, "Go to rapid fire!"

He remembered it in 1990 at a reunion but passed it off as just routine! I shall never forget when John came back to the Swanson, his duty completed and the Army on the radio thanking our Skipper, the late Captain E.L. Robertson, Jr., who died in 1992. He and John were very close. I was on the bridge with the Captain when John came up on the Bridge: Dirty, smelling, and a bad case jungle fever.

He said to our Captain, "Please forget my request for a transfer to where the action is!"

In 1989, Ensign Lindsay himself remembered the event:

JOHN V. LINDSAY 1989

MY DUTY ASHORE WITH THE FIRST CAVALRY

During the seizure of the Admiralty Islands, a volunteer was called for from the destroyers offshore to serve ashore as naval gunfire spotter, teamed up with the First Cavalry spotter. The Navy had supplied one during the landing of the first support troops on Los Negros, but he had been ill-advisedly withdrawn.

I got the job and took off in my steel helmet, etc., toward Los Negros Island, which had already been mainly secured.

The arrangement was that the Army spotter would have more knowledge of the turf and where to spot himself and the naval gunnery person would know the firing capacity of destroyers and could transmit the detailed orders. This is exactly what happened. The Army Lieutenant and I became good friends and stuck well together, as we had to.

I particularly can recall the bright moonlit night before we jumped off in the morning at dawn from Los Negros to Manus in landing barges, and more especially, I remember the church services that were held, in which obviously we were prayed over with hopes that most of us would survive. That was a very moving event under the moonlight.

I then recall most clearly two Australian guides in their floppy "digger" hats and short pants, going off in native canoes in the evening before to spread word among the natives that there would be a pulverizing bombardment in the morning at dawn and to move out. I'll never forget those two Australians with their two native paddlers, standing up in the dugout canoes as light was falling on their way to enemy territory. It was a brave business.

The next morning at dawn, we struck. B-25s came in low and repeatedly bombed the beachhead. Then came the strafers and fighter planes. I couldn't see how any living thing could have survived on the island of Manus. Then we went forward in the landing craft, with the landing craft that I and the Captain and the Army Lieutenant were riding on in the front ranks. Most of the Army had rifles, including my friend, and I was armed with a .45 revolver. We landed, got wet up to the knees, and dug in. I recall seeing my first dead Japanese soldiers—only they weren't Japanese, but Korean. I had wondered why they were so large. They had been pressed into service and I gathered that 100 percent of the Manus military population was Korean. But little did we know as they were all in Japanese soldier's dress and I'm quite sure if we hadn't slaughtered them in the bombardment that they would have slaughtered us.

Then I remember seeing immediately wounded men coming back on stretchers from sniper fire. The Japanese were good at that and apparently many of them had escaped the bombardment. That went on for quite a while and meanwhile my Army friend and I inched our way up forward and as dusk began to fall in the front ranks we dug in deep. It was the American military practice to dig in at nightfall, whereas the Japanese moved about. It was a long night and not without terror. At one time, both the Army Lieutenant and I were convinced that a Japanese had moved into our dugout and was about to let fly with a hand grenade, which meant we both quietly placed shells in the chambers of our guns and cocked them. It turned out to have been unnecessary.

And so it went, day after day, and we got more accustomed to it.

I do remember very strongly the terrible thirst I had. The canteen was quickly exhausted and we were encouraged never to drink the water on the grounds because it had been either deliberately poisoned or was poison anyway. Getting enough clean water turned into a fairly strong obsession with both of us.

One last thing, to get even with my dear colleagues on board I remember firing my ship, SWANSON, at intervals all night long. We worked them hard. But the Captain had zeroed in on just in front of us and all around us and it not only gave me some pleasure to know everybody was working as hard as we were back in the ship, but we thought it was highly necessary—and possibly was.

On my return to the Swanson, I hadn't bathed for a week and was dirty and smelly, but had survived.

Ensign Lindsay subsequently became an attorney. He was elected to the U.S. House of Representatives in 1958 and served there until 1965. In 1966, he was elected mayor of New York City and served until 1973.

ON LOS NEGROS the 5th, having taken Hill 260 earlier than expected, was plagued by snipers along the supply trail. F Troop of the 12th Cavalry was released from reserve at Papitalai Mission and ordered to advance southwest into the hills toward the supply trail. 1st Lt. Arthur Allen, leading the point platoon, was only 600 yards from the base when two enemy machineguns opened up on them. Allen personally turned his light machine-gun on the position and directed his riflemen on the visible enemy. Although Allen was killed, it allowed Troop F to withdraw. The squadron suffered thirty-seven casualties. The resistance being more than expected, General Chase revisited the 1st Brigade plans to clear Los Negros of the festering enemy.

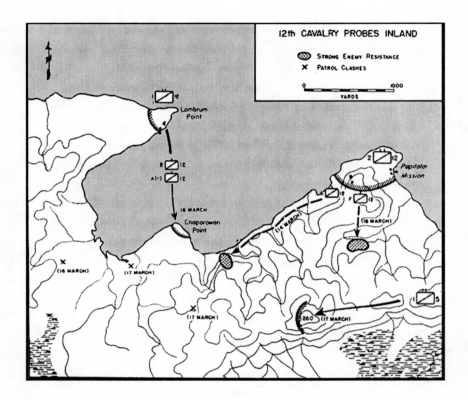

Sunday, March 19, 1944; Manus Island

Several artillery cub airplanes had landed at Momote. The Lorengau airfield was also operable and some of the Cubs were there. George asked Col. Chandler for permission to fly one of the Cubs over Road #2, leading to Old Rossum and on to Rossum, a few miles further south to locate targets, but he refused. George was disappointed, one because he liked to fly, but more importantly, the 2nd Brigade didn't realize the value of air cover. Refusing George's request to perform his reconnaissance proved to be an ill-fated decision. There was no strike request, so George and the 12th Air Liaison Party returned to Salami, since the 2nd Brigade no longer required their services.

On returning to Salami, George evidently voiced his irritation with the 2nd Brigade, since General Chase told him they would use air support and that he was giving him a letter of recommendation, commending him and the 12th ALP on their performance. George sent a message to 5th AAF Headquarters, requesting instructions. At midnight, the 12th ALP (F38) took over from the 8th ALP (G32) as the division station.

The conquest of Lorengau was easier than estimated. The original strength of Manus had been estimated at 2,000 enemy troops, thought to be located at Lorengau, but only a few hundred had defended the site, and the estimate of enemy strength was lowered to fewer than 500. Troop A was ordered to advance down Road #2 to Old Rossum, while Troop B was sent east along the coastal road. Troop B encountered only a few snipers and occasional machine-gun fire that was easily overcome. Another patrol was sent southwest on Road #1 and reached Tingo Village without encountering any enemy troops.

Troop A didn't fare as well. When 1st Lt. James M. Concannon was ordered down the Old Rossum road, he reviewed the enemy maps depicting the strongholds.

He realized he would agitate a hornet's nest and exclaimed, "Well, here goes Concannon to get himself a Purple Heart."

His prophecy came true as he entered the heart of enemy territory, not more than 200 yards from his own lines. His platoon was fired on by snipers and machine-gun fire. The fire was returned by spraying the trees with their own machine-guns. Five Japanese fell dead. When Concannon and one of his men were injured, his sergeant assumed command and attempted to flank Japanese bunkers that were at a bend in the road. Corporals Peter J. Armstrong and Amado V. Valencia set up their machine-guns no more than thirty yards from the enemy bunkers and started a steady stream of fire. Armstrong was wounded by a sniper but continued firing until he was knocked unconscious by a grenade explosion. Valencia continued firing until his machine-gun froze from being hit. He resumed his fire with a sub-machine gun until it too was knocked out of his hands by enemy fire. Both Armstrong and Valencia were awarded the Distinguished Service Cross for their heroism. Troop A only advanced 500 yards in the 94 degree heat and 84 percent humidity until they stopped for the evening.

Troop C came down the road to relieve the weary men of Troop A. While Troop C was organizing their position, they were attacked by eight Japanese with rifle grenades and small arms. By nightfall, the attack was stopped, but not before Troop C lost two men and had ten wounded.

Movement at night was dangerous. Throughout the night, Troop C was harassed by sniper and machine-gun fire, but the enemy didn't counterattack. As usual, cavalrymen stayed in their foxholes and fired at anything that moved. Troop C, having ten wounded, made the ill-fated decision to evacuate them on stretchers back to more friendly territory. Four stretcher bearers were killed and six more were wounded by their own not-so-friendly troops.

Since the Old Rossum road from Lorengau was well fortified, General Mudge decided to give the 8th Cavalry a rest and have them clear the way east to link up with the 1st Brigade. The 1st Brigade was still mopping up Los Negros, and the remaining enemy troops were retreating across to Manus. It was considered a light assignment for the 8th Cavalry. The 7th was assigned the tough assignment of advancing down the road to Old Rossum.

Monday, March 20, 1944

When Lt. McGowan learned that General MacArthur had presented the Distinguished Service Cross to Lt. Henshaw of the 1st Cavalry for being "the first to set foot in the Admiralty Islands" and for shooting the first Japanese, he was miffed. After all, he had actually been the first man to set foot in the Admiralties when they had conducted the dangerous mission of reconnoitering the island in advance of the 1st Cavalry landing.

On March 20, General Krueger flew to the Alamo Scout training center on Ferguson Island in southern Papua New Guinea and presented the Silver Star to McGowan and his team in a not-so-public display. General Krueger was extremely proud of the Alamo Scouts, and he told them so. The Alamo Scouts would go on to perform more than 100 missions behind enemy lines. None were ever killed or taken prisoner. The techniques and procedures they developed are still in use today, and even their very existence remained a military secret for nearly fifty years.

AT SALAMI, GEORGE received orders from 5th AAF Headquarters to have the 8th ALP return to "Red Herring" (the code name for Finschhafen, New Guinea) as soon as possible. The orders were for George and his 12th ALP to remain there until the 73rd RAAF Wing had established satisfactory communications. Their job would soon be over. George spent the morning sorting equipment and preparing to leave for New Guinea. He also wrote his mother.

52

Dearest Mother:

Well, it looks like I forgot your birthday, but I didn't really. I just have been so busy I haven't been able to write. The last letter I wrote I did forget to mention to wish you a happy birthday, but it was only because I was in a hurry to get it mailed.

I went on another operation on the 15th of this month, but it was mild compared to the first one. I sure wish I could tell you where it was, but you probably read in the papers what went on, on the 29th of Feb. and 15th of March. Incidentally, General Chase, the Cmdr of our task force, recommended me for the Silver Star, but I don't think I'll get it because as far as I'm concerned, I merely did my job and that shouldn't call for a medal, even if I did a good job in his opinion. One thing I'm glad of is that he gave a letter of commendation to the crew, at my suggestion, because it was because of them that we were able to do a satisfactory job. Did I tell you I got a Jap flag? Besides that, I have a lot of other stuff. Well, guess that's all, except to wish you a very happy birthday and here is a big kiss for you.

Loads of love,

George

ON MANUS ISLAND, the 7th Cavalry, as expected, ran into trouble trying to go down the road to Old Rossum. The road was narrow and flanked on each side by banks and dense jungle. The Japanese had taken every advantage of the terrain with hidden pillboxes, and snipers could hide anywhere. Capt. William C. Frey led Troop F of the 7th through the 8th Cavalry as they withdrew. They were aided by a light tank, a bulldozer, an artillery tractor towing a trailer of supplies, and a communications jeep. Troop F was able to advance within 800 yards of Old Rossum before they were repelled, suffering five deaths and ten wounded, including Capt. Frey. Corporal Grover S. Jordan, of Rose, Nebraska, stayed with Frey and three of the wounded. He placed himself in front of them and single-handedly stood off three determined enemy attacks before they were rescued.

The parade of vehicles couldn't turn around on the narrow road and were forced to back up several hundred yards. Meanwhile, the stealthy Japanese had sneaked in behind them and laid mines, blowing the tracks off the tractor and the tank. Under small arms fire, Pvt. Bill K. King, of Durant, Oklahoma, jumped from his bulldozer, coupled the tank to his bulldozer, and dragged the tank and its crew to safety. The other vehicles were abandoned, but not before taking the jeep radio with them. The 8th Cavalry moved in to form a defensive perimeter across the Rossum road and to hold the ground the 7th had gained.

While artillery bombarded the Japanese in front of them through the night, the 2nd Brigade's officers assembled at 2200 hours to revisit their plan for advancing into Old Rossum. With flashlights, they reviewed maps and planned the advance until the early morning hours, but the captured map depicting enemy positions wasn't revealed, nor was Capt. Frey's encounter or specific location discussed.[lxiv]

Tuesday, March 21, 1944

At Salami, George wrote in his morning report that it was just "normal routine work all day" and that there had been "no requests to handle." Based on the activity of the last few weeks, what constituted "normal routine work" was open to question. It was apparent that he was bored and discouraged about not being in the action.

On Manus, the 2nd Brigade decided to send out patrols to locate enemy positions and to prepare for a move inland against the Japanese. They arranged for natives to help guide the patrols through the jungle, looking for trails to flank the enemy. The patrols gained little new information and found no other trails. Using artillery spotter planes, they fired artillery at the enemy. At 1800 hours, the spotter planes dropped smoke shells to guide a strike of RAAF P-40s to the target.

On Los Negros, the 5th and the 12th Cavalry linked up, south of Papitalai Mission. A Japanese prisoner was captured, who told them that enemy ammunition was low and they were waiting for air support and reinforcements, but were giving up hope.

Wednesday, March 22, 1944

At Salami, George reported that it was still all quiet. He checked with the RAAF about their communications, but nothing had been done. As an afterthought, he reported that he'd had a request for air support and had succeeded in getting a dozen P-40s from the 75th Squadron to dive bomb Manus Island. The attack was for the evening before. George used the time to write letters home. It was his 5th letter home to his father and he wrote a similar letter to his mother. As explained in the letter, it was typed on equipment that he had with him.

53   *5*   *22 MARCH 44*

DEAR DAD;
   I FINALLY DISCOVERED A LETTER WITH YOUR ADDRESS ON IT SO I DON'T HAVE TO WAIT UNTIL I RETURN TO HEADQUARTERS TO WRITE YOU. I SENT TWO LETTERS TO MOTHER ADDRESSED TO LAUREL SPRINGS BECAUSE I FORGOT HER ADDRESS, BUT I FIGURED YOU BOTH WOULD BE

WONDERING WHAT HAPPENED TO ME UNLESS YOU FIG-URED I WAS DOWN IN SYDNEY HAVING A GOOD TIME AND NOT FINDING TIME TO WRITE BUT I WAS FAR FROM THERE, IN FACT, I GUESS WE ARE THE FURTHEREST NORTH OF ANY TROOPS IN THE SOUTHWEST PACIFIC AREA.

GUESS YOU CAN NOTICE I AM USING A SIGNAL CORPS TYPEWRITER, IT IS PART OF OUR SCR 299 RADIO EQUIPMENT AND SINCE THINGS ARE RATHER DULL AT THE MOMENT I AM TAKING TIME TO CATCH UP ON MY TYPING AND LETTER WRITING AT THE SAME TIME.

WE SURE HAD A HECTIC TIME HERE FOR A FEW DAYS. THE DAY WE LANDED WE HAD PLENTY OF FIRE FROM THE SHORE BUT AFTER WE REACHED SHORE THE SUR-PRISE WAS SO COMPLETE THAT THE JAPS COULDN'T ORGANIZE RESISTANCE UNTIL ABOUT FOUR O'CLOCK IN THE MORNING AND THEN IT REALLY BEGAN. I CAN'T TELL YOU MUCH OF WHAT HAPPENED BUT I THINK I CAN SAY THAT I WAS REALLY WONDERING WHETHER WE WOULD LAST THE NITE OUT BUT WE DID BECAUSE THE LORD WAS WITH US. AFTER I GET HOME I SURE WILL HAVE SOME STORIES TO TELL ESPECIALLY HOW I GOT TWO JAPS THE FIRST HOUR WE WERE ON SHORE AS A MATTER OF FACT THE COMMANDING GENERAL OF THE TASK FORCE HAS RECOMMENDED ME FOR THE SILVER STAR BUT I DOUBT IF I'LL GET IT BECAUSE IN MY OPIN-ION I WAS ONLY DOING MY JOB AND YOU DON'T GET MEDALS FOR THAT. I DID GET A COMMENDATION FROM GENERAL WHITEHEAD, MY BOSS, AND THE ENTIRE CREW GOT A COMMENDATION FROM THE GENERAL COMMANDING THE TASK FORCE AND THEY REALLY DESERVED IT BECAUSE ANY PRAISE THAT I GOT WAS ONLY DO TO THEM DOING SUCH A GOOD JOB UNDER DIFFICULT CONDITIONS WHICH INCLUDED

PAGE 2

NO SLEEP FOR FIVE DAYS AND NIGHTS BECAUSE THE JAPS WERE INFILTRATING OUR POSITION AT NIGHT AND DUR-

ING THE DAY WE HAD SO MANY PLANES IN SUPPORT THAT WE WERE IN CONSTANT TOUCH WITH THEM DIRECTING THEM TO TARGETS. IT REALLY WAS AN INTERESTING, IF TIRING JOB, AND WE GOT LITTLE REST EVEN AFTER THE REST OF THE FORCE ARRIVED AND RELIEVED THE TENSION A LITTLE. ONE NIGHT THE JAPS PULLED A BOMBING RAID AND ONE BOMB FELL 15 FEET AWAY FROM OUR DUGOUT WHICH ONLY WAS ABOUT 2 FEET ABOVE THE GROUND AND HAD A LOG AND SANDBAG ROOF WHICH PROTECTED US. WE WERE SHAKEN UP BUT THAT IS ALL SO THAT IS ANOTHER CASE WHERE THE LORD SURE WAS WATCHING OVER US.

ON THE 15TH OF THIS MONTH WE WENT OUT ON ANOTHER PHASE OF THIS OPERATION AND AGAIN WERE IN THE FIRST WAVE TO LAND BUT IT WAS MILD COMPARED TO THE OTHER ONE AND WE HAVE NOW COMPLETED OUR JOB AND HAVE RETURNED TO TASK FORCE HEADQUARTERS WHERE WE ARE MERELY WAITING FOR TRANSPORTATION BACK TO OUR OWN HEADQUARTERS, AND THIS TIME I REALLY EXPECT TO GET LEAVE.

I CAN'T TELL YOU WHERE WE HAVE BEEN BUT YOU HAVE BEEN READING ABOUT IT IN THE PAPERS AND I SAW GENERAL MACARTHUR THAT FIRST DAY. I'LL GIVE HIM CREDIT FOR REALLY GETTING OUT ON THE FRONT BECAUSE THE PLACE I SAW HIM WE LOST THAT NIGHT AND DIDN'T RECOVER IT FOR FOUR DAYS, SO NO ONE CAN SAY HE DOESN'T VISIT THE FRONT LINE TROOPS. THEY WERE REALLY IMPRESSED TOO, TO THINK THAT HE WOULD VISIT THEM AND TALK TO THEM.

WELL, GUESS THAT'S ALL THE NEWS. I'LL BE SURPRISED IF THE CENSOR DOESN'T CUT SOME OF THIS BUT IT SEEMS TO THAT IT DOESN'T REVEAL ANYTHING THE JAPS DON'T KNOW ALREADY.

HOPE YOU ARE WELL AND GET THE ASSIGNMENT YOU WANT AND A PROMOTION. WRITE WHEN YOU CAN, I'LL PROBABLY HAVE A FEW LETTERS WHEN I GET BACK AS I HAVEN'T RECEIVED ANY MAIL SINCE BEING HERE AND THAT WAS FEBRUARY 29TH.
LOVE, GEORGE

*P.S. I AM ENCLOSING A COUPLE OF THE PHAMPLETS WE
DROP ON THE NATIVES AND JAPS. THE NATIVES MORE OR
LESS FOLLOW INSTRUCTIONS BUT THE JAPS WON'T AS I
HAVE FOUND OUT, WHEN I ASKED THREE TO SURRENDER
AND THEY WOULDN'T DO IT. (THAT'S HOW I GOT TWO,
WHEN THEY STARTED TO RUN AWAY)*

```
                        OL BOI BILOG MANUS.
             SOLDIA BILOG YUMI AMERICA KOSUA PINIS LONG
             PAPITALAI BILOG RAUSIM JAPAN LONG OL MANUS.
    KIAP BILOG YUPELA I STAP ONTAIM SOLDIA BILOG YUMI.
    YU MAS KAM PAINIM KIAP, NA HARIM TOK.
    SIPOS BIPO JAPAN I PULIM YUPELA LONG WOK LONG HALIPIM OL, MASKI.
    MIPELA I NOGAT TOROVEL LONG BOI, TOROVEL LONG JAPAN DASOL.
    YU MAS KAM PAINIM KIAP NAU.
                        GUVMAN I TOK.
```

NOT MAKING ANY PROGRESS,
General Mudge ordered the full 1st
Squadron of the 7th Cavalry down
the Rossum road to attack Old
Rossum. The procession stopped
when it reached the defensive
perimeter held by the 8th Cavalry
while artillery and a rocket barrage
splattered on the enemy in front of
them. Without an observer, both the
artillery and the rocket fire, mounted
on a three-quarter-ton weapons carrier, was inaccurate, although it sounded impressive. Accompanied by a D-
7 bulldozer and a medium tank, the

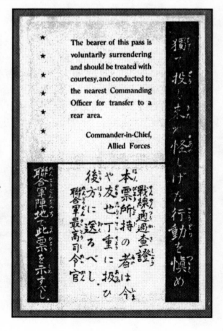

7th moved out at 0820. At first, they saw no sign of the enemy as they cautiously moved down the road, looking for snipers and land mines. The D-7 hit a mine and was disabled, and snipers wounded ten men, but the caravan kept moving down the road.

The 7th Cavalry soon learned that snipers hidden in trees were the most serious threat to the troops. The impact on morale was devastating, since they never knew when a sniper was directly overhead. The snipers would wait until troops passed them, looking for officers or a group. 1st Sgt. Haines was shot from directly overhead, suffering a shoulder wound while talking to the troop commander.

Snipers were well camouflaged and roped to trees or hanging in fish nets. Troops even had empty shell casings fall on them from snipers in the trees above them. It was suicide duty for the sniper, because as soon as they were discovered, they knew they'd be killed. Several methods were tried to eliminate the sniper threat, but none was totally effective. The troops tried standing still and silent to spot snipers, but they were so well hidden that they were seldom found. They tried spraying the trees with machine-gun fire, but the snipers used the racket to conceal their own intensified return fire. A formation with one platoon in front and another following with the sole mission of watching the trees also failed. The most effective method was a heavy concentration of artillery and fuse delay explosives, which reduced, but didn't eliminate, the sniper threat.

Four hundred yards north of Old Rossum, they were stopped by a machine-gun barrage from a hidden bunker. The leader of the point squad and two men were killed and three soldiers were wounded. The 7th Cavalry was surprised by the attack as the egomania of the 2nd Brigades commanders hadn't communicated the details of Capt. Frey's encounter, and no mention was made of the captured map detailing enemy positions.

An attempt to dislodge the concealed bunker was made with mortars, but that didn't work, since the mortars couldn't penetrate the dense forest. Troop C, leading the procession, withdrew and artillery was directed at the enemy obstacles in front of them. Bazookas were also brought forward and directed at the bunkers. Visibility in the dense forest was no more than fifteen yards, and smoke from the barrage of artillery, mortar, and grenades reduced visibility even more.

Corporals Conyers and Ortis moved forward and engaged two bunkers at point-blank range with light machine-guns. Conyers was killed and two other men injured before Sgt. Martinez was able to score four direct hits on the bunkers with bazookas. With the bunkers destroyed, the 7th Cavalry started their procession again, only to be stopped again fifty yards further down the road. As before, the troops were withdrawn as artillery fire, directed from artillery planes, was leveled on the enemy bunkers. By 1850, the 7th had finally reached the northern edge of Old Rossum. The cost for the few hundred yards gained was eleven killed and twenty-nine wounded. Except for harassment from snipers and a Japanese officer who stumbled inside the perimeter and lit a match to read a map, that night on the front was surprisingly quiet.

Thursday, March 23, 1944

At 0730, a new tactic to dislodge the enemy at Old Rossum was tried. Troop B moved forward along the ridges bounding the Rossum road on the right as Troop G did the same on the left side. Troop C was held in reserve. A bulldozer moved along the road, but was stopped by what at first was thought to be new mines the Japanese had apparently laid during the night. Later, it was learned that the mines had been missed from the night before. The Japanese had also destroyed the vehicles that had been abandoned during the March 19th debacle and then had used them to block the road. The cavalrymen made little progress. By noon, the 7th again called for artillery fire when they were pinned by sniper and machine-gun fire. In mid-afternoon they were again pinned down, but by mortar fire. By evening, they had advanced only 200 yards down the road. However, a patrol from Troop G was sent southeast and advanced 700 yards, where they found five empty bunkers. It had taken two days to advance 1,000 yards, at a cost of sixty-eight casualties, but they had destroyed twenty-one enemy bunkers. The 7th Cavalry was exhausted from the strain of battle in the heat and the humidity, and it looked like more of the same was ahead of them, since the Japanese had maximized their use of the terrain and their positions to make any Allied advance very costly.

ON LOS NEGROS, George went souvenir hunting. He ventured south to Hyane Harbor and Momote and found a Jap pack and an ammunition chest along the shore. He wrote to his sister Eleanor using the SCR typewriter.

6

23 MARCH 44

DEAR EL: 54

> *I THOUGHT BY THIS TIME THAT I WOULD BE ARRIV-ING BACK FROM SYDNEY AFTER WHAT I THOUGHT WOULD BE AN ENJOYABLE LEAVE BUT INSTEAD I AM SIT-TING UNDER A COCONUT TREE ON AN ISLAND IN THE SOUTHWEST PACIFIC WRITING A LETTER TO YOU.*
>
> *I WAS ALL SET TO GO ON LEAVE WHEN THIS SUDDEN NEW OPERATION CAME UP AND I WAS THE ONLY OFFI-CER AVAILABLE FOR THE JOB. LUCKILY I HAD A GOOD CREW ASSIGNED AND A GOOD LIEUTENANT FOR AN ASSISTANT, SO WE WERE ABLE TO DO A SATISFACTORY JOB. IN FACT, THE GENERAL COMMANDING THE TASK FORCE GAVE US ALL A CITATION AND I ALSO RECEIVED A PERSONAL CITATION FROM GENERAL WHITEHEAD, MY BOSS AT FIFTH AIR FORCE.*
>
> *WE SURE HAD A HECTIC TIME FOR A FEW DAYS AND I CAN REALLY SAY NOW THAT I SAW SOME ACTION. WE DIDN'T SLEEP FOR FIVE DAYS OR NIGHTS BECAUSE THE JAPS WERE ATTACKING EVERY NITE AND ALL DAY LONG I WAS BUSY DIRECTING THE PLANES TO TARGETS. I SUC-CEEDED IN GETTING TWO JAPS THE VERY FIRST HOUR AFTER WE LANDED AND I OBTAINED A JAP FLAG AND SOME OTHER SOUVENIRS I WILL BRING HOME WITH ME*

WHEN I FINALLY GET TO COME HOME. CAN'T TELL YOU ANYTHING ELSE ABOUT WHAT WENT ON, BUT I THINK YOU HAVE PROBABLY READ IN THE PAPERS OF THE TIME WE HAD AFTER WE LANDED.

I ALSO TOOK PART IN THE FINAL PHASE OF THIS OPERATION WHICH YOU HAVE READ HAS JUST BEEN COMPLETED. IN EACH CASE, WE WERE IN THE FIRST BUNCH THAT LANDED AND THIS SECOND ONE WAS QUIET, BUT THE FIRST ONE WE REALLY CAME ASHORE UNDER A HAIL OF BULLETS. WE WERE OUTNUMBERED AND REALLY HAD TO PUT UP A GOOD FIGHT, BUT THESE AMERICAN SOLDIERS OR RATHER TROOPERS ARE REALLY GOOD AND WE SUCCEEDED IN HOLDING ON UNTIL OUR REINFORCEMENTS ARRIVED.

I AM HOPING TO RETURN TO HEADQUARTERS IN A FEW DAYS AND FINALLY GET THAT LEAVE IN SYDNEY, WHICH IS LONG OVERDUE. I SURE HOPE I GET THE WHOLE FIFTEEN DAYS I AM ENTITLED TO, BUT IT WOULD JUST BE MY LUCK TO GET ONLY 7 DAYS OR EVEN BETTER GO OUT ON ANOTHER OPERATION. I WOULD-N'T CARE BECAUSE EACH OPERATION BRINGS ME NEAR-ER TO THE DAY I CAN GET HOME TO CLEO AND CLIN-TON AND YOU AND THE REST OF THE FAMILY SO THE MORE OPERATIONS THE MERRIER, AS FAR AS I AM CON-CERNED. HOWEVER, IF THERE ISN'T ANY THAT NEED ME THEN I WOULD LIKE THE LEAVE BECAUSE I NEED A LIT-TLE RECUPERATION FROM THIS CONSTANT STRAIN.

HOPE WARREN IS GETTING ALONG ALL RIGHT IN THE NAVY AND THAT YOU AND MARY ANNE AND WAR-REN ARE ALL IN GOOD HEALTH. I SHOULD HAVE A LET-TER FROM YOU WHEN I RETURN AS I GOT NO MAIL SINCE BEING HERE ON FEBRUARY 29TH.

LOTS OF LOVE AND KISSES,

George

Also on Los Negros, the 5th Cavalry had attempted for three days to move west off Hill 260, only to be deterred by the Japanese. Meanwhile, the 12th Cavalry by blocking the escape routes to Manus, believed they had killed a 100 of the enemy. Troops E and F had probed 800 yards inland from Papitalai Mission on the 22nd when the Japanese cut their supply line. Isolated during the night, they were attacked, but killed fifteen Japanese, two of them officers, and some wearing American fatigues and helmets. In the few days of attempting to break out from Hill 260 to clear the hills to the west, the 1st Brigade had suffered 102 casualties. The sniper-infested rain forest became denser as they advanced, compounding their already severe supply problems. The 1st Brigade spent the 23rd improving their supply lines. By that evening, Troops E and F were able to connect with the 5th at Hill 260 and to plan for a combined offensive to the west on the 24th.

Friday, March 24, 1944

The morning started the same as the previous five days for the 2nd Brigade—with an artillery concentration. A previously requested air strike along the Rossum road had been cancelled. A fourteen-man patrol of officers was sent down the Lorengau River to find a route to flank the enemy, but they were unsuccessful. While the patrol was looking for a route around the enemy, five troops of the 7th Cavalry, including the reserves, pushed down the road in a 300-yard front on both sides of the road. The troops were advancing blindly through the jungle and were susceptible to snipers and machine-gun fire. Artillery fire was used, but as soon as the fire stopped, the Japanese would come out from hidden bunkers, set up automatic weapons and fire on the advancing cavalrymen.

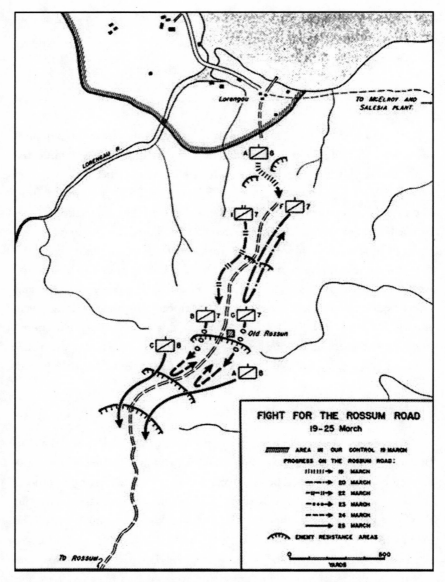

Capt. Roman D. Hubbell, leading Troop B, received the brunt of the enemy fire and was killed. A tank advancing down the road was more of a hindrance than help because of the mines on the road. By early afternoon,

Lt. Col. Kenneth L. Johnson, commanding the 99th Field Artillery Battalion, reported that his artillery fire was ineffective in the jungle. Lt. Col. John B. Maxwell II, the regimental executive officer, reported that the 7th Cavalry couldn't hold their present position without air cover. He also said that it was the fiercest and most difficult fighting on Manus to date, and they had only advanced 200 yards along a thickly-mined track that delayed any tank advance. The 7th had also lost eighty-seven percent of its officers and suffered twenty-four casualties as they retreated, marking their front lines with smoke pots.

At 1730, the RAAF strafed the enemy position and dropped a dozen 500-pound bombs. The air attack was followed by the 105mm guns of the 61st Artillery Battalion, stationed on Hauwei Island.

General Mudge's 2nd Brigade had suffered severe casualties, advancing only 2,000 yards in six days of fighting. Troop B had lost two of its commanders and most of its officers, and were facing high ground, more snipers, and more bunkers. The 8th Cavalry was called in from their "rest" at Salesia Plantation, where they were attempting to link up with the 1st Brigade, which was still fighting pockets of resistance on Los Negros.

On Los Negros, George received a request to have planes evacuate some

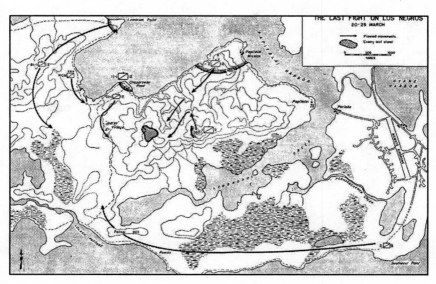

of the wounded back to New Guinea. Word was received back that two planes would arrive the next day.

In the afternoon he went to 2nd Brigade headquarters with Col. Corbett, RAAF Wing Commander Stoege, and his squad leader, Lomben. General Mudge, at the prompting of Lt. Col. Maxwell II, had finally budged and decided to try air cover to facilitate the advance. They met with General Mudge and Col. Finley, commander of the 1st Squadron of the 7th Cavalry, and plans were made for the 8th Cavalry to advance through the 7th Cavalry lines after the air attack, under cover of a subsequent half hour barrage from the artillery.

When George returned to Los Negros after the meeting, he wrote in his morning report for March 24th that there was "nothing much doing."

"Nothing much doing" wasn't the case for the 1st Brigade on Los Negros. Troops A and C of the 5th Cavalry and E and F of the 12th kicked off toward the enemy stronghold, preceded by an artillery hailstorm. The idea was that if one troop was held up, it would cover the adjacent troop in a leapfrog-style advance. After only a few hundred yards, they were stopped by machine-guns concealed in huts in a small village. Capt. Henry B. Greer, the ranking officer on the front line, called the commanders together and had them bring their machine-guns to the center and place them under cover on a hill overlooking the village. When the machine-guns started firing, all the men were to move forward, through or around the village.

The machine-guns fired and the troops charged, firing their carbines and BARs from the hip. The volume of fire was so great that the movement carried forward and beyond the village. When it was over, fifty Japanese had been killed.

Although supplies were short, they moved on and stopped 100 yards from a trail leading south from Chaporowan Point. That evening, it became evident that the remaining Japanese on Los Negros were out of ammunition when they started throwing sticks and mud clods into the cavalry foxholes. It was the last real battle on Los Negros, and except for those Japanese who escaped and lived like the natives, the battle was over.

Saturday, March 25, 1944

At 0530, George left with Lt. King, two men, and Sq. Leader Hannigan, of the RAAF, for Lorengau. At 0745, they arrived at the front lines of the 7th Cavalry. From the radio on their jeep, they made contact with "WINGO" (Wing Commander Stoege), who was leading the flights. The 7th Cavalry had set out smoke pots to mark their front lines.

At 0800, the twelve RAAF P-40s circled once and said they were ready. George went out in front of the smoke pots to be sure the planes were on target. One bomb hit 200 yards short of the objective and only 200 yards from George. The troops were moved back 500 yards and more smoke pots were laid out so the planes could bomb the front line. The rest of the planes came in dropping their bombs in front of their defensive perimeter.

At 0915, George set out another smoke pot 100 yards in front of the line so pilots could estimate targeted distances. The pilots reported that it worked and at 0930 the planes dive-bombed. At 0940, smoke pots were set off perpendicular to the front lines and George ordered the planes to dive-bomb in line with them. The procedure caused a five-minute delay, but the planes hit the target. Col. Bradley, Commanding Officer of the 8th Cavalry, requested the twenty-four planes in the air to use all their ammunition and strafe the enemy positions. In the meantime, General Mudge and Col. Chandler were anxious to start the artillery firing and kept asking when they could start. The planes stopped strafing at 1035 and George gave the clearance to fire artillery. Col. Bradley's troops moved out, under cover of the artillery fire, but some of it fell short and wounded two cavalrymen.

Despite the strafing and bombing, the going was still slow for the 8th Cavalry. Snipers, roped in trees and sitting in fish nets, who had survived the bombing and strafing were firing at the troops from hidden positions. Their location couldn't be traced from the noise of their weapons, since the artillery barrage hid the noise. The advance was also hindered by dense jungle growth, with visibility at times not more than ten feet. The tank progress, which some said was more of a hindrance than help, was also slow, since mines needed to be cleared before it could advance. Radio communication with the tank wasn't available, so troops walking with the tank would bang on the tank to direct it at targets, and the men themselves were prime targets, since they were doing the hazardous duty of clearing mines and directing the tank, which had more destructive power than the rifle troops.

George expressed his irritation with the 2nd Brigade again in his morning report, writing, "It took an hour and half before troops reached the line they had vacated with no opposition, but it was due to General Mudge's stubbornness, insisting on artillery fire after the bombing, so they lost the effect of the bombing and strafing. They sure need practice working with the Air."

He also reported that the radio worked fine and that he was in constant contact with the RAAF P-40s. At 1300, George returned to Los Negros with a request for bombing and strafing by A-20s or B-25s the next day. The aerial strike, although effective, would have been better if the light and medium bombers had been sent from the 345th for the mission.

By 1335, the 8th Cavalry was reaching their objective, a ridge south of Old Rossum occupied by a company of Japanese. They had knocked out two bunkers and four machine-guns. Troop B was stopped by a cliff and a swamp, but Troop C made it to the ridge at 1440 and was expecting a counterattack. Troop A, on the east, on their left flank, had also made it to their objective and was waiting for tank and mortar support. In getting to the objective, Troop A had suffered twenty-four casualties.

Mines stalled the tank Troop A was waiting for. A bulldozer pulled it out of the way while two more tanks drove around, firing at enemy bunkers while a 105mm concentration was hailed on the enemy. At 1600, Troop A advanced, with Troop C protecting their right flank. Capt. Walter M. Hart, in charge of the mortars, established his outpost ahead of the combat elements and was able to adjust mortar fire and high explosives into an area 50 by 100 yards. Under this cover, the troops were able to move ahead, firing their own machine-guns into the bunker slits and within grenade-throwing range.

Meanwhile, the two tanks moved ahead and assisted the charging cavalrymen by firing flame-throwers into the bunkers, followed by the bulldozer, which buried the bunkers. Japanese attempting to escape were cut down by rifle fire. No attempt was made to investigate the bunkers, since doing so would have endangered the troops.

By 1700, all resistance had ceased. The 1st Squadron was able to look out and see no enemy positions in front of them. The cost for the day was seven Americans killed and twenty-nine wounded, although 100 of the enemy were destroyed. The battle had gained the Rossum road and would be the last organized resistance on Manus Island, but pockets of Japanese remained on Manus and Los Negros, and mopping up in the dense jungle and hills was a task not to be taken lightly.

At 2000 George received word from General Mudge, through Col. Corbett at G-3 (operations), to cancel the air strike. George suggested an alternate target, different from the scheduled target, but it was also cancelled. George had radio difficulty and his message to cancel wasn't received, but he received word that A-20s would be over at 0845 the next morning.

The *Diary of the Admiralty Islands Campaign*, dated April 21, 1944, written by Headquarters, 1st Cavalry Division, concerning the efforts of George and the 12th ALP, said:

The jungle with its tangled mat of rain forest renders difficult the pinpointing of enemy position for an air strike. Several methods were tried. All of them were successful to some extent. But for each scheme our troops devised, the Japs would quickly introduce some counter-measure. For example, when the enemy position was marked by artillery or mortar smoke shell, the Japs would quickly fire one or two smoke shells into the cavalry lines. The pilot obviously would be, to put it mildly, slightly confused. When the front line of the troops was marked by smoke, the Japs immediately marked their own front line of the troops. The imitative Jap soon learned that the white star cluster code signal meant "you are bombing (strafing) your own troops, and during an air attack would discharge one of these signals, whenever they were available to him. However, the Jap was not successful in his use of counter ruses and stratagems. The troops of the 1st Cavalry Division were more resourceful, more clever, more ingenious than the Japs. They would devise useful, workable means far more rapidly than the Jap could counter. They would use different colored smokes, they would pinpoint a target by fixing its location as five hundred south on a perpendicular bisector of the smoke lines, and they would locate the target by firing its distance and direction from some visible or marked reference point.

In all air support missions, the Air Liaison Party proved a valuable and indispensable part of the team. Their position was normally on or in front of the front line of the troops. They willingly and cheerfully took every risk of combat in order to insure properly directed air support. These groups stand out among the many unsung heroes of any battle.

Sunday, March 26, 1944

Apparently, George related his annoyance with General Mudge and the 2nd Brigade to 5th AAF Headquarters "Daddy," as he asked that requests for air support be provided by the RAAF 73rd Wing, whose elements were stationed at Momote until the tactical situation became clear. George sent Capt. Eyman, with two men to the 2nd Brigade, to use their radio equipment and to establish an 8th ALP voice station, called "PREVADE."

For the air strike requested the day before, by the 2nd Brigade that hadn't been cancelled, George called to have the 76th RAAF Squadron place P-40s on alert, loaded with bombs. He also arranged for one P-40 to lead the scheduled A-20s to a new target, an enemy supply dump at Kawaliak, located at the end of Road #1 in the western section of Manus Island. The P-40 was able to rendezvous with the A-20s over Los Negros, but one A-20 lost its wing bombs over the 1st Brigade troops, although it caused no damage. Low on fuel another A-20 landed at Momote. The P-40 led the remaining A-20s to the supply dump and "it was really plastered." The change in target, developed overnight, emphasized that planes on the mission should check with the Division Air Liaison Party or the ALP at the front, in the event that there was a change in the tactical situation for a more favorable target.

Capt. Eyman called for a strafing mission by the P-40s at 1000, so the bombs were taken off the planes. Two reconnaissance missions were also requested and were run from a well-positioned command post at the front line. At 1500, a bombing mission was requested, so bombs were loaded onto the P-40s and Warembu was bombed, destroying four huts and one bunker.

There were no air strike requests for the next day.

Monday, March 27, 1944

George went to Manus Island and then to the front lines to check with Capt. Eyman and the 8th ALP on the radio set-up, which was found to be working fine. A seven-man patrol had been sent out toward Warembu, about two miles south of Rossum, but it was ambushed by four Japanese. The patrol suffered one man killed, but managed to kill three of the ambushers and take one of them prisoner. George caught up with the patrol just after the ambush and then they all pushed out again.

As George and the patrol followed the trail to Warembu, they found a dying Japanese lying alongside the trail. He was spotted just as he attempted to throw a hand grenade, but the patrol killed him before he could throw it. George was the first into Warembu when they reached it at 1530 hours. It appeared to be occupied by only the natives, since they found no foxholes or bunkers. George entered a hut and found a sick Japanese who was attempting to set off a hand grenade, but George knocked it out of his hand with a stick. The patrol tied the prisoner to a wheelbarrow and carted him back to squadron headquarters after setting fire to the village. The prisoner died in the ambulance as he was being evacuated to the division hospital.

At 1900, George returned to Salami and reported his findings to Division G-2 (Intelligence). He also received a message from 5th AAF Headquarters that C-47s would arrive the next day to transport the 8th ALP, Capt. Eyman, and his equipment back to New Guinea. G-3 (Operations) also confirmed that George's job in the Admiralties was finished and that the 12th ALP was to return to 5th AAF Headquarters as soon as the RAAF 73rd Wing established communications.

Lt. Booker, an ANGAU representative, sent a group of natives to Tong Island, along with a six-man patrol. They took rations for the day, and when the natives spotted a squad of Japanese soldiers, they offered them their rations. As the patrol was eating, the six-man squad moved in and captured all of them.

Tuesday, March 28, 1944

George spent the morning packing equipment, preparing to return to New Guinea. The SCR-299 radio set received from General Chase on March 3rd was given back to the 5th Cavalry. They had the SCR-193 radio that worked but it wasn't as good. He moved next to the Division Command Post at Salami point. In the afternoon, George conferred with Col. Finley, commanding the 7th Cavalry, regarding air support for the Pityilu Island show and volunteered himself and the 12th ALP to go with them. The 8th ALP left and returned to New Guinea as planned.

Wednesday, March 29, 1944

General Chase wrote a letter of commendation regarding the 12th Air Liaison Party. The letter was sent to General Swift, commanding the 1st Cavalry, to be forwarded to General Kenney.

The 12th ALP moved to Lorengau in preparation for the attack on Pityilu Island. They tested the communication channels. The 7th Cavalry had contact with division headquarters, who in turn had contact with the RAAF stationed at Momote, so communication channels were working.

Thursday, March 30, 1944 Pityilu Island

Patrolling activities on both Los Negros and Manus by March 30th indicated the battle in the Admiralties was over, except for clearing the outlying islands. Pityilu Island, three miles north of Lugos Mission, was the first to be cleared of Japanese troops. The island was three miles long and a maximum of 650 yards wide. A coconut plantation covered two-thirds of the western side, and a rain forest covered the eastern side. Pityilu could reach 135 degrees, with high humidity, and had an annual rainfall of 150 inches. It was the hottest spot in the 160-island Admiralty chain. The heat would steam the rain and it would rain when the sun was shining. The rain could come at any time, with exploding thunder and massive lighting, when the sky could no

HEADQUARTERS 1ST CAVALRY BRIGADE

APO 201
29 March 1944

Subject: Battle Commendation.

To : Commanding General. 5th Air Force, Advance Echelon, APO 713, Unit 1. Thru: Commanding General, 1st Cavalry Division, APO 201.

1. I wish to commend the following officers and enlisted men of the 12th Air Liaison Party for their work in coordinating the air support for the Brewer Reconnaissance Force in the capture of the Momote Airstrip on Los Negros Island, Admiralty Group. SWPA, between 29 February 1944 and 9 March 1944:

Captain George F. Frederick. 0372630
1st Lt. James C. King. 0418924
S/Sgt. Martin W. James, 13040947
Sgt. Mark D. Kohn, 16038033
Sgt. Hugh H. Bement, 39170125
Sgt. Roy H. Clark, 16043078
T/5th Gr Gordon R. Rule, 39837714

2. These men, bu their untiring efforts and efficiency of maintaining communications with Headquarters 5th Air Force, were responsible for the immediate placing of bombing and strafing attacks on enemy positions and installations which materially assisted this force in the successful accomplishment of its mission.

3. Captain Frederick from a position on top of a revetment, while under enemy small arms and mortar fire, personally directed the aircraft, in close-in bombing and strafing attacks on the enemy, and in the dropping of supplies to our own troops. This was the only means of supply for this force between 29 February 1944 and 3 March 1944.

/s/ Wm. C. Chase
WM. C. CHASE
Brigadier General, U. S. Army
Commanding

longer bear the weight of the water. However, it was a pleasant day for the island, with a temperature and humidity in the mid-80s. The breeze through the coconut trees emanated a musky smell, but the small island would bear the smell of death for the next month.

Pityilu Island

Before the landing, two destroyers prepared for the attack by shelling sixty rounds onto the island from 0630–0730. The destroyers and the 5th AAF had been intermittently shelling and bombing the island since before the Lugos Mission landing on March 15th. Immediately following the destroyer shelling, George controlled twenty-four P-40s and a dozen Spitfires from the RAAF 73rd Wing as they bombed and strafed the island. The entire island had been numbered, with target areas in circles approximately 100 yards in diameter and numbered from 601 through 642. The eastern rain forest beginning at the landing in the middle of the island's southern shore was 601, and proceeding to the northern shore and around the island until ending at 642, next to target 601.

After the air strike, landing barges fired rockets as they approached the beach, accompanied by artillery fire from the 61st Field Artillery Battalion, now stationed on the north side of the Lorengau airstrip. At 0900, they landed on a hard sandy beach on the southern shore, the only place suitable for a landing. Six waves of vehicle, mechanized, support, and tracked vehicles

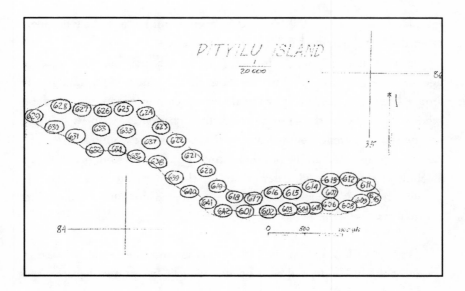

landed unopposed on the beach with Troops A, B, and C of the 7th Cavalry.

After landing, George controlled two more air strikes at 0947, directed at target 606, about 1,000 yards east of the landing. With Troop C on the left, A in the center, and B on the right, the cavalrymen didn't move out until 1000 hours, when some patrols were sent out, but no contact was made with the enemy. The reconnaissance platoon loaded into amphibious tanks and moved west through the coconut plantation. Troop C remained in reserve, but sent patrols into the interior. Troops A and B, with a tank, moved east into the rain forest. At 1020, one man was hit by a sniper and at 1030, litter bearers were called, because now two men had been shot. Troop B, moving along the south coast, was engaged at 1045 by enemy guns from a hut, but they were easily destroyed by the tank.

At noon, Troop A moved 1,500 yards east on a trail through the center of the rain forest, to position 615 on the north side of the island, where they ran into heavy resistance. They started to withdraw, but the Japanese followed so closely that it was impossible to evacuate the wounded until a light tank was brought up to cover their withdrawal. The tank and Troop A had passed a bunker in which the Japanese had withheld their fire. A fifty-six-

minute artillery barrage followed on the enemy position and the tank finally finished off the bunker, killing fourteen Japanese.

At 1400 hours, Troop B, following Troop A at position 603, adjacent
and southwest of target 615 on the south shore, came upon a hastily-con-
structed trench under a huge banyan tree containing twenty-one Japanese
who had given away their position with their chatter. Lt. John R. Boehme
and two privates went to investigate the chatter and were wounded. Pvt. Paul
A. Lahman advanced on the position, firing clip after clip from his BAR. Lt.
Boehme credited him with destruction of the entire force. Capt. Fred J.
Hughes, from 1st Squadron Headquarters, ordered three litter bearers and
was told they were on the way.

LT. JAMES KING, writing the 12th Air Liaison morning report, wrote that
the event at 1400 hours had been a counterattack. Twenty-two Japanese had
been killed. Ironically, in only a few hours the last battle of organized resistance in the Admiralties would be over, and in only a few days my father
would have the leave that he longed for, and a trip home to see Cleo and me,
the son he always wanted. But that was not what fate had dealt. My father,
Capt. George F. Frederick, was killed by a sniper at 1400 hours on March
30, 1944. He had volunteered for the mission. I was only four months old.

Lt. King reported George's death to the 5th AAF Headquarters and the
RAAF at Momote. At 1542, air observation reported Japanese walking about
in a dazed condition at points 606–608. A message was issued by General
Swift to chase out all sightseers and souvenir hunters immediately, and not
to allow anyone else to land that wasn't connected with the operation. An
hour later, the RAAF plastered the eastern tip of the island, strafing and
dropping eleven 500-pound bombs in a small area. The reconnaissance platoon returned from the western end of the island, reporting that they'd had
no contact with the enemy. At 1720, the 7th withdrew from the rain forest
and established a perimeter for the night.

The next morning, the RAAF bombed and strafed the northeast coast
again. The squadron advanced, but the dozen Japanese they found had all
been killed by the bombing. Lt. King returned to 1st Division Headquarters

at noon. The Japanese loss of fifty-nine troops cost six wounded and eight dead cavalrymen,[lxv] including my father. Lt. King reported that George was taken to Lorengau and buried in grave number 35, the middle grave south of the flag pole, in the third row. Lt. King took charge of George's personal gear.

EXCEPT FOR PITYILU, the remaining islands were found to be either unoccupied or harboring only a few Japanese who were hiding in the interior. Unknown to the Allies was a March 2nd directive that had called in all but a handful of troops from the outlying islands for the attack on Momote.

The amphibious assault on Koruniat Island was the first of its kind. The assault, made across a narrow 500-yard passage, was conducted by the 12th Cavalry in eighteen native canoes, four captured collapsible boats, and sixteen engineering boats. The troops landed unopposed after another coordinated air, artillery, and naval bombardment.

Lt. King directed the air strikes on Koruniat and Ndrilo. On April 3rd, King went to Rambutyo in a large invasion of the island and landed with the first wave at noon.

He directed air strikes on the island and received a message from General Swift, saying, "From Rambutyo, per schedule, Navy and RAAF cooperation and support perfect as usual."

A few Japanese escaped from Rambutyo Island and took a native canoe to Pak Island, where they were captured. The cavalry killed thirty Japanese and five more were captured on Rambutyo.

According to the 12th Air Liaison Party morning report, nothing important happened on April 4th, and on April 5th, the RAAF 73rd Wing took over. Air Support missions were now assigned to a different station, which could handle all traffic.

Sporadic mopping up by the 2nd Brigade would continue into June. Without food or ammunition, some of the remaining Japanese hid in the jungle and attempted to live off the land, but several cases of cannibalism were documented by members of the 7th and 8th Cavalries. On April 4th, the 5th Cavalry, which had been in battle for more than a month, moved to Koruniat Island while the 12th moved to Salami Plantation for rest and rehabilitation.

A diary found on a dead Japanese soldier suggests the fate of all the survivors:

28 March. Last night's duty was rather quiet except for the occasional mortar and rifle fire that could be heard. According to the conference of the various unit leaders, it has been decided to abandon the present position and withdraw. The preparation for this has been made. However, it seems as though this has been cancelled and we will firmly hold this position. Ah! This is honorable defeat and I suppose we must be proud of the way we have handled ourselves. Only our names will remain, and this is something I don't altogether like. Yes, the lives of those remaining, 300 of us, are now limited to a few days.

30 March. This is the eighth day since we began the withdrawal. We have been wandering around and around the mountain roads because of the enemy. We have not yet arrived at our destination but we have completely exhausted our rations. Our bodies are becoming weaker and weaker, and this hunger is getting unbearable.

31 March. Although we are completely out of rations, the march continues. When will we reach Lorengau? Or will this unit be annihilated in the mountains? As we go along, we throw away our equipment and weapons one by one.

1 April. Arrived at native shack. According to a communication, friendly troops in Lorengau cannot help but withdraw. Hereafter there is no choice but to live as the natives do."

AFTERMATH

Home Front

On Monday, April 10th, Cleo wrote to George's mother, telling her of a letter she had received from George. Cleo had just returned from the hospital after having her appendix removed and hadn't regained her strength.

Hiattville, Kansas
April 10th, 1944

Dear Mother,   55

I just mailed your letter a few minutes ago but I got a letter from George since. Told me to write you. I'll just quote most of it.
"I can't tell you where I am but I have been on an important operation and left for it on a notice of 12 hrs. I was supposed to go on leave but guess it will be a few weeks now. I don't care as it means ending this war sooner.

Incidentally, I can say now I took part in the war for sure. I was in the assault wave and immediately as we landed I rushed out with another officer and we got credit for the first two Japs killed. I got them both and have some souvenirs off of them to remember the occasion by. We had a hectic time but I am OK.

I may not be able to write again for a while as I am going out again in a few days so don't worry about it as I am OK."

That is all he says in regard to his work. Said he won't be able to write very often, so I won't get too uneasy if I don't hear as often. Incidentally, the letter was dated March 13th. The paper which he wrote was borrowed and it had Jap writing on it or something of that nature.

I surely hope when he finishes with that he'll get to come home afterward. I know he more than deserves coming back or leave.

I am rather uneasy until I hear again, but I trust the Lord to take care of him & bring him back. I am very, very proud of him.

Clinton is growing some hair now. Think I'll clip some off & send it to George. It is the same color as mine.

George said he hadn't gotten any mail since Feb 27th but would have a lot when he returned.

Love,

Cleo

His address is still the same APO 713. Won't he have a stack of letters from me, being that I write every day?

On Friday, April 14th, Harry Armstrong, the mail carrier from Hiattville, drove the fifteen miles along the gravel roads to deliver a telegram from the War Department to Cleo, announcing George's death. He knew the contents and was worried about delivering it. Along with the mail for

Cleo were several letters from George. His route takes him by Uncle Perry Dunn's place and around the mile section by the Johnson School District #6 schoolhouse. As he rounded the corner by the school, he saw several cars and recognized "Old Shaky," the '36 Chevy Cleo's folks drove. He assumed that Cleo was home alone. Continuing on for the next mile to deliver the mail to Cleo, he decided to come back with the telegram. He delivered the mail, leaving the letters from George. Then he continued his route and returned later that evening.

Without a word, Harry delivered the telegram to Cleo and my grandparents, Perry and Letha, watched as she opened it. Cleo read it, then handed it to her parents to read. She picked me up and sat down in a rocking chair. Letha went to the attic stairs, since Lavon was in the attic. Lavon saw her, and she knew.

Lavon later recalled, "Mom was as white as a sheet!"

"George has been killed," Letha said.

Downstairs, Cleo had read the telegram again, but not wanting to believe the news, she crushed the telegram and tossed it into the burning stove. She held me and cried as she rocked softly in the rocking chair.

On Sunday, Cleo wrote to George's parents.

Hiattville, Kansas
April 16, 1944   56

Dear Mother & Dad,

I surely hope you've learned of the news of George. I've wondered if they sent you a telegram as well as me of his death in the Admiralty Islands. I received a special delivery letter from Aalyce Callaway, who is one of George's and my friends. Her husband went over the same time George did & he told her that it was a sniper. It happened March the 30th & I've gotten letters from him as late as March 26th at that time he was waiting to go back to headquarters & expected his leave when he got there.

I really guess there isn't use to express how I feel except I am very proud of him and never regretted having the great honor of knowing him and also being his wife. I do know that he lived the last year of his life happy which I am grateful for. This little son of his has helped me very much. I just know if you folks could see him, you'd say it is another George Frederick. I hope I can help him to be as swell a fellow as George is.

I wished I had the strength to go back but it is no go. I rather feel I've had a load this winter but yet I've so much to be thankful for.

I think I'll attend college this summer. I don't know. I have enough saved in the bank to almost get my degree, then I can take better care of Clinton.

If you folks could get a chance, I still wish you could come here. I realize it is a long trip but I surely would like to see you.

I think Aalyce will come here for his memorial services. Wish you could, too—

Love,
Cleo

ON THE EAST COAST, George's parents also received the news in a telegram from the War Department. George's father was stationed in Charleston, South Carolina, placing radar installations up and down the East Coast. Mary had joined him in Charleston. A letter his mother had sent by V-Mail on March 2nd was returned. The envelope was stamped "Deceased." The letter was addressed to George at the 309th Bomb Wing and had a return address of Charleston, S.C. On receiving the news, Harry requested an emergency leave.

March 2, 1944

57

Dear George,

Received your letter, about your new job. They must think you are very valuable to them; maybe someday you will get your chance at flying. Since they need flyers so badly, they must consider you their No. 1 man, to take you off flying and give you this very important job.

They are making gliders at the Firestone aircraft plant at Willow Grove. They build CG-4A troop carrying gliders, and they are shipped to invasion ports in every theater of war, so they say, but I guess they don't have them where you are. Are you still someplace in New Guinea?

I got a letter from Harry yesterday and he told me your new address. It was a good thing he did, because your letter was so light, I couldn't hardly read it.

You say you received all the things we sent, did you get the box with the money belt in it and we have sent you two lots of film. Eleanor said you never mentioned the Digest that she and Warren sent you for Christmas, did you get it?

Cleo sent us a box of cheese. Wasn't that nice of her? We sure did appreciate her sending it to us, for I seldom buy any because of the [unintelligible].

I think Cleo is afraid that we will get the idea she is giving all her love to the baby and not saving any for you. She wrote us, how some mothers she knew gave all their love to the babies and that it could happen to her, because you are away. Only she said it won't with her, because the baby seems to bring you nearer. I told her the only thing about the baby, that looks like you was his eyes and his length. She said, she hopes he grows up to be as fine a man as his Dad, that she loves you very much. Cleo is a lovely girl and I'm proud to have her, the mother of my grandson.

Dad is still visiting around, but very busy. He sure got a dirty deal in Miami.

This paper is too short, must close.

Loads of love and good luck.

Mother

The Philadelphia Inquirer printed a picture of George on the front page, over the headline "South Jersey Flier is Killed in Action," but with the misinformation that he was a fighter pilot. The article also listed two other local airmen who were missing and a third who was reported as being a Nazi prisoner. At the end of the article, the casualty list for the day stated that 663 American souls had either been killed or were missing in action.

SOUTH JERSEY FLIER IS KILLED IN ACTION

War Fatality

CAPT. GEORGE F. FREDERICK

Two Other Airmen Missing: Ashland Man is Nazi Prisoner

A Laurel Springs fighter pilot was reported killed over New Guinea, two other fliers missing in the European area, and an Ashland bomber pilot, previously listed as missing, is now reported a Nazi prisoner, according to information sent their relatives today.

Two other South Jersey soldiers are reported wounded in the Central Pacific Theatre.

Killed:

Capt. George F. Frederick, 29, Beach and Lakeview Avenues, Laurel Springs.

Missing:

Lt. Donald F. Wagner, 23, of 424 North Sixth Street.

Staff Sgt. Howard R. Leconey, 22, of 48 Polk Street, Riverside.

Prisoner:

2nd Lt. John C. Marcotte, 21, Fourth Avenue, Ashland.

Wounded:

Pfc. Charles J. Laporta, 142 Chestnut Street, Williamstown.

Pvt. William R. Johnson, 824 Fern Street.

Captain Frederick, who participated in the capture of Lae and Salamaua and the first invasion of the Admiralty Islands, was killed March 30, according to a telegram received by his parents, Major and Mrs. Harry Frederick.

A personal letter of condolence was sent to Captain Frederick's relatives disclosing he has been recommended for the Silver Star for gallantry in action.

A graduate of Haddon Heights High School, he entered the service when the 44th Division, National Guard was federalized Sept. 16, 1940. He was a second lieutenant at that time and was commissioned a first lieutenant in April, 1941. He transferred to the air corps in February 1943, and was sent to Australia in April, last year.

Father in Service

Captain Frederick was secretary of the Laurel Springs Baptist Church Board of Trustees and superintendent of its Sunday school. His father, also a former National Guardsman, is stationed at Charleston, S.C.

Besides his parents, he is survived by a wife, Cleo, of Hiattville, Kansas; a five-month-old son, George C., and a brother Lt. Harry Frederick, Jr., stationed at the Aberdeen Proving Ground, Md.

Lt. Wagner recently was awarded the air medal and three oak leaf clusters. His last letter was dated April 4. He joined the air corps in March 1942, and received his basic training at Santa Ana, Calif. On Jan. 4, 1943, he received his wings and commission at Williams Field, Ariz. He has been overseas since Dec. 4, 1943. He was graduated from Riverside High school in 1938 and was employed at the RCA Manufacturing, Co., before going into the service. His father Louis is a veteran of World War I.

Missing Since April 13

Sgt. Leconey is the son of Mr. and Mrs. Thomas I. Leconey. He was a waist gunner on a B-17 bomber based in England. His family was notified he is "missing over Germany since April 13." On that date, 2000 American planes struck from Britain and Italy at Nazi aircraft and component factories along a 400-mile front through Schweinfurt and Augsburg in South Germany to Hungary.

Leconey entered the service Oct. 7, 1942. He went overseas in February, 1944. In his last letter April 10 he told his family he had completed six bombing missions. He attended Riverside High and was employed at Public Service before entering the air corps.

Lt. Marcotte was reported by the War Department last month as missing while on a bombing mission over Germany. His wife, Jennie, received a telegram Thursday saying he had been taken prisoner by the Germans.

Marcotte's commanding officer, who was on the flight, wrote Mrs. Marcotte her husband took part in a bombing attack on March 8 and after his plane was shot down he bailed out. That was the last seen of him.

Marcotte, son of Mr. and Mrs. Janvier J. Marcotte, of Woodcrest, enlisted in the Army Air Corps on Oct. 8, 1942. He received his wings on Sept. 30, 1943, at Napier Field, Ala., and went overseas Dec. 28, 1943. He was married Dec. 6 last year.

He attended St. Rose of Lima school, Haddon Heights, Camden Catholic High school and the Camden County Vocational school.

Private Johnson is a son of Mr. and Mrs. George Johnson. A brother, George E. Johnson, also serving in Italy, has written since that he visited his brother in a hospital and that he is now out of bed. William entered the Army in April of last year. He is in the field artillery.

LETTERS OF CONDOLENCE from George's buddies and superior officers poured in to Cleo. Also, on July 21, 1943, George had written an "In the Event of my Death" farewell letter, writing down his thoughts. Superstition among the troops held that writing such a letter when they were going into battle was bad luck. George had written the letter in July 1943, prior to the Lae invasion.

New Guinea
July 21, 1943

My dearest sweet Cleo,

 When you read this letter I will either be missing in action, killed or captured, and the last possibility is very remote because if I have any fight left in me, I will give my life to defend not only my country but the principles on which it was founded.

 I want you and our child to be able to live in freedom, as you want, wherever you want, and to do what you want. I want the opportunity for our child to be able to grow up and be kind, gentle and Christian, not barbarian like those we are fighting. To me, the Japs are worse than a pack of animals, because even so-called dumb animals have a sense of fairness.

 I want our child to be able to go to school and to college to learn whatever profession he or she wants to learn. If a boy, I want him to grow up and be a better man than his Dad. I want him to marry, if he chooses, a wife as kind and sweet as his mother. If a girl, I know she will be as fine a wife to some man as you have been to me.

 You will wonder why I have written this. I wonder myself, but last nite I lay thinking, what if I should be killed? Would Cleo know what my mind was thinking as to our future? I have no premonition of being killed and am trusting in the Lord to watch over me and keep me safe, but when He calls, I will be ready.

 It is a nice feeling, darling, to know that whatever happens to me, I will meet you again someday, but in a home that will be far nicer than any we could ever have had here on earth. So don't grieve, just think that I have gone away for a little while and I'll see you again.

 There is one favor that I ask. Back home, at my church, there is a plot of three lots that I had pictured fixing up someday as a children's playground with a tennis court, badminton court, swings, miniature golf and a sand pile for the little ones. I was hoping to be able to send enough money for that purpose from time to time so that when I get home I could fulfill my dreams, so, darling, if you will find out how much it will cost to do that and send the money to the church for that purpose if they want it. Of course, the whole lot will have a fence around it. Don't forget that.

One other thing comes to mind. You are young and beautiful and no doubt will meet several nice fellows that will want to marry you. The way I look at it, we said we were married until death do us part. Well, when you get this, we will have temporarily parted, but that won't prevent you from marrying again. In Heaven there is no marriage and no death, so we'll all be together anyway. Therefore, if you meet a nice young man who is willing to take you and provide a home for you and our child and probably some of his own, then you have my blessing and God be with you. All I ask that you make sure he is a Christian, because if he is, he will be kind and gentle and loving to you.

I have tried to be a Christian. I have sinned, but praise God, I know that He will forgive me my sins because I believe in Christ Jesus as my own personal Savoir and He watches over me always, until He is ready to take me home to Glory.

Farewell, my darling, until we meet again,

George

GENERAL HEADQUARTERS
SOUTHWEST PACIFIC AREA

A.P.O. 500,
April 6, 1944.

Mrs. Cleo V. Frederick,
Rural Free Delivery,
Hiattville, Kansas.

Dear Mrs. Frederick:

      I cannot express to you the poignancy of my regret at the death of your husband, Captain George F. Frederick.

      His service under me was characterized by his complete devotion to our beloved country and his noble death integrates him with its imperishable glory.

      I have lost a gallant comrade-in-arms and with you mourn a splendid gentleman.

Very faithfully,

Douglas MacArthur

Lt. Col. H. Carrington Smith RE (38861)
H.Q. 6 US Army
A.P.O. 442
6th April 1944

Dear Mrs. Frederick:

I am an Englishman serving in this theatre. I happened to be attached to the same Brigade as your husband and in fact was only a few yards from him when he was killed in action on 30th March.

I feel that I must write to tell you how inspiring his cheerfulness and courage were to all around him, both in hardship and in danger. In action his conduct was a shining example to all, and more than one man gained courage by his presence: at all times his cheerfulness and gay good humor put heart into everyone, and made them smile.

I only knew him for a few days but felt that I had lost a friend, and that your great country had lost a fine soldier and gentleman.

Please accept my deepest sympathy in what must be a most grievous loss.

Yours sincerely,

H. Carrington Smith

New Guinea
April 11, 1944

Dear Mrs. Frederick,

Of course by the time you receive this you will have been informed about your husband, Capt. Frederick. At a time like this there is little one can say in the way of helping but as one of "Freddie's" best friends,

I'll try to write what I think my wife would like to hear under the same circumstances.

When I first arrived in New Guinea I met "Freddie" & we were in the same section for 3 months. Only 5 of us were in the section and of course we became good friends as anyone would with him. He & I had many things in common, both flying officers, both married, and both with a child we had never seen. We often discussed our families & I think both felt like we knew each other's wives although we had never met them.

Speaking very truthfully, he was everyone's friend. This was very well proven when he received his promotion & everyone was very glad without any jealousy whatsoever.

His last operation was very efficiently handled as you can easily see when his citations & medals reach you & all justly earned. I'm sure you will be glad to know that he was very well & happy up to the day his accident occurred. I saw him only a short time before. It was a direct result of enemy action & happened very quickly, there being no suffering whatever on his part as is often the case.

He is buried on a small island about a mile from where he was killed along with 8 other good American boys. All died together in the same operation, fighting together for the same reason. It is a very beautiful island, peaceful now with the Japs entirely cleared from it. Before the war only about 6 or 7 white people lived on the island, a missionary & family and a plantation owner. I suppose there are about a hundred natives on the island. The little cemetery is on a knoll beside a coconut plantation & overlooking the Pacific Ocean. There is always much talk among men about whether they want to be taken back home if they should die overseas. I don't remember hearing "Freddie" express his opinion. Not in the form of giving advice but as my personal opinion, I don't think it advisable & don't think a better resting place could be found than where he is now with his friends with whom he fought side by side.

Perhaps I can see you sometime. I would like to meet you & have

*you meet my wife & family. When people are working & living togeth-
er they usually find friendship & become interested in each other's
friends & families. My wife's address is 720 Highland Ave., Princeton,
West Virginia. Feel free to write to either or both of us if you should like.*

*If there is anything you would like me to do, I would be very glad
to do it. Again, not knowing you personally, I don't know how much or
how little you would like to know about circumstances here. At present
because of censorship I couldn't name places or special events in relation
to "Freddie." But later, if you should desire, I could give you any little
minute details you might want to hear.*

*I hope you & family are well & can find some comfort and in
thought that the contribution to what we are fighting for represents the
most that can be given, or ever will be given by anyone.*

Sincerely,

1st Lt. John W. Guinn

HEADQUARTERS
ADVANCE ECHELON
FIFTH AIR FORCE
APO 713, UNIT 1

13 April, 1944.

Dear Mrs Frederick,

The officers and men who were George's closest friends and who were privileged to serve with him in combat have requested that I write you on behalf of all of us and express our deepest sympathy to you in your recent sorrow.

We fully realize that this letter will be small consolation, yet we sincerely feel that there are facts about George's life here that you and your son should know. We feel that you and Clinton will take pride in these facts as we have done here. Although we know that your loss is different from ours, nevertheless George's death was a severe shock and great loss to us too.

Lieutenant James C. King, his assistant, took charge of George's personal effects and has delivered them to Lieutenant Claude W. Shenkel of this headquarters. Lieutenant Shenkel has been offically appointed Summary Court, and has forwarded George's effects to Effects Quartermaster Kansas City, Missouri for forwarding to you.

George's record in this theatre has been more than impressive. On numerous occasions he has distinguished himself in combat with both American and Australian Troops. He possessed the rare ability of having a clear knowledge and full appreciation of both air and ground tactics. For this reason his services were invaluable to the Fifth Air Force. Surely promotion would have come to him as rapidly as the situation would have permitted. His ability as a staff officer actually was beyond his years. I have heard Major General Ennis Whitehead, Major General Ennis P. Swift, Brigadier General William C. Chase, Brigadier General Paul V. Wurtsmith, and many other high ranking officers of the Allied Forces in the Southwest Pacific, speak very highly of George and express their utmost confidence in him. I further know that his work has often come to the attention of Lieutenant General George C. Kenney.

Shortly before George's death he was recommended for the Distinguished Flying Cross and the Air Medal for extraordinary achievement while serving with the famous 7th Australian Infantry Division. During operations with this unit, George contributed invaluable service, in addition to his staff duties, by flying many important missions in light liaison aircraft. On numerous occasions the advance was planned on the information he brought back. Through his intrepidness and disregard for personal danger he gained the admiration and friendship of many Australians by flying wounded troops out of the front lines to rear echelon hospitals.

Enclosed you will find several letters of commendation which bears out the above statements. Unfortunately regulations prohibit forwarding the more explanatory communiques. I am sure however that in time, because these things do take time, that these medals will be duly presented to you.

Perhaps you may consider this somewhat of an empty gesture but I am sure that in the years to come these medals will be an inspiration to Clinton. When he must call upon his courage, these medals will remind him of the splendid fortitude and bravery that his father possessed.

George often spoke of his family, for whom he had the greatest devotion. If you care to, it would be appreciated by us if you will send a copy of this letter to his father. An extra copy is enclosed for this purpose.

As you know George was a very religious boy. Although he made no outward display of his beliefs, the manner that he lived his life each day was ample evidence of this fact. Without those beliefs I do not believe that he could have accomplished the things that he did. To the last his faith was never shaken.

For further information regarding (a) his effects, (b) his arrears and gratuity pay, and (c) his insurance, you may communicate directly with (a) The Effects Quartermaster, Kansas City, Missouri (b) The General Accounting Officer, Washington, D.C. and (c) The Veterans Administration, Washington, D.C.

In this sorrow our thoughts are with you particularly and if there is anything we can do or anything that you desire to know please do not hesitate to call upon us.

Very Sincerely Yours,

SPENCER SHROPSHIRE,
Major Air Corps.

Mrs George F. Frederick,
Hiatville, Kansas.

2 Incls:
  Incl #1-Ltr. Commendation fr Maj. Gen. Whitehead.
  Incl #2-Ltr. Commendation fr Maj. Gen. Vasey.

359

A LEGACY OF LETTERS

Cleo's father, Perry Campbell, was a most caring and compassionate person. His only vice was that he could swear up a storm when he was "talking" to his assortment of farm animals, particularly the mules, pigs, and cattle, but he could also deliver the most eloquent of prayers in church. He missed his calling, since he should have been a veterinarian, and his stock was always fed before he fed himself. On a stormy April 21st, he wrote a heartfelt letter to George's father, Major Harry Frederick.

Hiattville, Kan. April 21 – 44

Dear Major Frederick

I tho't I would drop you a line to let you know we share with you in sorrow of our son who has made the Supreme Sacrifice for his Country. I never got to see George very much as he was here a good many times when I was in the fields or threshing or haying, but he impressed me very much and the mail carrier commented on his faithful correspondence to Cleo. There acquaintance and courtship was rather short, but they were sure devoted to each other.

Cleo has stood up under shock better than I expected, as you perhaps know, she has not been home from hospital very long. She has the sweetest baby you ever saw, so good natured and considering what he has went through.

If you and your wife could make us a visit I am sure we would be glad to have you come anytime, either of you or both, as to particulars concerning Geo's death we don't know much yet. He wrote Cleo about 26th March that he was in first wave assault under one of greatest barrages he ever saw. He & other officer went got 2 first Japs in there outfit, said he had lost some weight otherwise he was OK & also said he expected to go back to Sydney on leave. Looks like they rushed him back in there.

We got a letter from a Lt. wife that George met death by a Jap sniper. The Admiralty Islands must been some pretty hard spots, as there are numerous casualty in this community reported from that theatre. I know it is terrible hot, I heard soldier say who was in New Guinea that sweat ran off their elbows while eating dinner. I never heard of George complaining about food. I got one letter from him I suppose when in New Guinea that he could buy whole valley for 200 & spoke about some things raised there, this may not be news to you.

Our oldest boy is working in Wichita on the Big 29 bomber, weights 131 ton can go to Japan & back to west coast on own fuel carried 75 mill cannon, holds 3 truck loads of ammunition. Things will soon be Germany as some ground crews have all ready went over seas. Our youngest boy Chester, navigator on B 24—stationed in Plymouth, England been battle ???? Lasted 4 days & nights he didn't say much about it, only said what fun he had. He is hoping to come home soon— has enough combat hours, I will close hoping the mother is better—we had time with Cleo for while, hoping this hellish war will soon end in a complete V.

P M Campbell

George's parents took Perry up on his offer. They boarded a train on the East Coast and went to Kansas. Letha had lived in the old farmhouse before the turn of the century. The first floor of the main house had two rooms. One was heated with a potbelly stove, the other they called the "summer room." The top floor had three bedrooms, one for the parents, one for the boys, and one for the girls. The kitchen was added in 1900 and had two porches, one on the west side and another on the east.

Having a small garden in New Jersey, the Fredericks were fascinated with the one-acre garden and size of the farm as they walked the pastures. Major Frederick, in his uniform, drove the Oliver 70 tractor, and Perry put on his

Sunday best overalls with white shirt, tie, and hat, and Cleo took their picture. The Fredericks stayed but a few days before they packed up Cleo and me and traveled back to New Jersey. They had a sleeper car. Cleo and I were in the top berth, with me the "happy, good natured" baby crying all the way.

Pappy Frederick received George's last letter, ironically postmarked March 30th, the day he was killed, telling about his boss, General Whitehead. Never shy about making a request, Harry wrote to General Whitehead, asking for as much detail as could be revealed concerning George's death and telling him that my grandmother, Mary wasn't taking the news very well. General Whitehead responded:

HEADQUARTERS
ADVANCE ECHELON
FIFTH AIR FORCE
APO 713 UNIT 1

9 May 1944

Major Harry Frederick,
P. O. Box 196,
Charleston, South Carolina.

My dear Major Frederick:

Your letter of April 21st concerning the recent loss of your son, George, has reached me. Please accept my deepest sympathy. I am very sorry that Mrs. Frederick has reacted so unfortunately to the news, though I can understand her grief.

While certain details must necessarily be withheld for a time for security reasons which I am sure you appreciate, I will gladly do what I can to answer your questions about George's death. He died as any soldier would wish to die: in direct contact with the enemy. On March 30th during operations in the Admiralty Islands he was leading his party in offensive work when he fell with two bullets through his left lung. Death was instantaneous. George was leading the fatal mission voluntarily and his participation in a mission of this nature was not a part of his regular assignment, but was far above his normal call of duty. The spirit he showed in undertaking such a hazardous task, when his orders did not require it, can well serve as an inspiration for every member of the Fifth Air Force.

It is true that George and his party were shortly to be relieved of duty in the combat area. They had served long in a most hazardous situation, and had received the highest commendations for their work, not merely from myself but from many high-ranking officers who were closely associated with them. It is ironic that George fell so near the end of his tour.

We here remember him with pride. In our view, George was a brave soldier, a courageous leader, and altogether a fine comrade. His loss is keenly felt by all of us.

Sincerely,

DENIS C. WHITEHEAD,
Major General, U. S. Army,
Deputy Air Force Commander.

Sunday, May 14, the 1st Baptist Church in Laurel Springs was filled to capacity for George's memorial service. Cleo and the Frederick family arrived early for the service. Two ladies were in a heated argument over where to place the candles in the church that were to symbolize George's passing. Reverend Bramhall announced to the congregation George's wish for a playground that he'd written about in his "farewell letter."

CAPTAIN GEORGE F. FREDERICK

MEMORIAL SERVICE

Sunday, May 14, 1944

CAPTAIN GEORGE F. FREDERICK

Born December 14, 1914 • Killed in Action March 30, 1944

Laurel Springs (N. J.) Baptist Church

REV. PAUL A. BRAMHALL, Pastor

MILITARY RECORD

Captain George F. Frederick enlisted in the National Guard of New Jersey, February 7, 1933, and attained the rank of Second Lieutenant, Infantry, N.G.U.S., November 28, 1938. He entered on active duty with the 57th Brigade, 44th Division, September 16, 1940, and was promoted to First Lieutenant April 30, 1941. For a time he took special training in Motor Transport at Fort Benning, Ga. After being transferred to the Air Corps February 25, 1942, he took his initial pilot training at Kelly Field, Texas, and primary training at Tulsa, Oklahoma; Ellington and Randolph Fields, Texas, and Pittsburg, Kansas. He received his wings on March 15, 1943, as a Glider Pilot at South Plains Army Flying School, Lubbock, Texas. He volunteered for foreign service and left for over seas April 21, 1943.

He was assigned to the 5th Air Force and attached to the 7th Australian Division. He later was assigned as Air Liaison Officer with the Advance Eschelon, 5th Air Force, with headquarters at Port Moresby, New Guinea. He was further promoted to Captain November 28, 1943, and participated in the assault and capture of Lae and Salamau as well as the battle of Ramu Valley. In these battles Captain Frederick served as Liaison Officer attached to the 7th Australian Division, who were nicknamed "The Cut-throats" by the Japs.

He was later transferred to the 309th Bomber Wing as co-ordinator of the air support. Soon afterward the Captain took part in the first invasion of Los Negros Island in the Admiralty group of the Bismrak Archipelago, Southwest Pacific Area and several other amphibious operations in that locality and was killed in action March 30, 1944.

For his gallantry in action, courage in danger, and accomplishments in operation, Captain Frederick was recommended by the Task Force Commander for the Silver Star and received a personal citation by the Commanding General of the Advance Eschelon of the Fifth Air Force.

He was laid to rest, on a small island about a mile from where he met his accident, along with eight other good American boys who died in the same operation; fighting together for freedom. The little cemetery is on a knoll beside a cocoanut plantation overlooking the Pacific Ocean. It is a very beautiful island, peaceful now with the enemy entirely cleared from it.

I Thess. 4:13—"I would not have you to be ignorant of those who sleep in Jesus, for the dead in Christ shall rise first. Wherefore comfort one another with these words."

PERSONAL RECORD

George F. Frederick was born in Phi'adelphia, Pa., December 14, 1914. His parents were Mr. Harry and Mrs. Mary Frederick. He graduated from the Laurel Springs (N. J.) Public School in June, 1928, and from Haddon Heights High School in June, 1932, afterward attending the Peirce School of Business Administration.

He became a member of the Laurel Springs Sunday School. Upon his confession of Christ as his Saviour, he was baptized June 26, 1932, and became a member of the church. From the start he was interested and active in everything. He became Financial Secretary of the church January 13, 1935, and a trustee April 8, 1935. He was the Secretary of the Board since 1935. As early as 1936 his interest in the Young People's Society was inspiring. He was not only President of the local society, he was also First Vice President of the Camden County B. Y. P. U. It was only his service in the Armed Forces which caused him to leave these. He was slated to become President of the Camden County B. Y. P. U.

George Frederick was Superintendent of the Laurel Springs Baptist Sunday School from July, 1940. He became Honorary Superintendent April 20, 1942, with the hope and expectation of his soon return.

He was married to Cleo Vista Campbell, of Farlington, Kansas, in the Post Chapel at South Plains Army Flying School, by an Army Chaplain, Kenneth B. Combs, on November 28, 1942.

His son, George Clinton Frederick, was born November 24, 1943.

He is survived also by his father, Major Harry Frederick, and mother, Mrs. Mary Frederick, and brother, Lieutenant Harry Frederick, and a sister, Mrs. Eleanor Mackara.

On April 20, 1944, we were all saddened by the news that George had been killed on March 30, 1944.

In one letter he wrote and said that he knows Jesus Christ as his own personal Saviour.

LETTER OF CONDOLENCE FROM
GENERAL MacARTHUR

General Headquarters

S. W. Pacific Area

A. P. O. 500,
April 6, 1944.

Mrs. Geo. F. Frederick,
Hiattville, Kansas.

Dear Mrs. Frederick:

I cannot express to you the poignancy of my regret at the death of your husband, Captain George F. Frederick.

His service under me was characterized by his complete devotion to our beloved country and his noble death integrates him with its imperishable glory.

I have lost a gallant comrade-in-arms and with you mourn a splendid gentleman.

Very faithfully,
DOUGLAS MacARTHUR.

IN MEMORIAM

Let each of us consecrate ourselves to his unfinished tasks, so that, as he dreamed and planned, we might not fail him.

After the service, the Fredericks were loading into the car, but Cleo said she wanted to walk home. Pappy Frederick sensed that something was bothering her, so Mary took me home in the Buick while Pappy walked with Cleo. Walking along the tranquil tree-lined streets of Laurel Springs, Pappy asked Cleo what was bothering her.

"I'm worried about the playground. If the old biddies at the church can't even agree where to put candles, how are they going to agree on the playground? What if a ball goes through a window, or a neighbor's window?" she asked. "I want to fulfill George's wish, but I can't see how the church can manage it if they can't agree on where to place candles."

Harry agreed, saying, "George wanted a playground, but the church needs an organ. I'm sure he wouldn't mind if you got an organ instead. The whole congregation, including the kids, will enjoy the music."

Cleo bought an organ for the church. Then she returned to Kansas not long after the memorial service. She received a letter from General Kenney and was notified that George had been awarded the Distinguished Flying Cross, Air Medal, and the Legion of Merit. The Legion of Merit was awarded in place of the Silver Star, although a letter from Major Shropshire had stated that he'd been awarded the Silver Star in addition to the other medals.

> **HEADQUARTERS**
> **FIFTH AIR FORCE**
> **APO 925**
>
> May 18, 1944.
>
> Dear Mrs. Frederick:
>
> Your husband, Captain George F. Frederick, who lost his life on March 30, 1944, while serving his country, has been awarded the Distinguished Flying Cross for extraordinary achievement during combat missions from August 22 to October 16, 1943.
>
> It is a tribute to the memory of a gallant officer paid by his country, by his colleagues, and by his commander in recognition of fearless and unselfish service to the ideals for which every American is fighting.
>
> I offer you my deepest sympathy in the loss of your husband; my sympathy and the promise that those of us left will keep on fighting for what your husband believed in: a world free of dictators and persecution, a world of peace.
>
> Very sincerely,
>
> GEORGE C. KENNEY,
> Lieutenant General
> Commanding.
>
> Mrs. Cleo V. Frederick,
> Hiattville, Kansas.

Pappy Frederick renewed his request to be transferred to the South Pacific directly to Major Shropshire. His request was approved and by July 16th, he was on a train headed west, with a stopover in Chicago. His route took him to Nevada, but he returned to New York, where he boarded a ship that took him through the Panama Canal. He arrived in New Guinea a few months later. He remained in the service after the war and was stationed in Japan, where he learned to speak Japanese.

USO
Chicago, Ill
17 July 1944

Dearest Mary:

Just a few lines to tell you, sweetheart, how much I miss you and the family after only such a short time away from you. I did not mind your tears yesterday when we parted. In fact, I appreciated your bravery and sacrifice in those tears, because when I think how long it will be until I see your dear face and hold your sweet self again in my arms, my heart fills with loneliness and longing for you.

It was a great comfort to talk to you over the telephone and you can rest assured I will make every effort to call you before going over. In the meantime, my every thought will be exercised to you by mail at every opportunity.

Right after I talked to you on the phone, I walked into the men's room here at the station, when a voice said, "What are you doing here?" It was Maj. Evans (formerly Capt. Evans) of the 114th Infantry, who was going back to his home in Camden after being in Alaska for nearly two years. He was on the regimental staff in Camden when I was there and we went to Fort Dix and several maneuvers together. He and George knew each other very well and he was deeply shocked to hear of his death. He did not know about it until I told him. He was slightly wounded at Attu last year but recovered all right. He has been ordered to the AMG School at Charlottesville, VA.

Took a street car to go uptown and when I offered my fare, the conductor said no charge for servicemen. The PTC or Public Service should do likewise.

Walked around awhile and when passing one of the department stores called "The Fair," it brought back fond memories and took me back to the year 1919 when you, George, Harry, and I were out here enjoying ourselves at the Zoo and along the lake. Little did I dream

371

then, I would be out here 25 years later alone on another mission. Let us hope and pray that this silly war will soon be over and we and our children and grandchildren can enjoy ourselves again and no more sad parting and heartaches.

You can, of course, realize too how much I miss my pals, two of the sweetest and best daughters in the world—I mean Eleanor and Mary Anne. They sure have filled the void in our home and with Warren sacrificing his time and money to be home, especially this past weekend, and Harry and Bonnie spending all their time with us on Saturday and Sunday, makes me appreciate what fortunate parents we are and what a future heritage we have as grandparents.

I could go on and on writing about the many incidents that have occurred to endear ourselves to George, to Harry, and to Eleanor, but it would take reams and reams of paper, and all we can do is to thank our Lord and Master for such wonderful memories and pray that our grandchildren will grow up into the same honest and faithful manhood and womanhood as their fathers and mothers.

Took in a movie this afternoon to pass the time away. It was called "The White Cliffs of Dover" and, as usual, was another war picture. However, I did enjoy the newsreel.

It has started to rain, but as I am here at the station to take the train for Denver in about an hour, I won't get wet.

Am anxiously awaiting your letters and to know if Pumkin misses me in addition to yourself and Eleanor, because I sure do.

Well, that's all now, my darling. Will write you from Denver tomorrow.

Your ever loving,

Harry

drh-2512

WAR DEPARTMENT
THE ADJUTANT GENERAL'S OFFICE
WASHINGTON 25, D.C.

IN REPLY REFER TO:
AG.201 Frederick, George F.
(18 Aug 44) PD-C 0372 630

18 August 1944

.Mrs. Cleo V. Frederick,

Hiattville, Kansas.

My dear Mrs. Frederick:

I have the honor to inform you that, by direction of the President, the Distinguished Flying Cross and the Air Medal have been posthumously awarded to your husband, Captain George F. Frederick, Air Corps. The citations relating to these awards are as follows:

DISTINGUISHED FLYING CROSS

"For extraordinary achievement while participating in aerial flights in the Southwest Pacific Area from 22 August 1943 to 16 October 1943. During this period, Captain Frederick participated in sustained operational activity against the enemy during which hostile contact was probable and expected. Supplies were dropped and troops transported to advanced positions. These flights involved flying at low altitudes over mountainous terrain under adverse weather conditions in an unarmed transport airplane and often necessitated landing within a few miles of enemy bases. Throughout these operations, Captain Frederick displayed outstanding courage and devotion to duty."

AIR MEDAL

"For meritorious achievement while participating in sustained operational flight missions in the Southwest Pacific area from 21 October 1943 to 23 December 1943, during which hostile contact was probable and expected. Supplies were dropped and troops transported to advanced positions. These flights involved flying at low altitudes over mountainous terrain under adverse weather conditions in an unarmed transport airplane and often necessitated landing within a few miles of enemy bases. The courage and devotion to duty displayed by Captain Frederick during these flights are worthy of commendation."

The decorations will be forwarded to the Commanding General, Seventh Service Command, Omaha, Nebraska, who will select an officer to make the presentation. The officer selected will communicate with you concerning your wishes in the matter.

May I again express my deepest sympathy to you in your bereavement.

Sincerely yours,

J. A. ULIO,
Major General,
The Adjutant General.

WAR DEPARTMENT

THE ADJUTANT GENERAL'S OFFICE

REPLY REFER TO:

AGFD-R 201 Frederick, George F. WASHINGTON 25, D. C.
(16 Oct 44) 0 372 630

16 October 1944.

Mrs. Cleo V. Frederick,

Hiattville, Kansas.

My dear Mrs. Frederick:

I have the honor to inform you that, by direction of the President, the Legion of Merit has been posthumously awarded to your husband, Captain George F. Frederick, Air Corps. The citation is as follows:

LEGION OF MERIT

"For exceptionally meritorious conduct in the performance of outstanding services at Los Negros Island, Admiralty Group, from 29 February to 9 March 1944. Captain Frederick was the leader of an air liaison party which established and maintained communications between initial landing forces, the ground commander and Air Forces. From a position on top of a revetment, while under enemy small arms and mortar fire, he personally directed our aircraft in bombing and strafing attacks on the enemy and in the dropping of supplies to our own troops. This was the only means of supply for this force for five days. By his initiative and courage in this hazardous undertaking, Captain Frederick performed a valuable service and contributed to the success of our attack."

The Legion of Merit will be forwarded to the Commanding General, Seventh Service Command, Omaha, Nebraska, who will select an officer to make the presentation. The officer selected will communicate with you concerning your wishes in the matter.

May I again extend my deepest sympathy to you in your bereavement.

Sincerely yours,

J. A. ULIO,
Major General,
The Adjutant General.

In November 1944, the first award ceremony for presentation of the medals to Cleo was held at the Farlington Methodist Church. George's younger brother, Harry, went to Kansas for the presentation. Nettie Pyle, a neighbor with a beautiful soprano voice, sang "America's Prayer," looked at me as Col. Carroll was presenting the medals to Cleo, and broke down in tears. An article buried in the Pittsburg Sun described the ceremony.

Hero's Medals Presented to Widow

A Distinguished Flying Cross and an Air Medal which were awarded to Capt. George F. Frederick who was killed in action in the South Pacific were presented to his widow, Mrs. Cleo V. Frederick at the Farlington Methodist Church Sunday afternoon by Col. Joseph F. Carroll of the Independence Air Base at Independence, Kansas. Col. Carroll also read the citation awarding the Legion of Merit medal to Captain Frederick posthumously, the medal to be presented to Mrs. Frederick later.

A brother of Captain Frederick, now a lieutenant in the Air Force, was present at the ceremony. Mr. and Mrs. Harry Dunn, the parents of cousin, Clyde Dunn, who was reported missing in the same area and at about the same time as the Captain, were also present.

The presentation service was sponsored by the Geo. C. Brown Post of the American Legion who arranged the following program: invocation, Rev. C.T. Cotton; song, "America's Prayer," by Mrs. Maxine Throndson, Mrs. Nettie Pyle, Don and Cliff Hewett with Mrs. Ethel McCracken accompanist; address, Rev. Cotton; song, "America the Beautiful," by quartet; presentation of decoration, Col. Carroll; benediction, Rev. Cotton. Geo. F. Beezley presided.

Don and Cliff Hewett were Cleo's cousins. Normally they were a trio of Don, Dean, and Clifford, but Dean was serving in the Navy. Occasionally their younger sister Ruthie joined them in the singing. Cleo returned to New Jersey with George's brother, Harry, and stayed with Mary in Laurel Springs until late January 1945. Mary was having a difficult time over the death of George, and I gave her comfort. My grandmother grieved for George the rest of her life.

The Legion of Merit award ceremony was held in Wilmington, Delaware. A car was sent to Laurel Springs to pick up Cleo, George's sister, Eleanor, and Aunt Carrie to attend the ceremony. Mary Anne and I stayed home with our grandmother. At the ceremony, an officer was assigned to escort Cleo through the proceeding.

Cleo receiving Legion of Merit

In addition to Cleo's receiving the Legion of Merit awarded to George, there were also medals presented to other widows or family members. Cleo was the first of those receiving medals. She remembered that some of the others receiving medals were for those killed in the Doolittle Raid of April 1942. The raid launched B-25s from the deck of the USS Hornet, some 650 miles from Tokyo. The original plan was to get within 450 miles of Tokyo, but they were spotted by a Japanese fishing boat. The planes wouldn't be able to return to the carrier, but they flew the mission anyway, with the intention of crash-landing in China when their fuel was exhausted. The raid caused little physical damage to Tokyo, but had a great demoralizing impact on the Japanese and built morale and confidence in America. Lt. Col. Doolittle, who led the raid, received the Medal of Honor for his participation, and each member also received the Distinguished Flying Cross. Two members received the Silver Star.

ON A COLD WINTER DAY in December 1945, Cleo was home alone on the farm in Kansas when a neighbor a half-mile away saw that the old farmhouse was on fire. He rushed to the house and was able to get Cleo and myself out of the house. Cleo made one trip back into the house and retrieved a picture of George and whatever else she could grab. She rushed back out and tried to go back in to get the letters and memorabilia George had sent her, but the neighbor restrained her and wouldn't let her go back. Except for a few letters regarding George's death and his farewell letter, which she had placed in a safe deposit box, all her letters and memorabilia from George were destroyed.

In June 1946, Cleo taught Sunday school at the Farlington Methodist Church. Letha was making lye soap and watching me. I was $2^1/2$ years old and was into everything. I reached in a bowl of lye soap my grandmother was making and swallowed a handful of the liquid. Letha, realizing what I had done, forced me to drink vinegar in order to dilute the lye soap. When Cleo returned home, they took me to a doctor in Girard. The doctor told them the vinegar should help and sent us home. I stopped eating and began to lose weight. Finally, on the first of August, Cleo took me to Dr. Rush in Pittsburg.

Dr. Rush examined me and told Cleo that there was only one hospital that treated lye victims, saying, "The hospital is called Jefferson Hospital, but I don't know where it's located. It might be Chicago, Philadelphia, or New York."

Luckily Jefferson Hospital was found to be located in Philadelphia. Cleo called Laurel Springs and boarded a train for Philadelphia. By that time, the scar tissue from the lye in my esophagus was closing to the point where I was becoming dehydrated from lack of liquid. Cleo fed me water with an eye-dropper on the train ride.

At the same time that Cleo was riding the train to Philadelphia, Pappy Frederick was returning home from Japan on another train to Philadelphia. The trains arrived at nearly the same time. From the train terminal, they went directly to the VA Hospital in Philadelphia, which Pappy Frederick thought they should try first, but the VA Hospital said there was nothing they could do for me.

They went on to the Jefferson Hospital, where Dr. Clerf examined me and told Cleo that she might as well return to Kansas, since I was going to be in the hospital for a long time. He also told her that feeding me water with the eye dropper had probably saved my life.

Cleo stayed with the Fredericks in Laurel Springs and visited me in the hospital daily. In order to feed me, Dr. Clerf cut a hole in my stomach so I could be fed by pouring food through a rubber tube. To keep my esophagus open, they ran a string through my nose, down the esophagus, and out through the tube in the stomach. The string was kept in place by taping it to my cheek and the tube in my stomach was taped to my belly when not being used. By attaching a dilator to the string and pulling it through my esophagus, the doctors gradually stretched my esophagus enough to allow me to eat. I still have trouble eating to this day.

After a few months, I recovered enough for Cleo to take me back to Laurel Springs, but she had to take me to the hospital for periodic treatments. In the fall of 1947, arrangements were made for me to be treated at the KU Medical Center in Kansas City. We returned to Kansas, and two years later, the tube in my stomach was finally removed, along with the string that had been taped to my cheek.

Cleo didn't remarry, although she came close a few times. In 1953, she moved to Pittsburg and finished college with a degree in home economics. Although she hadn't applied for a teaching position, the Carl Junction, Missouri, high school contacted her and offered her a position teaching home economics and art. For the next twenty-two years, she taught home economics at Carl Junction. After retiring in 1977, she moved to Ft. Scott, Kansas.

Cleo's sister, Lorene, married another soldier she'd met after Lt. Walls was killed in the Normandy D-Day invasion and moved to Omaha,

Nebraska. Lavon married a soldier who was in Kansas recovering from malaria and wounds he'd received in Guadalcanal and moved to Salt Lake City. My grandfather, Major Harry Frederick, stayed in the Air Force and was stationed in occupied Japan, Germany, the Philippine Islands, and then again in Japan. He retired as a colonel in 1954. Harry Frederick, Jr. stayed in the reserves and attained rank of lieutenant colonel. He remained in New Jersey and worked as a commodities broker. Eleanor and Warren remained in Laurel Springs, where Warren worked at the Navy yard and later in naval aviation supply in Philadelphia.

Admiralty Islands

The obliteration of Pityilu was the last organized resistance by the Japanese in the Admiralty Islands. Seizing the Admiralties marked a new high in cooperation among ground troops, Navy, and Air Corps, despite the ego and stubbornness of the 2nd Brigade commanders. Nearly 900 bombing missions and 1,400 tons of bombs were dropped on the Admiralties by the 5th AAF. The Navy transported troops and shelled targets on the beaches as identified by the 12th ALP and the 1st Cavalry. The 1st Cavalry secured the land and the Seabees constructed and rehabilitated airfields and harbors.

General Swift wrote, "The Navy didn't support us, they saved our necks." He also wrote to General Kenney, saying, "What we accomplished we could not have accomplished without your help and cooperation."

In 1955, the U.S. Air Force released *Historical Study 86, Close Air Support in the War Against Japan*. The study concluded:

The close support operations in the Admiralties were a great advance over anything which had preceded them in the SWPA. Marking of front lines and of targets, lead-in planes, control of support aircraft from front-line observation posts, air-ground radio: all of these techniques were used extensively. Cooperation between air and ground, despite poorly executed strikes on some occasions and failure of ground troops to follow them up on others, was almost as good as that practiced on Luzon a year later.

Yet little advantage was to be taken of this experience. The techniques developed in the Admiralties were not to be employed extensively again until landings on Luzon, nor was comparable efficient close support for SWPA troops to be forthcoming until that same operation. This neglect was perhaps in part due to a less acute need for close air support after the Admiralties campaign, for its subsequent actions Allied troops outnumbered the defending Japanese, but such explanation would hardly appeal to the men engaged in the bitter battles along the Drinimour, at Lone Tree Hill, and on Biak, where many ground support but few close support sorties were flown. A more probable explanation is that the death on Pityilu Island of Captain Frederick, who had in large measure been responsible for the great progress made in the Admiralties, prevented the dissemination of his experience to other Supporting Air Parties for use in future operations.

Seeadler Harbor, considered by some to be the largest and finest natural harbor in the world, became home to the 7th Fleet. The Navy base became one of the largest, if not the largest in United States history. Different ports throughout the islands catered to different types of ships: a submarine base at Manus, a liberty ship and PT boat overhaul base at Hyane Harbor, and a base for carrier units at Pityilu and Ponam. A hydroelectric power plant captured the power of the Lorengau River and 180 warehouses for supplies were constructed on Manus Island. Hospitals capable of servicing a city of 100,000 were constructed, and at any one time, more than 100,000 troops were stationed in the islands. Four airfields were constructed, and it became home to the 13th AAF in June, as well as the 73rd RAAF Wing.

Pityilu airfield was transformed into a practice and training field for aircraft carrier planes, and eighty acres were devoted to the construction of the finest recreation center in the Pacific Theater. The center could accommodate 10,000 men and included baseball diamonds, basketball and volleyball courts, shark-proof pools, a boxing ring, and "Duffy's Tavern," which could accommodate 200 thirsty customers. USO shows were staged every two or three weeks, and there were several visits by Bob Hope, where a special "Quonset Palace" was constructed for him with all the amenities available, although he never used it. Apparently, no one ever told him or his crew that the palace was for him, and he walked right past it on his way to and from the show.

From the Admiralties, bombing raids were conducted on the Caroline and Marianas Islands to the north and west up the north coast of New Guinea toward the Philippines. The Admiralties became the principal assembly point for the invasion of the Philippine Islands when, in October 1944, nearly 600 ships uncoiled from Seeadler Harbor as they sailed with 200,000 troops and into the greatest naval battle in history. The battle would cover more than 100,000 square miles and involve 282 ships. The Japanese lost four aircraft carriers, three battleships, nine cruisers, twelve destroyers, hundreds of planes, and thousands of lives in a stunning defeat.

Although small in comparison to many other battles, military historians consider the gains made from the Admiralty Islands invasion to be one of the most important battles of World War II as it stranded so many enemy troops.

WWII LEFT A FAMILY BEHIND—parents that grieved, along with a brother and sister, a most loving wife who lost her husband before a honeymoon, nieces, nephews, and grandchildren who never benefited from his humor, wisdom, and ethics. He also left me behind, a son he never saw or knew. How ironic. Fifty years later, a trunk in an attic would be opened, and there would be his letters, providing the opportunity for me to relish in his life and get to know him. I grieved for the father I never knew, but now I grieve more for the father I have come to know.

It's been said that WWII was "the last good war," But I would think that humanity would realize there is no good war. Wars are fought over greed or religious differences. There should always be an alternative to war and war should be invoked only as a matter of last resort.

I agree with my grandmother, who once said, "Put the world leaders on an island and don't let them come off until they have settled their differences."

THE END

APPENDIX 1 - Noted Acts of Heroism[lxvi]

There were many individual acts of heroism in WWII. These are only the ones that were compiled in April 1944 by the 1st Cavalry Division Headquarters. Note that some were omitted for whatever reason, most notably Sgt. Troy McGill, who received the Medal of Honor and whose story was told in the narrative of this book. In my opinion, all who served were heroes.

Date	Person	From	Act
2/29/44	S/Sgt Bobbie K. Horton	Alpine, TX	Replaced Navy gunner on landing craft after he had been killed and covered landing
	Pvt. George L. Sumpter	Mt. Holly, NC	Comrade in adjoining foxhole was stalked by two of enemy—he was also stalked—killed two stalkers—turned and killed his stalker
	Pvt. Walter E. Hawks	Wylie, TX	Killed eight of the enemy in group, exposing his position in outlying foxhole—was charged by twenty—held position despite grenade and fire—killed all that charged him (twenty-eight total)
3/1/44	Lt. Col. John R. Hall, Jr.	El Paso, TX	Rescued Capt. Joseph Q. Tuck, of Winterville, GA—was wounded in process—Tuck caught grenade while being drug out of way and tossed it back
	Pvt. Andrew R. Barnabei	Philadelphia, PA	Laid grenade outside his foxhole—killing five—exposed himself to enemy—received concentrated attack
	S/Sgt. Gilbert Newman	Mt. Enterprise, TX	Removed wounded officer from enemy emplacement while under small arms and grenade fire and subsequently helped destroy the stronghold
	Maj. Julio Chiaramonte	Gallup, NM	Enemy patrol penetrated command post and he led group that destroyed it—cool daring and inspiration to troops

3/2/44	Pvt. Leo W. Zoeller	Buffalo, NY	On patrol encountered enemy grenade mg emplacement – while Garvin covered Zoeller—threw two grenades into stronghold killing four of the enemy
	M/Sgt. David P. Garvin	Jacksonville, FL	Was NCO above—killed remaining enemy and recovered valuable documents and equipment that contributed to the continuing conduct of the operations (See enemy orders)
3/3/44	Lt. Col. Kenneth L. Johnson	Santa Barbara, CA	Commanded 75mm howitzer battalion on attack of perimeter—"extraordinary heroism" for placing guns in position to bring fire on enemy positions with disregard for heavy enemy fire directed at his exposed position
	Cpl. James R. Renfro	Kentucky	"Let's get 'em. Those guys don't even know the right words." Re: "Deep in the Heart of Texas" incident—group surrounded 100—thirty killed—seventy committed suicide "That saves a lot of ammunition"—Gen. Chase comment
	Cpl. Bill Alcine	*Yank Magazine*	Story of Cpl. Joe Hodonski of Chicago, IL—Japanese spoke English—"How you doin' Joe?" —Joe shot him.
	Cpl. Clarence W. Josephson	Bay City, WI	Transported artillery ammunition to battery position fifty yards through confused infiltrating enemy firing and defending troops enabled battery to maintain fire mission
	Maj. Don G. Gentry	Topeka, KS	Placed antiaircraft weapons in position while under fire—inspired troops—silenced enemy artillery and mortar fire
	Pfc. Harold E. Schmidt	Bellevue, IA	Manned light machine-gun in outer rim in midst of vicious sustained enemy assault—repulsed every enemy attack on his position
	Cpt. Carroll W. Seiber	Willis, VA	Effectively supported the attacks of ground troops while enemy field pieces made particular efforts to destroy his support—despite numerous casualties

			Seiber reorganized his battery on several occasions and his personal example was inspiration to his men
	Cpl. Jesse W. Keeton	McKinney, TN	Foxhole on the perimeter subjected to attacks by suicidal enemy groups—low on ammunition Keeton under enemy and defensive fire secured ammo from rear for his squad
3/4/44	Lt. Col. William E. Lobit	Galveston, TX	Extraordinary leadership and inspiration to men—his forcefulness, aggressiveness, cool courage, and determination resulted in suspension of assault and established defensive perimeter that defeated a numerically superior force
	Cpl. John E. Walkney	Pittsburgh, PA	Sustained enemy counterattack—Walkney's platoon forced to abandon a heavy machine-gun to secondary defensive position—Walkney returned—put gun in working order and killed many enemy in front of gun—Walkney found killed at the gun
	Cpl. Henry W. Patrick, Pvt. Carl E. Derringer	Big Sandy, TN, Wichita, KS	Disregarded heavy enemy fire that threatened to blow ammunition dump and continued to load ammunition for transport to battery gun positions
	Pfc. Frank J. Mitchell	Dorchester, MA	Same action as above except Mitchell at battery post after NCO left to bring forward ammunition—Mitchell continued fire against strong desperate enemy attack and repulsed it
	Lt. Horace E. Beaman	Indianapolis, IN	Saved a fellow officer's life by removing him from enemy fire despite being fired on himself
	S/Sgt. Clarence D. Sparks	Dallas, TX	Superior enemy force launched amphibious attack along beach—as barges neared shore fired until his machine-gun burned out—disregarding enemy fire left safety of emplacement retrieved another gun and started firing again forcing enemy to abandon barge—enemy killed wading ashore

	Capt. Charles C. Wright	Vernon, TX	Disregarded enemy fire and called for artillery fire over his observation post and adjusted fire that eliminated several enemy machine-gun positions
3/7/44	Cpt. William Cornelius	Nashville, TN	Regimental S-2, (Intelligence)—although duties didn't call for it, assumed command of a reconnaissance platoon—crossed from Porlaka to Papitalai with reconnaissance party to gain valuable information and was killed doing so
	S/Sgt. Frank W. Rye	Stamford, TX	Lead platoon spearheaded amphibious attack on Papitalai Mission—reached beach eliminated enemy machine-gun crew enabling rest of platoon to occupy beachhead—platoon leader a casualty and Rye assumed command and repulsed strong counterattack—was such a commanding figure he drew the concentrated fire of the enemy and was killed himself
	Lt. Alfred W. Prentice	El Paso, TX	Wounded early in the above engagement—ordered platoon to move in on a shack twenty-five yards from beach—one man killed in doorway—Prentice went in side and killed the Japanese—rejoined platoon as twenty-five enemy soldiers attacked—deployed platoon and firepower and killed twelve—seriously wounded, he killed seven but drove numerically superior force back and secured beachhead
3/10/44	Lt. Joseph Curtin	Location Unknown	G-3 Section—While on a souvenir hunt, a fact which he vigorously denied, discovered a Jap hiding in a bunker located about 100 yards from the Division CP—persuades him to surrender.
3/11/44	Pfc. Warren Pruitt	Huntington, TN	Hauwei Island battle—reconnaissance platoon ambushed—wounded Pruitt retained position and continued fire on enemy—advanced through jungle on enemy pillbox containing three machine-guns, drawing concentrated fire—attempt to destroy pillbox

			unsuccessful and Pruitt killed—although action permitted successful withdrawal for remainder of his squad—this was a particularly costly battle
3/14/44	Lt. Wm. H. Swan	Tucson, AZ	Troop B 5th Cavalry—platoon led by Lt. Ralph Hill was killed advancing 15 yards in front of enemy position—Lt. Swan, Executive officer of Troop D, close behind, was wounded—administered first aid to self came forward assumed command of the assault platoon and eliminated enemy strongpoint
	Cpl. Elmer L. Carlton	Arkansas City, KS	Stopped by heavy fire from enemy automatic weapons and due to casualties only machine-gun in action was a heavy water-cooled gun that was target of enemy fire—gun put out of action and two members of crew wounded—disregarding enemy fire, moved gun to a better position and assisted wounded crew member to deliver fire against enemy—enemy fire riddled Carlton's legs but he continued firing from a submachine-gun, enabling rest of troops to eliminate the enemy
3/15/44	Pvt. Garvin O. Presslar	Rogue River, OR	Enemy sniper held up the advancing troops—Presslar crawled along beach covered by shallow water and observed by enemy sniper that Presslar killed
	Pvt. Albert H. McDonald	Oakland, CA	Troops stopped due to terrain and dense jungle, but McDonald disregarded enemy fire and snipers crawled forward despite three wounds and threw a hand grenade into enemy entrenchment
	T/5 Clifford Briney	Detroit, MI	Briney mission was to locate approach for landing craft to beach—underwater reefs, mines and other obstacles—wounded by sniper, he disregarded enemy fire and completed his mission.
	Pfc. Elston B. Ferguson	Hillsboro, IN	Established wire communication between a forward mortar observation post and the mortar unit through an area being swept by enemy fire.

	1st Sgt. William J. Bretton	El Paso, TX	When the advance point was fired on from a concealed enemy position Bretton rushed forward under fire and rescued a wounded man lying directly in front of the enemy position
	S/Sgt. Jesse P. Johnson	Oakland, CA	Exposed himself to enemy fire in order to deploy troops to take out multiple enemy positions that had halted the advance.
	Pvt. Leslie A. Teter	St. Joseph, MO	On a reconnaissance patrol behind enemy lines enemy automatic fire was encountered that threatened annihilation of the patrol. Alone, Teter crawled forward and eliminated the automatic rifle nest. Enemy automatic fire was then encountered from another position. Teter continued his advance and while throwing hand grenades on the enemy position was killed.
	Sgt. Ervin M. Gauthreaux	White Castle, LA	When his platoon leader was wounded, Gauthreaux reformed the platoon and with great skill and leadership while under enemy fire moved them into effective tactical position preventing further casualties and enabled the platoon to complete their mission.
3/16/44	Pfc. Woodrow W. Chambers	Denham Springs, LA	Crawled to within five yards of enemy position attempting to destroy it when he was killed by enemy fire—enabled rest of platoon to advance while enemy occupied with Chambers
	Cpl. Richard L. Elliott	Turkey, TX	Led group of volunteers in attempt to eliminate by hand grenades enemy emplacement that had stopped troop advance—ten yards from emplacement, entire group became casualties but disregarding his own wounds, refused to withdraw until he effected removal of his comrades to safety
	Cpl. John A Freese	Madison, WI	Ran 100 yards with a wounded comrade over an exposed area, disregarding own safety under withering enemy fire saving comrade

388

Sgt. Virgil A. Hutchinson	Garrison, TX	Platoon stopped by enemy fire—advanced with light machine-gun through enemy fire and destroyed pillbox—enemy retreated—Hutchinson followed and killed enemy, enabling platoon to advance
Pfc. Carson Hall	Detroit, MI	Crawled within ten yards of enemy emplacement—wounded, he provided inspiration and stimulus to remainder of his unit on the assault although his attempt was not successful
Pvt. John J. Kriger	Santa Barbara, CA	Troops caught in crossfire—wire communication necessary for mortar fire—Kriger ran 200 yards and delivered message to platoon leader enabling withdrawal of remaining troops so artillery fire could destroy enemy—Kriger was killed in accomplishing the feat
Cpl. Doyce C. Price	Summitt, GA	Displayed outstanding gallantry and superb disregard of personal danger under heavy enemy fire reaching a point within ten yards of enemy emplacement—seriously wounded, he attempted to complete mission but was unable to do and was removed to safety—provided inspiration and courage to remainder of the troop
Pfc. Leo V. Tomlin	Union, MS	Over four-hour period, served as medical technician to 14 wounded soldiers saving their lives—outstanding devotion to duty under most arduous circumstances
Sgt. Virley L. Leonard	Tuscaloosa, AL	Left safety of his shelter and disregarding enemy fire, aided wounded comrades by moving them to safety, saving their lives
Pvt. Roy V. Little	San Bernardino, CA	Volunteered for suicidal mission with a small group to charge enemy emplacement preventing advance—wounded and disregarding fire, assisted two comrades back to safety

Pvt. Willard F. Meulbrook	Location Unknown	Caught in heavy concentration of enemy fire, continued to operate machine-gun, enabling squad leader to evacuate 4 wounded members—moved gun and contributed to defeat of the enemy
Pvt. Ivan J. Mudd	San Diego, CA	Unaided, left protected position—advanced under enemy fire to strongpoint and killed three of the enemy with hand grenade and a fourth with his trench knife, enabling platoon to advance
Pfc. Willard F. Russell	Caribou, MO	Wounded and with intense enemy concentration of fire on his tank and another disabled tank, abandoned the protection of his tank—coupled the disabled tank to his tank and towed it to safety
Cpl. Grady D. Sharber	Nashville, TN	Caught under intense concentration of enemy fire from hidden positions, removed the machine-gun and four wounded members of his squad to a position of safety—afterward returned to the assault on the enemy
S/Sgt. Leldon T. Webb	Childress, TX	Under enemy concentrated machine-gun and sniper fire and although wounded, removed other wounded crew members to safety—thereafter assumed machine-gunner's position and continued fire, resulting in elimination of enemy position
Pfc. James B. Roche	Somerville, MASS	Caught between two ridges and pinned to ground by enemy machine-gun fire from prone position with two companions advanced to within five yards of enemy pillbox and attempted to reduce it with hand grenades—both companions wounded—Roche maintained position and covered withdrawal of with automatic rifle fire—Roche killed in subsequent battle
T/5 Elmer J. Blanken	Loveland, CO	Learned a seriously wounded soldier was lying under heavy enemy fire within a few yards of an enemy bunker—another

			aid man who attempted to reach the wounded soldier was killed attempting to rescue him—Blanken crawled through heavy fire—reached the soldier and administered first aid and remained with him until they could be rescued
3/17/44	T/5 Harold P. Waldum	Black River Falls, WI	While delivering supplies from landing craft, observed casualties awaiting evacuation from the beach—under intense enemy sniper and machine-gun fire, he manned the automatic weapons of the landing craft and delivered fire on the enemy, enabling the landing craft to rescue the wounded men
	1st Lt. Clyde W, James	San Antonio, TX	Observing two enemy barges offshore—waded to a reef and under concentrated sniper fire to which he was exposed directed artillery fire on the barges that destroyed them
3/18/44	Sgt. Glen A. Prater	White Pigeon, MI	With a companion, rushed a concealed pillbox and destroyed it, enabling platoon to advance
	Pvt. Lee E. Wilkerson	Lebanon, KY	Same action as Prather, went to aid of five comrades that were wounded from attempt to storm enemy strongpoint—succeeded in removing the wounded to safety along with Prater
	Pvt. Codzy L. Curnutt	Fruitvale, TX	Led an advance against heavy fortification and assisted companion to set up machine-gun, operating with such effect as to cause withdrawal of the enemy
	Cpl. Vincent J. Zlotow	Chicago, IL	Accompanied platoon Sgt. forward under fire, found enemy strongpoint, and assisted in its elimination
	Pfc. Duane C. Irwin	San Francisco, CA	Leading an advance against enemy, encountered sudden barrage of enemy machine-gun and sniper fire from hidden positions—moved a machine-gun through enemy fire into position and fired at enemy, forcing their retreat

3/19/44	Cpl. Peter J. Armstrong,	Philadelphia, PA	
	Cpl. Armando V. Valencia	Tucson, AZ	On Rossum road set heavy gun in position at thirty-five feet from bunker in direct fire and laid a continuous burst of fire on the bunker—wounded by sniper fire, sustained fire until grenade knocked him unconscious by his gun—Valencia took over and continued fire at bunker slits—action of the two enabled squad to destroy bunker
	Lt. Allen F. Davis	Albany, GA	Led small patrol deep into enemy territory securing vital information of enemy dispositions and destroyed large stores of enemy supplies
	T/5 Elijah B. Bailey, Jr.	Drew, MS	Came upon a tank disabled by enemy land mines—exposed to enemy automatic and sniper fire, he dismounted from safety of bulldozer and assisted in coupling tank and dragging it to safety
	Pvt. Joe T. Blackburn	Gearhart, KY	Advance scout in group of three, killed two enemy soldiers who had wounded his companions and searched them for information while still under fire—assisted wounded in withdrawing, saving their lives—information gathered assisted in future operations against enemy
	Pvt. Maurice S. Noll	Easton, KS	Wounded in chest, covered the enemy fire on his position, enabling platoon to advance and destroy machine-gun nest
3/20/44	Pvt. Bill K. King	Durant, OK	Drove bulldozer and towed a disabled tank to safety while under enemy fire
	T/5 Earl Van Treese	Kansas City, MO	Treese and two other bulldozer operators, on patrol with troops, encountered heavy enemy fire and forced to withdraw—tank in patrol disabled by enemy land mine—operators drove bulldozer in front of disabled tank, dismounted while under fire and the three dozer operators pulled crippled tank and crew back to Lorengau Mission—during heavy enemy machine-gun fire, saw a wounded ANGAU Warrant Officer lying helpless

			on the trail—dashed across trail and dragged wounded man to safety
	Cpl. Grover S. Jordan	Rose, NE	Volunteered to stay with wounded platoon leader and three other wounded men—placed himself in front of wounded men and single-handedly repulsed three enemy attacks
3/21/44	Sgt. Herbert D. Zook	El Paso, TX	Platoon was advancing against enemy position and encountered heavy machine-gun and sniper fire—Zook, fully exposed to enemy observation, set up a machine-gun position and manned the gun with such effect that it silenced the enemy fire—maintained his position until other troops destroyed the enemy emplacement
	Master Sgt. Ottis C. Higgins	Plainview, TX	Performed many unheralded functions by supporting service on the front from 3/15–3/21 by serving as maintenance and dispatching equipment that he personally accompanied on several advance missions on foot patrol while under enemy fire
3/22/44	T/5 Diamon C. Dunzy	Wetunka, OK	Advancing with his troop along the shore to eliminate enemy, received intense machine-gun fire from a concealed enemy bunker preventing further advance—advanced alone to water's edge and was seriously wounded—continued and destroyed the bunker with hand grenades—his single-handed assault advanced the troops
	Sgt. Marion H. Young	Orange, TX	In command of building a supply road to advanced combat elements, was ambushed—dispersing his detail, he advanced under sniper fire and threw a hand grenade into a foxhole—grenade did not explode—raised off ground again and threw a second grenade, wherein he was killed—but the action enabled other men to reduce the strongpoint

	Pfc. Rosengrant	Lenox, IA	Member of a litter squad charged with evacuating wounded from the front lines—was under intense enemy machine-gun and sniper fire—other troops forced to withdraw because of artillery barrage, but Rosengrant accompanied his squad and evacuated the wounded
3/23/44	S/Sgt. John H. Smith	Harrisburg, IL	Caught in surprise mortar and sniper fire, he single-handedly destroyed enemy strong points with hand grenades and eliminated enemy resistance, allowing patrol to advance into enemy supply dump, which was methodically destroyed and expedited defeat of the enemy in that area
	Pfc. Joe E. Tyra	Tucson, AZ	Patrol suddenly under enemy mortar and sniper fire alone crawled forward and destroyed enemy positions with grenades and explosives
3/24/44	Lt. Col. John B. Maxwell		Encountered some of the fiercest and most difficult fighting in the Manus campaign, advancing only 200 yards south of Rossum township—thickly mined track delayed advance of tanks—fell back for air strike on enemy position in late afternoon
	12th ALP		In all air support missions, the ALP proved a valuable, an indispensable part of team—position was normally on or in front of the front line of the troops—willingly and cheerfully took every risk of combat in order to insure properly directed air support—stand out among the many unsung heroes of any battle
3/25/44	1st Lt. William H. Stone	Oklahoma City, OK	Met enemy force of comparable size along track leading south from his bivouac area—killed fifteen enemy soldiers before joining his troop perimeter—enemy began "banzai" chant prior to attack, but a well-directed mortar barrage broke up attack amid a chorus of shrieks and bloodcurdling yells—twelve of the enemy killed, but

		odor in the area for days afterward indicated many more had been killed that had escaped detection
Pvt. Johnson H. Crandall	Fort Smith, AR	During assault on enemy front lines, was with platoon when it received heavy fire from crest of a hill in front of advance—members of platoon protected themselves, but though wounded, Crandall delivered effective small arms fire against enemy from his position, rose to standing position and killed two of the enemy by accurate rifle fire, breaking enemy resistance
Cpl. John R. Sinclair	Pittsburgh, PA	Pinned to ground by machine-gun fire, crawled forward through the fire and destroyed the machine-gun with hand grenades
1st Lt. Arthur W. McGrath	Newton Center, MA	Directed tank fire while under fire to an important enemy position, thereby obliterating enemy position
Cpl. Clettus A. Daus	Haldeman, KY	Met by constant stream of enemy machine-gun fire, placed his own machine-gun squad in position to fire on enemy while under fire himself
Cpl. Jack F. Gates	Culver City, CA	Under severe and constant enemy automatic weapon and sniper fire, installed telephone circuits from forward lines to rear mortar positions and served as observer for mortar fire that destroyed enemy position while suffering from head wound
1st Sgt. Floyd J. Zientek	Tucumcari, NM	Encountered barrage of mortar and machine-gun fire from concealed positions—though wounded, he remained with troops in order to dispose his men most advantageously for their protection while at the same time locating enemy positions and directing fire on them
3/27/44 Lt. Booker	Australia	Booker, an ANGAU, sent a group of natives to Tong Island northeast of Seeadler Harbor, along with a six man

patrol—natives met small group of
Japanese and offered rations—entire
Japanese squad was captured while eating

3/30/44   Col. Glenn S. Finley

In charge of 7th Cavalry attacked
Pityilu Island—contact with enemy in
the forenoon and was attacked—
opposition so determined they
withdrew 100 yards at noon to allow
artillery concentration—advance
renewed immediately after the artillery
barrage, and by nightfall, forty-six
Japanese killed vs. fourteen wounds and
seven killed

APPENDIX 2 - Casualty List

The casualty list of those that gave their lives in the Admiralty Island conquest was compiled by 1st Cavalry Division Headquarters in April 1944.

NAME	RANK	ORGANIZATION	DATE
Baldwin, Frank	1st Lt.	Btry B 99th FA Bn	29 Feb
Ferea, Tony R.	Pfc	Tr E 5th Cav	1 Mar
King, Everett W.	Maj	5th Air Force	1 Mar
Olsen, Silas J.	Pfc	Tr E 5th Cav	1 Mar
Ray, Wayman T.	Pvt	Tr F 5th Cav	1 Mar
Spires, Bernice	Pvt	Tr E 5th Cav	1 Mar
Croom, Allen R	1st Sgt	Tr H 5th Cav	2 Mar
Davis, Ernest A	Pvt.	Tr E 5th Cav	2 Mar
Duensing, W.A.	Pfc	Tr E 5th Cav	2 Mar
Hall, Elton J.	Cp;	Tr E 5th Cav	2 Mar
Neal, Francis E.	Pfc	Tr F 5th Cav	2 Mar
Patrizio, Raymond	Pvt	Tr H 5th Cav	2 Mar
Reil, Clarence	Pvt	Tr A 5th Cav	2 Mar
Roach, Henry C.	Pvt	Tr F 5th Cav	2 Mar
Rodriquez, Raymond R.	Pfc	Tr G 5th Cav	2 Mar
Shyrer, Roy J.	Pvt	Tr H 5th Cav	2 Mar
Tobin, David R.	Pfc	673d AAA MG Btry	2 Mar
Underwood, Van Dyke	Pvt	Tr H 5th Cav	2 Mar
Weber, Jacob E.	Pvt	673 AAA MG Btry	2 Mar
Anderson, James H.	Pvt.	Tr H 5th Cav	3 Mar
Appleton, Lonnie	Tec 4	Tr F 5th Cav	3 Mar
Buckley, John F.	S/Sgt	Co A 592d Engr B&S Reg	3 Mar
Clanton, Donald	Pvt.	Tr H 5th Cav	3 Mar
Clewes, Ernest	Cpl.	Tr G 5th Cav	3 Mar
De Angelies, Joseph	Pvt	Tr G 5th Cav	3 Mar
Delgado, Felix	Pfc	Tr G 5th Cav	3 Mar

Gunby, Kenneth E.	T/4	Tr H 5th Cav	3 Mar
Horvath, Joseph	Pfc	Tr G 5th Cav	3 Mar
Kramer, Robert W.	Pvt	Tr F 5th Cav	3 Mar
Loop, William G.	Cp;	Bty B 99th FA Bn	3 Mar
Loring, Terance E.	Pvt	Co A 592d Eng B&S Reg	3 Mar
Manchester, Madison	2nd Lt	Co A 592d EBSR	3 Mar
McGill, Troy A.	Sgt.	Tr G 5th Cav	3 Mar
Murningham, Paul L.	Pvt	Tr G 5th Cav	3 Mar
Noonon, Ernest	Pfc	Tr G 5th Cav	3 Mar
Ochoa, Rudolph R.	S/Sgt	Tr H 5th Cav	3 Mar
Rodriguez, Arcadio S.	Pvt	Tr G 5th Cav	3 Mar
Scofield, Monty L.	Pfc	Tr A 5th Cav	3 Mar
Sether, Myrone	Pfc	Tr F 5th Cav	3 Mar
Williams, Everett L.	Pvt	Tr H 5th Cav	3 Mar
Amm, Fred J.	Pvt.	Btry A 99th FA Bn	4 Mar
Carmona, Daniel	Pvt.	Tr G 5th Cav	4 Mar
Davis, J.A.	Pfc	Tr G 5th Cav	4 Mar
Degruttala, L.R.	Pvt	Tr G 5th Cav	4 Mar
Denney, Audie M.	Pfc	Btry A 211th CA Bn	4 Mar
Frie, Andrew	T/Sgt	Bty C 99th FA Bn	4 Mar
Gillett, Newell E.	1st Lt.	Btry A 211th CA Bn	4 Mar
Gondek, Joseph W.	T/5	Tr G 5th Cav	4 Mar
Leske, Gerhart	Pfc	Tr G 5th Cav	4 Mar
Madden, James	Cpl.	Tr H 5th Cav	4 Mar
Maier, Vernon R.	Pvt	Wpns Tr 5th Cav	4 Mar
McLochlin, Albert	Pvt	Tr E 5th Cav	4 Mar
Moreno, Albert	Pfc	Tr G 5th Cav	4 Mar
Natvig, Gerald C.	Pfc	Wps Tr 5th Cav	4 Mar
Rahr, Gustavo	S/Sgt	Tr E 5th Cav	4 Mar
Simpson, William O.	Pvt	Tr H 5th Cav	4 Mar
Sumpter, George	Pvt	Tr E 5th Cav	4 Mar
Tucker, Arlie C.	Pvt	Btry A 99th FA Bn	4 Mar
Walkney, John E.	Cpl.	Hq Co 592d EBSR	4 Mar

Anderson, Thomas M.	Pvt.	Btry C 168th AAA Bn	5 Mar
Albert, Monroe B	Pvt.	Tr G 12th Cav	7 Mar
Chadwell, Austin	Sgt.	Tr E 12th Cav	7 Mar
Cornelius, William C.	Capt	Hq 5th Cav	7 Mar
Day, William C.	Cpl.	Tr G 12th Cav	7 Mar
Engle, Howard J.	T/4	Co C 583d Sig AW Bn	7 Mar
Eubank, Charles E.	Pvt	Tr G 12th Cav	7 Mar
Hale, James O.	Pfc	Btry CC 168th AAA Bn	7 Mar
Jones, Fred	Pvt	Btry B 82d FA Bn	7 Mar
McClain, Elmer T.	Pfc	Tr G 12th Cav	7 Mar
McDowell, Edward	Sgt.	Tr G 12th Cav	7 Mar
Phillip, Leo J.	Pvt	Bty C 168th AAA Bn	7 Mar
Rye, Frank W.	S/Sgt	Tr G 12th Cav	7 Mar
Sanchez, Louis B.	Pfc	Btry C 168th AAA Bn	7 Mar
Williams, Delbert	Pfc	Wpns Tr 12th Cav	7 Mar
York, Dane F.	Pvt	Btry C 82d FA Bn	7 Ma
Ware, Thomas W.	Pvt	Tr B 5th Cav	8 Mar
Myers, Carl S.	T/5	27th Ord Co	9 Mar
Rosen, Albert A.	Pvt	Tr F 8th Cav	9 Mar
Aughtman, Clanton	Pvt.	Tr F 5th Cav	10 Mar
Gallegos, Ramon A.	Pvt	Tr F 5th Cav	10 Mar
Granzin, Raymond Y.	Pvt	Tr G 5th Cav	10 Mar
Guerra, Luis B.	Pfc	Tr E 5th Cav	10 Mar
Johnson, William	Pvt	Tr G 5th Cav	10 Mar
Johnston, George T.	Pfc	Hq Tr 7th Cav	10 Mar
Ramer, Armond C.	Pvt	Tr E 5th Cav	10 Mar
Slutter, Frank K.	1st Lt.	Hq 1st Sq 12th Cav	10 Mar
York, Robert E. Lee	S/Sgt	Tr F 5th Cav	10 Mar
Coyle, James B.	Pvt.	302d Cav Ren Tr	11 Mar
Pruitt, Warren	Pfc	302d Rcn Tr	11 Mar
Schaff, Jack	S/Sgt	302d Rcn Tr	11 Mar
Vaden, Carter S.	Maj.	Wpns Tr 12th Cav	11 Mar
Wilson, Jesse J.	Pvt	302d Rcn Tr	11 Mar

Cunningham, Daniel E.	Pvt.	Tr G 7th Cav	12 Mar
Kroll, Eldon	Pfc	302d Rcn Tr	12 Mar
Coughlin, C.J.	Pvt.	Tr B 7th Cav	13 Mar
Davis, James R.	Pvt.	Tr F 12th Cav	13 Mar
Hejna, Lewis	Pfc	Tr D 5th Cav	13 Mar
Hill, Ralph E.	1st Lt.	Tr B 5th Cav	13 Mar
Graman, Urban	Pfc	Tr F 12th Cav	14 Mar
Parson, John W.	Pvt	Tr B 5th Cav	14 Mar
Pendell, Roy C.	Pfc	Tr A 5th Cav	14 Mar
Vessel, Virgil L.	Pvt	Tr G 12th Cav	14 Mar
Alexander, Thorton	Pvt.	Tr A 5th Cav	15 Mar
Bishop, James M.	Pvt.	Tr B 5th Cav	15 Mar
Douglas, Robert D.	Pfc	Tr D 5th Cav	15 Mar
Harkey, Vincent	Pvt	Tr A 5th Cav	15 Mar
Jones, Jesse L.	Pfc	Tr E 8th Cav	15 Mar
Kimble, Samie R.	Pfc	Tr B 8th Cav	15 Mar
Yancy, D.H.	S/Sgt	Tr A 8th Cav	15 Mar
Chambers, Woodrow M.	Pfc	Tr C 8th Cav	16 Mar
Ciangiela, James	Pvt.	Tr B 8th Cav	16 Mar
Dugen, William A.	Pfc	Tr B 8th Cav	16 Mar
Jones, Harold S.	Pvt	Tr E 5th Cav	16 Mar
Kowal, Bruno M.	Pvt	Tr B 8th Cav	16 Mar
Kriger, John J.	Pvt	Tr C 8th Cav	16 Mar
LaRue, Edward L.	Pfc	Tr F 5th Cav	16 Mar
Lemon, William D.	Cpl.	Tr B 8th Cav	16 Mar
Perdue, Herman M.	Pvt	Med Det 8th Cav	16 Mar
Perkins, Robert M.	Capt	Tr B 7th Cav	16 Mar
Fakestraw, William B.	Pvt	Tr B 8th Cav	16 Mar
Ramirez, D.G.	S/Sgt	Tr A 7th Cav	16 Mar
Sircy, Luther H.	Pfc	Tr B 8th Cav	16 Mar
Spalding, Robert L.	Pfc	Tr B 8th Cav	16 Mar
Sullivan, Thomas J.	Pvt	Tr D 8th Cav	16 Mar
Teter, Leslie A.	Pvt	Hq Tr 5th Cav	16 Mar

Whelehel, Doyle	Cpl.	Tr A 7th Cav	16 Mar
Williams, Joseph D.	Pvt	Tr B 7th Cav	16 Mar
Williams, Wilbur	Pfc	Tr A 7th Cav	16 Mar
Willis, Franklin A.	Pfc	Tr B 8th Cav	16 Mar
Bowling, Woodrow W.	Pfc	Tr C 5th Cav	17 Mar
Fournier, Frank	Maj	Hq 1st Sq 5th Cav	17 Mar
Goforth, Sammy	Pfc	Tr B 12th Cav	17 Mar
Johnson, Jessie	S/Sgt	Tr C 8th Cav	17 Mar
Lervold, Carl	Capt	Tr D 5th Cav	17 Mar
Myers, Charles C.	Pvt	Med Det 5th Cav	17 Mar
Waddell, Lester	Cpl.	Tr B 12th Cav	17 Mar
Alaniz, Eduardo	Pvt.	Tr. E 12th Cav	18 Mar
Bennett, Milton A.	Pfc	Tr E 12th Cav	18 Mar
Busalachi, Anthony C.	Pfc	Tr E 12th Cav	18 Mar
Capone, Michael G.	Cpl.	Tr F 12th Cav	18 Mar
Gayaso, Lester R.	Cpl.	Hq Btry 82d FA Bn	18 Mar
Hargrove, Bennie F.	Pvt	Tr F 8th Cav	18 Mar
Phipps, Floyd M.	Pvt	Hq Tr 8th Cav	18 Mar
Reneau, Edward L.	T/4	Tr H 12th Cav	18 Mar
Risinger, Clarence M.	Cpl.	Tr F 12th Cav	18 Mar
Boyboa, Antonio B.	Cpl.	Tr F 7th Cav	20 Mar
Dwinell, Ralph E.	Pvt	Tr C 8th Cav	20 Mar
Filippene, Michael, J.	Pvt	Tr H 8th Cav	20 Mar
McCarray, Hiskell J.	Cpl.	Tr G 7thCav	20 Mar
Parks, Arlie C.	Pfc	Tr C 8th Cav	20 Mar
Roberts, Cornelius F.	T/4	Tr F 7th Cav	20 Mar
Shull, Lester H.	Sgt.	Tr F 8th Cav	20 Mar
White, Glenne	Pvt	Med Det 7th Cav	20 Mar
Wilson, Carl L.	S/Sgt	Tr F 7th Cav	20 Mar
Balfe, Thomas L.	Tec 4	Tr C 12th Cav	21 Mar
Barhill, Ottis	Tec 4	Hq Tr 12th Cav	21 Mar
Bell, Frank J.	Pfc	Tr D 12th Cav	21 Mar
Shields, J.P.	Pfc	Tr F 12th Cav	21 Mar

Waters, Kenneth	Pvt	Tr F 12th Cav	21 Mar
Williams, Ostlek	S/Sgt	Tr D 5th Cav	21 Mar
Bustamente, Gustave	Pvt.	Tr C 7th Cav	22 Mar
Callaway, Orlin L.	2nd Lt	Hq Btry 271st FA Bn	22 Mar
Cogliani, Vicente A	Pvt.	Tr C 7th Cav	22 Mar
Conyers, Charles M.	Cpl.	Tr C 7th Cav	22 Mar
Cox, Myrada C.	Pvt.	Tr B 5th Cav	22 Mar
Curnyn, John R.	Pfc	Tr H 12th Cav	22 Mar
Donahue, Richard	Sgt.	Tr F 12th Cav	22 Mar
Edwards, Glenn E.	Pfc	Tr F 12th Cav	22 Mar
Jameson, Travis	Pvt	Med Det 7th Cav	22 Mar
Jones, Charles A.	Pvt	Tr C 12th Cav	22 Mar
King, George W.	Pfc	Tr G 12th Cav	22 Mar
Lamerson, Blenn W.	Cpl.	Tr H 5th Cav	22 Mar
Manville, Owen	Pfc	2d Col Tr 1st Med Sq	22 Mar
Mauricio, Francisco	Pvt	Tr C 7th Cav	22 Mar
Miller, Earl J.	S/Sgt	Tr H 12th Cav	22 Mar
Olson, Harold G.	Pvt	Tr B 5th Cav	22 Mar
Phillips, William	Pvt	Tr H 12th Cav	22 Mar
Rodriguez, Benjamin C.	Pfc	Tr B 7th Cav	22 Mar
Roe, Arthur F.	Pvt	Tr A 12th Cav	22 Mar
White, Charles B.	Cpl.	Tr C 7th Cav	22 Mar
Young, Marion H.		Ser Tr 12th Cav	22 Mar
Andrews, Donald E.	Pvt.	Tr G 5th Cav	23 Mar
Centretto, S.P.	Pvt.	Tr G 5th Cav	23 Mar
Hesse, Albert A.	T/4	Tr E 12th Cav	23 Mar
Maniscalco, Jake	Pvt	Tr E 12th Cav	23 Mar
Schroeder, B.A.	Pvt	Tr G 5th Cav	23 Mar
Talley, Joseph	Pvt	Tr G 7thCav	23 Mar
DePinto, Radames	Pvt	Tr B 7th Cav	24 Mar
Hubbell, Roman D.	Capt	Tr E 7th Cav	24 Mar
Madison, Martin	Pvt	Tr B 7th Cav	24 Mar
Miler, Bruce	Pfc	Tr B 7th Cav	24 Mar

Renfro, James R.	Cpl.	Tr A 5th Cav	24 Mar
Speight, William E.	S/Sgt	Tr E 12th Cav	24 Mar
Bloom, Howard W.	Pvt.	Tr A 8th Cav	25 Mar
Bollman, Beryl L.	Pvt.	Tr A 8th Cav	25 Mar
Connel, Carlis	Pvt.	Tr A 8th Cav	25 Mar
Mason, Warren T.	Pvt	Tr B 8th Cav	25 Mar
Roche, James P.	Pfc	Tr C 8th Cav	25 Mar
Snyder, Lorenzo J.	Pfc	Tr A 8th Cav	25 Mar
Zollinger, James M.	Pvt	Tr B 12th Cav	25 Mar
Brown, Irving	Pvt.	Tr D 5th Cav	27 Mar
Finn, John F.	Capt	Tr G 7thCav	27 Mar
Tennant, Gordon S.	Pfc	Hq 1st Sq 8th Cav	27 Mar
Gotheridge, Ernest A.	T/5	Tr B 5th Cav	28 Mar
Lovett, John E.	Pvt	Tr B 8th Engr Sq	28 Mar
Wisuiewski, Benjamin S.	Pvt	Tr H 5th Cav	29 Mar
Bruner, Eric	Pfc	Med Det, 7th Cav	30 Mar
Davis, William C.	Sgt.	2d Col Tr 1st Med Sq	30 Mar
Farley, Talmadge	Sgt.	Tr A 7th Cav	1 Apr
Frederick, George F.	Capt	12th ALP 5th Air Force	30 Mar
Hamrick, Oval B.	Cpl.	Tr A 7th Cav	30 Mar
Jinks, Will R.	T/4	2d Col Tr 1st Med Sq	30 Mar
Thomason, William H.	Cpl.	Tr A 7th Cav	30 Mar
Wilson, Ransome R.	Pvt	Tr A 7th Cav	30 Mar
Parker, Norma S.	Pfc	Tr F 7th Cav	10 Apr
Lingfelter, Robert E.	Pvt	Tr E 8th Cav	13 Apr

INDEX

INDEX

O

Oklahoma
>Ardmore 103, 104, 105, 106
>Gene Autry 106
>Oklahoma City 89, 90, 394
>Tulsa 36, 37, 38, 40, 41, 42, 43, 48, 53, 55, 56, 57, 60, 67, 70, 73, 106

Operation FS 45, 46
Ortis, Corporal 324
Ough, Pvt. Webster J. 298

P

Panama 9, 20, 52, 370
Panama Canal 9, 20, 370
Patton, General George S. 25
Pearl Harbor 7, 20, 22, 23, 24, 31, 45, 46, 47, 59, 77, 193, 230, 231
Pease, Captain Harl 82, 83, 418
Pennsylvania
>Philadelphia 1, 2, 6, 7, 8, 24, 25, 29, 65, 89, 114, 125, 222, 348, 377, 378, 379, 383, 392

Philadelphia Inquirer 348
Philippine Islands 10, 24, 26, 31, 34, 223, 379, 381, 418
>Bataan Peninsula 31, 52
>Corregidor 33, 35, 46
>Luzon 31, 379, 380, 414, 418
>Manila 20, 242, 414, 418

Phoenix cruiser 33, 177, 179, 185, 187, 189, 198, 208, 209, 212, 423, 427
Pierce Business College 6, 7, 12
Prentice, Lt. Alfred W. 262, 263, 267, 386
Purple Heart Medal 315
Pyle, Nettie 375

Q

Queen Mary 258

R

RAAF 73rd Wing 271, 334, 335, 338, 341
Ramirez, Sgt. 184, 400, 419
Rawolle, Major Franklin M. 189
Red Herring 317
Reed, Major 55, 214
Robertson, Commander Edward L. 307, 311
Rooke Island 195
Roosevelt, President Franklin 22, 23, 31, 34, 47, 105, 121, 235, 417, 423
Rough Riders 227
Royal Australian Air Force 81, 127, 155, 156, 179, 271, 273, 278, 281, 283, 288, 293, 294, 317, 319, 329, 330, 331, 332, 334, 335, 336, 338, 340, 341, 380
Royce, General Ralph 81
Rush, Dr. 71, 109, 159, 258, 291, 302, 377
Rusmusson, Commander I.S. 225

S

Samoa 45, 47
SAUCEPAN 289
Scanlon, General 'Mike' 79, 80
Schefendecker, Earl 84
Seabees 180, 209, 223, 225, 228, 231, 234, 238, 239, 252, 255, 256, 262, 272, 273, 278, 309, 379
Second Air Tactical Force 139, 153
Secretary of State Hull 20
Shokakua Aircraft Carrier 45
Shore, Major Moyer S. 294
Shropshire, Major Spencer 128, 281,

INDEX

USS Nicholson 243, 251, 264
USS Oyster Bay 283
USS Reid 187, 188, 205
USS Sands 187, 188, 196, 197, 420
USS Saratoga 77
USS Smith 124, 127, 188, 243, 304, 355, 394, 395, 424, 430
USS Stevenson 188, 243
USS Stockton 188, 212, 218
USS Swanson vii, 118, 119, 242, 243, 244, 246, 247, 249, 259, 263, 264, 265, 266, 267, 268, 273, 301, 307, 309, 310, 311, 313, 429
USS Warramunga 228, 243, 244, 250
USS Wasp 77
USS Welles 188, 197, 243
USS Wilkes 243, 264, 266, 268, 273
USS Yorktown 44, 47

V

VA Hospital 378
Vaden, Major Carter S. 282, 283, 399
Valencia, Corporal Amado V. 315, 392
Vasey, General George A. 78, 117, 142, 148, 149, 153, 155
Vitiaz Strait 160, 165, 199

W

Waco CG-4A Glider 100, 101, 107, 347
Wainwright, General 34, 35
Walker, General Ken 79, 81
Walls, Lt. Frank 59, 60, 62, 88, 106, 107, 378
War Department 124, 344, 346, 351
Whitehead, General Ennis C. 52, 79, 124, 172, 173, 178, 180, 185, 187, 248, 279, 280, 290, 325, 362, 417
Willoughby, General Charles 174, 175, 177, 180

Wooten, General G. F. 142, 149, 156

Y

Yamamoto, Admiral 45, 46
Yank Magazine v, 117, 201, 212, 384
Yankee Diddler 217, 218, 225, 260

Z

Zuikaku Aircraft Carrier 45

i   Exhibits of Joint Committee, Exhibit No. 1, intercepted diplomatic messages sent by the Japanese government between July 1 and December 8, 1941.

ii   JCS, after March 1942, consisted of Generals Marshall and Arnold, and Admirals King and Leahy. Leahy served as chairman. The JCS reported directly to the president and interfaced with the British Chiefs of Staff.

iii   Personal interview with Dan Kruszyna and research of USS Canopus, www.destroyerhistory.org.

iv   Lt. Harl Pease would later earn the Medal of Honor for a bombing flight.

v   Lt. Laird also remembered the incident in early 2005.

vi   George C. Kenney, General Kenney Reports, 1949, p.359; John Miller, Jr. CARTWHEEL: The Reduction of Rabaul, 1959, p. 320.

vii   "The Fifth Air Force in WW II," http://www.kensmen.com/history.html#articles; The Army Air Forces in World War II: Combat Chronology, 1941–1945, the Office of Air Force History, Headquarters USAF, 1973. See also R. H. Spector, Eagle Against the Sun, 1985, p. 281. Although Capt. Frederick didn't actually participate in the meeting, he was engaged in the planning. He had flown missions into the Admiralty Islands and his "desk job," as he called it, consisted of planning for the invasion. Actual meeting was in Brisbane and didn't include General Whitehead, who was notified by courier. See General Kenney Reports, p. 359.

viii   John Miller, Jr., CARTWHEEL: The Reduction of Rabaul, 1959, p. 320.

ix   Cf. par. 1a (2) of BREWER TF FO 2, 25 Feb 44, with Annex I, Intel. In ALAMO ANCHORAGE Jnl, 3, 24–26, Feb 44, ALAMO FO 9, and BREWER TF FO 1 are orders prepared for the one-division invasion of the Admiralties scheduled for 1 April.

x   Thomas J. Cutler, The Battle of Leyte Gulf, 1994, p. 7.

xi   W.F. Craven and J.L. Crate, The Army Air Forces in World War II, Vol. IV, The Pacific: Guadalcanal to Saipan, August 1942 to July 1944, 1950, p. 559.

xii   Donald M. Goldstein, Ennis C. Whitehead: Aerospace Commander and Pioneer (PhD dissertation, University of Denver, 1970).

xiii   George C. Kenney, General Kenney Reports, 1949, pp. 35, 41.

xiv   John Miller, Jr. CARTWHEEL: The Reduction of Rabaul, 1959, p. 22.

xv   John Miller, Jr. CARTWHEEL: The Reduction of Rabaul, 1959, p. 320.

xvi   Planes allocated to the 5th Air Force would be diverted to Nimitz for "emergency operations," to the chagrin of General Kenney. See General Kenney Reports 1949, p. 128.

xvii   R. H. Spector, Eagle Against the Sun, 1985, p. 125. JCS provided balance of the Army and the Navy and forestalled the danger of Roosevelt succumbing to the opinion that MacArthur be given the position of overall supreme military commander.

xviii   R. H. Spector, Eagle Against the Sun, 1985 p. 276. The JCS was correct in that Rabaul was defended so heavily by the Japanese that "Tarawa, Iwo Jima and Okinawa would have faded to pale pink in comparison with the blood which would have flowed if the Allies had attempted an assault on Rabaul." See also Morison, Breaking the Bismarck's Barrier, pp. 403–09.

xix   BREWER was the code name given for the Admiralty Island invasion.

xx   Col. James F. Sunderman, USAF, WW II in the Air, the Pacific, 1962. p. 87. The generals were Maj. General Innis P. Swift, Commanding General of the 1st Cavalry, and his right arm, Brig. General William C. Chase, Commander of the 1st Brigade.

xxi   ULTRA named by the British was the acronym given for the code breaking of

ENDNOTES

	Japanese and German intercepted communications.
xxii	Code named BREWER, the invasion of the Admiralties was scheduled for April 1, 1944.
xxiii	Walter Krueger (Lieutenant General) served as commander of the Blue Third Army during the Louisiana maneuvers. Krueger took command of that army in May 1941 and soundly defeated the opposing Red Army. Krueger was a professional soldier, beginning his military career as a private in 1898. Krueger was recognized as one of the U.S. Army's best educated and perceptive officers, and kept pace with the changes of the art of war. In February 1943, Krueger was promoted to Commanding General of the Sixth Army in the Southwest Pacific Theater of Operations, including the Philippine Islands. Krueger was promoted to the rank of full general in March 1944, due to his outstanding leadership in the Pacific.
xxiv	George C. Kenney, General Kenney Reports, 1949, p. 359.
xxv	W.F. Craven and J.L. Crate, The Army Air Forces in World War II, Vol. IV, The Pacific: Guadalcanal to Saipan, August 1942 to July 1944, 1950, p. 557.
xxvi	John Miller, Jr. CARTWHEEL: The Reduction of Rabaul, 1959, p. 320.
xxvii	The original invasion plans for April did call for assistance from Admiral Nimitz.
xxviii	James, Years of MacArthur p. 380; George C. Kenney, General Kenney Reports, 1949, p. 360.
xxix	George C. Kenney, General Kenney Reports, 1949, p. 360.
xxx	John Miller, Jr. CARTWHEEL: The Reduction of Rabaul, 1959, p. 321.
xxxi	APD is a High-Speed-Destroyer-Transport.
xxxii	W.F. Craven and J.L. Crate, The Army Air Forces in World War II, Vol. IV, The Pacific: Guadalcanal to Saipan, August 1942 to July 1944, 1950, p. 561.
xxxiii	R. H. Spector, Eagle Against the Sun, 1985 p. 281.
xxiv	Innis P. Swift (Major General) served in the Louisiana maneuvers as the Commanding General of the 1st Cavalry Division. The Louisiana maneuvers was the last campaign for the mounted cavalry units of the U.S. Army. Swift commanded his cavalry troopers through all the battles and skirmishes, including the crossing of the Sabine River as the 1st Cavalry attacked the Red Second Cavalry at Zwolle, Louisiana, and starting turning the Western Flank for Krueger. After the maneuvers, Swift led the 1st Cavalry to the Southwest Pacific where they engaged in the fighting for the Admiralty Islands in 1943–1944. In 1945, the division entered the fighting in the Philippine Islands as General MacArthur fulfilled his promise to return and liberate the Philippine people. Swift was promoted to Commanding General, I Corps, on Luzon in 1945. His old cavalry division was one of the best units under the command of Douglas MacArthur. The 1st Cavalry helped liberate Manila. The tactics and training received during the Louisiana maneuvers greatly contributed to the success of this division and to Swift's leadership capability, http://www.army.mil/cmh-pg/matrix/1CD/1CD-WW2-OB.htm. (Note: At a reunion of the 1st Cavalry in Texas in 2003, the veterans of WWII commented that he always signed his full first name and never used initials.)
xxxv	Center for Military History, United States Army, The Admiralties, Operations of the 1st Cavalry Division, 1946, p. 12.
xxxvi	ALAMO, actually the Sixth Army, was theoretically a task force directly under GHQ.
xxxvii	Latin phrase meaning "First among equals."

xxxviii   "Recon on Los Negros: Alamo Scouts First Mission," M. F. Dilley and L.Q. Zedric http://www.alamoscouts.org.

xxxix   The team consisted of Lt. John McGowen, Tech. Sgt. Caesar J. Ramirez, Sgt. Walter A. Mc Donald, Sgt. J. A. Roberts, Private 1st Class John P. Legoud, and Private Paul V. Gomez, http://www.alamoscouts.org.

xl   "Recon on Los Negros: Alamo Scouts First Mission," M. F. Dilley and L.Q. Zedric, http://www.alamoscouts.org. Most information concerning the Alamo Scouts was obtained from this article.

xli   Pvt. Gomez, as well as all members of the McGowen team, subsequently received the Silver Star.

xlii   George C. Kenney, General Kenney Reports, 1949, p. 144. General Kenney wanted more firepower, so he modified the B-25 by placing .50-caliber machine-guns in the nose with 500 rounds of ammunition each.

xliii   George C. Kenney, General Kenney Reports, 1949, p. 361.

xliv   The 12th Air Liaison Party consisted of Capt. George F. Frederick, 1st Lt. James C. King, S/Sgt. Martin W. James, Sgt. Mark D. Kohn, Sgt. Hugh H. Bement, Sgt. Roy H. Clark, and T/5th Gr. Gordon R. Rule.

xlv   USAF Historical Studies: No. 86, "Close Air Support in the War Against Japan," USAF Historical Division; Research /studies Institute, Air University, February 1955, pp. 89–90.

xlvi   According to John Miller, Jr., CARTWHEEL: The Reduction of Rabaul, 1959, Glossary, G-1 is Personnel, G-2 Intelligence, G-3 Operations, and G-4 is Supply.

xlvii   Morning Report, Capt. George F. Frederick, 12th Air Liaison Party.

xlviii   Center for Military History, United States Army, The Admiralties, Operations of the 1st Cavalry Division, 1946, pp. 4–5.

xlix   "Recon on Los Negros: Alamo Scouts First Mission," M. F. Dilley and L.Q. Zedric, http://www.alamoscouts.org. Most information concerning the Alamo Scouts obtained from this article.

l   Center for Military History, United States Army, The Admiralties, Operations of the 1st Cavalry Division, 1946, p 21.

li   W.F. Craven and J.L. Crate The Army Air Forces in World War II, Vol. IV, The Pacific: Guadalcanal to Saipan, August 1942 to July 1944, 1950, p. 563.

lii   Journal 12th Air Liaison Party, as supplied from AFHRA/RSA, Maxwell AFB, AL, E, "Aboard USS Sands. Check party and equipment. Have Lt. King and five men."

liii   Direct Quote from McGowen: "Recon on Los Negros: Alamo Scouts First Mission," M. F. Dilley and L.Q. Zedric, http://www.alamoscouts.org.

liv   See also: "Recon on Los Negros: Alamo Scouts First Mission," M. F. Dilley and L.Q. Zedric, http://www.alamoscouts.org.

lv   The Army Air Forces in World War II , p 564.

lvi   Both received Bronze Stars for their actions at Los Negros.

lvii   AAF references indicate barbed wire was dropped; however, infantry references indicate barbed wire was desperately needed and not dropped.

lviii   The morning report kept by the 12th Air Liaison Party and the book The Admiralties, Operation of the 1st Cavalry Division. 29 February–18 May 1944, written by the Center of Military History 1 December 1945 is in conflict on three accounts on the events of March 1st and March 2nd. First, according to the

ENDNOTES

morning report, the 1st Squadron arrived on March 1st. However, the Center for Military History has them arriving on March 2nd. Second, the number killed by the strafing and machine-gun fire was placed at 100 and not 400. Perhaps the 400 figure counts the Japanese killed also in the battles the night of March 1st, since an accurate count isn't given of combining the two. The third conflict occurs on March 2nd, concerning the attack by Captain Baba. The morning report has the events surrounding Captain Baba occurring on March 2nd, and the Center for Military History on March 1st. The machine-gun incident referred to in the morning report was ten feet away from their dugout, but the Captain Baba incident occurs thirty-five yards from their dugout, so the events must be separate incidents.

lix   For his action, McGill was awarded the Congressional Medal of Honor. "His intrepid stand was an inspiration to his comrades and a decisive factor in the defeat of a fanatical enemy."

lx   Severely wounded, he died the next day. For his courage and leadership, he was awarded the Distinguished Service Cross.

lxi   Capt. Kawato subsequently performed a solo record flight across the pacific to further the friendship between Japan and the United States. During WWII he shot __ down Maj. Gregory "Pappy" Boyington of "Black Sheep" fame. After WWII Kawato and Boyington became close friends.

lxii   As stated in The Army Air Forces in World War II, Volume IV, Craven & Crate state: "The capable Captain Frederick worked out the air support plan for D-Day with General Swift…" page 569. See also CARTWHEEL; The Reduction of Rabaul, John Miller, Jr., p. 340.

lxiii   S/Sgt. Erwin M. Gauthreaux was subsequently awarded the Silver Star and promoted to 2nd Lieutenant.

lxiv   Major Houck Spencer, (Personal Experience of a Troop Commander) Advanced Department for Advanced Infantry Officers Class No. 2, The Infantry School, Fort Benning, GA., wrote: "Planning for this operation, on the squadron level, was untimely and incomplete. In view of the fact that the efforts of the 7th Cavalry were directed by Brigade order, against the Rossum Track commencing 19 March, some effort should have been initiated to prepare for possible commitment. Hence, two extremely valuable sources of enemy and terrain intelligence—liaison aircraft and patrolling—were not utilized. Further, the information recorded on the captured Japanese map was neither considered in advance on the squadron level nor was it even made available to the troop commanders. As a result, small-unit leaders were plunged into the attack with only the most fragmentary knowledge of the situation. No plan whatsoever was formulated in advance for squadron employment in event of enemy contact. The late hour and date at which troops were alerted resulted in a hurried briefing of personnel after dark."

lxv   Also killed March 30, 1944 were Sgt. William C. Davis, T/4 Will R. Jinks, Pfc. Eric Bruner, all from the medical detachment; Sgt. Talmage Farley, Cpl. Oval B. Hamrick, Cpl. William H. Thomason

lxvi   From "Diary of the Admiralty Islands Campaign," Headquarters, U.S. Forces, APO 324, April 21, 1944, a previously classified document that was unclassified on Oct. 19, 1989.

BIBLIOGRAPHY

Following are sources used for *Legacy of Letters*. The sources used were books in my possession and from websites on the internet.

Books:

The Admiralties: Operations of the 1ˢᵗ Cavalry Division 28 February–18 May 1944, Center of Military History, United States Army 1946 CMH Pub 100-3, also available from: http://www.army.mil/cmh

The Admiralties At War, 1944–1945, Robert Manning Smalley, Special Research Bryan Cleary for The Admiralty Group, USA Trafford Publishing Co. Inc. Victoria, B.C., Canada 1994.

Papuan Campaign: The Buna-Sanananda Operation, 16 November 1942–23 January 1943, Center of Military History, United States Army 1945 CMH Pub 100-1.

CARTWHEEL: The Reduction of Rabaul, John Miller, Jr., Center of Military History, United States Army 1959, CMH Pub 5-5.
The Army Air Forces in World War II: IV The Pacific: Guadalcanal to Saipan

BIBLIOGRAPHY

August 1942 to July 1944, Edited by W.F. Craven and J.L. Cate, Office of Air Force History 1950, The University of Chicago Press, Chicago.

History of United States Naval Operations in World War II: Vol. VI, Breaking the Bismarck's Barrier: 22 July 1942–May 1944, Samuel Eliot Morison, Little Brown and Company, Boston, New York, London, Toronto, 1950.

General Kenney Reports: A Personal History of the Pacific War, George C. Kenney, Duell, Sloan and Pearce, New York, 1949.

Pacific War Stories: In the Words of Those Who Survived, Rex Alan Smith and Gerald A. Meehl, Abbeville Press, New York, London, 2004.

MacArthur's Navy: The Seventh Fleet and the Battle for the Philippines, Edwin P. Hoyt, Orion Books, a division of Crown Publishers, New York, 1989.

Eagle Against the Sun: The American War With Japan, Ronald H. Spector, The Free Press, A Division of Macmillan, Inc., New York, 1985.

Fifth Air Force Story, Kenn C. Rust, A Historical Aviation Album Publication, Templeton, CA, 1973.

War in the Pacific: 1937–1945, Ross Burns, Brompton Books Corp., Greenwich, CT, 1991.

World War II in the Air: The Pacific, Edited by Co. James F. Sunderman, USAF, Van Nostrand Reinhold Co., New York, Cincinnati, Toronto, London, Melbourne, 1963.

Air Force Combat Units of World War II: History & Insignia, Edited by Maurer Maurer, USAF Historical Division, Air University, Department of the Air Force, Zinger Publishing Co., Inc., Washington, D.C., 1961.
Silent Wings At War: Combat Gliders in World War II, John L. Lowden,

Smithsonian Institution Press, Washington and London, 1992.

The Glider Gang, Milton Dank, Cassell, London, 1977.
Pacific Microphone, William J. Dunn, Texas A&M University Press, College Station, TX, 1988.

The Battle of Leyte Gulf: 23–26 October 1944, Thomas J. Cutler, Harper Collins Publishers, New York, NY, 1994.

Warpath Across the Pacific: Eagles Over the Pacific, Vol. I, Lawrence J. Hickey, International Research and Publishing, Co. Boulder, CO, 1984.

Reminiscences: General of the Army Douglas MacArthur, Douglas MacArthur, McGraw-Hill Book Company, New York, Toronto, London, 1964.

Roosevelt and Churchill 1939–1941, Joseph P. Lash, W.W. Norton & Co., New York, NY, 1976.

The Best from Yank, the Army Weekly, Selected by the Editors of Yank, E.P. Dutton & Co., Inc., New York, NY, 1945.

Yank, The Army Weekly, Steve Kluger, St. Martin's Press, New York, NY, 1991.

From Fiji Through the Philippines with the Thirteenth Air Force, Lt. Col. Benjamin E. Lippincott, Historian, Thirteenth Air Force, Newsfoto Publishing Co., San Angelo, TX, 1948.

Bye, Bye, Black Sheep, Capt. Masajiro "Mike" Kawato, Associated Lithographers, Phoenix, AZ, 1978.

The Greatest Generation Speaks: Letters and Reflections, Tom Brokaw, Random House, New York, NY, 1999.

From Maxwell AFB, Historical Studies:

BIBLIOGRAPHY

Historical Studies were prepared by the AAF and subsequent USAF Historical Office. The following are available on line from: http://www.au.af.mil/au/afhra. The studies were classified previously as Secret, Confidential, and/or Restricted documents. Also contained in the documents supplied to me from Dr. Kitchens at Maxwell AFB was the "morning report" of the 12th Air Liaison Party.

The AAF in the South Pacific to October 1942, USAF Historical Study 101, January 1946.

Close Air Support in the War Against Japan, USAF Historical Study 86, February 1955.

The Fifth Air Force in the Huon Peninsula Campaign, January to October 1943, USAF Historical Study 113, January 1946.

The Fifth Air Force in the Huon Peninsula Campaign, to February 1944, USAF Historical Study 116, April 1947.

The Fifth Air Force in the Conquest of the Bismarck Archipelago, November 1943 to March 1944, USAF Historical Study 43, January 1946.

Air Action in the Papuan Campaign: 21 July 1942 to 23 January 1943, USAF Historical Study 17, August 1944.

MacArthur's Victory: The War in New Guinea, 1943–1944, Harry A. Gailey, Presidio Press, 2004.

Internet Websites:

The following websites were used in my research. The sites shouldn't be considered as all-inclusive, since many of the sites directed me to other sites that I may have used.

Air Force Historical Research Agency, http://www.au.af.mil/au/afhra

Army Air Forces, http://www.armyairforces.com

308th Bombardment Group, http://www.308thbombgroup.org

345th Bomb Group Association,
http://web.cortland.edu/van/345thBombGroup.htm

38th Bomb Group, http://home.st.net.au/~dunn/38thbomb.htm
Web- Birds, http://www.web-birds.com

43rd Bomb Group, http://www.kensmen.com/contents.html

317th Troop Carrier Group, http://home.st.net.au/~dunn/317thtg.htm

National Museum of the United States Air Force,
http://www.wpafb.af.mil/museum

39th Troop Carrier Association,
http://www.39thassociation.org/pages/1/index.htm

The Flying Knights, 9th Fighter Squadron, 49th Fighter Group,
http://www.flyingknights.net

The United States Army Air Forces in World War II,
http://www.usaaf.net/index.html
USAF, http://www.usaf.com/index2.htm

BIBLIOGRAPHY

Wings of Valor, http://www.homeofheroes.com/wings/index.html

United States Army Air Force Resource Center, http://www.warbirdsre-
sourcegroup.org/URG/index.html

Alamo Scouts, The US 6th Army Special Reconnaissance Unit of World
War II, http://www.alamoscouts.org/index.htm

Australian War Memorial, http://www.awm.gov.au/index.asp
"World War II Campaigns: Bismarck Archipelago," "The Admiralties:
Operations of the 1st Cavalry Division (29 February–18 May 1944),"
"Guadalcanal: The First Offensive," "Papuan Campaign: The Buna-
Sanananda Operation (16 November 1942-23 January 1943)," "WWII
Campaigns: Western Pacific," "WWII Campaigns: Papua," "WWII
Campaigns: New Guinea," http://www.army.mil/cmh

The First Cavalry Association, http://www.1cda.org

The Second World War Encyclopedia,
http://www.spartacus.schoolnet.co.uk/2WW.htm

U.S. Army Air Forces in World War II: Combat Chronology 1941–1945,
https://www.airforcehistory.hq.af.mil/PopTopics/chron/contents.htm

American Battle Monuments Commission, http://www.abmc.gov

Camden County War Dead,
http://www.dvrbs.com/CamdenCountyWarDeadIndex.htm

National WWII Memorial,
http://www.wwiimemorial.com/default.asp?page=home.asp
USS Swanson DD 443 Association, http://www.geocities.com/swan-

sondd443/swanmen.html

Admiralty Island Invasion, USS Bush DD 529,
http://www.ussbush.com/admralty.htm

USS Phoenix (CL-46), http://www.ussbush.com/admralty.htm

20th Century History, http://history1900s.about.com

Australia @ War, http://home.st.net.au/~pdunn/index.htm

Chronology of World War II,
http://www.onwar.com/chrono/1941/oct41/f06oct41.htm

Documents of World War II,
http://www.mtholyoke.edu/acad/intrel/ww2.htm

General Douglas MacArthur in Australia During WW2,
http://home.st.net.au/~dunn/macarthur.htm

Manus Province (also includes other Admiralty Islands), http://www.pacificwrecks.com/provinces/png_manus.html

Military.com (Source for Maps),
http://www.military.com/Resources/HistorySubmittedFileView?file=history_worldwarii_asia_maps.htm#japaneseoffensive

The National Archives, http://www.archives.gov/index.html

Officer Training School Curriculum Assistance,
http://www.au.af.mil/au/aul/school/ots/ots.htm

WWII Resources, http://www.ibiblio.org/pha

Naval Historical Center, http://www.history.navy.mil/nhc6.htm

The American War Library,
http://members.aol.com/veterans/warlib46.htm

BIBLIOGRAPHY

United States Army Military History Institute,
http://carlisle-www.army.mil/usamhi

http://www.pbs.org/wgbh/amex/bataan/peopleevents/p_mucci.html

From Military History Institute and National
Archives and Records Administration

Historical Report of the 7th Cavalry, National Archives.

Clippings of the Admiralty Island Campaign

Operations of Troop C, 7th Cavalry: 1st Cavalry Division 22–24 March 1944,
Academic Department, The Infantry School, Personal Experience of a
Troop Commander, Major Houck Spencer.

Operations of A Troop, 8th Regt; 1st Cavalry Division 14–24 March 1944,
Academic Department, The Infantry School, Personal Experience of a
Troop Commander, Major Raymond J. Jennings.

Diary of the Admiralty Campaign, HQ 1st Cavalry Division, April 21, 1944
The Approach to the Philippines, Robert Ross Smith, Office of the Chief of
Military History, Department of the Army.

"Papers of Chaplin Charles V. Trent," Unpublished article, 1962.
"Hell for Leather," *True War Magazine*, Richard Dennis, publication date
unknown.

*Of Garry Owen in Glory: The History of the Seventh United States Cavalry
Regiment*, Written and Compiled by Lt. Col. Melbourne C. Chandler.

58 letters

Printed in the United States
142684LV00002B/12/A

9 780977 849307